The Genocide Convention

The Genocide Convention

The Legacy of 60 Years

edited by

H.G. van der Wilt, J. Vervliet, G.K. Sluiter
and J.Th.M. Houwink ten Cate

MARTINUS
NIJHOFF
PUBLISHERS

LEIDEN • BOSTON
2012

If the Whole Body Dies, by Robert Skloot, copyright Parallel Press. Reproduced with permission.

Library of Congress Cataloging-in-Publication Data

The genocide convention : the legacy of 60 years / edited by H.G. van der Wilt ...[et al.].
p. cm.
Includes bibliographical references.
ISBN 978-90-04-15328-8 (hardback : alk. paper) -- ISBN 978-90-04-22131-4 (e-book) 1. Convention on the Prevention and Punishment of the Crime of Genocide (1948) 2. Genocide. I. Wilt, Harmen van der, 1955-
KZ7180.A61948G46 2012
345'.0251--dc23

2012015174

ISBN 978 9004 15328 8 (hardback)
ISBN 978 9004 22131 4 (e-book)

This book is printed on acid-free paper.

Table of Contents

Foreword

Johannes Houwink ten Cate and Harmen van der Wilt

On 7 and 8 December 2008 the Centre for Holocaust and Genocide Studies, the Peace Palace Library and the Amsterdam Centre for International Law held a conference in commemoration of the 60th birthday of the Genocide Convention.

It is common knowledge that the Genocide Convention has largely been modeled after the archetypical genocide, the mass murder of the Jews by the Nazi-regime. Ever since, the world has wrestled with the concept. There is an undisputable gap between the popular perception and rigid legal analysis of genocide. It is of paramount importance to achieve a proper balance between inflation of the concept (calling each and every massacre 'genocide') and making the concept practically redundant. Solid academic analysis and dissemination of the results are key instruments to accomplish this goal. The organizers were of the opinion that an encounter between historians and lawyers would serve this purpose.

Now historians and lawyers do not speak the same languages, nor do they share an epistemological framework. Historians try to reconstruct partial truths and realities and they do not eschew open-ended narratives. Lawyers, straitjacketed by rigid evidentiary standards and requirements of legal certainty, on the other hand, search for mathematical outcomes. Hannah Arendt's stern admonition that courts should stick to their core business of distinguishing the guilty from the innocent and should not indulge in writing history is well known. Nonetheless, international criminal tribunals have brushed these warnings aside. And indeed, 'history in the courtroom' is less of an anathema than in Arendt's days. It is more widely acknowledged that historical records in judgments may serve the purpose of putting international crimes in a broader context, will help to keep the memory alive and may even have some cathartic effect.

The participants and speakers of the conference found the encounter productive and rewarding. This volume contains a number of contributions, reflecting a wide variety of social, legal and political aspects of the crime of genocide. A special place is dedicated to the founding father of the Genocide Convention, Raphael Lemkin, who succeeded in reconciling the socio-political framework of genocide with its legal elements. Both the short biography by Jeroen Vervliet and Bob Skloot's stage play 'If the Whole Body Dies' pay tribute to this remarkable man.

The play 'If the Whole Body Dies' was actually performed during the conference. The event made a deep impression on the audience, as the play reveals Lemkin's personal struggles as he reflected on the dismal topic.

The play is reproduced – free from charges - with kind permission of the original publisher, Parallel Press.

Raphael Lemkin (1900-1959) and the Genocide Convention of 1948. Brief Biographical and Bibliographical Notes

Jeroen Vervliet

1. Biographies on Raphael Lemkin

Samantha Power's "A Problem from Hell. America and the Age of Genocide"[1] has been the first publication to introduce to a wider audience the jurist Raphael Lemkin and his influential effort to settle the new word 'genocide' and its intrinsic adoption in international legal cases, to the establishment of the Genocide Convention and to the ratification thereafter by members states of the United Nations. Samantha Power discusses as well Cambodia, Iraq, Bosnia, Rwanda, Srebrenica and Kosovo, and "Lemkin's Courtroom Legacy".[2]

Raphael Lemkin and the Struggle for the Genocide Convention[3] by John Cooper is the most extensive biography. The book also touches upon Raphael Lemkin's more personal life and his endeavours in the province of the history of genocides, but the main focus is Lemkin's struggle for the Genocide Convention. It draws on Lemkin's archival heritage.

William Korey, a human rights scholar and former director of International Policy Research for B'nai B'rith, authored the first Lemkin biography, *An Epitaph for Raphael Lemkin*[4] – making reference to Lemkin's dearest wish with respect to the Genocide Convention, namely to be "an epitaph on my mother's grave".[5] It contains as well chapters leading to the appreciation of the 'Lemkin-heritage' in the United States of America and more contemporary international criminal law issues. This

---

1 Samantha Power, A Problem from Hell. America and the Age of Genocide, New York 2002, viz. Chapters 2-5, pp. 17-85.

2 Id., Chapter 13, pp. 475-502.

3 John Cooper, Raphael Lemkin and the Struggle for the Genocide Convention, London 2008.

4 William Korey, An Epitaph for Raphael Lemkin. A Publication of the Jacob Blaustein Institute for the Advancement of Human Rights. s.l., 2001. URL: http://www.ajcarchives.org/AJC_DATA/Files/7A16.PDF + http://www.ajcarchives.org/AJC_DATA/Files/7A17.PDF + http://www.ajcarchives.org/AJC_DATA/Files/7A18.PDF + http://www.ajcarchives.org/AJC_DATA/Files/7A19.PDF + http://www.ajcarchives.org/AJC_DATA/Files/7A20.PDF , accessed 13 June 2011.

5 Id., p. 115.

book is 'A publication of the Jacob Blaustein Institute for the Advancement of Human Rights of the American Jewish Committee'; its goal, according to the 'Foreword' by Robert S. Rifkind, is to describe that "the Convention on the Prevention and Punishment of the Crime of Genocide is one of the fruits of" ... "the effort to find legal mechanisms to restrain at least the more extreme manifestations of state barbarism" and it serves as "an homage to the man who was father and midwife to the word genocide, and brought into being the Genocide Convention", and who "tirelessly worked to give a name and legal existence to a new crime" and "[b]y the force of his own will, [...] functioned as a one-person non-governmental organization to change the landscape of international law".[6]

Lemkin was seven times unsuccessfully proposed as a Nobel Peace Prize laureate between 1950 and 1959.[7] Whenever a nomination had been endorsed, Lemkin had not been relegated to obscurity, best examplified by the very few attenders to Lemkin's funeral in 1959.

However, Raphael Lemkin has been rescued from oblivion because of the current trend of humanization of international law, and since courts and tribunals for international criminal law cases came into being in the 1990s, e.g. the International Criminal Tribunal for the Former Yugoslavia and the International Criminal Tribunal for Rwanda, i.a. focusing on the genocides that took place, and the International Criminal Court, entitled to launch an indictment against perpetrators of genocide. Of course, the gatherings to commemorate the 1948 Genocide Convention in 2008 have as well been instrumental in the revival of the remembrance of Raphael Lemkin.

2. Life and Work of Raphael Lemkin

Raphael Lemkin was born in 1900 in a farmers family in the region near Wolkowysk, at that time still in tsarist Russia; after the undoing of the partitions it became Eastern Poland; nowadays it is Belarus. Lemkin was of Jewish descent, was raised as a Jew and knew Hebrew, as well as many other languages, for he was a linguistic genius. His mother acted as the home teacher and as his intellectual mentor, with whom Lemkin, – an event of seminal importance for his life and values –, could discuss Henryk Sienkiewicz's *Quo Vadis* on the perpetrators and bystanders of slaughterings of Christians in Nero's Rome.

As a student of philology in Lvov Lemkin was profoundly impressed by the revengeful assassination of Talaat Pasha, the Turkish Minister of the Interior, living freely in Berlin, who was held responsible for the Armenian massacres of 1915. The Armenian murderer, Soghomon Tehlirian, was brought to court but acquitted for he was considered to be insane. Lemkin still wondered why it was a crime to kill one man while it was not a crime for that man to have killed a million. The professor with whom Lemkin disputed rebutted with the statement of applicable national

6 Id., p. iii.

7 Samantha Power, p. 77; John Cooper, p. 266 -267; William Korey, pp. 57-58.

sovereignty rights, legitimately excluding a foreign country to intervene. This caused a rearrangement of Lemkin's mental disposition and he redirected his studies to law.

Lemkin became a criminal law practioner (he took the office of a public prosecutor) and scholar, drafting codes and legal texts, and writing commentaries, e.g. *Commentary on the Polish Penal Law of 1932*. He also spent time on international criminal law, even promoting an international criminal court (where he became acquainted with the French professor Henri Donnedieu de Vabres and the Romanian lawyer Vespasian Pella). In 1933 Lemkin had prepared a report within the domain of international criminal law domain to be presented at the 'Association Internationale de Droit Penal' in Madrid. His proposal concerned the outlawing of "barbarity" (physical human destruction) and "vandalism" (destruction of cultural and artistic works of ethnic groups). The furious German delegation to the conference left the venue.

During the odyssey Lemkin had embarked upon, escaping the German armies, he stayed in Sweden in 1941, where he started to collect documentation on policy and practice of the German occupation of European nations. Having travelled through Russia, Siberia and Japan Lemkin arrived in the United States of America. At Duke University Law School Lemkin resumed academic work and the documentary elaboration of what was going to be his epoch-making *Axis Rule in Occupied Europe. Laws of Occupation, Analysis of Government. Proposals for Redress*, finished in 1943, published in 1944 by the Carnegie Endowment for International Peace. The word 'genocide' appears for the first time in this book, a neologism invented by Lemkin himself and composed of the Greek 'genos', meaning 'people', 'origin', 'race' or 'tribe', and of the Latin 'cide', meaning killing, a combination as is known of words, such as infanticide, patricide or tyrannicide.

Winston Churchill spoke about a crime without a name,[8] Raphael Lemkin created a name for a crime without an equal. In Lemkin's words: "Genocide is directed against the national group as an entity, and the actions involved are directed against individuals, not in their individual capacity, but as members of the national group"[9] and "Genocide has two phases: one, destruction of the national pattern of the oppressed group; the other, the imposition of the national pattern of the oppressor. This imposition, in turn, may be upon the oppressed population which is allowed to remain, or upon the territory alone, after removal of the population and colonization of the area by the oppressor's own nationals".[10]

Axis Rule in Occupied Europe was well-received in the New York Times Book Review, Lemkin wrote articles on genocide in the "Free World"[11] and in "American Scholar",[12] contributing to an even wider proliferation of the word and in 1947 Lem-

8 Samantha Power, p. 29.

9 Raphael Lemkin, Axis Rule in Occupied Europe. Laws of Occupation, Analysis of Government. Proposals for Redress". Washington, 1944, p. 79.

10 Id., p. 79.

11 Raphael Lemkin, Genocide – A Modern Crime. In: Free World, Vol. 9 (1945), pp. 39-43.

12 Raphael Lemkin, Genocide. In: American Scholar Vol. XV, No. 2 (1946, April), pp. 227-230.

kin published on genocide in the "American Journal of International Law".[13] On 11 December 1946 the United Nations declared in a unanimous vote genocide to be an international crime. Lemkin started his relentless enterprise to seek agreement upon a universal anti-genocide treaty, even applicable in peacetime situations.

In the meantime however, Lemkin had to survive several disappointments. Disappointment (Lemkin's "blackest day"[14]) over the judgment at Nuremberg, because the word genocide did not occur in the verdict, and solely wartime massacres were accepted as excrescences of aggressive warfare. Disappointment because Lemkin's co-authors of the Genocide Convention, his 1930s acquaintances Henri Donnedieu de Vabres and Vespasian Pella, were no longer in favour of the cultural element of genocide, because it would unduly extend the definition of genocide beyond the justifiable physical and biological coining.[15] Nevertheless Lemkin continued his unrestricted canvassing for the Convention. On 9 December 1948 the Convention on the Prevention and Punishment of the Crime of Genocide was unanimously accepted in Paris, the first United Nations human rights treaty; the day after the Universal Declaration of Human Rights was on the table. On 12 January 1951 the Genocide Convention got legal force.

The years to come were dedicated to furthering the ratification of the Convention. Another project was the compilation of a three volume history on genocides from ancient times up to the 20th century,[16] not on the holocaust in particular. Genocide in relation to colonialism of settler societies of the newly discovered world, e.g. in the Americas and in Australia and New Zealand. Genocide committed during the German colonization of the Herero-population and by Belgium in Congo. Genocide inflicted by the Soviets,[17] e.g. in the Ukraine.[18] These studies on colonialism and mass murder provided Lemkin with the 'conceptual framework for analysing the German policy of occupation and extermination in Eastern Europe during World War II'.[19] The voluminous book however remained a manuscript.

---

13 Raphael Lemkin, Genocide as a Crime Under International Law. In: American Journal of International Law. Vol. 41, No. 1 (1947), pp. 145-151.

14 Samantha Power, p. 50.

15 John Cooper, pp. 90-91.

16 Dominik J. Schaller and Jürgen Zimmerer (Eds.), The Origins of Genocide. Raphael Lemkin as a Historian of Mass Violence. London, New York, 2009.

17 Anton Weiss-Wendt, Hostage of Politics: Raphael Lemkin on "Soviet Genocide". In: Dominik J. Schaller and Jürgen Zimmerer (Eds.), The Origins of Genocide. Raphael Lemkin as a Historian of Mass Violence. London, New York, 2009, pp. 107-115.

18 Roman Serbyn, Lemkin on Genocide of Nations. In Journal of International Criminal Justice, Vol. 7 (2009), pp. 123-130.

19 Dominik J. Schaller, Raphael Lemkin's View of European Colonial Rule in Africa: Between Condemnation and Admiration. In: Dominik J. Schaller and Jürgen Zimmerer (Eds.), The Origins of Genocide. Raphael Lemkin as a Historian of Mass Violence. London, New York, 2009, pp. 87.

Parts of the manuscript have been published thereafter. Steven L. Jacobs edited "Raphael Lemkin's Thoughts on Nazi Genocide. Not Guilty?" in 1992.[20] These "Thoughts on Nazi Genocide" were probably to become a chapter in the abovementioned 'History of Genocide'. Although this merely legal document contains a couple of mistakes, it also touches in a forecasting way on future historiographical issues, namely the role of the Wehrmacht in the extermination of the Jews, plunder and robbery of Jewish property and objects of art, Jewish genocide in order to pave the way for eastbound colonization, and ordinary men as perpetrators.[21] Among the archival material there is as well 'a sketchy first draft entitled "The Hitler case"'[22] with which Lemkin was dissatisfied.[23]

"Totally Unofficial" (most likely an allusion to the informal position Lemkin fulfilled or was forced to take during the realization of the Genocide Convention) is the title of a autobiographical book that Lemkin had commenced to write, but was not yet ready for publication around the day of Lemkin's death on 28 August 1959.[24]

3. Concluding remarks

Scholars within the field of genocide studies or international criminal law frequently honour Raphael Lemkin in their writings. Chapters, paragraphs and various other references committed to Lemkin.[25]

In 2008 conferences and symposia were organized in order to commemorate the 60th anniversary of the Genocide Convention. The products of these meetings – other than the present – consist of a book presented on 9 December 2008, *La Résistance aux génocides. De la pluralité des actes de sauvetage*, edited by Jacques Séme-

20 Steven L. Jacobs (Ed.), Raphael Lemkin's Thoughts on Nazi Genocide. Not Guilty? New York, 1992.

21 Dan Stone, Raphael Lemkin on the Holocaust. In: Dominik J. Schaller and Jürgen Zimmerer (Eds.), The Origins of Genocide. Raphael Lemkin as a Historian of Mass Violence. London, New York, 2009, pp. 95-106.

22 Id., p. 97.

23 John Cooper, p. 254.

24 John Cooper, pp. 1, 265-266, 271; Tanya Elder, What You See Before Your Eyes: Documenting Raphael Lemkin's Life by Exploring His Archival Papers, 1900-1959. In: Dominik J. Schaller and Jürgen Zimmerer (Eds.), The Origins of Genocide. Raphael Lemkin as a Historian of Mass Violence. London, New York, 2009, pp. 46-47.

25 Cf. Hirad Abtahi and Philippa Webb, The Genocide Convention, The Travaux Préparatoires. Leiden, Boston, 2008, passim; Paola Gaeta (ed.), The UN Genocide Convention – A Commentary. Oxford 2009, p. 3-8; John Quigley, The Genocide Convention. An International Law Analysis. Aldershot (etc.), 2006, pp. 4-5;

William Schabas, Genocide in International Law. The Crime of Crimes. Cambridge, 2009 (2nd ed.), pp. 28-34, 60-64; Donald Bloxham and A. Dirk Moses (Eds.), The Oxford Handbook of Genocide Studies. Oxford 2010, esp. A. Dirk Moses, Raphael Lemkin, Culture, and the Concept of Genocide, pp. 19-41.

lin, Claire Andrieu and Sarah Gensburger,[26] and *The Genocide Convention, Sixty Years After its Adoption* conference proceedings, edited by Christoph Safferling and Eckart Conze.[27]

James J. Martin, a Holocaust denier who has tried to characterize Lemkin as unreliable and as a suspicious author and informant,[28] wrote the revisionist biography *The Man Who Invented Genocide. The Public Career and Consequences of Raphael Lemkin.*[29]

Raphael Lemkin, as a passionate promoter of an inescapable objective, deserves more than this short introduction. Convincingly, Bob Skloot, an American playwright, has conferred dignity upon Raphael Lemkin in a different way in his drama "If the Whole Body Dies: Raphael Lemkin and the Treaty Against Genocide".[30]

26 Jacques Sémelin, Claire Andrieu and Sarah Gensburger (Eds.), La Résistance aux génocides. De la pluralité des actes de sauvetage. Paris, 2008.

27 Christoph Safferling and Eckart Conze (eds.), The Genocide Convention, Sixty Years After its Adoption. Cambridge, 2010. Raphael Lemkin is omnipresent in "Part One: Historical Development": William A. Schabas, Genocide in International Law and International Relations Prior to 1948, pp. 19-34; John Q. Barrett, Raphael Lemkin and 'Genocide' at Nuremberg, 1945-1946, pp. 35-54; Jost Dülffer, The United Nations and the Origins of the Genocide Convention 1946-1948, pp. 55-68.

28 John Cooper, p. 2; Tanya Elder, What You See Before Your Eyes: Documenting Raphael Lemkin's Life by Exploring His Archival Papers, 1900-1959. In: Dominik J. Schaller and Jürgen Zimmerer (Eds.), The Origins of Genocide. Raphael Lemkin as a Historian of Mass Violence. London, New York, 2009, pp. 29-30.

29 James J. Martin, The Man Who Invented Genocide. The Public Career and Consequences of Raphael Lemkin. Torrance, 1984.

30 Bob Skloot, If the Whole Body Dies: Raphael Lemkin and the Treaty Against Genocide. Madison, 2006.

About the Authors

Aartsen, Jozias van, Mayor of The Hague since 27 March 2008, liberal politician and party leader in parliament from 2003 till 2006, served as Minister of Foreign Affairs from 1998 till 2002.

Ambos, Kai, Chair of Criminal Law, Criminal Procedure, Comparative Law and International Criminal Law at the Georg-August-Universität Göttingen since May 2003, educated at the Universities of Freiburg im Breisgau, Oxford and Munich, research fellow at the Max-Planck-Institute for Foreign and International Criminal Law, Freiburg im Breisgau, in charge of the sections "International Criminal Law" and "spanish-speaking Latin America" (1991-2003).

Donia, Robert, Ph.D. in history from the University of Michigan in 1976, author of *Sarajevo: A Biography* (2006), and of *Islam under the Double Eagle: The Muslims of Bosnia and Hercegovina*, 1878-1914 (1981), historical expert witness providing testimony in the trial of former Yugoslav President Milošević and ten other trials at the International Criminal Tribunal for the Former Yugoslavia in The Hague.

Fleischer, Hagen, received a Ph.D. in History in 1978 in Berlin, at present a professor of modern history at University of Athens, focuses mainly on contemporary Greek history, World War II and its legacy and cultural policies abroad.

Herik, Larissa van den, is Professor of Public International Law at Leiden University since 2011, Editor in Chief of the *Leiden Journal of International Law*, studied law at VU University Amsterdam, defended her PhD thesis 'The Contribution of the Rwanda Tribunal to the Development of International Law' in 2005.

Houwink ten Cate, Johannes, Professor of Holocaust and Genocide Studies at the University of Amsterdam, graduated in History in 1978 at the University of Utrecht, from 1985 to 2002 research on Nazi persecution of Jews on Dutch occupied territories at the Netherlands Institute for War Documentation in Amsterdam.

Ketelaar, Eric, is Emeritus Professor of Archivistics in the Department of Media Studies (Faculty of Humanities) at the University of Amsterdam (and Leiden University), leader in the field of social and cultural archivistics (or: archival science) advocating a postmodern, interdisciplinary and comparative approach (social and collective memories, individual and group identities, social and cultural contexts of records creation and use), General State Archivist (National Archivist) of The Netherlands from 1989-1997.

LeBlanc, Lawrence, is a full Professor and Department Chair at the University of Iowa, Visiting Fulbright Scholar at the Universiti Kebangsaan Malaysia for 2003-04 and recipient of The John P. Raynor Award for Teaching Excellence in 2005, specializes in international politics, international law and organizations, US foreign policy, and on the implementation of United Nations human rights conventions.

Leydesdorff, Selma, is an oral historian (oral history of the Jewish proletariat of Amsterdam, published as *We Lived With Dignity*, 1994), is principal editor of the international series *Memory and Narratives*, since 2002 her research has focused on the survivors of Srebrenica (*Surviving the Bosnian Genocide; The Women of Srebrenica Speak*, 2011).

Lippman, Matthew, Professor at the Department of Criminology, Law and Justice of the University of Illinois, Chicago, educated at Harvard Law School, PhD in Political Science, legal expert on the Nazi holocaust, the legal profession in Nazi Germany, the extradition of Nazi war criminals and on the Genocide Convention.

Marrus, Michael, is the Chancellor Rose and Ray Wolfe Professor Emeritus of Holocaust Studies in the Department of History at the University of Toronto, he has been a visiting fellow of St. Antony's College, Oxford, the Institute for Advanced Studies of the Hebrew University of Jerusalem, and has taught as a visiting professor at UCLA and the University of Cape Town, South Africa, he has written widely in the areas of modern European history and the Holocaust, is an expert on the history of French Jewry and anti-semitism.

Mennecke, Martin, Department of Holocaust and Genocide Studies of the Danish Institute of International Studies, his fields of interest are international criminal law and genocide education.

Moreno-Ocampo, Luis, lawyer from Argentina (as prosecutor involved in precedent-setting prosecutions of top military commanders for mass killings and other large-scale human rights abuses from 1984 till 1992, "Trial of the Juntas"), Prosecutor of the International Criminal Court (ICC) since 2003.

Mulder, Dirk, since 1986 director of Memorial Center Camp Westerbork (former transit camp for Dutch Jews during WWII), taught history at high schools for 15 years, member of the Dutch delegation of the International Task Force for Cooperation on Holocaust Education, Remembrance and Research, and chair of its Memorials and Museums Working group, and he is on the advisory board of the Masterplan Sobibor and the Potocari Memorial Center in Bosnia and Herzegovina.

Schabas, William, international criminal and human rights law specialist (*Genocide in International Law: The Crime of Crimes*, 2nd ed. 2009; *An Introduction to the International Criminal Court*, 4th ed. 2011; *The Abolition of the Death Penalty in International Law*, 3rd ed. 2003; *The International Criminal Court: A Commentary on the Rome Statute*, 2010; he has also published more than 300 articles in academic journals), Professor of International Law at Middlesex University in London since 2011, Professor of International Law and Director of the Irish Centre for Human Rights at the National University of Ireland, Galway (2000-2011), Professor of Human Rights Law and Criminal Law at the Département des Sciences Juridiques of the Université du Québec à Montréal (1991 to 2000).

Skloot, Robert (Bob), Emeritus Professor of Theater and Drama and Jewish Studies, contributed to his field with *The Theater of Genocide: Four Plays about Mass Murder in Rwanda, Bosnia, Cambodia and Armenia*, *The Darkness We Carry: the Drama of the Holocaust*, and the one-act play *If the Whole Body Dies: Raphael Lemkin and the Treaty Against Genocide* (persons or groups who would like to arrange for a reading should contact the author at rskloot@wisc.edu for information and permission).

Sluiter, Göran, Professor of International Criminal Law, in particular the Law of International Criminal Procedure at the University of Amsterdam, Judge at the District Courts of Utrecht and The Hague (Van Anraat case, the first genocide case in the Netherlands), co-founder and co-editor (with Prof. André Klip) of the series *Annotated Leading Cases of International Criminal Tribunals*.

Tromp, Nena, is a researcher with the Leadership Research Team for the Office of the Prosecutor at the ICTY and works at the University of Amsterdam as an Associate Professor at the Department of Eastern European Studies.

Vervliet, Jeroen, Director of the Peace Palace Library in The Hague, studied history and law at the University of Amsterdam.

Voorhoeve, Joris, liberal politician and party leader (1986-1990), Minister of Defence between 1994 and 1998 (during the Srebrenica-massacres of 1995), and Professor in International Relations.

Vriend, Koen, historian and lawyer, University of Amsterdam, Criminal Law-researcher.

Weiss-Wendt, Anton, Ph.D. in Judaic Studies from Brandeis University, worked on comparative genocide studies, heads the Research Department at the Center for the Study of the Holocaust and Religious Minorities in Oslo.

Wilt, Harmen van der, since 2004 full Professor of International Criminal Law at the University of Amsterdam, research interests in the concepts of criminal responsibility in International Criminal Law, the principle of complementarity at the ICC, criminal procedure of the international criminal tribunals and cooperation between states and the international criminal tribunals as well as European arrest warrant and harmonisation of criminal law in Europe, has been involved in professional training programs for judiciary and public prosecutors in Addis Abeba (Ethiopia) and training programs for young staff-members of Lobatchevski University of Nijni Novgorod (Russia).

Zegveld, Liesbeth, works at Böhler Advocaten, specialises in legal remedies for war victims, is also a professor of International Humanitarian Law at Leiden University since 2006, focuses on the Rights of Women and Children in Armed Conflict, her scholarly works address diverse issues such as victims of chemical warfare in Iraq, kidnapping in Colombia, torture in Afghanistan, and accountability.

Speech by the Mayor Mr van Aartsen at the conference on '60 Years Genocide Convention', 8 December 2008

Ladies and gentlemen,

On 25 June 1995 a young girl in the besieged town of Sarajevo had had quite enough of being forced to sit indoors. Her parents finally give way to her pleas: Sidbela Zimic was allowed to go out and play with her skipping rope in the playground, near the flat where she lived. A few minutes later, a Serbian grenade brought her brief life to an end, along with the lives of three of her playmates. That brought the total number of children who had died on Bosnian territory since the start of the war to 16,771. It is with this heart-rending story that Samantha Power begins her famous book about genocide and the reactions to it, *A Problem from Hell.*

More than thirteen years later, on 30 July 2008, the man who is seen as the architect of the siege of Sarajevo - and thus the death of that nine year old Bosnian girl - arrives in The Hague: Radovan Karadzic. A day later he is led before the International Criminal Tribunal for the former Yugoslavia. Together with the Rwanda Tribunal, the ICTY was the first of its kind to be set up after the General Assembly of the United Nations had adopted the "Convention on the Prevention and Punishment of the Crime of Genocide" in 1948.

Since the founding of the Yugoslav Tribunal and later, too, the International Criminal Court, our city has grown to be a centre of international criminal law. This is partly because in the preceding decade The Hague, as city of peace and justice, had evolved to become a centre of legal knowledge. In recent years, the Hague infrastructure in the domain of international criminal law has been further strengthened by the activities of the International Criminal Law Network that celebrated its fifth anniversary last year.

With the founding of the International Criminal Court, international criminal law has embarked on a new chapter of its existence. For the first time in history there is a permanent court that can call perpetrators of crimes against humanity to account. A place where judgement is handed down in the event of a state being unable or unwilling to do so. The Hague feels itself privileged to be home to this unique institution.

The International Criminal Tribunals for the former Yugoslavia and Rwanda, and also the Special Court for Sierra Leone, will close their doors within the foreseeable future. The arrest of Karadzic has admittedly postponed the date of closure of the ICTY but not, of course, *ad infinitum*.

The question that arises, however, is what happens after that? We can't just pull the plug on the whole thing. For decades to come, for instance, the detention of those sentenced has to be supervised and people may take their cases to higher appeal. Some witnesses are in a witness protection programme that naturally cannot come to an end from one day to the next.

So what have been called 'residual mechanisms' will have to be put in place to perform the residual functions of these tribunals. I can imagine that the residual mechanisms of the ICTY will be located in The Hague. There is also a conceivable scenario for the residual functions of different tribunals to be combined, with or without satellite offices abroad.

And then we have the question of what to do with the tribunal records. The residual mechanisms could very well manage these archives. That sounds like a logical solution, though one might ask whether it is a realistic one in the long term. The fact is, that there will come a time when the residual mechanisms are no longer needed either.

And talking about the archives of these ad hoc tribunals, we have to bear three things in mind. Firstly, that we are dealing in part with items of evidence that have to be properly and, above all, securely maintained. There are plenty of parties who would stand to gain if that evidence to be mislaid.

We must also realise that the records and documents are part of our legal and historical heritage. A heritage that in principle belongs to the world community, the same global community that took the decision to set up the tribunals in the first place. By taking that step the world community ensured that the Genocide Convention, Raphael Lemkin's legacy, is more than just a paper tiger.

Lastly, we have to be constantly aware of the immense emotional charge of these archives. They contain, after all, the oral and written records of witnesses to the most horrific crimes. Crimes that have traumatised, once and for all, not only individuals and their next of kin, but often whole nations or tribes as well. And all those who are familiar with the inventory of the archives of the Nuremberg trials, placed in the custody of the International Court of Justice, know that the accompanying material evidence can be infinitely worse than the witnesses' own gruesome verbal testimony.

Some sections of the archives are in the public domain and, in the case of the ICTY, can soon be consulted via the internet by anyone who is interested. The confidential archives, needless to say, remain the preserve of the judicial authorities.

In a digital age, one may, of course, rightly ask oneself whether the actual location of an archive really matters, certainly a public one. Once it has been digitalised, it is globally accessible. In the case of the confidential archives, I can imagine that they should be kept as close as possible to the residual mechanisms. And all the originals, public or confidential, have to be stored somewhere where they can be secure and properly maintained.

These criteria cannot be fulfilled to the same degree all over the world. The Netherlands Ministry of Foreign Affairs and the local authority of The Hague take the view that The Hague meets all the requirements for eligibility as the definitive location of the archives of the ad hoc tribunals. The Hague and the surrounding metropolitan region have thorough knowledge of both preservation techniques and digitalisation. Moreover, the existing infrastructure of legal knowledge, to be expanded in the near future with a University College, is a strong argument in favour of The Hague.

Naturally, it is not up to The Hague or the Netherlands to decide on the future location of the archives. Should they ultimately be accommodated elsewhere, then the Netherlands can, of course, offer assistance in preserving and accessing these archives. There is also the option of keeping a so-called 'mirror archive' in The Hague with authenticated copies.

I think there is no need for me to say in this company how valuable these archives are for academic research. But the preservation and the accessing of the archives are also extremely important for another group of people: the next of kin of the victims. For example, the parents and elder sister of the little girl Sidbela Zimic, whose tragic death I spoke about at the beginning of my speech.

We must never forget that we are talking about crimes perpetrated against individuals. Sometimes they may have been in large groups, but the victims were and remain individuals. That is the special thing about international criminal law, that it affects people individually. Crimes and retribution all involve people. Even when the last witness is no longer alive, his or her testimony must be preserved for their descendants. The Netherlands government and the city of The Hague regard it as their task to help to ensure that this happens.

60 Years Genocide Convention, Opening Remarks

Joris Voorhoeve

1. Introduction

The Genocide Convention of 1948 was a major step towards protection of the right of population groups and recognition of their right to be different from others on religious, ethnic, racial or other grounds. All groups have a right to live and develop in peace, to not being destroyed in war or civil war, or eliminated by other policies such as starvation. The Convention makes those persons aiming at the destruction of such groups punishable under international law. The general concept of crimes against humanity which played already a key role in the Nuremberg and Tokyo Tribunals was specified by this convention against wilful destruction of specific population groups.

It is regrettable that the Convention was not put into practice for several decades, and that a leading Western democracy delayed ratification till 1988, perhaps mainly because of a doctrinal issue concerning the obligations which follow from international law for its citizens and priority over national law. As a multicultural, multiracial and multilingual democracy, the Unites States embodies the right to be different and as a leading member of the Security Council, being the second largest democracy after India, it has a major responsibility for getting the Convention implemented.

It is fortunate that the Genocide Convention could play an important role in the indictments before the International Criminal Tribunal for the former Yugoslavia. Hopefully, all major suspects will be sentenced before this Tribunal is formally disbanded by the Security Council.

2. Prevention

Even more important than successful prosecution, arrest and trial of suspects, is prevention of genocide. The doctrine of the responsibility to protect aims to achieve this. Results till now are disappointing, however. The Security Council is generally not willing to apply this new norm. State sovereignty prevails over human security. Only when other national interests and values of main members of the Security Council support the upholding of the security of a particular population group in danger, the Council may be willing to act. This was the case with the Kurdish people in the north of Iraq after the first intervention against Saddam Hussein. The enforcement of the zone north of Bagdad by airplanes of three veto-holding states created a more or less protected area which saved many lives.

In the war in the former Yugoslavia between 1991 and 1995, the Security Council introduced safe areas by resolution, covering Sarajevo, Srebrenica, Tuzla, Zepa, Gorazde and Bihac. Among these, Srebrenica and Zepa fell to aggressors, as these enclaves were not defended by blue helmet soldiers. Most of the captured males of both enclaves were executed. The fate of these enclaves and the earlier killings of civilians in Sarajevo and Tuzla in 1994-5 seriously discredited the concept of safe areas or safe havens. Of these safe areas, four survived, however, thanks to the Dayton Peace agreement as well as the threat of deterrent air force by main military powers. Noteworthy is the case of Gorazde, which tells us how an endangered enclave can be saved.

After the fall of Srebrenica and Zepa in July 1995, the UN and troop contributing countries met in London to see how the imminent attack on Gorazde could be halted. NATO members issued a stern new message to the leaders of the attack in Belgrade and Pale: If Gorazde will be overrun, NATO members would attack by airstrikes sensitive targets of the opponent elsewhere, far away from Gorazde itself, which was not defensible on the ground. This re-introduced defence by deterrence, which had saved West Berlin in 1948 and more generally the peace in Europe during the Cold War.

I submit to you that enforcing protected humanitarian zones in countries at war or in civil war, is an idea which should not be discarded on the basis of its failure in Srebrenica and Zepa. Its success in Gorazde, and also the case of Northern Iraq, shows what conditions should be met to make the idea work. More important than a UNSC resolution declaring an area to be safe, will be credible deterrence of aggression against large concentrations of refugees and other civilians. This requires that main UNSC members, at least one veto-holding power, possibly a coalition, and even better an alliance, should put its prestige on the line and deter attack of the area by holding military targets hostage, such as the enemy's headquarters, munitions storage, airfields and other carefully chosen, non-civilian targets.

Next to the condition of credible deterrence, the safe area should be clearly delineated and be geographically defensible for some time by conventional forces. Ideally, the UN should augment, or temporarily take over, the administration of the area, provide some basic legal order for the refugees, supply the area with essential goods and services to the refugees and indigenous population, and control the in- and outflow of persons carrying weapons by disarming them. The area should not be a recruiting ground for war parties, not serve as a base from which to attack, and be demilitarized, with a zone around it in which heavy weapons are forbidden. This would need to be enforced by a coalition of the willing, ideally mandated by the Security Council. One may add other conditions, such as an exit strategy and a political plan for the future of the area. My remarks are not yet a complete list of conditions needed to prevent genocidal campaigns against enclaves.

The point I want to make is that in present and future forms of contemporary armed conflict the concept of what I want to rename internationally protected safe humanitarian zones may help to save many lives of civilians, in case the UN and a relevant coalition of main military powers are really prepared to support the zone when it comes under attack, also with deterrent air power against enemy targets elsewhere. This may help to reduce the risk of genocide and other gross crimes against humanity in the area concerned.

Prevention of war crimes, crimes against humanity and genocide will also be augmented by growing relevance of the International Criminal Court. Its arrest warrants are a message to all perpetrators of such crimes, be they political or military leaders, militia, armed gangs, and major administrators engaged in such crimes.

Let us hope that the US under its new leadership will overcome its previous hesitations against the ICC and come to recognise the significance to the interests and values of the US itself in joining the ICC.

3. The Responsibility to Protect

My last remark concerns the doctrine of the responsibility to protect. This doctrine is debated and criticized particularly by non-Western countries as assuming a more or less imperialist, neo-conservative or neo-colonial responsibility that might justify armed interventions against governments of developing countries. This criticism is incorrect. The opponents try to score a point against Western preponderance and neo-colonial humanitarianism. But the doctrine follows from universal human rights thinking.

Invoking this non-binding R2P in the case where the Birmese government obstructed urgent humanitarian assistance to its own population was not needed and not helpful, however. I submit it would have been wiser to invoke the Convention for the Protection of Social, Economic and Cultural Rights. This Convention stipulates that governments have to take care of the basic needs of their peoples. It has been ratified by the vast majority of states and is binding international law, even though its world-wide implementation is still deficient.

Governments which deny their people food, medical and other basic care necessary to survive are in blatant violation of basic human rights. This applies unfortunately to many governments in the world, as the number of hungry and malnourished has reached 975 million according to FAO. It may well rise further as a result of the recession in many countries. I make this point about basic human economic rights to suggest that the R2P is in a way a specification of the general responsibility of governments to take care of their populations' basic needs, as tasks grounded in the global human rights treaties. This approach may make its application in specific cases less vulnerable to political criticism.

I conclude by wishing you all a very fruitful conference, strengthening the future of the Genocide Convention. I congratulate the Peace Palace Library, the Amsterdam Center for International Law and the Center for Holocaust and Genocide Studies for this initiative and express my appreciation for the authorities and institutions which made this important conference possible.

Speech by Luis Moreno-Ocampo at the conference on '60 Years Genocide Convention', 7 December 2008

Ladies and Gentlemen,

Thank you for the opportunity to be with you today. As Prosecutor of the International Criminal Court (ICC) with the power and the duty to investigate massive crimes, including Genocide, I welcome the opportunity to build upon lessons learnt by a diversity of actors and to work towards strengthening the network of individuals and organizations working to prevent and punish acts of genocide.

The 1948 Convention on Genocide is a founding text for the ICC; it is also a visionary text which already envisaged the creation of an international tribunal.

In 1998 in Rome, the adoption of the Statute of the ICC was the culmination of efforts of the international community to establish such a permanent Court.

In 2008 the Court is in operation. As Prosecutor, on 14 July, I requested to the Pre-Trial Chamber I the issuance of an arrest warrant against Sudanese President Al Bashir for genocide, crimes against humanity and war crimes.

Today, I will address three issues:

- The significance of the Genocide Convention as a founding text of the ICC;
- The role of the ICC, and;
- The Darfur challenge.

1. The Genocide Convention and the ICC

As you know, the definition contained in Article II of the Convention has been copied literally into the Rome Statute. But the contribution of the drafters to the ICC Statute is even greater.

The adoption of the Genocide Convention was the first expression of a worldwide consensus that crimes of this nature should no longer go unpunished; in addition, the drafters recognized that, for the law to be effective, an independent judicial enforcement mechanism would be required.

To that end, Article 6 refers to the authorities with jurisdiction over the crime: "a competent tribunal of the State in the territory of which the act was committed, or by such international penal tribunal".

The reference to an international penal tribunal was a revolutionary novelty in international law. That idea, and the lessons learnt from the political hesitations that allowed genocides such as the ones in Srebrenica and Rwanda to happen, laid the foundations for the ICC.

2. The Rome Statute as the foundation of a global criminal justice system

The goal of the Rome Statute is to end impunity for the most serious crimes of international concern and to contribute to the prevention of such crimes.

To achieve its goal, the Rome Statute integrates sovereign States and an international criminal court in one legal system. The Rome Statute incorporates detailed definitions of genocide, crimes against humanity and war crimes in one text, defining the prosecution and prevention of these crimes as a national and international obligation.

In the words of the Preamble, the Rome Statute consolidates the "duty of every state to exercise its criminal jurisdiction over those responsible for international crimes" and establishes a system of international cooperation. The Rome Statute is more than a Court. National States remain primarily responsible for investigating and prosecuting crimes committed within their jurisdiction but in addition they have to support an independent and permanent International Criminal Court whenever and wherever the Court decides to intervene. States Parties have to "guarantee lasting respect for and the enforcement of international justice".

The Rome Statute created a truly international criminal justice system based on two main principles: complementarity and cooperation.

It took more than a century to develop this model. In 1873, Louis Gabriel Gustave Moynier, the Swiss lawyer who co-founded the International Committee of the Red Cross, proposed a similar concept, recognizing the challenge of compliance. Moynier stated: "a treaty was not a law imposed by a superior authority on its subordinates (but) only a contract whose signatories cannot decree penalties against themselves since there would be no one to implement them. The only reasonable guarantee should lie in the creation of international jurisdiction with the necessary power to compel obedience".

The Court as an independent and permanent mechanism provides a different dynamic, compared with other areas of international criminal law such as drugs trafficking, money laundering, arms dealing or terrorism. The mere existence of the Court produces incentives to take action at the national level. Additionally a ruling of the ICC will not only decide on the guilt or innocence of the accused, but it will reverberate with at least 108 States and citizens all around the world. The Judges' decisions will contribute to establish the rule of law in the world. Even before our first trial, for example, in Sri Lanka and Colombia there have already been discussions about the use of child soldiers by local militias.

We need to further explore the possibilities and constraints of such a novel system, always bearing in mind that much of the activities could and should take place at the national level.

There have already been significant achievements in the implementation of the Rome "system" by different actors. National legislation has been approved in more than 50 countries. Diplomats and negotiators are increasingly excluding amnesties for the crimes covered by the Rome Statute. Armies around the world, even from non signatory States, are adjusting their regulations to the Rome Statute. They are seeking to prevent their personnel from committing acts falling within the jurisdiction of the ICC. This is the way to stop crimes. The law makes the difference between a soldier or a terrorist, a policeman or a criminal.

All past genocides, in World War II in Europe, in Rwanda and the Former Yugoslavia, have been committed and have been carefully planned by organizers; now the planners know that we can go after them; although the effect of such a new approach cannot be assessed yet in terms of preventing genocides, there are already some signs of the impact of the ICC Statute.

In this context, I would note that the United Nations (UN) Security Council, in referring the Darfur situation to the ICC in March of 2005, has recognized that lasting peace and security in Darfur will require justice and accountability. In a few years, the UN system for peace and security was connected with the permanent system of justice. The Darfur case is a test for the international community and the coming months will be critical.

3. The Darfur case

Since June 2005, my Office has carried out an investigation under difficult circumstances. I have a duty to protect the persons called as witnesses and I cannot protect those living in the Sudan. Thus we had to investigate Darfur without visiting Darfur. We received information from many sources, including the Government of the Sudan, and were helped by thousands of documents collected by the UN Commission of Inquiry. We contacted victims all over the world and interviewed more than 100 witnesses in 18 countries. And the victims, those who escaped from Darfur, in spite of all the pain, told us their stories. One woman described how they killed her baby and then raped her. A man told us: "They forced me to watch as they raped my 8-year-old daughter. I was asking: 'why?'"

Those stories are evidence. On this basis, in April 2007, Pre-Trial Chamber I of the ICC issued an arrest warrant against Ahmed Harun and Ali Kushayb for 51 counts of crimes against humanity and war crimes.

The evidence showed that the Sudanese Armed Forces, acting in concert with Militia/Janjaweed, attacked hundreds of villages predominantly inhabited by the Fur, Masalit and Zaghawa. Helicopters or aircraft dropped bombs. Ground forces killed, tortured and raped thousands of civilians. The attackers destroyed all means of survival, sources of water, and stripped the villages, destroying schools, mosques and hospitals.

As a result of the attacks, at least 35,000 people have been killed. The UN says that almost 300,000 of those who fled the attacks died of starvation and diseases. More than 200,000 people managed to reach refugee camps in Chad or Central African Republic. Almost 2.5 million people went to the outskirts of bigger cities that would become camps for Internally Displaced Persons (IDPs).

This first Darfur case confirmed one fact: the attacks against civilians in their homes, the massive campaign of rapes, the forced displacement of almost 3 millions people, were not the product of autonomous self-defence militias or the result of "inter tribal fighting". They were the actual goal of an operation planned and implemented by the Sudanese state apparatus, executed by the Army, the Air Force and Reservist forces integrating tribal militias called "Janjaweed".

The mobilization of local militia allowed Mr. Al Bashir for years to disguise the conflict as a tribal one that had nothing to do with state forces. Mr. Al Bashir created the illusion of Militia/Janjaweed autonomy, and this helped him to continue to carry out the genocide in the face of international scrutiny. The victims were attacked by those same officials who were supposed to protect them.

On 14 July of this year, I presented to the Judges my second case in the Darfur situation covering crimes committed from March 2003 to the present. I requested an arrest warrant against Mr. Al Bashir for 3 counts of genocide, 5 counts of crimes against humanity and 2 counts of war crimes.

The evidence in this second case highlights three aspects, all of them known but all of them denied: Al Bashir ordered the crimes; it is genocide; and it is happening now.

Al Bashir ordered the crimes

He ordered the attacks on the villages and he orders today the attacks on the camps for internally displaced persons, the rapes and the hindering of humanitarian assistance. He publicly ordered to "take no prisoners; I only want scorched earth". He ensured the implementation of his decision. He removed commanders and soldiers that refused to follow his illegal orders and appointed those who were ready to commit a genocide.

Al Bashir has genocidal intent

Al Bashir assessed that the Fur, Masalit and Zaghawa ethnic groups constituted a threat to his power. They challenged the economic and political marginalization of their region, and members of the groups engaged in armed rebellion. Al Bashir's goal was not simply to defeat a rebellion, but to destroy those ethnic groups whose members challenged his power. His motives were largely political. His pretext was a "counterinsurgency". His intent was genocide. This is not new. In 2004 already, Professor Alex de Waal wrote "This is the routine cruelty of a security cabal, its humanity withered by years in power: it is genocide by force of habit."

The Genocide is being committed now

The Fur, Masalit and Zaghawa are systematically attacked, first in their villages and now in the camps.

The mass displacement operations in Darfur were conducted in conditions which, during the deliberations preceding the adoption of the Genocide Convention, were found to constitute genocide:

> "Mass displacements of populations from one region to another [...] do not constitute genocide [...] unless the operation were attended by such circumstances as to lead to the death of the whole or part of the displaced population. If for example, people were driven from their homes and forced to travel long distances in a country where they were exposed to starvation, thirst, hunger, cold and epidemics".

As indicated in January 2005 by the UN Commission of Inquiry, there would be no policy of genocide if "*the populations surviving attacks on villages ... live together in areas selected by the Government...where they are assisted*". The evidence shows that the target groups, far from being assisted, are also attacked in the camps.

President Al Bashir is providing no meaningful assistance to those millions displaced and is hindering the humanitarian efforts of the international community. Fear, rape and hunger are the main weapons of the current phase of the genocide. One victim of rape explained:

> "They kill our males and dilute our blood with rape. [They]...want to finish us as a people, end our history".

Another victim in the desert overheard one attacker say:

> "Don't waste the bullet, they've got nothing to eat and they will die from hunger".

Since September 2005, Mr. Al Bashir appointed Ahmed Harun as the Minister of State for Humanitarian Affairs, to continue attacking his victims. He is still a critical piece in the implementation of Al Bashir's plan. The Humanitarian Aid Commission (HAC), within his Ministry, works in close association with the intelligence and security apparatus; they block the delivery of aid, expel relief staff, deny visas and travel permits to aid workers. As a consequence, 2.5 million people in the camps today are subjected to conditions of life calculated to bring about their physical destruction.

The Court is doing its part. The Pre-Trial Chamber will decide. But States have to be prepared: the Judges will decide on the arrest warrant sooner and later and States should adjust to this simple fact sooner than later.

There is a need to better integrate the judicial, humanitarian and political efforts. For almost one year, the first arrest warrant, issued against Harun, was ignored by mediators and political leaders in their discussions on Darfur. They ignored the Court's decision, and they ignored the facts. They ignored Harun's role in the HAC—the main obstacle to humanitarian assistance; they ignored Harun's membership of the African Union/United Nations Hybrid operation in Darfur (UNAMID) oversight committee, affecting the deployment of peacekeepers. In August 2007, Harun was appointed head of a committee to investigate human rights abuses, thus providing certainty to the other members of the Government that crimes are condoned.

A new comprehensive strategy is needed to factor in the information contained in our Applications and the fact of the arrest warrants.

Arrest warrants have to be executed. They not only serve the interests of justice; they can help alleviate the humanitarian situation, facilitate the deployment and operation of UNAMID and reach lasting political agreements. It is about justice and it is about realpolitik. Massive crimes are not just a moral problem; massive crimes cross borders, destabilize entire regions and affect world security.

Given the international attention on Darfur, imposing conditions calculated to bring about the physical destruction of the target groups, combined with a studied misinformation campaign, was, and is still the most efficient strategy to achieve complete destruction. By preventing the truth about the crimes; concealing the crimes under the guise of "inter tribal clashes", or the "actions of lawless autonomous militia"; threatening Sudanese citizens and humanitarian workers into silence, and blackmailing the international community with the threat of derailing the North-

South peace agreement, Mr. Al Bashir made possible the continuation of the genocide.

The Darfur case represents a unique opportunity for the international community to come together, to establish a new framework to protect individuals. As the UN Secretary General, Mr. Ban Ki-Moon said, peace and justice have to work hand in hand. The Court is fulfilling its judicial mandate, the Court is unveiling the truth and is creating the possibility of collective action against the crimes, but it will not be enough. International justice relies on cooperation. States and multilateral institutions have to create the conditions to implement arrest warrants and to update and harmonize old conflict management strategies with the new reality.

4. Conclusion

We are celebrating 60 years of the Genocide Convention; we celebrated 10 years of the creation of the permanent International Criminal Court envisaged in the Convention, but in the coming months the destiny of 2.5 millions Darfuris will be decided. "Never again" should no more be a promise: it is time to transform it into a reality. Darfur is our test.

It is easier to talk about past genocides, to say "never again" about the Holocaust, or to talk about the failures in Srebrenica or Rwanda, but it is not easy to talk about today's problems. There are different interests at stake in Darfur. You could have an important role in explaining today the lessons of past genocides. As demonstrated in the past by the work of Raphael Lemkin, even one person without official functions can contribute meaningfully to ending the crimes.

General

1. Genocide and Crimes against Humanity: Clarifying the Relationship

William Schabas

The Convention for the Prevention and Punishment of the Crime of Genocide was adopted in Paris, on December 9, 1948, at the third session of the United Nations General Assembly.[1] It entered into force slightly more than two years later, on January 12, 1951, after obtaining the requisite twenty ratifications. But despite its importance in the general scheme of international human rights treaties, and a willingness to accept many of its provisions as declaratory of customary international law, it still only has about 140 states parties, a comparatively low number. This event is one of several being held around the world to mark the sixtieth anniversary of the adoption of the Convention. A decade ago, there was scant attention for what was arguably a more significant commemoration. Interest in the Convention and in the legal aspects of genocide has grown dramatically in the past ten years, a part of the proliferation of activity in the field of international criminal law. There have been more important judicial pronouncements on genocide in the past five years than in the previous fifty-five.

At the same time, the legal significance of genocide has probably declined, a phenomenon related to the dramatic expansion of the related category of crimes against humanity. Today, there are few if any legal consequences to identifying an act as genocide, as opposed to describing it with the somewhat broader and more flexible label of crimes against humanity. Yet for victims of atrocity, describing their persecution as genocide is viewed as a badge of honour, and denying this to them is often treated as trivialization. A contemporary manifestation of the phenomenon can be seen in the rather spectacular and extravagant charge levelled by the Prosecutor of the International Criminal Court (ICC) against the sitting president of The Sudan,[2] a matter currently being examined by Pre-Trial Chamber I.

The Genocide Convention was the first human rights treaty of the modern system, codifying an international norm that protects the right to life and to the exis-

1 Convention on the Prevention and Punishment of the Crime of Genocide (1951) 78 UNTS 277.

2 *Situation in Darfur, The Sudan* (Case No. ICC-02/05), Summary of Prosecutor's Application under Article 58, July 14, 2008.

H.G. van der Wilt, J. Vervliet et al., *(eds.)* The Genocide Convention: The Legacy of 60 Years.
Copyright 2012 Koninklijke Brill NV. ISBN 978 9004 15328 8. pp. 3-14.

tence of national, ethnic, racial, and religious minorities. The Convention establishes important principles in the areas of prosecution and prevention that have since been amplified and developed in other instruments and institutions. Article VI constitutes the starting point of the subject jurisdiction defined by the Rome Statute. Many have argued that the Convention has serious gaps, and that it needs to be "repaired" or "completed". But questioning the "gaps" in the Genocide Convention is like speculating on "improvements" to Picasso's Guernica, Marc Anthony's eulogy, Seigfried's funeral music, or asking whether new ingredients should be added to a classic dry martini or whether one can make oysters Rockefeller using chicken. The Genocide Convention is what it is: a seminal development in international law, an affirmation of important principles, a reflection of the values and standards of its time, but at the same time the clear inspiration for much that has followed. It has no gaps.

Genocide is, first and foremost, a legal concept. Like many other terms—murder, rape, theft—it is also used in other contexts and by other disciplines, where its meaning may vary. Many historians and sociologists employ the term genocide to describe a range of atrocities involving killing large numbers of people. But even in law, it is imprecise to speak of a single, universally recognized meaning of genocide. There is a widely accepted definition, first set out in Article II of the 1948 Convention for the Prevention and Punishment of the Crime of Genocide. Like most legal definitions, its language is subject to various interpretations, and important controversies remain about the scope of the concept, even within the framework of what is a concise and carefully worded definition. The crime of genocide has been incorporated within the national legal systems of many countries, where domestic legislators have imposed their own views on the term, some of them varying slightly or even considerably from the established international definition. As a result, even in law, one can speak of many definitions or interpretations of the concept of genocide.

The term itself was invented by a lawyer, Raphael Lemkin. He intended to fill a lacuna in international law, as it then stood in the final days of the Second World War. For more than two decades, Lemkin had been engaged at an international level in attempts to codify new categories of international crimes involving atrocities committed against vulnerable civilians. Even before Lemkin's time, international law recognized a limited number of so-called international crimes. As a general rule, they were so designated not because of their shocking scale and extent, but for more mundane reasons, namely because they escaped the territorial jurisdiction of states. Piracy is the classic example, a crime committed on the high seas. Lemkin and others argued from a different perspective, proposing the recognition of international crimes where they represented serious human rights violations.

The beginnings of this were already apparent at the time of the First World War, when Britain, France, and Russia warned that they would hold perpetrators to account for "these new crimes of Turkey against humanity and civilization." But the idea that a state could be held liable for atrocities committed against its own nationals remained extremely controversial, and it was this gap in the law that Lemkin worked to fill. His initial proposal evidenced a much broader concept of genocide than what was eventually agreed to in the 1948 Convention. Lemkin actively participated in the negotiations leading to the Convention's adoption, and while he would no doubt have hoped for a somewhat different result, he cannot be detached from the Convention's definition. Indeed, following its adoption he campaigned aggressively for its ratification.

Lemkin's famous proposal, contained in a chapter entitled "Genocide" in his book *Axis Rule in Occupied Europe*, called for the "prohibition of genocide in war and peace". Lemkin insisted upon the relationship between genocide and the growing interest in the protection of peoples and minorities that was manifested in several treaties and declarations adopted following the First World War. He noted the need to revisit international legal instruments, pointing out particularly the inadequacies of the *Hague Convention* of 1907, which he noted was "silent regarding the preservation of the integrity of a people". According to Lemkin:

> The definition of genocide in the *Hague Regulations* thus amended should consist of two essential parts: in the first should be included every action infringing upon the life, liberty, health, corporal integrity, economic existence, and the honour of the inhabitants when committed because they belong to a national, religious, or racial group; and in the second, every policy aiming at the destruction or the aggrandisement of one of such groups to the prejudice or detriment of another.[3]

The legal concept of genocide was forged in the crucible of post-Second World War efforts to prosecute Nazi atrocities. Its development took place in conjunction with that of other international crimes, especially crimes against humanity, with which it bears a close, but complex and difficult, relationship. The development and history of genocide as a legal concept cannot be properly understood without considering the parallel existence of crimes against humanity. Although the participants in the United Nations War Crimes Commission, established in November 1943, and in the London Conference, which met from late June to early August 1945 to prepare the Nuremberg trial of the major war criminals, opted to use the term crimes against humanity in the prosecutions, they also employed the word genocide as if it was more or less synonymous. In his "Planning Memorandum distributed to Delegations at Beginning of London Conference, June 1945," where Justice Robert Jackson outlined the evidence to be adduced in the Nuremberg trial, he spoke of:

> Genocide or destruction of racial minorities and subjugated populations by such means and methods as (1) underfeeding; (2) sterilization and castration; (3) depriving them of

3 Raphael Lemkin, *Axis Rule in Occupied Europe: Laws of Occupation, Analysis of Government, Proposals for Redress* (Washington: Carnegie Endowment for World Peace, 1944), 90-93. On Lemkin, see: William Korey, *An Epitaph for Raphael Lemkin* (New York: Jacob Blaustein Institute for the Advancement of Human Rights, 2001); John Cooper, *Raphael Lemkin and the Struggle for the Genocide Convention* (Basingstoke, United Kingdom: Palgrave Macmillan, 2008).

> clothing, shelter, fuel, sanitation, medical care; (4) deporting them for forced labour; (5) working them in inhumane conditions.[4]

The indictment of the International Military Tribunal charged the Nazi defendants with "deliberate and systematic genocide, viz., the extermination of racial and national groups, against the civilian populations of certain occupied territories in order to destroy particular races and classes of people, and national, racial or religious groups, particularly Jews, Poles, and Gypsies".[5] The term "genocide" was also used on several occasions by the prosecutors during the trial itself. Sir David Maxwell-Fyfe, the British prosecutor, reminded one of the accused, Von Neurath, that he had been charged with genocide, "which we say is the extermination of racial and national groups", or, as it has been put in the well-known book of Professor Lemkin, "a co-ordinated plan of different actions aiming at the destruction of essential foundations of the life of national groups with the aim of annihilating the groups themselves".[6] Lemkin later wrote that "[t]he evidence produced at the Nuremberg trial gave full support to the concept of genocide".[7]

Nevertheless, the Charter of the International Military Tribunal did not use the word genocide, nor does it appear in the final judgment issued on September 30 and October 1, 1946. The legal concept of crimes against humanity, as defined at Nuremberg, suffered from a very serious limitation, in that it was confined to atrocities committed in association with an aggressive war. This was quite intentional on the part of those who drafted the legal provisions governing prosecutions, especially the four great powers—the United States, the United Kingdom, France, and the Soviet Union. Indeed, extending international law from classic war crimes, involving battlefield offences and various forms of persecution of civilians in an occupied territory, so that it would also cover atrocities committed by a government against its own civilian population was not only novel and unprecedented, it was also threatening to the very states who were organizing the prosecution. The distinctions were set out quite candidly by the head of the United States delegation, Robert Jackson, at a meeting of the London Conference on July 23, 1945:

> It has been a general principle of foreign policy of our Government from time immemorial that the internal affairs of another government are not ordinarily our business; that is to say, the way Germany treats its inhabitants, or any other country treats its inhabitants is not our affair any more than it is the affair of some other government to interpose itself in our problems. The reason that this program of extermination of Jews and destruction of the rights of minorities becomes an international concern is this: it was a part of a plan for making an illegal war. Unless we have a war connection as a basis for reaching them, I

4 *Report of Robert H. Jackson, United States Representative to the International Conference on Military Trials* (Washington: US Government Printing Office, 1949), 6.

5 *France et al. v. Goering et al.*, (1946) 22 IMT 45-6.

6 (1947) 17 IMT, 61. See also: (1947) 19 IMT 497, 498, 509, 514, 531.

7 Raphael Lemkin, "Genocide as a Crime in International Law," 41 *American Journal of International Law* 145 (1947), 147.

> would think we have no basis for dealing with atrocities. They were a part of the preparation for war or for the conduct of the war in so far as they occurred inside of Germany and that makes them our concern.[8]

Speaking of the proposed crime of "atrocities, persecutions, and deportations on political, racial or religious grounds," which would shortly be renamed "crimes against humanity," Justice Jackson indicated the source of the lingering concerns of his government:

> Ordinarily we do not consider that the acts of a government toward its own citizens warrant our interference. We have some regrettable circumstances at times in our own country in which minorities are unfairly treated. We think it is justifiable that we interfere or attempt to bring retribution to individuals or to states only because the concentration camps and the deportations were in pursuance of a common plan or enterprise of making an unjust or illegal war in which we became involved. We see no other basis on which we are justified in reaching the atrocities which were committed inside Germany, under German law, or even in violation of German law, by authorities of the German state.[9]

There is little doubt that the British, the French, and the Soviets had reasons of their own to share these concerns. As a result, the definition of crimes against humanity in Article VI(c) of the Nuremberg Charter requires that atrocities be committed "in furtherance of or in connection with any crime within the jurisdiction of the International Tribunal".[10] In its final judgment, the International Military Tribunal made a distinction between pre-war persecution of German Jews, which it characterized as "severe and repressive", and German policy during the war in the occupied territories. Although the judgment frequently referred to events during the 1930s, none of the accused were found guilty of an act perpetrated prior to September, 1 1939, the day the war broke out.

Following the judgment, there was considerable outrage about the severe restriction upon the concept of crimes against humanity. A member of the Nuremberg prosecution team, Henry King, described meeting Raphael Lemkin in the lobby of the Grand Hotel in Nuremberg in October 1946, a few days after the International Military Tribunal completed its work:

> When I saw him at Nuremberg, Lemkin was very upset. He was concerned that the decision of the International Military Tribunal (IMT)—the Nuremberg Court—did not go far enough in dealing with genocidal actions. This was because the IMT limited its judgment

8 "Minutes of Conference Session of 23 July 1945", in *Report of Robert H. Jackson, United States Representative to the International Conference on Military Trials*, (Washington: US Government Printing Office, 1949), 331.

9 Ibid, 333.

10 *Agreement for the Prosecution and Punishment of Major War Criminals of the European Axis, and Establishing the Charter of the International Military Tribunal (IMT)*, annex, (1951) 82 UNTS 279.

> to wartime genocide and did not include peacetime genocide. At that time, Lemkin was very focussed on pushing his points. After he had buttonholed me several times, I had to tell him that I was powerless to do anything about the limitation in the Court's judgment.[11]

The disappointment soon manifested itself in the United Nations General Assembly, which was meeting at Lake Success, in the New York suburbs, at the time. India, Cuba and Panama proposed a resolution that they said would address a shortcoming in the Nuremberg trial by which acts committed prior to the war were left unpunished.[12] One of the preambular paragraphs in the draft resolution stated:

> Whereas the punishment of the very serious crime of genocide when committed in time of peace lies within the exclusive territorial jurisdiction of the judiciary of every State concerned, while crimes of a relatively lesser importance such as piracy, trade in women, children, drugs, obscene publications are declared as international crimes and have been made matters of international concern ...[13]

This paragraph never made it to the final version of Resolution 96(I), adopted in December 1946, because the majority of the General Assembly was not prepared to accept universal jurisdiction for the crime of genocide. Nevertheless, the resolution, somewhat toned down from the hopes of those who had launched it, launched a process that concluded two years later with the adoption of the Convention on the Prevention and Punishment of the Crime of Genocide.[14] Proposals that the Genocide Convention make reference to crimes against humanity as a related concept, or as some kind of broader umbrella under which the crime of genocide was situated, were rejected by the drafters so as not to create any confusion about the fact that genocide could be committed in time of peace as well as in wartime. This could not be said with any certainty about crimes against humanity at the time, precisely because of the Nuremberg precedent.

Thus, the recognition of genocide as an international crime by the General Assembly of the United Nations in 1946, and its codification in the 1948 Convention, can be understood as a reaction to the narrow approach to crimes against humanity in the Nuremberg judgment of the International Military Tribunal. It was Nuremberg's failure to recognize the international criminality of atrocities committed in peacetime that prompted the first initiatives at recognizing and defining the crime of genocide. Had Nuremberg affirmed the reach of international criminal law into peacetime atrocities, the Genocide Convention might never have been adopted. The

11 Henry T. King Jr., "Origins of the Genocide Convention," 40 *Case Western Reserve Journal of International Law* 13 (2008), 13.

12 United Nations, Doc. A/C.6/SR.22.

13 United Nations, Doc. A/BUR/50.

14 Convention on the Prevention and Punishment of the Crime of Genocide (1951) 78 UNTS 277.

term "genocide" would probably have remained a popular or colloquial label used by journalists, historians and social scientists, but one absent from legal discourse.

The Convention on the Prevention and Punishment of the Crime of Genocide was adopted unanimously by the United Nations General Assembly on December 9, 1948. It provides the following definition of the crime of genocide:

> In the present Convention, genocide means any of the following acts committed with intent to destroy, in whole or in part, a national, ethnical, racial or religious group, as such:
> (a) Killing members of the group;
> (b) Causing serious bodily or mental harm to members of the group;
> (c) Deliberately inflicting on the group conditions of life calculated to bring about its physical destruction in whole or in part;
> (d) Imposing measures intended to prevent births within the group;
> (e) Forcibly transferring children of the group to another group.

In one sense, the definition is considerably narrower than that of crimes against humanity, which can apply to a broad range of acts of persecution and other atrocities committed against "any civilian population." On the other hand, the definition is manifestly broader because of the absence of any requirement of a link with aggressive war.

Besides defining the crime, the Convention imposes several obligations upon states that ratify it. They are required to enact legislation to provide for punishment of persons guilty of genocide committed on their own territory. The legislation must not allow offenders to invoke in defence that they were acting in an official capacity. States are also required to cooperate in extradition when persons suspected of committing genocide elsewhere find refuge in their territory. They may not treat genocide as a political crime, which is an historic bar to extradition. Disputes between states about genocide are automatically subject to the jurisdiction of the International Court of Justice (ICJ).

The title of the Convention speaks of prevention, but aside from a perfunctory undertaking "to prevent" genocide there is nothing to suggest the scope of this obligation. In 2007, in a case filed by Bosnia and Herzegovina against Serbia (the Bosnia and Herzegovina case), the ICJ said there had been a breach of the Genocide Convention because Serbia failed to intervene with its allies, the Bosnian Serbs, so as to prevent the Srebrenica massacre of July 1995. The Court said that in view of Serbia's "undeniable influence," the authorities should have "made the best efforts within their power to try and prevent the tragic events then taking shape, whose scale, though it could not have been foreseen with certainty, might at least have been surmised."[15] The judgment clarifies that the obligation to prevent extends beyond a country's own borders. The principle it establishes should apply to other states who take little or no action to respond when mass atrocity posing a risk of genocide is

15 Application of the Convention on the Prevention and Punishment of the Crime of Genocide (Bosnia and Herzegovina v. Serbia and Montenegro), Judgment of February 26, 2007, para. 438.

threatened. This pronouncement is in the same spirit as an emerging doctrine in international law expressed in a unanimous resolution of the United Nations General Assembly, adopted in 2005, declaring that states have a "responsibility to protect" populations in cases of genocide, crimes against humanity, war crimes, and ethnic cleansing.[16]

The Convention specifies that genocide is to be prosecuted by the courts of the country where the crime took place or "by such international penal tribunal as may have jurisdiction with respect to those Contracting Parties which shall have accepted its jurisdiction." The original General Assembly resolution proposed by Cuba, India and Panama called for recognition of universal jurisdiction over genocide. This would mean that the courts of any state could punish the crime, no matter where it was committed. The idea was rejected by the General Assembly in favour of an approach combining territorial jurisdiction and an international institution. The promised international court was not established for more than half a century, when the Rome Statute of the International Criminal Court entered into force on July 1, 2002.[17] Despite the Convention's rejection of universal jurisdiction, in the A-G Israel v. Eichmann prosecution the Israeli courts decided that it was accepted by customary international law.[18] Although no treaty authorizes universal jurisdiction over genocide, and there is as yet no determination of its legitimacy by the ICJ, there now seems little doubt that it is permitted by international law. In 2006 and 2007, the International Criminal Tribunal for Rwanda authorized transfer of suspects for trial on the basis of universal jurisdiction with the approval of the United Nations Security Council, further evidence of the broad acceptance of universal jurisdiction over genocide.[19]

The definition of genocide set out in Article II of the Convention has frequently been criticized for its narrowness. For example, it applies to a limited number of protected groups, and it requires intent directed at physical destruction of the victimized group. There was disappointment when the ICJ, in the Bosnia and Herzegovina case, dismissed attempts to broaden the definition by interpreting the words "to destroy" so as to encompass the notion of "ethnic cleansing." The Court said that "ethnic cleansing," which it described as the "deportation or displacement of the members of a group, even if effected by force," was not necessarily equivalent to destruction of that group, and that destruction was not an automatic consequence

---

16 United Nations, Doc. A/RES/60/1, "2005 World Summit Outcome," paras. 138-139.

17 *Rome Statute of the International Criminal Court* (2002) 2187 UNTS 90. In the *Bosnia and Herzegovina case*, the ICJ held that the International Criminal Tribunal for the former Yugoslavia was an international court contemplated by article 6 of the Convention.

18 A-G Israel v. Eichmann (1968) 36 ILR 5 (District Court, Jerusalem), paras. 20-22.

19 Prosecutor v. Bagaragaza Decision on Prosecutor's Request for Referral of the Indictment to the Kingdom of the Netherlands, (Case No. ICTR-2005-86-R11bis), April 13, 2007. For Security Council acquiescence, see: United Nations, Doc. S/PV.5697.

of such displacement.[20] The relatively conservative approach to interpreting the definition, and a resistance to broadening the scope through judicial action rather than amendment of the Convention, is also reflected in judgments of the International Criminal Tribunal for the former Yugoslavia (ICTY),[21] and an authoritative report by a United Nations fact-finding commission.[22]

Nor has there been any serious effort at the political level to amend or modify the definition in Article II of the Convention. The ideal opportunity for such a development would have been the adoption of the Rome Statute of the International Criminal Court, when the definitions of the other core international crimes, crimes against humanity and war crimes, were quite dramatically modernized. But when it came to genocide, there were a few modest proposals, and these did not gain any traction during the negotiations.[23] At the Rome Conference, only Cuba argued for amendment of the definition, proposing it be expanded to include social and political groups.[24]

There is some evidence of innovation by national lawmakers when the provisions of the Genocide Convention are translated into domestic criminal legislation. The French Code pénal, for example, defines genocide as the destruction of any group whose identification is based on arbitrary criteria.[25] The Canadian implementing legislation for the Rome Statute states that "genocide means an act or omission committed with intent to destroy, in whole or in part, an identifiable group of persons, as such, that, at the time and in the place of its commission, constitutes genocide according to customary international law," explaining that the definition in the Rome Statute, which is identical to that of the Convention, is deemed a crime according to customary international law. The legislation adds, in anticipation: "This does not limit or prejudice in any way the application of existing or developing rules of inter-

20 Case Concerning the Application of the Convention on the Prevention and Punishment of the Crime of Genocide (Bosnia and Herzegovina v. Serbia and Montenegro), Judgment of February 26, 2007, para. 190.

21 Prosecutor v. Krstić, Judgment of Apri 19, 2004, Case No. IT-98-33-A. Also: Prosecutor v. Stakić, Judgment of July 31, 2003, Case No. IT-97-24-T; Prosecutor v. Brđanin, Judgment of September 1, 2004, Case No. IT-99-36-T). Prosecutor v. Blagojević et al., Judgment of May 9, 2007, Case No. IT-02-60-A).

22 United Nations, Doc. S/2005/60, "Report of the International Commission of Inquiry on Darfur to the United Nations Secretary-General, Pursuant to Security Council Resolution 1564 of 18 September 2004," Geneva, January 25, 2005.

23 United Nations, Doc. A/50/22, "Report of the Ad Hoc Committee on the Establishment of an International Criminal Court," para. 61. United Nations, Doc. A/AC.249/1998/CRP.8, 2; Herman von Hebel and Darryl Robinson, "Crimes Within the Jurisdiction of the Court," in Roy S. Lee, ed., *The International Criminal Court: The Making of the Rome Statute, Issues, Negotiations, Results* (The Hague, London and Boston: Kluwer Law, 1995), 79-128, 89, n. 37.

24 United Nations, Doc. A/CONF.183/C.1/SR.3, para. 100.

25 *Code pénal* (France), Journal officiel, July 23, 1992, Article 211-1.

national law."[26] Recently, the European Court of Human Rights (ECHR) acknowledged some of this variation at the national level, ruling an expansive interpretation of the definition of genocide by German courts not to be inconsistent with the prohibition of retroactive criminality.[27] Still, at the international level, a relatively strict reading of the Convention definition remains the rule.

The Genocide Convention continues to fascinate jurists, politicians, journalists, and human rights activists. For most of its first fifty years, it lived in a state of tension with crimes against humanity. There was much frustration with the narrowness of the definition of genocide. Schwarzenberger famously remarked that the Genocide Convention was "unnecessary when applicable and inapplicable when necessary."[28] Frank Chalk and Kurt Jonassohn wrote that "the wording of the Convention is so restrictive that not one of the genocidal killings committed since its adoption is covered by it."[29] Many, therefore, argued for a dynamic interpretation of the concept of genocide that would include a range of other protected groups, such as political and social groups, and that would apply to a broader range of acts.[30] But what they were proposing, in reality, was equivalent to crimes against humanity without the nexus to armed conflict.

In early 1945, genocide and crimes against humanity were cognates, terms devised to describe the barbarous acts of the Nazi regime. Though not identical in scope, they neatly overlapped and could be used more or less interchangeably to describe the great crime of the era, the attempted extermination of Europe's Jewish population. By late 1946 an important rift developed, and it was not healed until the end of the century. Eventually, the nexus disappeared from the definition of crimes against humanity, but it would take half a century for the evolution to become evident. In 1995, the Appeals Chamber of the ICTY declared that the requirement that crimes against humanity be associated with armed conflict was inconsistent with customary law.[31] It offered the rather unconvincing explanation that the Security Council had included the nexus in Article 5 of the Statute of the International Criminal Tribunal for the former Yugoslavia as a jurisdictional limit only.[32] The more plausible

26 Crimes Against Humanity and War Crimes Act, 48-49 Elizabeth II, 1999-2000, C-19, s. 4.

27 Jorgić v. Germany (Application no. 74613/01), Judgment of July 12, 2007.

28 Georg Schwarzenberger, *International Law*, Vol. I, (London: Stevens & Sons, 1957, 3rd ed.) 143.

29 "The Conceptual Framework," in eds. Frank Chalk and Kurt Jonassohn, *The History and Sociology of Genocide* (New Haven and London: Yale University Press, 1990), 3-43.

30 Example: United Nations, Doc. E/CN.4/Sub.2/1985/6, "Revised and Updated Report on the Question of the Prevention and Punishment of the Crime of Genocide."

31 Prosecutor v. Tadić, Decision on the Defence Motion for Interlocutory Appeal on Jurisdiction, Case No. IT-94-1-AR72, October 2, 1995, para. 141; Prosecutor v. Tadić, Judgment of July 15, 1999, Case No. IT-94-1-A, para. 251; Prosecutor v. Kordić et al., Judgment of February 26, 2001, Case No. IT-95-14/2-T para. 23.

32 Prosecutor v. Šešelj Decision on the Interlocutory Appeal Concerning Jurisdiction, August 31, 2004, Case No. IT-03-67-AR72.1) para. 13.

explanation is that the lawyers in the United Nations Secretariat who drafted the Charter believed the nexus to be part of customary law, and the Council did not disagree.[33]

Nevertheless, there can today be no doubt that the flaw in the Nuremberg concept of crimes against humanity, something that prompted Lemkin's genocide-related initiatives at the General Assembly, has been corrected. The authoritative definition appears in Article 7 of the Rome Statute, which contains no reference to armed conflict as a contextual element. The only real remaining uncertainty is precisely when the nexus disappeared from the elements of crimes against humanity. As far as the International Law Commission was concerned, it was present as late as 1950, and perhaps after that. In 1954, the Commission experimented by removing the nexus, replacing it with another contextual element, the State plan or policy.[34] There is also some recent authority from the ECHR supporting the view that the nexus was absent as early as the 1950s.[35] In a September 2008 decision, a Grand Chamber of the Court said cautiously that a nexus with armed conflict "may no longer have been relevant by 1956."[36] The issue directly confronts the Extraordinary Chambers of the Courts of Cambodia in their current efforts to prosecute Khmer Rouge atrocities.

The distinction between genocide and crimes against humanity is still of great symbolic significance, of course. Many Bosnians were shattered that their suffering during the 1992-95 war was not labelled genocide, save for the very specific case and ultimately anomalous case of the Srebrenica massacre. This was reflected in many negative comments from international lawyers about the judgment of the ICJ.[37] Similarly, there was much disappointment when the Commission of Inquiry set up pursuant to a Security Council mandate determined that Sudan was not committing genocide in Darfur.[38] And yet the essence of the Bosnian war has been described on countless occasions in the case law of the ICTY as a crime against humanity, and the Darfur Commission did the same for the ethnic cleansing in Sudan, urging that the situation be referred to the ICC for prosecution:

33 See the Secretary-General's report: "Crimes against humanity are aimed at any civilian population and are prohibited regardless of whether they are committed in an armed conflict, international or internal in character." United Nations, Doc. S/25704, "Report of the Secretary-General Pursuant to Paragraph 2 of Security Council Resolution 808 (1993)," para. 47. See: Larry D. Johnson, "Ten Years Later: Reflections on the Drafting," 2 *Journal of International Criminal Justice* 368 (2004), 372.

34 United Nations, Doc. A/CN.4/SER.A/1954/Add.l, *Yearbook...1954*, Vol. II, 150.

35 Kolk v. Estonia (App. no. 23052/04), Kislyiy v. Estonia (App. no. 24018/04), Admissibility Decision, January 17, 2006; Penart v. Estonia (App. No. 14685/04), Admissibility Decision, January 24, 2006.

36 Korbely v. Hungary (App. No. *9174/02*), Judgment, September 19, 2008, para. 82.

37 Antonio Cassese, "A Judicial Massacre," *The Guardian*, February 27, 2007; Ruth Wedgwood, "Bad Day for International Justice," *International Herald Tribune*, March 8, 2007.

38 United Nations, Doc. S/2005/60, "Report of the International Commission of Inquiry on Darfur to the United Nations Secretary-General, Pursuant to Security Council Resolution 1564 of 18 September 2004," Geneva, January 25, 2005.

> The conclusion that no genocidal policy has been pursued and implemented in Darfur by the Government authorities, directly or through the militias under their control, should not be taken in any way as detracting from the gravity of the crimes perpetrated in that region. International offences such as the crimes against humanity and war crimes that have been committed in Darfur may be no less serious and heinous than genocide.[39]

If their victimization is acknowledged as crimes against humanity, the Bosnian Muslims and the Darfur tribes are in good company. After all, even though today we speak of the Armenian and Jewish genocides, at the time when they were committed crimes against humanity was the applicable terminology. Perhaps in the years to come, now that the legal difficulties distinguishing genocide and crimes against humanity have been resolved, the more popular connotation of these terms will tend to evolve in the same direction.

The legal significance of the Genocide Convention has declined over the past decade or so, but not because it is inapplicable to specific circumstances or out of a perceived conservatism of diplomats and judges. Rather, new instruments and new institutions have emerged. Foremost among them is the ICC. In a different way, it accomplishes much the same thing as the Genocide Convention, but in a manner applicable to crimes against humanity as well. Moreover, the recent "responsibility to protect" doctrine extends the duty of prevention found in Article I of the Genocide Convention to crimes against humanity. The only legal consequence of describing an atrocity as genocide rather than as crimes against humanity is the relatively easy access to the ICJ offered by article IX of the 1948 Convention. But Article IX has generated more heat than light, and the recent ruling of the Court in Bosnia v. Serbia should discourage resort to this remedy except in the very clearest of cases.[40] In a legal sense, there is now slight importance, if any, to the distinction between genocide and crimes against humanity. The importance of the Genocide Convention can probably be found not so much in its contemporary potential to address atrocities, something that is largely superseded by more modern texts, as in its historic contribution to the struggle for accountability and the protection of human rights.

39 Ibid, 4.

40 Case concerning Application of the Convention on the Prevention and Punishment of the Crime of Genocide (Bosnia and Herzegovina v. Serbia and Montenegro), Judgment of February 26, 2007. On the judgment, see: William A. Schabas, "Genocide and the International Court of Justice: Finally, a Duty to Prevent the Crime of Crimes," 2 *Genocide Studies and Prevention* (2007), 101.

2. The Drafting and Development of the 1948 Convention on Genocide and the Politics of International Law

Matthew Lippman

1. Introduction

The prevention and punishment of genocide was a subsidiary, but animating purpose of the United Nations and was the first human rights instrument adopted by the fledgling organization. The Treaty boldly proclaims that genocide does not fall within the sovereign prerogatives of States and that the perpetrators of this atrocity are not insulated from international accountability.

The Convention on the Prevention and Punishment of the Crime of Genocide is one of the legal instruments that promises to be emblematic of our era. The document affirms that individuals possess human rights and are active subjects rather than passive objects of international law. The Convention also affirms that in this globalized world groups possess rights that transcend those provided by the nation-state and that all of humankind benefits from the protection of diversity.

The Genocide Convention was an unprecedented progressive step in the history of international law. The treaty was part of a wave of international human rights and humanitarian reform and almost two decades would pass before similar efforts would prove successful. This paper provides historical overview of the development of the legal concept of genocide, briefly reviews the impact of the Cold War on the drafting process and offers reflections on the contemporary politics of genocide.

2. The Historical Foundation of Genocide

The Martens Clause in the Preamble to the Hague Convention of 1907 provides that until a more complete code of the humanitarian law of war is drafted individuals remain under the protection of the usages established among civilized peoples, public conscience and the laws of humanity. Similar phraseology, in fact, had been invoked by Western European regimes seeking to justify their right to intervene to safeguard their religious brethren in the Ottoman Empire. This broad language suggested that

H.G. van der Wilt, J. Vervliet et al., *(eds.)* The Genocide Convention: The Legacy of 60 Years.
Copyright 2012 Koninklijke Brill NV. ISBN 978 9004 15328 8. pp. 15-25.

there are unarticulated, transcendent and evolving principles that protect individuals in time of war and presumably in time of peace.[1]

The notion of laws of humanity was incorporated into the report of the Commission on Responsibility appointed in 1919 by the Versailles Peace Conference. The Commission determined that the Central Empires and their Allies were guilty of barbarities heretofore unknown during the course of armed conflict. Many of these later came to be viewed as characteristic of genocide. The Commission took the unprecedented step of proposing that individuals whose crimes transcended national boundaries should be brought before mixed international tribunals applying the laws and customs of war and the laws of humanity. The Commission's proposals were incorporated in generality into the Versailles Peace Treaty. These anticipated prosecutions foundered on the shoals of practical politics. Only nine trials were conducted before the Penal Senate of the Reichsgericht and, by 1933, all the defendants either had been acquitted or released.[2]

The notion of laws of humanity appeared to have been intended, in part, to extend criminal liability to the Turkish perpetrators of the atrocities against the Armenians. Efforts to bring Turkish perpetrators to justice also proved unsuccessful.[3] Reflecting on this experience, historians have concluded that the international community stumbled in their first tentative steps towards the creation and punishment of the crime of genocide.[4]

The League of Nations, concerned with creating a prophylactic against the type of ethnic explosion that led to World War I created a minority protection system. This structure could not contain centrifugal communal forces and was washed away by World War II.[5] The United Nations Secretary-Generals when queried whether this system should be reinstated perhaps somewhat hopefully noted that human rights rather than group rights was the central concern of the new world order.[6]

This triad of trends—transcendent principles that reflected the laws of humanity, criminal prosecution and group rights—was the foundation on which Raphael Lemkin constructed the neologism genocide. Lemkin believed that minority groups were the engine of creativity and culture in the world. But, they were also the subject

1 Convention Respecting the Law and Customs of War on Land, Oct. 18, 1907, preamble, 36 Stat. 277, T.S. No. 539, 1 Bevans 631.

2 Commission on the Responsibility of the Authors of the War and on Enforcement of Penalties, Report Presented to the Preliminary Peace Conference, Mar. 19, 1919, *reprinted in* 14 Am. J. Int'l L. 95 (1920).

3 *See* Treaty of Peace Between the Allied Powers and Turkey (Treaty of Sèvres), Aug. 10, 1920, art. 230, *reprinted in* 15 Am. J. Int'l L. 179 (Supp. 1921); Treaty With Turkey and Other Instruments Signed At Lausanne, Jul. 24, 1923, Dec. VIII (Declaration of Amnesty), *reprinted in* 18 Am. J. Int'l L. 1 (1924).

4 James F. Willis, *Prologue to Nuremberg; The Politics and Diplomacy of Punishing War Criminals of the First World War*, 163 (1982).

5 Patrick Thornberry, *International Law and the Rights of Minorities*, 42-46 (1991).

6 *See Study of the Legal Validity of the Undertakings Concerning Minorities*, Commission On Human Rights, at 70, U.N. Doc. E/CN.4/367 (1950).

of repression which created a continuing source of instability. Lemkin's solution was to urge the creation of an international convention on genocide.[7]

The concept of 'laws of humanity' became increasingly identified with the inchoate crime of genocide. President Franklin Delano Roosevelt, in his statement of March 24, 1944, affirmed that the Allies were determined to prosecute and punish Nazi war criminals. He singled out Hitler's "crimes against humanity" for condemnation, particularly "the wholesale systematic murders of the Jews of Europe."[8]

The term genocide entered the lexicon of international law when the Nuremberg Tribunal indicted Nazi war criminals for genocide under both the Crimes against Humanity and War Crimes counts.[9] Genocide was referenced by both the French and British prosecutors during their closing arguments. The French prosecutor noting that the crimes of the Nazis were so atrocious that a new term, genocide, had to be invented to capture the horror.[10] The Judgment did not mention the term genocide. Instead, it dealt with genocide as aggravated mass murder, even when describing the crimes of a defendant like Hans Frank who was alleged to have been responsible for the extermination of as many as three million Jews in Poland. Perhaps the most significant conviction at Nuremberg in regards to the history of genocide was the conviction of Julius Streicher, the editor of the "hate-sheet" Der Sturmer. Streicher was convicted of the Crime against Humanity of persecution based on his incitement to the extermination of the Jews at the time that atrocities were being carried out in the East.[11] The Tokyo Tribunal also avoided the term genocide in discussing the "Rape of Nanking."[12]

The Nuremberg Judgment possessed the flaw of limiting Crimes against Humanity to acts connected to War Crimes and to Crimes against Peace. The judgments in the Einsatzgrupen and Justice cases issued under Control Council Law 10, however, held that Crimes against Humanity were subject to punishment whether committed in a time of war or in a time of peace. The American tribunals' explained that the extension of Crimes against Humanity to encompass the pre-war period was based on considerations of history, policy and public conscience.[13] The Tribunal in the Justice case noted that genocide was the exemplar of Crimes against Humanity. In another significant decision in the Zyklon B case, a British Military Court, in con-

7 *See* Raphael Lemkin, *Axis Rule in Occupied Europe* (1944).

8 *War Refugees, Statement of the President (Roosevelt), Mar. 24, 1944*, VI Doc. AM. Foreign Rel., July 1943-June 1944, 191, 192 (1945).

9 *See* United States v. Hermann Goring, II *Trial of the Major War Criminals Before The International Military Tribunal* 30, 45-46 (1947) (Indictment).

10 *Id.* at 497, 531.

11 22 *id.* at 547-549.

12 The Tokyo War Crimes Trial (Nov. 1948), *reprinted in* II *The Law of War; A Documentary History*, 1029, 1079 (Leon Friedman ed., 1972).

13 United States v. Otto Ohlendorf, *IV Trials of War Criminals before the Nuremberg Military Tribunals under Control Council Law No. 10* , 411, 497-98 (1950); United States v. Josef Altstoetter, III *Trials of War Criminals before the Nuremberg Military Tribunals under Control Council Law No. 10*, 954, 973 (1951).

victing industrialists for providing toxic chemicals to the Auschwitz Concentration Camp, noted that crimes of such significant magnitude were subject to universal jurisdiction.[14] In the Justice case, the first two defendants in history were convicted of genocide. Both defendants Ernst Lautz and Oswald Rothaug were determined to have transformed the Nazi judicial system from engines of justice into engines of extermination.[15]

Prosecutions also were initiated before domestic tribunals across Europe and Asia. These trials generally avoided reference to genocide. The significant exception is the Supreme National Tribunal of Poland which in three separate prosecutions convicted Nazi operatives of the physical, spiritual and cultural genocide of the Polish people.[16]

3. The United Nations

Parallel to these developments was the effort undertaken in the United Nations to define and prohibit the crime of genocide. General Assembly Resolution 96(I) sponsored by Panama, Cuba and India called on the Social and Economic Council to explore the drafting of a document prohibiting genocide. The resolution noted that genocide had inflicted great damage to the people and cultures of the world. The document went on to note that just as homicide was the denial of the right of an individual to live that genocide was the right of a group to live.[17] The drafting process was intricate, involved and lengthy. Finally, on December 9, 1948, Mr. Evatt, the President of the General Assembly, announced the adoption of the Convention on the Prevention and Punishment of the Crime of Genocide. He noted that this marked the triumph of international law and an attitude of mind that should guide the United Nations in all future deliberations. Mr. Azkoul of Lebanon praised the document as the first formal recognition of group rights under international law.[18] A review of the drafting process reveals several factors influencing the Convention's drafting.

3.1 The Cold War

The United States generally favored a narrowly focused document while the Soviet Union advocated a broad-based approach. Both countries, however, opposed the creation of any institutions that could serve as a forum for criticism and commen-

---

14 *See* Zyklon B Case (U.K v. Tesch, et. al.) 1.L.R. 93,94 (U.N. War Crimes Comm'n Brit. Milit.Ct., Hamburg 1946).

15 United States v. Otto Ohlendorf, *supra* note 13, at 995-96, 1151-56.

16 *See* Trial of Gauleiter Artur Greiser, XIII L. Rep. Trials of War Crim. 70, 113-14 (U.N. War Crimes Comm'n Sup. Nat'l Trib. Poland 1949). The other prosecutions were brought against Amon Leopold Goeth (Commandant at Plaszow) and Rudolf Franz Ferdinand Hoess (Commandant at Auschwitz).

17 G.A. Res. 96(I), U.N. GAOR, 1st Sess., at 189, U.N. Doc. A/64/Add.1 (1946).

18 3 U.N. GAOR ,179th plen mtg, at 852 (1948).

tary of their actions. The Soviet Union used the drafting process to appeal to its constituency in the Third World while the United States aligned herself with Western and Northern European democracies. The two superpower rivals also used the debate to engage in ideological disquisitions.[19]

The Soviet Union had suffered mightily at the hands of the Third Reich and tended to view the crime of genocide through the lens of World War II. The Soviet's took the position that the International Law Commission should be charged with considering the crime of genocide in conjunction with the drafting of the Nuremberg Principles. The Soviet Union also favored reference in the Preamble to Nazism and fascism as causes of genocide and initially favored Article One referring to genocide as Crime against Humanity rather than an international crime in order to align the Convention with Nuremberg. A similar motivation appears to explain the Soviet Union's proposal that Article Four specifically abrogates the superior orders defense and that the intent standard for the crime of genocide should be broadened. The United States adopted a much narrower approach to the Convention and primarily was concerned with limiting the Treaty's interference with her sovereign prerogatives. The American representative persistently opposed on ideological grounds inclusion of incitement to genocide. This same commitment to civil liberties helps to explain the United States' vociferous opposition to Soviet proposals for the punishment of preparatory acts, the prohibition on racist and Nazi organizations and the criminalization of propaganda for genocide. The Soviet Union predictably opposed the protection of religious groups and the categorization of ethnic cleansing and the forced movement of peoples as genocide, Soviet's endorsement of a narrow provision prohibiting cultural genocide seems to have been intended to solidify support among the Soviet Union's diverse ethnic populations and to demonstrate solidarity with the developing world. A similar motivation seems to explain the Soviet sponsorship of an unsuccessful proposal to extend automatic application of the Convention to 'non self-governing territories'.

In the last analysis, both superpowers shared an interest in limiting international and universal jurisdiction over genocide. The United States did not want to risk international recrimination for the country's continued practice of racial segregation and mistreatment of Native Americans and the Soviet Union bore the burden of the strangulation of satellite States. Both countries opposed the creation of a broad-based international criminal court and a stronger extradition provision and universal jurisdiction. The Soviet Union supported vesting exclusive jurisdiction in the Security Council. The Soviets were against a role for the International Court of Justice while the United States asserted that the court's jurisdiction should be

19 These observations are based on my study of the drafting process. *See* Matthew Lippman, *The Drafting of the 1948 Convention on the Prevention and Punishment of the Crime of Genocide,* 3 B.U. Int'l L. J. 1-60 (1984); Matthew Lippman, *The 1948 Convention On The Prevention And Punishment Of The Crime Of Genocide: Forty-Five Years Later,* Temple Int'l & Comp.. L.J. 1-73 (1994); Matthew Lippman, *The Convention On the Prevention and Punishment of the Crime of Genocide: Fifty Years Later,* 15 Arizona J. Int'l & Comp. L. 415-463 (1998) [hereinafter *Fifty Years Later*].

limited to extraterritorial acts of genocide. Both States also importantly opposed extending protection under the Convention to political groups. The important point is that the United States and Soviet Union at a significant and seminal moment in time declined to truly transform the world order. This might be compared to the lost opportunity following World War II to place the nuclear genie 'back in the bottle.' We can only speculate as to the contours of a Genocide Convention that might be drafted by the contemporary United Nations.

4. Reform of the Genocide Convention

Concern with genocide was eclipsed by the political calculations of the Cold War. The most significant exception was the controversial and questionable prosecution of Adolf Eichman, which resulted in important strides in the jurisprudence of the crime of genocide. Claims that American or Soviet nuclear strategies or prosecution of the wars in Vietnam or Afghanistan were genocidal were brushed aside as romantic rhetoric. The two Superpowers tolerated and justified the genocidal excesses of their client states and, as a result, genocides in African, Asia and Latin America were subjected to little international scrutiny.

The 1978 report of the Special Rapporteur on genocide concluded that the Convention bemoaned the fact that the Convention lacked effective international measures to prevent and punish genocide, resulting in the unimpeded perpetration of this barbarous crime.[20] The Special Rapporteur's 1985 report reached a similar conclusion, determining that

> all too much evidence continues to accumulate that acts of genocide are still being committed in various parts of the world... [I]n its present form, the Convention (...) must be judged to be inadequate. Further evolution of international measures against genocide is necessary and indeed overdue.[21]

The Special Rapporteur recommended that these additional measures be included in a supplementary Convention or Protocol.[22] The reports made several specific proposals for reform.

---

20 *Study of the Question of the Prevention and Punishment of the Crime of Genocide*, U.N. ESCOR, 31st Sess, 120, U.N. Doc. E/CN.4/Sub.2/416 (1978) [hereinafter 1978 Special Rapporteur].

21 *Review Of Further Developments In Fields With Which The Sub-Commission Has Been Concerned, Preliminary Revised and Updated Report on the Question of the Prevention and Punishment of the Crime of Genocide Prepared by Mr. Whitaker, Review of Further Developments in Fields with which the Sub-Commission has been concerned*, U.N. ESCOR, Human Rights Sub-Commission on the Prevention of Discrimination and Protection of Minorities, 38th Sess., 37, U.N. Doc. E/CN.4/Sub.2/1985/6 (1985) [hereinafter 1985 Special Rapporteur].

22 *Id.* at 40-41.

The Special Rapporteur, in 1978, stressed the need for universal jurisdiction over genocide as an antidote to the failure to create an international criminal court.[23] The Special Rapporteur also advocated prohibiting reservations to Article IX.[24]

The 1978 report also called for the creation of an 'early warning system' administered by a Special Rapporteur or by a newly-created Genocide Committee. This 'early warning system' would monitor volatile situations that might degenerate into genocide as well as request reports and sponsor research.[25] Professor William Schabas has advocated a reporting system similar to the International Labour Organization. States Parties to the Convention would be required to submit periodic reports. The reports would be submitted to a committee of experts which would recommend steps that might be taken to counteract situations that present an 'early warning' of genocide.[26] An inchoate step towards Professor Schabas's proposal for monitoring the actions of States to prevent genocide was the United Nations Secretary General's appointment of a Special Advisor on the Prevention of Genocide. An important part of the Special Advisor's responsibility is to bring situations that could result in genocide to the attention of the Secretary-General and to the Security Council. The great oversight in the Treaty regime remains a lack of attention to the victims of genocide.

5. The Contemporary Developments in the Jurisprudence of Genocide

Despite the failure to reform the Convention, the Rwandan and Yugoslavia war crimes tribunals and International Court of Justice have made important contributions to the jurisprudence of the law of genocide. It must be cautioned that the decisions of the Rwandan and Yugoslav courts are based on the statutes that established these Tribunals and have limited precedential authority in regards to other tribunals. In interpreting the elements of genocide and of the Genocide Convention, international tribunals have responded to the admonition of the International Court of Justice in the 'reservations' case. The Court stressed that the humanitarian object and purpose of the instrument dictates that the Convention should be expansively interpreted and amended. As noted by the International Court of Justice in its advisory opinion, "[t]he Convention was ... adopted for a purely humanitarian and civilizing purpose ... The high ideals which inspired the Convention provide ... the foundation and measure of all its provisions."[27] The four dissenting judges stressed that the "enormity of the crime of genocide can hardly be exaggerated" and requires that the Convention should be accorded the "most generous interpretation." Gen-

23 1978 Special Rapporteur, *supra* note 21, at 56.

24 *Id.* at 83-84.

25 *See* 1985 Special Rapporteur, *supra* note 29, at 42-43.

26 William A. Schabas, *Genocide in International Law* 549 (2000).

27 ICJ, Reservations to the Convention on the Prevention and Punishment of the Crime of Genocide, ICJ Reports, 1951, 15, 23.

erally, international court judgments have accorded a broad interpretation to the terms of treaty to enhance the protection of human rights.[28]

Genocide now has been recognized as an independent and autonomous crime that complements Crimes against Humanity and War Crimes and which is associated with global rights and responsibilities on the international community. The International Court of Justice in the judgment on the merits in Bosnia and Herzegovina v. Yugoslavia held that States Parties to the Genocide Convention possess obligations under Article One to "employ all means reasonably available to them, so as to prevent genocide so far as possible." This includes steps beyond those specified in the Genocide Convention. Responsibility is incurred if the "State manifestly failed to take all measures to prevent genocide which were within its powers and which might have contributed to preventing genocide." The obligation to act to prevent genocide arises at the "instant that the States learns of, or should normally have learned of, the existence of a serious risk that genocide will be committed." The decision, while subject to criticism, provides a strong complement to the responsibility to protect.[29] Another conspicuous example is the recognition of rape as a constitutive act of genocide.[30] Other exemplars of this expansive methodology in interpreting the Genocide Convention include a flexible approach to the analysis of genocidal intent and to the standard for determining whether individuals who are victimized constitute a group protected under the Treaty as well as a liberal approach to complicity in genocide and to conspiracy to undertake genocide and to incitement to genocide. Various judgments also point to the destruction of cultural objects and to ethnic cleansing as constituting circumstantial evidence of a genocidal intent.[31]

6. The Politics of Genocide Denials

Despite the developments in the jurisprudence of genocide, the unhappy reality is that genocide remains a crime that is rarely prosecuted before domestic or international tribunals and which infrequently results in convictions.

As for international intervention, the international community has been condemned for failing to act against genocide. In the case of the Balkans, Ad Hoc Judge Hershel Lauterpacht went so far as to observe in 1993 in the International Court of Justice's indication of special measures proceedings that the U.N. Security Council's imposition of an arms embargo had implicated the Council as an "accessory to genocide." Judge Lauterpacht went on to suggest that complicity in genocide rather than condemnation of genocide was the international norm.[32]

28 *Id.* at 27.

29 ICJ, Application of The Convention On The Prevention And Punishment Of The Crime Of Genocide (Bosnia and Herzegovina v. Yugoslavia) ICJ Rep. 2007 at 425-438.

30 *Prosecutor v. Jean-Paul Akayesu,* Case No. ICTR-96-4-T, T. Ch. I, Judgement, September 2 1999.

31 See for example, *Prosecutor v. Jelisic,* ICTY-95-10-A, App. Ch., Judgement, July 5, 2001.

32 Application of the Convention on the Prevention and Punishment of the Crime of Genocide, Provisional Measures, Order of 13 September 1993, 1993 I.C.J. 324, 441.

Genocide, of course, is a collective crime and any prosecution likely will prove partial and incomplete and ultimately fail to quench the thirst for justice. The impunity accorded to government officials makes the legal pursuit of genocide particularly problematic. The failure to pursue and to prosecute genocide generally is attributed to problems of proof and to political calculations.[33]

There, however, may be a deeper psychological explanation for the relatively low-profile of genocide prosecutions. The Genocide Convention is of 1948 remains a 'first generation' human rights instrument that lacks the enforcement mechanisms of contemporary instruments. The Convention was a symbolic effort to atone for the failure to prevent the acts of genocide committed during World War II rather than a document that was designed to punish future acts of genocide. The constrained content of the Genocide Convention, of course, also reflects the calculations of the Cold War. The Treaty, rather than marking the triumph of international law, reflects the fragile foundation of the newly-founded United Nations.

The very term and definition of genocide reflects Raphael Lemkin's tragic experiences during World War II. The Treaty remains a 'museum piece' which was intended symbolically to punish and to respond to past acts of genocide rather than to act against those atrocities that may occur in the future. It was neither legally logical nor politically persuasive to have excluded economic or social or political groups from the definition of Convention. The recognition of territorial jurisdiction and lack of effective enforcement mechanisms seems at odds with the proclamation of genocide as an international crime punishable during war as well as peace.

The Genocide Convention remains a 'prisoner of the past.' The identification of genocide with the Holocaust provides the concept of genocide with immense emotional and moral weight which results in a reluctance to reference the term. The invocation of genocide reminds us once again that there are victims, victimizers and bystanders. The notion of genocide also raises the reality that there are constraints on our compassion and limits on our resources. It is to acknowledge that there are primordial forces in the world which call into question our faith in the perfectibility of human beings and in the inevitability of liberal democracy and in human rights. There can be little confidence in progress when confronted by contemporary genocides involving mass mobilizations and crude and callous face-to-face killings that are far removed from Hannah Arendt's banality of bureaucratic evil. We are reluctant to acknowledge that 'never again' continues to ring hollow when confronted by the reality that the world 'once again' experiences a genocide. The expressions of concern articulated by political leaders and their humanitarian sentiments seemingly falter when confronted by the challenges and conundrums of global action or military intervention.

The paradigm of genocide remains the barbarities of the Nazi 'Super-State.' The Shoah at times appears to consume our exclusive compassion and concern. Genocide seems more a matter of politics than analytical precision. The silent and 'invis-

33 The remainder of the paper is broadly based on Matthew Lippman, *Fifty Years Later, supra* note 19, at 468-514. *See generally,* Matthew Lippman, *Genocide,* I *International Criminal Law* 589, 2nd ed. (Cherif Bassiouni ed. 1999).

ible' genocide visited upon powerless, invisible and semi-literate indigenous people proceeds without noticeable protest. This is part of the seeming lack of urgency in responding to genocides directed against 'people of color.' These 'slow motion' genocides are excruciatingly detailed in the media and unfold before the eyes of the world. The conflicts are portrayed as the result of inevitable ethnic conflict and there is said to be little that can be done to halt the killings. Both sides are viewed as equally guilty, the killing is inevitable and intervention is 'too little too late.' These savage schisms are portrayed as humanitarian crises rather than as criminal conspiracies and are dismissed as regional rather than as international concerns. Existing victims all too often are compelled to characterize their plight in terms of less morally emotive and compelling neologisms such as 'ethnic cleansing.'

The bystanders resort to verbal acrobatics and to tortuous distinctions to avoid the term genocide. There is no better example than the U.S. Department of State's evasive rhetoric in regards to Bosnia and Rwanda. Statistics on death and dying and eyewitness reports are dismissed as hyperbole and the motives and judgment of those who denounce the killings are questioned and dismissed as naïve idealism. The calculations of economic self-interest are elevated over human life. Genocide in the end seems more symbol than substance. It is metaphorically speaking a 'victimless crime'; a crime without victims, victimizers or morally culpable bystanders. Claims of genocide are more often an occasion for measured rhetoric and academic analysis than an occasion for urgent moral condemnation. In light of this global genocidal denial, there is a temptation to view the Genocide Treaty as yet another product produced by the global human rights industry. This skepticism is heightened by the fact that the Convention has attracted fewer signatories than most other major human rights conventions. It also should be noted that despite the Treaty's significance that it is not been recognized by the United Nations as part of the 'International Bill of Rights.'

Genocide is the most elemental of human rights violations and serves as a catalyst for the wholesale violation of civil and political rights. Genocide institutionalizes distinctions and discrimination. It is an inversion of morality in which the most vulnerable are the first to suffer and to die. Genocide privileges power and privilege over humanitarianism, equality and democracy. A genocidal regime inevitably is compelled to conceal its crimes, limit freedom of expression and ransom the truth. Protests are suppressed and dissidents interned and made to disappear. The elimination of one group makes other minority groups vulnerable to the genocidal instinct towards national uniformity. History is revised, rewritten and reconfigured. The costs of genocide are not merely measured in the loss of human life, the killings extinguish culture and community and cosmopolitanism.

The 'new revisionists' contend that genocide and the narrative of human rights and international law is employed by Western Powers to subordinate the developing world. The former colonial powers that call for humanitarian intervention and the enforcement of human rights are themselves accused of involvement in mass violence against civilians under the banner of counter-insurgency and counter-terrorism. International institutions in the view of these 'new revisionists' are a vehicle for 'human rights fundamentalists' to selectively impose their values. The victims in developing societies that do not appear on the menu of concern are left to be extinguished without champions or concern. The solution for these 'new revisionists' lies in truth commissions and in other local solutions rather than in transnational initiatives.[34]

The 'new revisionism' highlights the complex issues surrounding race and genocide. The revisionist's case nonetheless is overstated and exaggerated. The victimizers cannot credibly be cast as victims of a post-colonial conspiracy and regimes relying on violence have demonstrated little interest in self-examination. In the end, the 'new revisionism' remains a variant of the global trend towards 'genocide denial'.

There undoubtedly is merit in the criticism that the crime of genocide at times is drawn too broadly and too often is employed to rally political support for a cavalcade of causes. Nonetheless, this seems much less a threat than the studied indifference of the global community to the crime of genocide and the victims of genocide. The question remains, in light of this 'global genocide denial,' whether the crime of the past century will be characteristic of the next.

There is an extensive literature on the larger social forces that are a catalyst for genocide. These causal characteristics include a sense of historical grievance and revenge, a serious social shock, an insular and an uncontested exclusionary ideology, and a reservoir of social stereotypes that fuels the resort to scapegoating along with the human instinct towards collective solidarity and personal advancement. There is no single theoretical approach that is fully compelling or convincing. Existing theories seem closer to description than to explanation. The literature does clearly indicate that a failure to condemn and criticize mass violence is an invitation to genocide. This suggests that our silence when confronted with genocide implicates the entire international community in the perpetuation of this horrible crime.[35]

Let me conclude by paraphrasing Primo Levi's observation on Chaim Rumkowski, the morally compromised head of the Lodz Ghetto in German-occupied Poland. Levi writes that like Rumkowski we are so dazzled by 'power and prestige' that we forget our 'essential fragility' and that outside the fence the train is waiting. I should add that the train is waiting, for you, for me, for all of us.[36]

34 The exemplar of the "new revisionism" is Mahmood Mamdani, *When Victims become Killers; Colonialism, Nativism and the Genocide in Rwanda*, 2001.

35 See, *James* Waller, *Becoming Evil; How Ordinary People Commit Genocide and Mass Killing*, 2002.

36 Primo Levi, *The Drowned and the Saved*, 1989, 69.

3. Understanding the Milošević Case: Legacy of an Unfinished Trial

Nena Tromp

1. Introduction

This paper will address the question: what is the value of the record left by a trial that never came to conclusion? The expectations of the Milošević trial, for justice and accountability, were never met. His guilt was never formally established in the court and, in a legal sense, he died an innocent man. This paper argues that mass atrocities trials have not only a legal, but also an extralegal function purpose. Although the traditional objectives of criminal law—such as retribution and deterrence—were not achieved in Milošević's case, no verdict was pronounced, and no judgment was written, the trial procedures, testimonies, expert reports, and documents produced as evidence left a comprehensive record to be studied by researchers from many different fields. The importance of this record should be understood in its relevance to societies in transition in the region, its contribution to the historical interpretation of the period, and for its role in shaping the collective memory. However, this will be a longstanding process where the same competing narratives as those heard at the trial will continue the contest: prosecution narrative vs. defense narrative.

This paper also argues that the trial record of Slobodan Milošević should not be used to ascertain a fixed view on the history of the causes and nature of the recent wars, or on his guilt or innocence. The trial record shows that there is an overlap between legal, political, and historical responsibility, and although Milošević's legal responsibility will never be determined, the trial record provides material which can aid in more understanding of the extent of his political and historical responsibility.

2. Legal/Criminal, Political and Historical Responsibility

It is important to stress from the outset that, as the Milošević trial did not finish, one should not expect that a study on the trial has any unspoken or implied ambition to substitute a judgment that was never pronounced. Although every trial record is based on evidence intended to prove the guilt or innocence of those accused, the dominant view among modern day historians is that history "should not concern itself with ascribing praise or blame to individuals, but rather with tracking long-term

H.G. van der Wilt, J. Vervliet et al., *(eds.)* The Genocide Convention: The Legacy of 60 Years.
 ISBN 978 9004 15328 8. pp. 27-37.

social and institutional change."[1] Indeed, historians and social scientists in the last several decades have increasingly minimized the significance of individuals, preferring to study group identity, group behaviour, and long-term structural and institutional change. Slobodan Milošević is something of an exception, as his political and historical role in the disintegration of Yugoslavia has already been the subject of many studies since the 1980s.

International criminal justice focuses on individual criminal responsibility and thus contributes to the record of the political and historical responsibility of an individual. The view advanced in this paper is that, given the unique position of Slobodan Milošević in the political system of Serbia and later in the Federal Republic of Yugoslavia (FRY, 1992-2003), expressed in his de jure and de facto powers, his personal criminal, political, and historical responsibilities are also core issues in understanding the processes that led to the disintegration of Yugoslavia and the violence that followed.

However, the exact nature of Milošević's role and strategy, as well as the role and strategy of the other actors involved, remain a matter of dispute.[2] The record left by the Milošević trial will inevitably contribute to a more comprehensive historical record to assist historians, and legal and other scholars in their research...

Milošević's political life has been the subject of a number of books in which Milošević was cast as a central political figure in the former Yugoslavia in the period preceding and during the wars of the 1990s.[3] Historians and political scientists ascribe a leading role to Milošević in the emergence of post-communist ideological movements and ideologies such as nationalism, which depend on a strong leadership.[4] Those who critically assess his role in these processes, as well as those more supportive of it, all agree that his leadership was an undisputed fact. The historical value of the trial is augmented by the fact that Milošević took such a prominent role

1 Mark Osiel, *Mass Atrocities, Collective Memory and the Law* (Piscataway, NJ: Transaction Publishers, 1997), 101.

2 Jasna Dragović-Saso, "Why did Yugoslavia Disintegrate? An Overview of Contending Explanations," in *State Collapse in South-Eastern Europe: New Perspectives on Yugoslavia's Disintegration*, Leonard J. Cohen and Jasna Dragović-Saso eds. (West Lafayette, IN: Purdue University Press, 2007), 14.

3 See, for example: Slavoljub Djukić, *Milošević and Marković: A Lust for Power* (Montreal: McGill-Queen's University Press, 2001) [note: this is a translation of a work that originally appeared in Serbian]; Lenard Cohen, *Serpent in the Bosom: The Rise and Fall of Slobodan Milošević* (Boulder, CO: Westview Press, 2001); Louis Sell, *Slobodan Milošević and the Destruction of Yugoslavia* (Raleigh, NC: Duke University Press, 2002); Adam LaBor, *Milošević : A Biography* (London: Bloomsbury, 2002); Dusko Doder and Louise Branson, *Milošević : Portrait of a Tyrant* (New York: Free Press, 1999); and Vidosav Stevanović, *Milošević : The People's Tyrant* (London: IB Tauris, 2002).

4 See, for example: "The actions of Slobodan Milosevic were...important, not just for developments within Serbia, but also outside of it.... The role of political leadership in general, and its instrumental uses of nationalism in particular, were very important." in Valerie Bunce, *Subversive Institutions: The Design and the Destruction of Socialism and the State* (New York: Cambridge University Press, 1999), 149.

in it, testing the Prosecutor's evidence in cross-examination, and selecting and conducting the examination of his own witnesses.[5]

By its nature the ICTY places the individual at the centre of the criminal investigation and accountability. In reality, the dividing line between individual criminal responsibility on the one side, and collective and state responsibility on the other, remains an issue of importance.[6] The documents produced by the state and used at the trial in open sessions will contribute to establishing a historical and public record about both the criminal responsibility of Milošević and the policies of the states involved. Normally, such documents would remain sealed in state archives for thirty to thirty years, or longer, before being made public and accessible for historical or other research.

Although historians and legal scholars such as Douglas (2001), Marrus (2002), Teitel (2000), Osiel (1997), and Simpson (1997 and 2007)—who have addressed the relationship between the legal and extralegal purposes of mass atrocities trials—see no contradiction between a trial's legal function and its didactic and historical effects, they do emphasize that legal judgments and proceedings should never be looked to for definitive historical interpretations of the events concerned. Marrus sees the records produced at trials as yet another historical source, like any other. He underlines the fact that historians must evaluate every source with an eye to its derivation, since all sources are in some sense "tainted," and war crimes trial records are no exception. This means that a judgment, though the final stage in legal proceedings, does not represent finality of the position in history of the events that were judged.

Moreover, the material used in the court is limited by the legal standards and requirements for excluding evidence that would commonly be used by historians and thus is vital in shaping historical opinion. Although hearsay is allowed at the International Criminal Tribunal for the Former Yugoslavia (ICTY) under certain circumstances, other material used by historians—such as third party accounts, reports about the general political atmosphere, and the tone set by leaders—is part of the historical account but may not be allowed as evidence in the courtroom.[7] While Marrus sees the records from war crimes-related trials as a historical source, similar to any other source used by historians, Teitel stresses the fact that all legal responses

5 Human Rights Watch, "Weighing the Evidence: Lessons from the Slobodan *Milošević's* Trial," The Balkans 18, no. 10(D) (New York: HRW, 2006), 1.

6 See, for discussion on individual, state, and collective responsibility: G. Nice, "Uska granica izme|u pojedinca i dr`ave," *Helsinki Charter*, no. 107-108 (May/ June 2007), 12-18; Simpson, *Law, War and Crime*, 54-78; Steven R. Ratner and Jason S. Abrams, *Accountability for Human Rights Atrocities in International Law: Beyond the Nuremberg Legacy*, 2nd ed. (New York: Oxford University Press, 2001), especially Chapter 1: "Individual Accountability for Human Rights Abuses: Historical and Legal Underpinnings;" and Norman Cigar and Paul Williams, *Indictment at The Hague: The Milosevic Regime and Crimes of the Balkan Wars* (New York: New York University Press, 2002).

7 Marrus, "History and the Holocaust," 228.

produce transitional narratives and, explicitly or implicitly, there is always a historical account.[8]

3. The Trial Record as a Historical Source

By the nature of a legal proceeding which deals with individual criminal responsibility, the Milošević trial record contains a comprehensive—and possibly the largest—collection of materials pointing not only to the criminal but also to his historical and political responsibility for the disintegration of Yugoslavia and the subsequent wave of violence. In the scholarly literature some argue that the question of guilt or innocence belongs exclusively in the courtroom. Other scholars, such as Charles Maier, however, do not see much difference between the work of lawyers and historians as according to him the mass atrocities trials deal with the responsibility of individuals—which is what historians do as well. According to Maier, a historian confronts responsibility precisely because it helps to measure the degree of freedom of choice within a given institutional context. Maier asserts that "doing justice" and "doing history" are related activities. A historian endeavors to "do justice" by voicing the aspirations of the protagonists and exploring their choices.[9] In literature that addresses the collapse of Yugoslavia, as well as in the writings of journalists and policymakers involved in the wars, there is a near consensus on the centrality of the role played by Slobodan Milošević in the violent processes of disintegration.[10]

4. History in the Courtroom

One of the first studies on the topic of the use of history in the courtroom—relating to judgments by the ICTY—was written by Richard Wilson, a human rights scholar.[11] Wilson states that the judgments in two ICTY cases he analyzed "are characterized by detailed contextualization of criminal acts and extensive historical interpreta-

8 Teitel, *Transitional Justice*, 117.

9 Charles S. Maier, "Doing History, Doing Justice: The Narrative of the Historian and of the Truth Commission" in *Truth v. Justice: The Morality of Truth Commissions*, Rotberg, R. I. and Thompson D. eds., (Princeton: Princeton University Press, 2000), 261-278.

10 See, for example: James Gow, *The Serbian Project and its Adversaries: A Strategy of War Crimes* (Montreal: McGill-Queen's University Press, 2003); Marko Attila Hoare, *How Bosnia Armed* (London: Saki, 2004); Susan L. Woodward, *Balkan Tragedy: Chaos and Dissolution after the Cold War* (Washington, DC: Brookings Institution, 1995); Christopher Bennett, *Yugoslavia's Bloody Collapse: Causes, Course and Consequences* (London: Hurst, 1995); and Catherine Samary, *Yugoslavia Dismembered* (New York: Monthly Review Press, 1995).

11 Richard Wilson, "Judging History: The Historical Record of the International Criminal Tribunal of the Former Yugoslavia," *Human Rights Quarterly* 27 (2005): Wilson's analysis also deals with Holocaust trials held in France. The ICTY cases analyzed are: the Tadić case (No. IT-94-1-T) and the Krstić case (No. IT-98-33), both Bosnian Serb perpetrators.

tion."[12] He explains that international tribunals are less influenced by the distorting narratives of national identity, but that charges such as genocide, which emphasize the collective nature of the crimes tried, compel the court "to situate individual acts with long-term, systematic policies."[13] The Milošević trial illustrates that in some cases it is desirable, or even essential, for the courtroom to be a place where there is an understanding of history, for several reasons. First, it is necessary for establishing and proving the real state of mind—mens rea in legal terminology—of the accused, and of his fellow high-level officials involved in articulating and executing the political plan which eventually led to the commission of crimes. A (criminal) plan often derives from ideological concepts conceived in the past. The plan as charged in the indictments against Milošević developed over decades, even centuries. A proper understanding of how such an ideology was applied contemporaneously is best achieved, or perhaps can only be achieved, when placed in its broader historical context. Second, a historical context is needed in the courtroom to assist the judges in comprehending the political dynamics that led to the occurrence of mass atrocities. In this particular case, history of political events was necessary in the courtroom in order to provide the background for understanding how the political elites in Yugoslavia moved from being ordinary politicians to those who could, and did, use violence to conquer, consolidate, or retain power. For these purposes, i.e. to establish mens rea and to provide the historical and political context in which the crimes occurred, the prosecution and defense may call expert witnesses on history and politics, as happened at the Milošević trial.[14]

5. The Narrative of the Courtroom

Maier argues that in a trial, as in the writing of history, the judge, like the historian, aspires to produce a coherent narrative: one that explains and interprets as well as records.[15] There is a difference in focus between jurists and historians when examining trial records, though. Jurists focus on their precedential value of the legal principles and their potential contribution to international and national law, while his-

12 Wilson, "Judging History," 908.

13 Ibid.

14 Audrey Budding was called by the Prosecution as an expert witness on history, while Ton Zwaan was called as an expert witness on genocide. The defense called several expert witnesses: Slavenko Terzić was called as an expert on history of the Kosovo conflict; Kosta Mihailović was called to testify about Serbia's economic disadvantages in Yugoslavia from 1918-1991; Čedomir Popović was called as expert on Greater Serbia. The Defense was also to call several other expert witnesses, such as historian Vasilije Krestić, who would testify on the history of genocide on Serbs in Croatia, and Kosta Čavoški, who wrote an expert report, "Budding vs. Budding," refuting the Prosecution's expert on history.

15 Maier, "Doing History, Doing Justice," 271.

torians concentrate on the historical narrative as told in the courtroom.[16] By reason of the legal system applied at the international criminal courts, the prosecution and defense are likely to present competing historical narratives, or "two truths" about the conflict. The Anglo-Saxon adversarial legal system gives both parties the opportunity to set out their evidence before the judges. Consequently, every trial record produces at least two accounts of the past: that of the defence and that of the prosecution. This means that there is not only not a single version of events, but possibly more than two depending on how many persons are on trial.[17] Otto Kirchheimer, a legal scholar who wrote an authoritative study on political justice, described the gamble that polarized narratives in the courtroom can introduce. He called it an "irreducible risk" as the inevitable sine qua non of a just trial. This risk, that every decision to submit traumatic history to criminal law is, in a sense, a "double wager," means that not only might a defendant prevail, but that even if the trial ends in a conviction it might fail in its didactic aim.[18]

In the debate over the prevailing narrative of the Holocaust, Douglas acknowledges that, at times, the law succeeded and, at times, it failed in this wager. Nevertheless, he sees the Nuremberg and Eichmann trials as "powerful, imaginative, and socially necessary responses to extreme crimes."[19]

Simpson is similarly aware of this risk, noting that even successful prosecutions can cause cultural upheaval and unease. He offers the example of Klaus Barbie, who was put on trial and eventually convicted of having committed crimes against humanity in 1944 in occupied France. His trial became an ordeal for the French nation, because at times it was as though France was a codefendant for having carried out crimes against humanity in Algeria during the colonial struggle there.[20] The focus of attention of the public was successfully shifted to the topic identified by the defense, and occasionally it seemed as if Barbie were no longer the defendant at all.[21] The Eichmann trial produced a dissident text by Arendt, which arose from the revelation of details about the Jewish leadership in wartime Europe, that allowed Arendt to claim that the leadership always cooperated with the Nazis.[22]

The trial of Milošević had all the characteristics of a "double wager." The stakes were further raised by Milošević defending himself and lacking any real interest in a legal defense. Instead, he used the courtroom to advance his political position by

16 Leora Bilsky, *Transformative Justice: Israeli Identity on Trial* (Ann Arbor, MI: University of Michigan Press, 2004), 7.

17 "At Nuremberg, with 22 defendants, including Martin Bormann who was tried in absentia, the accused quite often disagreed among themselves in describing what had happened in Nazi Germany and reacted quite differently to accounts of the persecution and murder of European Jews." See: Marrus, "History and the Holocaust," 229.

18 Otto Kirchheimer, *Political Justice: The Use of Legal Procedure for Political Ends* (New York: Princeton University Press, 1961), 324.

19 Douglas, *The Memory of Judgement*, 5.

20 Simpson, "Didactic and Dissident Histories," 802-803.

21 Ibid, 834.

22 Ibid.

making political speeches, addressing the large domestic audience which received the live trial broadcast throughout the region. Distorting both the legal and historical narratives, he attempted to shift the focus from individual criminal responsibility to collective, or rather state, criminal responsibility, as well as to accuse Western powers of committing crimes.

Milošević was allowed in his trial to address issues such as the alleged criminality of the North American Treaty Organization (NATO) campaign against the Federal Republic of Yugoslavia in 1999, in efforts to divert attention from crimes that occurred under his political authority. For instance, he blamed NATO attacks for the mass exodus of Albanians from Kosovo, thus to refute allegations of systemic expulsions and ethnic cleansing of Kosovar Albanians from Kosovo by Serbian armed forces:

> I repeat, the population from Kosovo was expelled by the KLA because they ordered people to do so. They beat them and they killed them. That was number one. Number two, NATO, through their airstrikes. That is the truth behind your story about deportations. And I want to say here something that everybody in Serbia knows. In the Serb tradition and in the tradition of the Serb military, a prisoner of war and an unarmed person are held sacred. Whoever violated this sacred principle has to be held accountable. However, this was not done by the military or by the police.[23]

These words and many others will allow historians and other researchers in search of evidence on topics such as the victimhood of Serbs, the martyrdom of Slobodan Milošević, and a global conspiracy against Serbia led by the United States, to find enough material to advance the counter narrative as presented by the defense. Milošević was frequently allowed to advance his interpretation of the Yugoslav conflict and his role in it, ascribing responsibility for the outbreak of war and for criminal war violence in the former Yugoslavia to Slovenian and Croatian leaders, to Muslim fundamentalists, to the Kosovo Liberation Army, to Germany, The Vatican, The United States, and even to NATO.[24] In his opening speech for the defense in August 2004, Milošević advanced his position claiming a distortion of history by the outside world, a theme which would be repeated throughout the trial in different forms:

> In the international public, for a long time and with clear political intentions an untruthful, distorted picture was being created in terms of what happened in the territory of the former Yugoslavia. Accusations leveled against me are an unscrupulous lie and also a tireless distortion of history. Everything has been presented in a lopsided manner so - in order to protect from responsibility those who are truly responsible and to draw the wrong conclusions about what happened and also in terms of the background of the war against Yugoslavia.[25]

23 ICTY Trial Transcript (February 14, 2002), 253, lines 1-17.

24 See, for example: ICTY Trial Transcript (February 14, 2002), 287, lines 7-16; ICTY Trial Transcript (August 31, 2004), 32170, lines 8-24.

25 ICTY Trial Transcript (August 31, 2004), 35218, line 1; 35215, line 10.

This interpretation of events may not have been the best legal defence, but it certainly had a huge impact on the public in the former Yugoslavia, who viewed live television broadcasts of trial proceedings.

6. Transformative Trials and Collective Memory

The value of the Milošević trial record could be categorized as a "transformative trial", a term coined by Leora Bilsky. She sees transformative trials as political trials, placed somewhere between the political and the legal.[26] On the one hand, a transformative trial has to remain loyal to the basic liberal value of the rule of law, and on the other hand, it performs a unique function as a legal forum in which society's fundamental values can be examined in light of competing counter stories as presented in the courtroom.[27] The trial of Slobodan Milošević was indeed about individual criminal responsibility according to the international criminal law legal system, but it also had a story to tell to the domestic and the international audience about which mechanisms trigger and make possible political violence of the kind that occurred in the former Yugoslavia.

In traditional societies or states with long histories, the formation of collective memory is achieved through a long, diffuse process and through religious and communal rituals that have nothing to do with the law. In the transition periods that follow any occurrence of mass atrocities or long standing abuses of human rights, legal proceedings instituted against the members of the abusive regimes will inevitably contribute to shaping collective memory about that period of history.[28] Rutie Teitel sees trials as long-standing ceremonial forms of collective history and the primary way of processing events in controversy. In her view, the purpose of a criminal trial is both to adjudicate individual responsibility and to establish the truth about an event in controversy.[29]

It is fair to say that the political leadership in post-war societies of Yugoslav successor states did not embrace the concept of transitional justice with enthusiasm. There has been a reluctance to admit to crimes committed against "others" (i.e. those of other ethnicities). In the case of Serbia one might even talk about an orchestrated campaign of denial regarding responsibility for the war and for crimes committed by the Serbian armed forces in Croatia, Bosnia-Herzegovina, and Kosovo. Even after the fall of Slobodan Milošević in 2000, political and intellectual elites in Serbia did not give up ambitions of expanding their western border by the inclusion of Republika Srpska, the Serbian entity in neighbouring Bosnia-Herzegovina. In the same period, since 1999, many attempts were made to keep Kosovo within Serbian borders, ultimately with no success. The state borders of Serbia have been altered since the independence proclamation of Kosovo in February 2008. One could argue that

---

26 Leora Bilsky, *Transformative Justice: Israeli Identity on Trial* (Ann Arbor, MI: University of Michigan Press, 2004), 7.

27 Ibid, 8.

28 Ibid, 7.

29 Teitel, *Transitional Justice*, 72.

political stability and consensus among the Serbian ruling elites, needed in a society where the wrongs of the past must be addressed, have not been achieved and thus no conditions for the transitional justice processes have been met.

The trial of Slobodan Milošević was held against the backdrop of a polarized Serbian society. On one side were the pro-European political forces, led by the late Serbian Prime Minister Zoran Đinđić, who understood the political necessity and obligation of cooperation with the ICTY. This political orientation resulted in the extradition of Milošević to The Hague on June 28, 2001. But Serbian politics of this ilk came to an abrupt end in March 2003 with the assassination of Đinđić by those who opposed cooperation with the ICTY. These forces, on the other side of the political spectrum in Serbia thus maintained an anti-European and anti-ICTY orientation, were led by Vojislav Koštunica and Vojislav Šešelj, and were supported by intellectual elites close to the Serbian Academy of Sciences and Arts (SANU, or Srpska akademija nauka i umetnosti). They were also proponents of the Serbian nationalist state project, which advocated the extension of Serbia's western borders.[30] Since the assassination of Đinđić, Serbian foreign and domestic politics have shifted from a pro- to an anti-European stance, and "vital national interests" have been used to justify keeping rom the ICJ and from the public eye evidence that could implicate the state of Serbia in the crimes committed in Croatia and Bosnia-Herzegovina.[31] The impact of Milošević's trial on Serbia confirmed the polarization that already existed in Serbian politics and society. The trial also demonstrated that Serbian nationalistic ideology and its expansionist state project has survived the political tenure of Milošević. The same ideologues of Serbian nationalism in the 1980s that led the country into the war testified as defense witnesses, still defending the divisive positions they articulated and promoted. Mihailo Marković, Smilja Avramov, Kosta Mihajlović, Čedomir Popović, Slavenko Terzić, and Ratko Marković testified, while two other academy members, Kosta Čavoški and Vasilije Krestić, who were scheduled to testify, were prevented from doing so only by the death of the accused.[32]

The trial had a very different effect in Croatia, Bosnia–Herzegovina and Kosovo, where crimes by Serbian armed forces took place and where the victims were expecting the trial not only to do justice, but also to shed more light on the political and military responsibility of those who led their countries into war. These expectations were only partially met and it is still to be seen how the trial record will be explored and used by those who will research the causes and conduct of the wars in the former Yugoslavia.

30 Sonja Biserko, "The Serbian Elites and Genocide in Bosnia," *Helsinki Charter*, no. 109-110 (July/August 2007), 16-17, available at: http://www.helsinki.org.rs/hcharter_t16.html.

31 See Hugh Griffiths and Ana Uzelac, "Justice at What Price?," *IWPR Tribunal Update*, no. 407 (May 17, 2005), http://iwpr.net/report-news/justice-what-price.

32 Biserko, "Serbian Elites," 18.

7. Bibliography

Bilsky, Leora, Transformative Justice: Israeli Identity on Trial (Ann Arbor, MI: University of Michigan Press, 2004).

Biserko, Sonja, "The Serbian Elites and Genocide in Bosnia," Helsinki Charter, no. 109-110 (July/August 2007), 1-19.

Cohen, Lenard J. and Dragović-Soso, Jasna, eds., State Collapse in South-Eastern Europe: New Perspectives on Yugoslavia's Disintegration (West Lafayette, IN: Purdue University Press, 2007).

Douglas, Laurence, The Memory of Judgment: Making Law and History in the Trials of the Holocaust (Yale University Press: New Haven and London, 2001).

Kirchheimer, Otto, Political Justice: The Use of Legal Procedure for Political Ends (New York: Princeton University Press, 1961).

Maier, Charles, "Doing History, Doing Justice: The Narrative of the Historian and of the Truth Commissions," in Truth v. Justice: The Morality of Truth Commissions, Rotberg, R. I., Thompson D. eds., (Princeton: Princeton University Press, 2000), 261-278.

Marrus, Michael R., "History and the Holocaust in the Courtroom," in Lessons and Legacies Volume 5: The Holocaust and Justice, ed. Smelser, Ronald M. (Evanston, IL: Northwestern University Press, 2002).

Osiel, Mark, Mass Atrocities, Collective Memory and the Law (Piscataway, NJ: Transaction Publishers, 1997).

Peterson, Jeremy D., "Unpacking Show Trials: Situating the Trial of Saddam Hussein," Harvard International Law Journal 48 (2007).

Scharf, Michael, Balkan Justice: The Story behind the First International War Crimes Trial since Nuremberg (Durham, NC: University of North Carolina Academic Press, 1997).

Scharf, Michael D. and Schabas, William A., Slobodan Milošević on Trial: A Companion (New York: Continuum International Publishing, 2002).

Shklar, Judith, Law, Morals and Political Trials (Cambridge, MA: Harvard University Press, 1964).

Simpson, Gerry, "Didactic and Dissident Histories in War Crimes Trials," Alabama Law Review 60, no. 3 (1997), 801-839.

Simpson, Gerry, Law, War & Crime (Cambridge: Polity Press, 2007).

Stephen, Chris, Judgement Day: The Trial of Slobodan Milosevic (London: Atlantic Monthly Press, 2005).

Stover, Eric, The Witnesses: War Crimes and the Promise of Justice in The Hague (Philadelphia: University of Pennsylvania Press, 2007).

Welsh, Helga, "Political Transition Processes in Central and Eastern Europe," Comparative Politics 26, no. 4 (July 1994), 379-394.

Wilson, Richard, "Judging History: The Historical Record of the International Criminal Tribunal of the Former Yugoslavia," Human Rights Quarterly 27 (2005).

Internet Sources

Griffiths, H. and Uzelac, A., "Justice at What Price?" IPWR Tribunal Update, no. 407 (May 17, 2005).

Jungvirth, G., "Croat Anger at 'Lenient' Sentences for Vukovar Three," IWPR Tribunal Update, no. 519 (September 28, 2007).

Sadović, M., "Serbian Anger at Haradinaj Acquittal," IWPR Tribunal Update, no. 545 (April 4, 2007).

"Slobodan Milošević's Trial is a Political Case," The Voice of Russia, 3 January 2002, http://www.vor.ru/Opinion/008_eng.html (accessed: March 10, 2008).

Reports

Human Rights Watch, "Weighing the Evidence: Lessons from the Slobodan Milošević's Trial," The Balkans 18, no. 10(D) (New York: HRW, 2006).

United Nations Security Council, "The Rule of Law and Transitional Justice in Conflict and Post-Conflict Societies: Report of Secretary General," S/2004/616 (August 23, 2004).

Procedure and Substance

4. Between Hate Speech and Mass Murder: How to Recognize Incitement to Genocide

Harmen van der Wilt

1. Introduction

In December 2008, a Trial Chamber of the International Criminal Tribunal for Rwanda (hereafter ICTR) pronounced judgment in the case of Simon Bikindi, a popular musical composer and singer.[1] The most salient question was whether the Trial Chamber would hold this 'Rwandese Michael Jackson' criminally responsible for writing and performing seditious lyrics, thus circumscribing the artistic freedom which Bikindi was inclined to invoke.

According to the Prosecutor, charging Bikindi with incitement to genocide, the accused had intoxicated his audience with his songs, fanning hatred and violence amongst the Hutu population against Tutsis and moderate Hutus. The Trial Chamber, assisted by linguistic experts and numerous witnesses, took great pains to analyze the lyrics. Some of the witnesses praised their poetic quality, while others pointed at arcane passages which irrefutably were saturated with ethnic hatred. All agreed that the songs were highly complex and equivocal, adding that it would be impossible to capture all allusions and metaphors without a thorough knowledge of Kinyarwanda.[2] The Trial Chamber, although acknowledging that some songs had certainly advocated Hutu unity against a common foe and had incited ethnic hatred, concluded that the evidence did not evince beyond all reasonable doubt that Bikindi composed the lyrics with the specific intent to incite attacks and killings, even if they were used to this effect in 1994.[3] Bikindi, however, did not get away with it. He was convicted, on another count, and sentenced to fifteen years in prison. [4]

1 *Prosecutor v. Bikindi*, Judgment, Case No. ICTR-01-72-T, 2 December 2008.

2 *Prosecutor v. Bikindi*, §§ 187-255.

3 *Prosecutor v. Bikindi*, §249 and § 255.

4 The Trial Chamber found that Bikindi had publicly addressed a crowd of Hutus by loudspeaker at a roadblock, charging "the majority" to "rise up and look everywhere possible" and not to "spare anybody", immediately referring to the Tutsi minority. According to the Chamber this *did* constitute direct and public incitement to commit genocide; *Prosecutor v. Bikindi*, § 423.

H.G. van der Wilt, J. Vervliet et al., *(eds.)* The Genocide Convention: The Legacy of 60 Years.

ISBN 978 9004 15328 8. pp. 41-50.

It is interesting to contrast the Bikindi judgment with another landmark decision of the ICTR, colloquially called the Media case. In this case a Trial Chamber convicted three accused, who allegedly served as masterminds behind a media campaign spreading hatred amongst the Hutu population against the Tutsis, for incitement to commit genocide.[5] The accused had been involved in the founding of the Radio Télévision Libre des Milles Collines, RTLM (Nahimana and Barayagwiza) or of the newspaper Kangura (Ngeze). Leading articles in Kangura had over a protracted period capitalized on feelings of inferiority and fear among the Hutus against the dominant Tutsis who had been given preferential treatment by colonial powers. Broadcasts by RTLM had actively fueled the violence by naming specific individuals who should be harassed and killed.

The judgment raised the hopes and spirits of human rights activists, who have always claimed that genocide does not emerge out of the blue, but is meticulously prepared and orchestrated by power elites, using the mass media to poison the minds of the general populace, which ultimately results in the annihilation of an ethnic, racial or religious minority.[6]

Simultaneously, the Media-judgment has evoked a number of critical comments. They point at shortcomings and inconsistencies in the Trial Camber's legal reasoning in general and, in particular, censure the unwarranted extension of temporal jurisdiction and the Trial Chamber's failure to identify explicit instances of calls to violent action in newspaper articles or radio broadcasting.[7]

The Appeals Chamber partially redressed the legal flaws, but ultimately upheld the conviction of Nahimana (on the basis of superior responsibility, Article 6(3) ICTR-Statute) and Ngeze, while acquitting Barayagwiza on this count. [8]

One may wonder why the outcome of both decisions is so different. Is it conceivable that Bikindi was simply smarter in concealing his true intentions? One thing is certain, though: the requirements for 'incitement to commit genocide' are rigid and demanding. The intent of the accused to exhort others to commit mass murder must be unambiguous and the audience must have clearly understood the message.

In this short essay I will give some reflections on the criminal law features of incitement to commit genocide. I will argue that it is a highly complicated concept

5 *Prosecutor v. Nahimana, Barayagwiza and Ngeze,* Judgment and Sentence, Case No. ICTR-99-52-T. T. Ch. I, 3 December 2003.

6 An exponent of these human rights activists is Alison des Forges, *Leave None to Tell the Story; Genocide in Rwanda*, New York: Human Rights Watch,1999, who served as an expert witness during the *Media*-trial and died in an airplane crash in February 2009.

7 Compare Gabrielle Della Morte, "De-Mediatizing the Media Case," *Journal of International Criminal Justice,* 3 (2005), 1019-1033 and Alexander Zahar, "The ICTR's *Media* Judgment and the Reinvention of Direct and Public Incitement to Commit Genocide," *Criminal Law Forum,* 16 (2005), 33-48.

8 *Prosecutor v. Nahimana, Barayagwiza, Ngeze,* Appeals Judgment, Case No. ICTR-99-52-A, 28 November 2007. For a survey, see Sophia Kagan, "The 'Media case' before the Rwanda Tribunal: The *Nahimana et al.* Appeal Judgment," *Hague Justice Journal*, 3, no. 1 (2008) 83-91.

which—apart from some obvious and notorious cases like Streicher[9] and Goebbels—is very difficult to apply in practice as it labors under a number of tensions. Squeezed between 'hate speech' and 'actual (physical) genocide,' incitement to genocide displays features of both 'crimes of expression' and 'risk crimes.' Nevertheless, it should not be conflated with either of the adjacent categories, because, as an inchoate and separate crime, it has standing of its own. I will try to demonstrate how the inconsistencies in the judgment of the ICTR's Trial Chamber can be attributed to the multi-faceted nature of incitement to commit genocide. And finally, although I do not pretend to resolve the quandary, I will venture to discuss some possibilities to identify 'incitement to commit genocide' as a meaningful concept which can be applied in practice.

2. The Dual Character of 'Incitement to Commit Genocide'

To a certain extent, incitement to commit genocide can be considered as a 'crime of expression,' as it insults or offends people because of their specific racial, ethnic or religious features. In this respect it shares some common ground with 'hate crimes.' Concerns have been raised that criminalization of 'hate speech' and incitement to commit genocide would trespass on the much cherished freedom of expression, but those objections are farfetched. After all, both the European Convention on Human Rights and the International Covenant on Civil and Political Rights subject the exercise of this freedom to restrictions or penalties, prescribed by law and necessary in a democratic society, 'for the protection of the reputation or rights of others.' [10] Besides, both the Human Rights Committee and the European Court of Human Rights have emphasized in their case law the need to criminalize hate speech.[11]

However, incitement to genocide is much more than a simple hate crime. It derives its bad reputation as a very serious international crime from its potential to inspire the actual destruction of a group. It is generally presumed that inflammatory propaganda denouncing minorities as inferior beings substantially enhances the risk that massive violence will materialize. From this perspective incitement to genocide can be qualified as a 'risk crime,' the reprehensibility of which is largely predicated on the actualization of another crime. Although this element is not completely ab-

---

9 Julius Streicher was the infamous owner and general editor of *Der Stürmer* who stood trial at Nuremberg and was convicted, and sentenced to death for his vituperative attacks on the Jews which presaged and paved the way for the Holocaust. For a succinct 'biography', see *Prosecutor v. Nahimana et al.* (Tr. Ch.), § 981. See also Ann and John Tusa, *The Nuremberg Trial* (New York: Atheneum, 1984) 333-37.

10 ECHR, Article 19(2), ICCPR, Article 19(3).

11 For a short survey, see: Wibke K. Timmermann, "The Relationship between Hate Propaganda and Incitement to Commit Genocide: A New Trend in International Law Towards Criminalization of Hate Propaganda?" *Leiden Journal of International Law* 18 (2005), 257, 264-266 and (more extensively) ICTR Trial Chamber in *Prosecutor v. Nahimana, Barayagwiza and Ngeze*, §§ 984-999.

sent in hate speech, it is much more pronounced in incitement and therefore the two should not be confused. [12]

The distinction between hate speech and incitement to genocide has been confirmed by the Appeals Chamber in the Media-case:

> The Appeals Chamber considers that there is a difference between hate speech in general (or inciting discrimination or violence) and direct and public incitement to commit genocide. Direct incitement to commit genocide assumes that the speech is a direct appeal to commit an act referred to in Article 2(2) of the Statute (of the ICTR); it has to be more than a mere vague or indirect suggestion. In most cases, direct and public incitement to commit genocide can be preceded or accompanied by hate speech, but only direct and public incitement to commit genocide is prohibited under Article 2(3),c of the Statute. This conclusion is corroborated by the travaux préparatoires to the Genocide Convention.[13]

3. Incitement as a Separate and Inchoate Crime

Whereas the 'risk crime'-nature of incitement stresses the (potential) connection with ensuing calamities, other features, reversely, point at the distinctiveness of the crime. Incitement to genocide is a separate offence; neither in the Genocide Convention, nor in the Statute of the ICC and the Statutes of the ad hoc-tribunals has it been categorized as a form of participation in another offence.[14] Cooperation between 'partners in crime' is an entirely foreign concept. As already emerged in the introduction, the mens rea of incitement to genocide is the specific intent to destroy a group in whole or in part.[15] However, the mens rea in respect of incitement is not a derivative of the mental element of genocide. It is a separate requirement which is unrelated to the similar mens rea of the actual perpetrator(s).

---

12 In the same vein Susan Benesh, "Vile Crime or Inalienable Right: Defining Incitement to Genocide," *Virginia Journal of Int. Law,* 48 (2008), 487-88: "Incitement to genocide is not the same as hate speech, and conflating these crimes (as some of the recent decisions have done) or even confusing incitement to genocide with protected speech can lead to both wrongful convictions and improper exonerations." For a different view, see Timmermann, "The Relationship between Hate Propaganda and Incitement to Commit Genocide," 281: who seems to consider hate speech as a predecessor or gateway to incitement.

13 *Prosecutor v. Nahimana et al.* (Appeals Chamber), § 692.

14 See also G. Werle, *Principles of International Criminal Law* (The Hague: Asser Press, 2005) 211: "It (the provision on incitement to commit genocide) provides a separate ground for criminalizing a separate form of complicity, namely inducing – or even merely attempting to induce – others to commit genocide. A completed genocide is not required."

15 *See Prosecutor v. Akayesu,* Judgment, Case No. ICTR-96-4-T, 2 September 1999, § 560; Prosecutor *v. Ruggiu,* Judgment, Case No. ICTR-97-32-1, 1 June 2000, § 14.

Moreover, and this even reinforces the distinct character of the offence, incitement to genocide is an inchoate crime.[16] This means that the person who endeavors to prompt others to engage in genocide incurs criminal responsibility, even if the desired results do not materialize. The obvious aim is to forestall or prevent genocide, recognizing the particular dangerousness of the acts because of the high risk they carry for society, even if they fail to produce results.

By implication, a causal link between incitement and actual genocide is not required. This is obvious in those cases in which genocide does not follow, but it equally holds true for those situations in which the incitement apparently succeeds. [17]

4. Inconsistencies in the Media-case: Consequences of the Janus-face of Incitement to Genocide

The dual nature of incitement to genocide—as a separate offence, bearing resemblance to 'hate speech,' as it sets the scene and nurtures the minds and as a crime which is far more intimately connected with actual genocide since it serves as a catalyst or precursor to genocide—has been conducive of some flawed decisions in the Media-case.

4.1 Confusion between the Dichotomies Inchoate/ Non-inchoate and Continued/ Instantaneous Offence

The Trial Chamber has erroneously expanded its temporal jurisdiction by including acts of incitement which were performed before 1 January 1994. The Trial Chamber reasoned as follows:

> The Chamber notes (...) that the crime of direct and public incitement to commit genocide, like conspiracy, is an inchoate offence that continues in time until the completion of the acts contemplated. The Chamber accordingly considers that the publication of Kangura, from its first issue in May 1990, through its March 1994 issue, the alleged impact of which culminated in the events that took place in 1994, falls within the temporal jurisdiction of the Tribunal to the extent that the publication is deemed to constitute direct and public incitement to genocide. Similarly, the Chamber considers that the entirety of RTLM broadcasting, from July 1993 through July 1994, the alleged impact of which

16 *Prosecutor v. Akayesu*, Judgment, Case No. ICTR-96-4-T, 2 September 1999, § 562. Confirmed in *Prosecutor v. Nahimana et al.* § 1013 (Trial Chamber) and § 678 (Appeals Chamber).

17 This was, perhaps redundantly, stressed by the Trial Chamber in the *Media*-case: "In considering whether particular expression constitutes a form of incitement on which restrictions would be justified, the international jurisprudence does not include any specific causation requirement linking the expression at issue with the demonstration of a direct effect. (...) Rather, the question considered is what the likely impact *might* be, recognizing that causation in this context might be relatively indirect." (Emphasis added). *Prosecutor v. Nahimana et al.* § 1007.

> culminated in events that took place in 1994, falls within the temporal jurisdiction of the Tribunal to the extent that the broadcasts are deemed to constitute direct and public incitement to genocide.[18]

This is an obvious logical error. One cannot, on the one hand, assert that incitement is a separate offence, while on the other hand deduce or measure its continuous character from the fact that it has produced the desired result. In the opinion of the Trial Chamber, the character of incitement as a continued offence is predicated on the materialization of the actual genocide which precisely denies its inchoate and separate/ independent nature.[19]

The Appeal Chamber has corrected this flawed reasoning:

> The Appeals Chamber is of the opinion that the Trial Chamber erred in considering that incitement to commit genocide continues in time 'until the completion of the acts contemplated.' The Appeals Chamber considers that the crime of direct and public incitement to commit genocide is completed as soon as the discourse in question is uttered or published, even though the effects of incitement may extend in time. The Appeals Chamber accordingly holds that the Trial Chamber could not have jurisdiction over acts of incitement having occurred before 1994 on the grounds that such incitement continued in time until the commission of the genocide in 1994.[20]

In other words, incitement to genocide cannot simultaneously be qualified as an inchoate crime and a continuous offence. The Trial Chamber apparently had confused both concepts.

4.2 Determination of Mens Rea

In determining the mens rea of the accused in the Media-case, the Trial Chamber in a similar vein advanced the actual occurrence of genocide as evidence of the inciter's special intent, thus again ignoring the distinct nature of the latter crime. After having concluded that "with regard to causation, the Chamber recalls that incitement is a crime regardless of whether it has the effect it intends to have," the Trial Chamber subsequently (and quite surprisingly) added:

> In determining whether communications represent an intent to cause genocide and thereby constitute incitement, the Chamber considers it significant that in fact genocide occurred. That the media intended to have this effect is evidenced in part by the fact that it did have this effect.[21]

18 *Prosecutor v Nahimana et al.* (Trial Chamber) § 1017.

19 In the same vein: Della Morte, "De-Mediatizing the Media Case," 1024, note 16.

20 *Prosecutor v. Nahimana et al.* (Appeals Chamber) § 723.

21 *Prosecutor v. Nahimana et al.* (Trial Chamber) § 1029.

The distinctive character of incitement is again put into question, as the mens rea is derived from the completed genocide. Or, in the words of Della Morte:

> This reasoning seems to imply that the intent of an inchoate crime would be demonstrated by the occurrence of a non-inchoate offence. The mens rea of direct and public incitement is deduced (better induced) from the actus of genocide.[22]

This time the Appeals Chamber's criticism was less crushing. Apparently, it shared the Trial Chamber's view that the occurrence of genocide could shed a light on and serve as (partial) evidence of the inciter's intent:

> (...) in some circumstances, the fact that a speech leads to acts of genocide could be an indication that in that particular context the speech was understood to be an incitement to commit genocide and that this was indeed the intent of the author of the speech. The Appeals Chamber notes, however, that this cannot be the only evidence adduced to conclude that the purpose of the speech (and of its author) was to incite the commission of genocide.[23]

By taking this conciliatory approach, the Appeals Chamber strayed from its former rigid logic and failed to disprove the Trial Chamber's inconsistency.

5. In Search of the Essence of Incitement to Genocide

There is an obvious tension between the risk-crime nature of incitement to genocide and the qualification of incitement as a separate and inchoate offence. How can this tension be explained or attenuated? In the opinion of the present author, the gist of the problem is that, in search of the essence of incitement to genocide, we pursue several aims which are largely incompatible. On the one hand, it is important to distinguish between simple 'hate crime' and incitement to genocide, in order to preserve the special serious nature of the latter and guard against trivialization. On the other hand, we have noticed the distinction between incitement as an inchoate crime and auxiliary forms of participation, like instigation. Perhaps the quandary can best be defined as follows: the effort to contrast incitement to genocide with 'hate speech' inevitably procures that incitement draws nearer to genocide. But the conceptual fusion of incitement to genocide and actual genocide makes it more difficult to perceive the former as a separate and inchoate crime—witness the strange meanderings of the Trial Chamber in the Media-case. The challenge then is to carve out a special niche for incitement, distinguishing the concept sufficiently from 'hate speech', while safeguarding its separate existence vis à vis genocide.

In a recent article, Susan Benesh has proposed the Reasonably Possible Consequences Test, which entails a six-prong inquiry on the basis of which incitement to genocide might be identified. These six elements are to be considered as additional

22 Della Morte, "De-Mediatizing the Media Case," 1025.

23 *Prosecutor v. Nahimana et al.* (Appeals Chamber) § 709.

conditions which should be met.[24] The six elements serve to distinguish incitement to genocide from simple 'hate speech,' while the prefix *Possible* obviously denotes the inchoate nature of the crime. Although the Test does not provide the final answer, it is, in my view, a step in the right direction and I will therefore shortly discuss the elements, highlighting the criminal law aspects.

a) Was the speech understood by the audience as a call to commit genocide?

Although there is no need that the inciter and the (potential or would-be) perpetrators of genocide cooperate, communication is obviously vital. The audience must have grasped the meaning of the message, which does not necessarily imply that the call was blunt or unambiguous. Even masked or cryptic language can do the trick. 'Direct incitement' need not be explicit, as was recognized by the Trial Chamber in the Akayesu-case.[25] It all depends on the cultural context in which the speech or broadcast was delivered.[26] The most difficult question is obviously how a court can assess that the audience perceived the message as a call to genocide, especially if that court is linguistically, culturally and geographically far removed from the event. It might serve as an argument in favor of involvement of local courts.[27]

b) Was the speaker able to influence the audience, and was the audience able to commit genocide?

Those who convey the message must have the authority to influence their audience and those receiving the message must be capable of carrying out their dismal task. People may be imbued by racial hatred and express the most gruesome desires to annihilate entire groups, but their endeavors will come to naught if the transmitter is not taken seriously or even ridiculed, or if the (willing) audience is too weak or disorganized to perform the hideous work.

In criminal law terms one would speak in such a case of an absolute or relative unsound attempt.

---

24 Benesh, "Vile Crime or Inalienable Right," 519-25.

25 *Prosecutor v. Akayesu*, Judgment, Case No. ICTR-96-4-T, 2 September 1998, § 557: "The Chamber further recalls that incitement may be direct, and nonetheless implicit. Thus, at the time the Convention on Genocide was being drafted, the Polish delegate observed that it was sufficient to play skillfully on mob psychology by casting suspicion on certain groups, by insinuating that they were responsible for economic or other difficulties in order to create an atmosphere favorable to the perpetration of the crime."

26 *Prosecutor v. Akayesu*, § 558: "The Chamber will therefore consider on a case-by-case basis whether, *in light of the culture of Rwanda and the specific circumstances of the instant case*, acts of incitement can be viewed as direct or not, by focusing mainly on the issue of whether the persons for whom the message was intended immediately grasped the implication thereof." (Emphasis added)

27 On this point, see especially Zahar, "The ICTR's *Media* Judgment," 41.

c) Did the speaker dehumanize the target group and justify killing?

Genocide is a creeping process. The minds of the future génocidaires must be ripened and therefore they must conquer their natural inhibitions to kill fellow human beings. Media campaigns preceding actual genocide display a number of conspicuous features which aspire to accomplish this aim. First, they tend to dehumanize victims, depicting them as subhuman, parasites and vermin. Another well-known tactic is the 'accusation in a mirror', The perpetrators change roles with their victims, blaming the latter for their violent inclinations and invoking self-defense as the only measure to ward off annihilation.[28] And finally, calls to commit genocide are usually cloaked in euphemistic language, justifying massacres in the light of 'historical necessity' or even qualifying the measures as 'humane.'[29]

d) Had the target group suffered recent violence?

Mass violence usually does not break out all of a sudden. Small isolated incidents accumulate and genocidal propaganda will thrive in such an explosive and violent climate. Inflammatory speech may aggravate an already volatile situation, giving the final boost to a fully-fledged genocide.[30]

e) Was the 'Marketplace of Ideas' still functioning?

Alternative opinions denouncing discrimination of and violence against ethnic, racial or religious minorities, serve as an effective counter-poison. Therefore, militant factions, disseminating ethnic hatred, aim at monopolizing the means of communication. As soon as the 'voices of reason' are silenced, the genocidal propaganda machine will hold the reins.

f) Had the audience already received similar messages?

Repetition is a vital prerequisite, as people will not be convinced all of a sudden. One witness at the Media trial captured the condition in a plastic metaphor, speaking of 'spreading petrol little by little' so that finally it took a small spark to ingnite the genocidal apocalypse.

From a criminal law perspective, the three conditions last mentioned are slightly problematic, as they are usually beyond the power of the inciter. In other words, the

28 Ph. Gourevitch, *We wish to inform you that tomorrow we will be killed with our families,* New York: Farrar, Straus and Giroux, 1998) 157: refers to this tactic: "From the start of the war with the RPF in 1990, Hutu extremists had promoted their genocidal aspirations with the world-upside-down rhetoric of Hutu victimization. Now Hutu Power had presided over one of the most outrageous crimes in a century of seemingly relentless mass political murder, and the only way to get away with it was to continue to play the victim."

29 Benesh, "Vile Crime or Inalienable Right," 506: a good example of the use of euphemistic language are the code words 'to work' (*travailler*) and 'to clean up' (*nettoyer*) which concealed the intent to kill Tutsis. see L. Reydams, "Belgium's First Application of Universal Jurisdiction: the Butare Four Case," *Journal of Int. Criminal Justice,* 1 (2003), 428-436.

30 Benesh, "Vile Crime or Inalienable Right," 522-23.

accused cannot influence their occurrence. They are, however, not entirely foreign to criminal law, as definitions of criminal offences sometimes contain 'additional conditions for criminal responsibility.' A good example in Dutch criminal law is Article 101 of the Dutch Penal Code, which considers as a criminal offence the entering into the military service of a foreign state by a Dutch man in the prospect of war, if the war indeed breaks out.

6. Some Concluding Observations

The famous words of Justice Stewart "I know it, when I see it," referring to hard core pornography, may not be so easily applicable to incitement to commit genocide—especially not, if actual genocide does not occur.[31] The thin line between hate speech and incitement to genocide has tempted courts and scholars alike to blur the two concepts. For the reasons expounded above, it is essential to distinguish between the two crimes. Incitement to genocide is far more intimately connected to genocide and serves as a preparatory act to the main event. However, one may easily lose track of the distinctive and separate nature of incitement to genocide if the relationship with the main crime is emphasized.

The Reasonably Possible Consequences Test, as proposed and elaborated by Benesh, is a useful tool to identify incitement to genocide as an autonomous crime, reconciling the specific (dual) nature of the crime with its feature as a separate and inchoate crime. The problem is that the additional conditions—apart from the first one: was the call understood by the audience?—are not explicit elements of the crime. From the perspective of the nullum crimen principle this is not a matter of great concern, as additional elements tend to limit the field of application of the offence. In other words, the accused has no reason to complain that he did not receive fair warning.

The test may especially come in handy 'to nib genocide in the bud' which obviously augments the preventative capacities of criminalization of incitement to genocide as an inchoate crime. To my knowledge, no one has ever been convicted for incitement to genocide without actual genocide having materialized. The current attempts to trigger criminal proceedings against the incumbent president of Iran, Ahmadinejad, for his shameless appeals to destroy the state of Israel, may provide an interesting test case. Whether these efforts stand any chance of success is a question which requires careful legal analysis and lies beyond the scope of this short paper. [32] Suffice to say, at this point our phenomenological understanding of genocide may not fully square with the current fashion amongst psychotic heads of state who threaten other states with complete extinction.

31 These famous words are quoted by Bob Woodward and Scott Armstrong, *The Brethren; Inside the Supreme Court* (New York: Avon Books, 1981) 229.

32 Benesh, "Vile Crime or Inalienable Right," 526: applying her own test to the case is skeptical: "Although Ahmadinejad's speech is despicable, at this point there does not seem to be a reasonable possibility that it will cause genocide."

5. The Meaning of the Word "Destroy" and its Implications for the Wider Understanding of the Concept of Genocide

Larissa van den Herik

1. Introduction

The occasion of the sixtieth anniversary of the Genocide Convention (the Convention) provides momentum to both commemorate the past and reflect on what the future may bring. A first observation at this juncture is that the Genocide Convention has seemingly not lost any of its relevance over the past sixty years. This is a sad conclusion to draw in light of the axiom "never again" that underlies the Convention. The continuing relevance of the Genocide Convention for legal purposes is demonstrated by the fact that the crime of genocide has featured and continues to feature in quite some indictments before national and international criminal courts and tribunals. These cases address Second World War crimes, but also—and perhaps even in their majority—other situations of mass crime.

Most likely, back in 1948 the drafters of the Genocide Convention did not envisage that the Convention would be applied to a range of new situations. As Professor Schabas remarked ten years ago at the Convention's fiftieth anniversary, the drafters of the Convention probably envisaged the erection of a monument looking back at the Holocaust, rather than conceiving that the Convention would apply to genocides yet to occur.[1] As a result, the legal definition of genocide was tailored on past events rather than being forward-looking. The definition, in a way, is the legal narrative of the Holocaust, rather than one that was specifically created for future application to yet unknown situations that are in essence comparable to the Holocaust. Even though the Holocaust has not been repeated in scale, form and character, the qualification of genocide has been invoked in quite a number of situations, ranging from the massacres in Rwanda, Srebrenica and Darfur, to the annihilations of Indians in the Americas and the transfer of Aboriginal children in Australia.

The question is: are all these situations in essence comparable, and is the qualification of genocide the most adequate one? Phrased in more abstract terms: to what extent is the definition of genocide—as included in the Genocide Convention—ap-

1 W.A. Schabas, *The Genocide Convention at Fifty*, United States Institute of Peace, http://www.usip.org/files/resources/sr990107.pdf, viewed June 24, 2009.

H.G. van der Wilt, J. Vervliet et al., *(eds.)* The Genocide Convention: The Legacy of 60 Years.
Copyright 2012 Koninklijke Brill NV. ISBN 978 9004 15328 8. pp. 51-58.

plicable to new situations, and what can recent jurisprudence teach us about the future application of the Convention? In this essay, it is argued that the essence of the legal definition of genocide is captured in the word "destroy"—part of the mental element of the crime—, namely, that an act is committed with the specific intent to destroy a group. A review of recent jurisprudence on the meaning of the word "destroy" will indicate to what extent, if at all, the definition of genocide, as applied by international judges, has moved beyond its original conceptualization.

2. The Traditional Approach

There is general agreement that the qualification of genocide applies to the mass violence that occurred in Rwanda from April to June 1994. The International Criminal Tribunal for Rwanda (ICTR) was a pioneer in that it was the first international criminal tribunal to apply the definition of genocide to a specific case resulting in a conviction. Given that Rwanda was such a clear case of genocide, the ICTR did not have to stretch the limits of the law. The ICTR adhered to the traditional interpretation of the word destroy, as explained by the International Law Commission (ILC) in its 1996 Report:

> As clearly shown by the preparatory work for the Convention, the destruction in question is the material destruction of a group either by physical or by biological means, not the destruction of the national, linguistic, religious, cultural or other identity of a particular group. The national or religious element and the racial or ethnic element are not taken into consideration in the definition of the word "destruction", which must be taken only in its material sense, its physical or biological sense.[2]

The ICTR Trial Chambers thus emphasized that the word "destroy" should be understood as "the material destruction of a group either by physical and biological means and not the destruction of the national, linguistic, religious, cultural or other identity of a particular group."[3]

The word "destroy" is part of the mental element. This means that genocide occurs if specific crimes are committed with the intention to destroy a group. Hence, the destruction does not need to materialize.

3. An Attempt to Broaden the Notion of "Destroy"

The count of genocide did not feature as a central charge in the indictments before the International Criminal Tribunal for the Former Yugoslavia (ICTY). It was gener-

2 United Nations, Doc. A/51/10, May 6, 1996 to July 26, 1996, 90-91.

3 Prosecutor v. Jean de Dieu Kamuhanda, Trial Chamber Judgement, Case No. ICTR-95-54A-T, January 22, 2004, para. 627; Prosecutor v. Laurent Semanza, Trial Chamber Judgement, Case No. ICTR-97-20-T, May 15, 2003, para. 315; Prosecutor v. Sylvestre Gacumbitsi, Trial Chamber Judgement, Case No. ICTR-2001-64-T, June 17, 2004, para. 253; Prosecutor v. Mikaeli Muhimana, Trial Chamber Judgement, Case No. ICTR-951B-T, April 28, 2005, para. 497.

ally agreed that the practice of ethnic cleansing was better qualified as persecution as a crime against humanity. One early ICTY case in which genocide was charged was the case of Goran Jelisić. This case concerned crimes committed at the police station and a detention camp in Brčko, a town and municipality in northeastern Bosnia and Herzegovina. Jelisić did not commit his crimes in a general context of genocide, but was rather prosecuted as a lone génocidaire.[4] One of the questions before the judges in this case was whether Jelisić had acted with the intent to destroy a group. Leaving all legal intricacies of this case aside, it is important to note that the Chambers made a distinction between "discriminatory intent" and "intent to destroy". An act committed with discriminatory intent does not qualify as genocide unless it is also committed with the specific intent to destroy a group.[5]

The subsequent question, at the heart of our enquiry, is what exactly the word "destroy" refers to. The ICTY Trial Chambers, the ICTY Appeals Chamber and Judge Shahabuddeen in particular provided views on this in a number of cases concerning crimes committed in Bosnia and Herzegovina in which a charge on genocide featured.

Genocide was in particular, but not exclusively, charged in relation to crimes committed in Srebrenica in 1995. The first and so far only conviction on a genocide charge came forth in the case against Krstić. Referring to the United Nations (UN) General Assembly Resolution 96(I) on genocide, the UN Secretariat, International Court of Justice (ICJ) jurisprudence, the ILC, and ICTR jurisprudence, the ICTY Trial Chamber underlined that genocide principally targets a group as such, and not only one or several individuals.[6] Subsequently, the Trial Chamber discussed what kind of envisaged destruction would qualify as genocide. By way of general reflection, it held:

> The physical destruction of a group is the most obvious method, but one may also conceive of destroying a group through purposeful eradication of its culture and identity resulting in the eventual extinction of the group as an entity distinct from the remainder of the community.[7]

In the particular context of the Genocide Convention, however, the Chamber observed the following as regards the appropriate interpretation of the word "destroy":

4 The negotiators of the Statute of the International Criminal Court have forestalled the possibility of charging a "lone *génocidaire*" with genocide by including in the "Elements of Crime" the following requirement: "the conduct took place in the context of a manifest pattern of similar conduct directed against that group or was conduct that could itself effect such destruction."

5 Prosecutor v. Goran Jelisić, Trial Chamber Judgement, Case No. IT-95-10-T, December 14, 1999, paras. 62-66; Prosecutor v. Goran Jelisić, Appeals Chamber Judgement, Case No. IT-95-10-A, July 5, 2001, paras. 42-55.

6 Prosecutor v. Radislav Krstić, Trial Chamber Judgement, Case No. IT-98-33-T, August 2, 2001, paras. 551-553.

7 Ibid., para. 574.

> Although the Convention does not specifically speak to the point, the preparatory work points out that the 'cultural' destruction of a group was expressly rejected after having been seriously contemplated. The notion of cultural genocide was considered too vague and too removed from the physical or biological destruction that motivated the Convention.[8]

The Chamber noted some recent developments that might point to an acceptance of cultural or social genocide, but it still acknowledged that:

> (...) Customary international law limits the definition of genocide to those acts seeking the physical or biological destruction of all or part of the group. Hence, an enterprise attacking only the cultural or sociological characteristics of a human group in order to annihilate these elements which give to that group its own identity distinct from the rest of the community would not fall under the definition of genocide.[9]

The Appeals Chamber quoted this excerpt approvingly on appeal.[10] In applying this legal standard to the situation in Srebrenica, the Chamber seemingly broadened the concept of physical destruction of a group to a situation where a group would not be able to reconstitute itself in a given area:

> (...) forcible transfer could be an additional means by which to ensure the physical destruction of the Bosnian Muslim community in Srebrenica. The transfer completed the removal of all Bosnian Muslims from Srebrenica, thereby eliminating even the residual possibility that the Muslim community in the area could reconstitute itself.[11]

In a Partial Dissenting Opinion, Judge Shahabuddeen agreed that if the requirement were to prove intent to physically or biologically destroy the group, this could be proven by the "disastrous consequences for the family structures" that the transfer of women, children and elderly people had.[12] However, in his opinion Shahabuddeen actually advocated a different understanding of the word "destroy". He proposed to distinguish more clearly between the acts of genocide and the mental element. Whereas the acts obviously had to be of a physical or biological nature, "it is not apparent why an intent to destroy a group in a non-physical or non-biological way should be outside the ordinary reach of the Convention."[13] Judge Shahabuddeen argued that, whereas certain genocidal acts require or imply intent to destroy physi-

8 Ibid., para. 576.

9 Ibid., para. 580.

10 "The Genocide Convention, and customary international law in general, prohibit only the physical or biological destruction of a human group": Prosecutor v. Radislav Krstić, Appeals Chamber Judgement, Case No. IT-98-33-A, April 19, 2004 (*Krstić Appeals Judgement*), para. 25.

11 Ibid., para. 31.

12 *Krstić Appeals Judgement*, see n 11, para. 47.

13 Ibid., para. 49.

cally or biologically,[14] other acts do not specify this.[15] In other words, the definition of genocide does not articulate that the physical act of killing members of the group should occur with the intent to physically destroy that group.[16] Shahabuddeen noted in this context that a group "is constituted by characteristics—often intangible—binding together a collection of people as a social unit."[17]

In a Rule 98 bis decision in the case against Slobodan Milosević, the Trial Chamber adhered to the more traditional view and held that "it is the material destruction of the group which must be intended and not the destruction of its identity."[18] Subsequently, and in contrast, in the case of Prosecutor v. Vidoje Blagojević and Dragan Jokić the Trial Chamber endorsed Shahabuddeen's position while trying to adhere to the formal obligation it had to respect legal precedents set by the Appeals Chamber. It came to the puzzling finding that "physical or biological destruction of a group is not necessarily the death of group members."[19] While the broad interpretation led to a conviction of Blagojević for complicity in genocide at first instance, the conviction was overturned on appeal. The Appeals Chamber held that without knowledge of the mass killings, it could not be proved that Blagojević had knowledge of the principal perpetrators' genocidal intent.[20] In a footnote, the Appeals Chamber added:

> The Trial Chamber's conclusion to the contrary may have been based on a view that in removing a group from a particular location, the removers are 'destroying' a group.... The Appeals Chamber emphasized, however, that displacement is not equivalent to destruction.[21]

In Prosecutor v. Momčilo Krajišnik, the Trial Chamber continued Shahabuddeen's line of reasoning, and held that the word "destroy" as used in the mental element was not limited to physical or biological destruction of the group's members, as the group could also be destroyed in other ways, such as transferring children or severing the bonds among its members.[22]

---

14 Such as subsection (c): "deliberately inflicting on the group conditions of life calculated to bring about its physical destruction in whole or in part", or subsection (d): "measures intended to prevent births within the group."

15 Namely, subsection (a): "killing members of the group" and subsection (b): "causing serious bodily or mental harm to members of the group."

16 *Krstić Appeals Judgement*, see n 11, paras. 48-49.

17 Ibid., para. 50.

18 *Prosecutor v. Slobodan Milosevic*, Decision in Motion for Judgement of Acquittal, Case No. IT-02-54-T, June 16, 2004, para. 124.

19 *Prosecutor v. Vidoje Blagojević and Dragan Jokić*, Trial Chamber Judgement, Case No. IT-02-60-T, January, 17, 2005, para. 666.

20 *Prosecutor v. Vidoje Blagojević and Dragan Jokić*, Appeals Chamber Judgement, Case No. IT-02-60-A, May 9, 2007 (*Blagojević and Jokić Appeals Judgement*), para. 123.

21 Ibid., footnote 337.

22 *Prosecutor v. Momčilo Krajišnik*, Trial Chamber Judgement, Case No. IT-00-39-T, September, 27, 2006, para. 854.

The ICJ did not pursue this thought, but rather endorsed the more traditional view as set forth in the Krstić Appeals Judgement, which drew a clear distinction between the physical destruction and the mere dissolution of a group. Quoting the Stakić Trial Judgement, the ICJ held that expulsion is not sufficient to qualify as genocide.[23] Following the lead of the ICTY Appeals Chamber, the ICJ further found that the destruction of historical, religious or cultural heritage does not in itself qualify as genocide, but it can be considered as evidence of intent to physically destroy a group.[24] In the most recent Popović Trial Judgement, the ICTY Trial Chamber agreed with these more restrictive findings that attacks on cultural property and forcibel transfer could be relevant considerations when assessing genocidal intent, but could not qualify directly as genocidal acts.[25]

The discussion above was echoed in the International Criminal Court's (ICC's) decision on the Prosecution's Application for a Warrant of Arrest against Al-Bashir.[26] In this decision, the majority of the Pre-Trial Chamber endorsed the more traditional view that clearly distinguishes between ethnic cleansing, deportation and transfer on the one hand, and a genocidal policy on the other.[27] Pursuant to this view, only in extreme cases can the practice of ethnic cleansing result in genocide. In a Separate and Partly Dissenting Opinion, Judge Ušacka paid tribute to the more expansive approach suggested by Shahabuddeen in an attempt to keep the discussion on this point open. The negative decision by the majority has been appealed by the Prosecutor.[28] On appeal, it was decided that the evidentiary threshold at this stage of the proceedings was lower[29] and subsequently an arrest warrant was issued also for the genocide charges.[30]

23 *Blagojević and Jokić Appeals Judgement*, see n 21, para. 190, quoting *Prosecutor v. Milomir Stakić*, Trial Chamber Judgement, Case No. IT-97-24-T, July 31, 2003, para. 519.

24 *Bosnia and Herzegovina v. Serbia and Montenegro*, Judgement on the Case Concerning the Application of the Convention on the Prevention and Punishment of the Crime of Genocide, January 26, 2007, para. 344.

25 *Prosecutor v. Vujadin Popović* et al., Trial Chamber Judgement, Case No. IT-05-88-T, 10 June 2010, para. 822 and 824.

26 *The Prosecutor v. Omar Hassan Ahmad Al Bashir (Omar Al Bashir)*, Decision on the Prosecution's Application for a Warrant of Arrest against Omar Hassan Ahmad Al Bashir, Pre-Trial Chamber I, Case No. ICC-02/05-01/09, March 4, 2009.

27 Ibid, paras. 141-145.

28 *Omar Al Bashir*, Prosecution's Application for Leave to Appeal the "Decision on the Prosecution's Application for a Warrant of Arrest against Omar Hassan Ahmad Al Bashir", Case No. ICC-02/05-01/09, March 10, 2009.

29 *Prosecutor v. Omar Al Bashir*, Case No. ICC-02/05-01/09, Judgment on the appeal of the Prosecutor against the "Decision on the Prosecution's Application for a Warrant of Arrest against Omar Hassan Ahmad Al Bashir", 3 February 2010.

30 *Prosecutor v. Omar Al Bashir*, Case No. ICC-02/05-01/09, Second Warrant of Arrest for Omar Hassan Ahmad Al Bashir, 12 July 2010.

4. A Domestic Push for a Broader Interpretation

In some domestic cases, perpetrators have also been charged with genocide for crimes committed in Bosnia and Herzegovina, other than the Srebrenica killings. Most notable is the German case against Jorgić. In this case, the German Court concluded that genocide also encompasses the situation where group members survive but the group ceases to exist as a social unit. Pursuant to this view, the practices of ethnic cleansing in Bosnia and Herzegovina were qualified as genocide. The European Court of Human Rights (ECHR) held that this finding did not violate the principle of legality, as the German Courts' interpretation was consistent with the essence of the offence of genocide. The Court did not give any further insight into what precisely it understood the "essence of the offence of genocide" to be. Remarkably, the ICTY Trial Chamber in its Krstić Judgment referred to these German findings, but held that it could not adopt this line of reasoning, as that would violate the legality principle. It thus concluded quite the opposite to what the ECHR had found on the legality principle. The disparity in the application of this fundamental principle of criminal law can be explained by the different roles that the ECHR and the ICTY have been assigned with, and by the fact that the ECHR does not function as an appeal court, but rather undertakes a marginal review, leaving national courts with a certain margin of appreciation.

In its finding permitting the broader German approach in the understanding of the word "destroy," the ECHR relied on a textual and contextual interpretation. The Genocide Convention does not specify the kind of destruction that is envisaged, and thus it could bear an interpretation that encompasses social destruction.[31] The authority on the law of genocide, William Schabas, has indicated that the German interpretation does not trespass the letter of the law.[32] Schabas explains that ethnic cleansing and genocide may share the same goal, namely to cleanse a given area. But he also points to the difference between these two criminal practices, namely, that a policy of ethnic cleansing tolerates the existence of the group elsewhere, whereas a genocidal policy has the ultimate objective of erasing the group from earth. To quote Schabas: "Isn't there a meaningful difference here?"[33]

In the specific case of Jorgić, the charge on genocide may well have been inspired by the lack of jurisdiction over crimes against humanity. It may be argued that the current absence of a convention on crimes against humanity similar to the Genocide Convention has tainted the jurisprudence on genocide, in particular at the domestic level. The implementation of the ICC Statute in the jurisdictions of state parties has undercut this development to some extent. Therefore, the need for a broad construction is less apparent, as those crimes that fall outside the definition of genocide can still be qualified as crimes against humanity. This need may only exist at the inter-

31 W.A. Schabas, "National Courts Finally Begin to Prosecute Genocide, the 'Crime of Crimes'", 1J. *International Criminal Justice* (39, 2003), 58-59.

32 W.A. Schabas, *Genocide in International Law: The Crime of Crimes* (Cambridge, 2nd ed. 2009), 270-273.

33 Ibid., 234.

national level in the context of state responsibility and access to the ICJ, due to the current lack of a Convention on crimes against humanity providing a jurisdictional basis for access to the ICJ.[34]

5. Concluding Observations

To conclude, we may observe at this sixtieth anniversary of the Genocide Convention that the original intention of the drafters of the Genocide Convention—to restrict the scope of genocide to intended physical and biological destruction—has generally been respected. Given the coexistence of genocide with crimes against humanity and, in particular, persecution as a crime against humanity, there is no great legal need for an expansive interpretation of the crime of genocide. Moreover, if we understand international criminal law as a tool that, while punishing individuals, also provides a legal narrative of what happened, it is important that this tool clearly distinguishes between situations that are essentially different.

Making this distinction is, in practice, an increasingly difficult task, given the enormous focus on genocide outside the courtroom. The genocide discussion has practically become routine in situations of mass violence, and the Darfur situation illustrates that positions taken in this discussion tend to be rather black and white, as if genocide is the only international crime; as if Darfur is either characterized as genocide or not as an international crime at all. Macabre as it is, the term genocide now has an almost attractive value, and it is perceived as having specific legal consequences. For instance, the term is perceived as creating a legal duty for the international community to intervene militarily. Furthermore, given that genocide is sometimes called the crime of crimes, it almost seems to place victims of genocide in some kind of higher position than victims of other international crimes. The misplaced focus on genocide outside the courtroom is worrisome, as it not only overlooks the existence of crimes against humanity as a separate international crime, but it also risks diverting attention from where it should be, namely on what is actually happening in a given situation, such as Darfur, or from what has happened factually. From a human perspective, is it eventually not more important to have some insight into the factual situation and to acknowledge the complexity of the situation, rather than to know whether this one qualification—"genocide"—does or does not apply? Is it not, even in a criminal trial, ultimately most important that we establish and acknowledge the facts properly, rather than focus exclusively on the genocide charge? In the end, we must realize that, in general, the word "genocide"—however we conceptualize it—does not in itself provide us with a full picture of what has happened.

34 The Washington University St. Louis project of forging a Crimes Against Humanity Convention aims to fill this gap. For more, see: http://law.wustl.edu/crimesagainsthumanity/index.asp?id=7111, viewed June, 25 2006.

6. Criminologically Explained Reality of Genocide, Structure of the Offence and the 'Intent to Destroy' Requirement *

Kai Ambos

"Certainement qui est en droit de vous rendre absurde, est en droit de vous rendre injuste"[1]

Voltaire, *Questions sur les miracles* (1765)

1. Introduction

I have argued elsewhere[2] that the traditional understanding of the "intent to destroy" requirement in the genocide offence as a purpose based special or specific intent (dolus specialis) with regard to all participants in a genocidal enterprise should be replaced by a combined structure- and knowledge-based approach distinguishing according to the status and role of the (low-, mid- and top-level) perpetrators. Thus, the purpose based intent should only be upheld with regard to the top- and mid-level perpetrators while for the low-level perpetrators' knowledge of the genocidal context should suffice. Apart from doctrinal considerations related to the peculiar structure of the genocide offence and its relationship with crimes against humanity, I have argued that this reading of the "intent to destroy" requirement better fits the criminological reality of genocidal campaigns. From this reality it follows, so I argued, that a genocide cannot be committed by a few crazy individuals alone but needs intellectual masterminds and an organizational apparatus to be carried out. The low-level perpetrators, i.e., the easily interchangeable "foot soldiers" of a genocidal campaign, normally lack the means to destroy a group alone and sometimes do not act with a purpose or desire to destroy. In fact, although these individuals cannot solely contribute in any meaningful way to the ultimate destruction of a group, they can either express any meaningful, act-oriented will as to the overall result. These low-level perpetrators, albeit carrying out the underlying genocidal acts with their own hands,

* Reprinted with permission and previously published in: "Collective Violence and International Criminal Justice," Intersentia 2010.

1 "Those who can make you believe absurdities, can make you commit atrocities."

2 Ambos 2009.

H.G. van der Wilt, J. Vervliet et al., *(eds.)* The Genocide Convention: The Legacy of 60 Years.
Copyright 2012 Koninklijke Brill NV. ISBN 978 9004 15328 8. pp. 59-79.

are, in terms of their overall contribution to the genocidal campaign, only secondary participants (accessories), more precisely aiders or assistants. In other words, while they are the direct executors of the genocidal plan and therefore should be convicted as such (i.e., as principals) their acts receive only their full "genocidal meaning" because there exists a genocidal plan in the first place. As the low-level perpetrators were not involved in designing this plan but are, in a normative sense, only used as mere instruments to implement it, they need not possess the destructive special intent themselves but only know of its existence. In addition, I argued, that, as to the direct perpetrator's (hostile) attitude towards the group, it does not make a difference if he acts with the purpose or knowledge of the overall genocidal purpose.[3] He may even act with a kind of indirect purpose by not distancing himself completely from the overall genocidal purpose.

In this paper I will put my theory through a criminological reality check by examining the following questions: Do my arguments correspond to the criminological reality of genocidal acts and campaigns? Is the threefold distinction between low-, mid- and top-level perpetrators or participants in genocide too simplistic in the light of the more sophisticated models of recent criminological research? Finally, does the criminological reality of genocide support the reinterpretation of the intent to destroy requirement or does it speak against it?

2. Typologies in Criminology

As Smeulers has correctly pointed out, relying on the results of the majority of the case studies,[4] perpetrators are "ordinary people within extraordinary circumstances".[5] In these extraordinary circumstances they are actually acting in a "continuum of destruction" where the ordinary social rules and the ordinary law are restructured:

> 'Genocide and mass killing do not directly arise from difficult life conditions and their psychological effects. There is a continuum of destruction. People learn and change by doing, by participation, as a consequence of their own actions. Small, seemingly insignificant acts can involve a person with a destructive system.'[6]

Thus, law-abiding citizens can convert into perpetrators and lawful activities may ironically lead to the perpetration of crimes.[7] This is confirmed by the idea of a "reversal of morality" according to which killing members of the other (protected)

3 Here and in the following I use the masculine pronoun *he* while referring to the male and female form.

4 See for individual and group case studies Arendt 1964; Gupta 2001; Haritos-Fatouras 1993.See for general studies Staub 1989; Bandura 1999: 200 ('Given appropriate social conditions, decent, ordinary people can be led to do extraordinarily cruel things.'); Smeulers 2004; Welzer 2005. See also Smeulers 2008: 234 with more references.

5 Smeulers 2008: 234.

6 Staub 1989: 17. See also Smeulers 2008: 235.

7 Smeulers 2008: 237.

group comes to be seen as morally right, and even desirable. So, "new group norms evolve, and institutions are established in the service of genocide or mass killing."[8] Jamieson asserts that in times of war, emergency, and social transformation a rearticulation of concepts of "crime" and morality takes place at the levels of both law and ideology.[9] I would add that this rearticulation also exists in genocidal situations since the genocidal ideology transforms crime categories as well. Yet this triggers the question of how one can say that genocidal perpetrators commit crimes if their acts are considered as being in conformity with the prevailing socio-legal values? The answer is that it is not the perpetrators or their personality structures that change, but rather the societal rules to which they must adapt. There is a cognitively redefined morality of killing[10] and the perpetrators of genocide adapt to the newly established rules.[11] It is for this reason that genocidal actions cannot be satisfactorily explained by traditional criminology.[12]

The typology offered by Michael Mann is a very useful starting point. The author distinguishes nine common motives found among perpetrators:[13]

1. Ideological killers believe in the "righteousness of murderous cleansing" and characterize themselves as victims. They justify killing as "self-defense";
2. Bigoted killers, more mundane in their ideology, often share the prejudices of their social environment and react to the physical disgust provoked by disliked minorities;
3. Violent killers feel attracted to murder and experience violence as a release;
4. Fearful killers do not really want to kill, but they "feel credibly threatened" and fear harm to life or limb if they do not kill;
5. Careerist killers work for organizations involved in murderous cleansing and garner a professional benefit because of their compliance with killing;
6. Materialist killers feel motivated by the idea of "direct economic gain" e.g., by taking the job of the victim or his or her property;

8 Staub 1989: 18.

9 Jamieson 1998: 493.

10 See Bandura 1999: 195.

11 In the same vein Jager 1985: 7 et seq.

12 On the difficulties and challenges of genocide for criminological studies see Brannigan 1998: 257–276, explaining the limitations of the mainstream criminology for the research on genocide and suggesting more history-based criminological analysis. In the same token Jamieson (1998: 488) who claims that "we need a criminology that can problematize the relationship between moral and immoral acts and social order in conditions of peace and war." See also Yacoubian 2000, explaining the limited possibilities of traditional criminology and suggesting more exchange between criminology and international criminal law. See in the same vein Woolford 2006, advocating a criminology of genocide 1. reflexive and nonredemptive, 2. undisciplined and critical, and 3. responsible. Also calling for more criminological analysis on genocide see Day & Vandiver 2000. See in general on the problems of the reductionist comprehension of "crime" Jager 1989: 20 et seq.; Neubacher 2005: 158 et seq.

13 Mann 2005: 27–29 (emphasis in the original).

7. Disciplined killers feel pressure by organizational authority and have the necessity to act in conformity with directives;
8. Comradely killers feel pressure by the peer group to kill because they do not want to lose the group's emotional support;
9. Bureaucratic killers are caged within "the bureaucracies of modernity" and are motivated by habitual obedience.

Mann explains, however, that these characterizations are "only ideal types" while "almost all perpetrators ha[ve] mixed motives".[14] Also Raul Hilberg, in his seminal work on the destruction of the European Jews, identifies different kinds of perpetrators but does not classify them according to different categories. He distinguishes between "Hitler"[15] and "the participants" ("Die Beteiligten"),[16] i.e., between the mastermind and the (willing) executors of his diabolical plan. Among the participants the author distinguishes are the bureaucrats who merely comply with the orders and instructions within their formal competences,[17] and the " fanatics" who are eager to go beyond the instructions of their superiors.[18] Further, there are the "sadists"[19] that enjoy making their victims suffer and, in contrast, the "skeptics" ("Zweifl er") who are plagued by doubts and do not really want to get involved.[20]

In turn, Dipak Gupta identifies three decisive motivations for an individual's choice: ideology (group preference), greed (selfish interest) and fear (cost). Subsequently, three kinds of participants in collective actions follow: true believers are motivated primarily by the goals of the collective enterprise; mercenaries are motivated mainly by their own narrow self-interests; and captive participants are motivated primarily by the cost of non participation, i.e., by fear. Together, these three basic motivations explain the reasons for non participation in collective criminal actions: conscientious objectors do not participate because of ideology; collaborators do not participate in the collective action of their own group but cooperate with the other group because of greed, i.e., because they think that they can pursue their own selfish interests better by assisting the other group; and easy riders do not take part in the collective action because of fear.[21]

14 Mann 2005: 29.

15 Hilberg 1992: 15 et seq.

16 Hilberg 1992: 33 et seq.

17 Hilberg 1992: 37 and 66.

18 Hilberg 1992: 64 et seq. ('Fanatiker an ihren Schreibtisch' ['fanatics at their desks'], p. 69).

19 Hilberg 1992: 67 et seq. ('vollig gefuhllosen Killer vor Ort' ['totally unfeeling killer on site'], p. 69).

20 Hilberg 1992: 69. See a similar typology Crelinsten 1993: 64 et seq., distinguishing three types of torturers: the true believers, the professional or careerist, and the sadist (at pp. 67–68). It is worthwhile pointing out, however, that as to torture perpetrators – in contrast to genocide perpetrators – the categories of "sceptics" and "compromised" perpetrators are excluded.

21 Gupta 2001: 103 et seq.

These three motivational patterns are also confirmed by Kressel with regard to the participants in the Nazi machinery:

> 'From their statements after the war, one might conclude that few Nazi leaders agreed with Nazi ideology, fewer still knew about anything outside of their direct organizational responsibilities, and that virtually none disliked the Jews. One might be led further to the conclusion that even those who committed the most heinous war crimes did so out of soldierly obedience and with a deep sense of guilt, oft en because they perceived no way out of difficult situations. To the extent that they acted out of personal motives, these were: (1) to be good soldiers; (2) to move up the career ladder; (3) to save their own skins.'[22]

These patterns do not only explain the involvement of leaders in genocidal acts, but also of other lower mid- and even low-level perpetrators. In this sense, it is not always possible to distinguish reasons for a certain conduct with a view to the rank of the perpetrator. As correctly pointed out by Kressel recalling explanations of the "major war criminals" Wilhelm Keitel, Albert Speer, and Hermann W. Goering:

> 'Some truth may remain in the explanations offered by Nazi leaders. They square rather well with the findings of some social science studies (...). And if obedience, career ambition, and fear constituted the primary motivation of these top dogs, shouldn't we conclude that they played an even greater role for mid-level bureaucrats and low-level grunts?'[23]

It seems then that the motivation of the perpetrators depends on personal characteristics rather than on factors of hierarchy.[24] These characteristics, often indicating the true motives for participation in genocide, must not be confused, however, with intent as the required mental element in criminal law. In fact, motives are only to be taken into account at the sentencing level but not, as intent, at the level of allocation of responsibility for the criminal acts.[25]

Regarding the relationship, if any, of motives and intent, Smeulers' types (the criminal mastermind, the fanatic, the criminal/sadist, the profiteer, the careerist, the devoted warrior, the followers and the conformist, the compromised perpetrator, and the professional), which remind us especially of Mann's typology, show that

22 Kressel 1996: 124.

23 Kressel 1996: 125.

24 23 See Brewster-Smith 1968.

25 See Drost 1959: 83 et seq., who does not accept motives as criminal elements of genocide, but seems to confuse them with the purpose ("Whatever the ultimate purpose of the deed, whatever the reasons for the perpetration of the crime, whatever the open or secret motives for the acts or measures directed against the life of the protected groups, whenever the destruction of human life of members of the group as such takes place, the crime of genocide is being committed", at p. 84). See also LeBlanc 1991: 80 et seq.; Verhoeven 1991: 19; Bassiouni & Manikas 1996: 528; Ratner et al. 2009: 40 and Vest 2002: 109–110. See also Ambos 2008: §7 marginal number 158 with further references of the case law of the ICTY and ICTR.

motives and intent may differ, i.e., that the same motives may entail different intents. For example, the perpetrator could have material reasons and pursue material goals, e.g., the property of the murdered neighbor (i.e., the profi teer perpetrator), but he could also be motivated by hate of the other group and could then aim at the destruction of the members of this group (i.e., the fanatic perpetrator); he could be motivated by fear and pursue the destruction of the group out of (putative) self-defense assuming and strongly believing that the group poses a threat to his people and his country (i.e., the devoted warrior), or, out of the same motive, he could merely want to protect his own life and in order to avoid to be seen as a traitor and become a target of the violence, he could attack members of the other group (this would be a compromised perpetrator – the motive for his conduct is still fear, but his intent is not directed at the destruction of the group); he could merely act because of the professional reason to keep his job or to even get a better one (i.e., the careerist perpetrator), or only because he is accustomed to obeying orders without asking further questions (i.e., the follower and conformist perpetrator); he could also become involved in genocidal acts because of a mental disorder and a feeling of individual pleasure or satisfaction (the sadist), or because he acts upon orders and is trained to do so (the professional) or, last but not least, he is doing more than expected because of his strong ideological commitment (i.e., the devoted warrior).

Criminologists and sociologists often distinguish between motive and intent when studying genocidal crimes. Yet, as already pointed out, for the question of individual criminal responsibility it is not important why, i.e., for which motive, an act was carried out (fear, hate, etc.), but only that the act can be attributed to the actor, i.e., that he, inter alia, acted with intent.[26] In any case, the dividing line between intent and motive is sometimes difficult to draw, especially in the context of genocide because of the (ulterior) intent to destroy requirement. Take for example the following quote:

> 'Where an attacker rapes a victim solely as an act of vengeance or hostility toward the victim, the rape is not genocidal, even if the attacker has selected the victim on the basis of her religion or ethnicity. On the other hand, if evidence suggests that the attacker committed the rape as part of an effort to drive the victim or members of her group into mental states that the attacker hopes will lead to the group's destruction, a finding of genocide is justifiable [...]. The line between intent, a relevant factor, and motive, an irrelevant one, may thus prove thin in practice.'[27]

As shown in this example, while motives must not be confused with criminal intent they may constitute indicia as to the genocidal intent to destroy. It also follows from the typology of (genocidal) perpetrators that there may be a series of reasons or "motives" to commit genocide, oft en going beyond or different from the destruction of the group. Thus, the question arises how these different motives relate, if at all, to the "intent to destroy" requirement.

26 See *supra* note 24 and main text.

27 Ratner et al. 2009: 44–45.

3. The Significance of the Criminological Typology of Perpetrators for the Offence of Genocide

The "intent to destroy" requirement of the genocide offence has always been understood by case law as a "special intent" or "dolus specialis" with a view to the destruction of the group – in the words of the seminal Akayesu Trial Chamber, as "the specific intention, required as a constitutive element of the crime, which demands that the perpetrator clearly seeks to produce the act charged".[28] According to a dissenting view in the doctrine – the so called knowledge-based approach – knowledge as to the genocidal intent of the main perpetrators or as to the possibility of the destruction of the group is sufficient to establish liability.[29] In this vein, it has been argued that "principal culpability should extend to those who may lack a specific genocidal purpose, but who commit genocidal acts while understanding the destructive consequences of their actions for the survival of the relevant victim group".[30] In my view, as explained at the beginning of this paper,[31] the knowledge-based approach must be combined with the traditional approach, which takes into account the different status and role of the perpetrators.

Indeed, the criminological studies on genocide show that a flexible approach is needed. It seems quite unlikely that a participant acts with "intent to destroy" in a volitional, purpose-based sense if he has no special feelings towards the targeted group or, for example, if he does not follow the genocidal ideology. According to Smeulers, the hate towards the victims often only comes after the fact and serves to justify the criminal conduct, first of all before oneself.[32] If this is correct, many perpetrators act without a purpose-based intent to destroy. This purpose may, at best, be deduced from the negative feelings that may arise, if at all, after the fact; yet these feelings operate as pure ex post facto neutralization techniques vis-a-vis the criminal acts and the ensuing intent would, in terms of criminal law doctrine, not be more than an irrelevant dolus subsequens.

The criminological findings also demonstrate that a knowledge-based intent will oft en not exist. Many participants in genocidal campaigns are simply unaware of the final aim pursued by the masterminds and leaders of the campaign. The corresponding knowledge cannot be deduced without more evidence of the participant's awareness of a campaign's general policies since each contribution depends on the

28 *Prosecutor v. Akayesu,* Trial Judgment, Case No. ICTR-96–4-T, 2 September 1998, para. 498.

29 See Bassiouni & Manikas 1996: 527; Gil Gil 1999: 258 et seq.; Vest 2002: 104 et seq. See also Greenawalt 1999: 2259–2294. See for a discussion and further references Ambos 2009.

30 Greenawalt 1999: 2265.

31 See *supra* note 1.

32 Smeulers 2008: 239: 'many people do not start to kill and torture because they hate their victims or perceive killing and torturing them as justifiable but they start to hate their victims and start to believe in the ideology because it justifies the killing and torture in which they have become involved.'

specific circumstances surrounding the genocidal campaign. These circumstances must be considered in context, taking into account that genocide usually develops within structural changes in the social order.[33] The "intent" of the participants must therefore be examined from a twofold perspective: observing the particular factual circumstances surrounding their individual conduct (indicated by the motives and goals) and considering the context in which this conduct takes place (as official state duty, or isolated from other actions, or in groups, etc.). Both levels constitute what John Steiner called social and moral intelligence, and role margin: the manner and degree of accountability that an interacting individual assumes for the consequences and welfare of others, and the area of authority over the choice span that is available to any role one undertakes in social interaction, respectively.[34]

In the same token and going even further, Martin Shaw proposes that genocide studies should focus not on the intentions of the perpetrators but on the structure of the conflict situations.

> 'Intentionality does not therefore provide an overall framework for understanding genocide. We need to move, I propose, to the main stage of sociological conceptualization, structural concept formation. This means moving away from the subjective meaning of genocidal action (for the perpetrators) to understanding the typical social relations of genocide (not only among perpetrators, but crucially between them and the victims, and indeed among victims), and therefore the structure of social conflict that these set up.'[35]

While Shaw accepts the intentionality underlying genocidal conduct,[36] he claims that the legal understanding of intent is too narrow and moves away from a realistic concept.[37] For Shaw it is "unrealistic", from a sociological perspective, to use concepts like collective intention to capture the collective nature of genocide.[38] As Post puts it: "Groups don't make decisions; individuals do".[39] In other words, the collective genocidal act (Gesamttat) consists of the individual contributions and intents (Einzeltaten) that, in turn, make up the Gesamttat. In this view then the "collective intent" concept only seems to serve as a theoretical vehicle or tool to grasp the complexity of the genocide offence.[40] Accordingly, it may be more correct to draw attention to the social conflictive "context" than to search for a collectively carried out

33 Smeulers 2008: 235.

34 Steiner 2000.

35 Shaw 2007: 81–82.

36 Schabas 2009: 256: 'it is inconceivable that an infraction of such magnitude could be committed unintentionally'.

37 Shaw 2007: 82 et seq.

38 Shaw 2009: 83.

39 Post 2004: 16.

40 See against this idea Hagan & Rymond-Richmond 2009: 162 et seq., who offer a detailed analysis of the individual- and collective-level dynamics of the racially intentional and targeted violence in the Darfur genocide.

intention. Thus, a sociological structural approach considers the individual intent contextualized in the genocidal relationships.

Collectivity in subjective terms is, however, not rejected by all scholars. Thus, Smeulers seems to identify a collective motive when she writes

> '(...) the masses aim to get rid of the alleged privileged classes or minorities whom they blame for their misfortune. Ideologies usually serve as motivating forces which at the same time incite and instigate the masses while justifying the violence.'[41]

This description would fit a very collective phenomenon in which almost everyone, as part of the mass, is engaged as perpetrator. Similarly, Mann explains the Rwanda genocide as follows:

> 'Ethnic hatreds may transpose this threat-humiliation-rage triad to a collective level: Hutus feel threatened and humiliated by Tutsi power, and they strike out, enraged at any Tutsi.'[42]

The obvious problem with this position is that genocide does not always manifest itself in the same way. Indeed, the public is not always involved at all or to the same extent. The Nazi-genocide, for example, was almost exclusively carried out by way of a hierarchically organized state apparatus which did not depend on the involvement of normal citizens.[43] This is a clear difference to the genocide in Rwanda, which turned into a "collective violence" where civilians killed other civilians, either unknown to the killers or their neighbors and friends.[44] Against this background it is

41 Smeulers 2008: 235.

42 Mann 2005: 28.

43 So, for example Niewyk (2009: 129): "Violent attacks on Jews were uncommon... The exception... was the 'Crystal Night' (Kristallnacht) pogrom of November 9–10, 1938, when Nazi thugs physically attacked thousands of Jews... These actions were clearly the work of virulent anti-Semites in the Nazi Party, supported by government officials who found pogroms useful in advancing economic objectives." See also Niewyk (2009: 130): 'Only when Hitler invaded the Soviet Union in 1941 did emigration give way to extermination. Believing that the German people would not understand such a ghastly policy, the Nazis carried out the genocide of the Jews in secrecy and under cover of war. Accordingly, responsibility for mass murder was placed in the hands of the SS (*Schutzstaffel*), Hitler's special guard of policemen and soldiers that had grown into the central agency of terror in Nazi-dominated Europe.'

44 See Lemarchand (2009: 489): 'Despite many exceptions to the rule, one cannot fail to notice the number of journalists, medical doctors, agronomists, teachers, university lecturers, and even priests who were identified by survivors as accomplices in the massacre of innocent civilians. At the other end of the social spectrum were the hundreds and thousands of landless Hutu peasants and unemployed city youth whose prime motivation for killing was to steal their victims' property, their land, their furniture, their radio, or what little cash they happened to carry.' See in this sense also Jamieson (1999: 136) who analyses genocide as "social exclusion" and argues that an individual-

important to distinguish between acts carried out by the state and its agents (or non-state actors organized in armed groups[45]) and acts carried out by normal citizens. In the former case there is usually a direct chain of command and the genocidal policy is generally known, at least as a policy against a certain group or persons. In this case the acts of genocide can be understood as "crimes of obedience".[46] In the latter case of "private" violence the perpetrators are not necessarily aware of the genocidal purpose but rather "believe"[47] that their acts are promoted or approved by the authorities.

4. Correspondence of Categories of International Criminal Law with Criminological Typologies of Perpetrators

The typologies of perpetrators and the intent analysis of the criminological studies on genocide suggest a more realistic approach with regard to the categories of imputation in international criminal law. Concretely speaking, it seems advisable to add a further distinction to the combined structure- and knowledge-based approach explained above.[48] First of all, it can be noted that the basic threefold classification of top-, mid- and low-level perpetrators is confirmed by criminological studies. For example, Jamieson refers to the cases of division of labor and the chain of responsibility in Bosnia and Rwanda, "with the planners at the top overseeing the 'middle men of genocide' – the coordinators and tacticians who, in turn, directed those who implemented the policy on the ground".[49] In particular, the threefold classification is reflected in the case of genocidal campaigns by state actors. The case of the Holocaust is paradigmatic in this respect because the objective three-level-distinction is also reflected in the intent of the Nazi elite (including Hitler), the mid-level bureaucrats (who were not always Nazis), and of the low-level police or death camp personnel:

---

izing juridical approach overlooks that exclusionary projects (e.g. ethnic cleansing in Bosnia-Herzegovina) are only achievable with the complicity and the support of the whole community. It is, however, not exactly the same to act as principal perpetrator (regardless of whether high-, mid- or low-level perpetrator) or mere accomplice. This distinction must be always kept in mind when analyzing the different grades of involvement in crime.

45 Under International Humanitarian Law *armed groups* are recognized as legal subjects if they fulfill certain requirements such as a minimum degree of organization, i.e. a certain level of organizational coherence and hierarchy, a command structure and the capacity to sustain military operations (cf. La Rosa/ Wuerzner 2008). In this sense most references to the state and state actors in the text equally apply to *armed groups* (and their members).

46 Smeulers 2008: 236.

47 Smeulers 2008: 236.

48 See *supra* notes 1 and 28 and main text. See on this discussion also Kres 2005.

49 See Jamieson 1999: 138 with further references.

> 'An ideological commitment to exterminate the Jews, a careerist concern on the part of bureaucrats, an adaptation to extraordinary circumstances and peer conformity on the part of perpetrators, contributed to the lethal dynamic of the Holocaust.'[50]

From this analysis, it clearly follows that the ideological commitment to exterminate the Jews, i.e., the purpose-based intent "to destroy", is located at the top-level of the hierarchy. Mid- and low-level perpetrators, on the contrary, do not necessarily share this purpose. They may at best know about its existence because of their functions: they receive orders and are aware of internal instructions and guidelines, they talk to colleagues of other hierarchical levels, they receive information about the activities and tasks of other officials; in sum, they do not act in an isolated manner but as interconnected links.[51] Of course, it is possible to imagine situations in which the low-level state agent is not actually aware of the genocidal state plan. Thus, the character of Hanna in Bernhard Schlink's novel "The Reader" was unable to know the details about her job and its relation to the Nazi genocide because of her illiteracy. She did not tell her colleagues and superiors because she was ashamed of her illiteracy. Such cases are, however, just the exceptions to the rule.

In any case, the threefold classification cannot be transferred without further ado to the case of non-state, private actors. First of all, as non-state, private actors do not receive direct and structural state support they can hardly implement a full-fledged genocidal plan, even if they belong to the top-level of the respective group or organization. Second, their knowledge of a genocidal plan, at the mid- or low-level, cannot be simply inferred from their formal involvement or role in the power apparatus but rather depends on their factual status and role in the group and their access to the top level individuals or to the information at the disposal of these individuals. Thus, one should apply the threefold classification in a more flexible way to non-state actors.

The following table encompasses the perpetrators' types resulting from the criminological studies[52] and intends to relate them to the threefold classification of International Criminal Law, in particular with regard to the mental requirement (knowledge and purpose). First, the table shows different categories of perpetrators differentiated according to level (high, middle and low) and status (state agent or private actor). The distinction as to the state or private perpetrator's type (see the extreme left and right columns, respectively) shows that these must also be treated differently from a legal perspective. If we take, by way of example, the top-level, we

50 Friedrichs 2000: 27.

51 See for example on the Armenian genocide Adalian (2009: 65): 'The chain of command that put the Armenian genocide into motion joined every link in the administration of the Ottoman state'; on the Nazi genocide and their microphysical distribution of tasks and responsibilities through all different state links Niewyk 2009: 134: 'each department and individual was accountable for only one small segment of the program, diff using personal responsibility.'

52 In this table are considered the above mentioned typologies by Smeulers 2008; Mann 2005; Hilberg 1992; Gupta 2001 and Jamieson 1998.

can see that there exist only state perpetrator's types (as mastermind, leader, and planner) but no private perpetrator's types. At the mid- and low-level there are both state and private perpetrator's types, yet oft en a perpetrator type appears in a different level and status categories. The "true believer", for example, could be a mid- or low-level state agent or private actor, i.e., there are four types of true believers. However, the differences between level and status and their influence on the legal classification appear more significant in the case of perpetrator's types that are not represented in both the extreme left and right (state/private) columns. At the mid-level, for example, one finds state agents acting because of their institutional career (compromised type, or careerist type), yet these perpetrator's types do not exist for private actors; a midlevel private actor may act for reasons of profit (profiteer, materialist type) or because of ideology (true believer type), but not pursuant to a command chain (e.g., the professional type state agent). Moreover, a mid-level private actor would neither act because of fear (fearful type) nor professional pressure (captive participant type), and this distinguishes him/her further from private low-level perpetrators, who may possibly act with the group out of fear or pressure. Secondly, the table shows what kind of mental requirement would be necessary and sufficient in each case (knowledge and purpose, only knowledge, knowledge in a general or specific form) depending on the category (level and status) of the perpetrator. This second aspect of the table is further explained in the following.

Table. International criminal law categories in comparison with criminological typology of perpetrators

Perpetrator's type (state)	Perpetrator is state agent		Perpetrator's level	Perpetrator is a private actor			Perpetrator's type (private)
	Knowledge	Purpose		Knowledge		Purpose	
mastermind; leader; planner	X	X	top-level	–		–	----
fanatic; careerist; devote warrior; bigot; true believer; compromised; professional	X	–	mid-level	X		–	criminal/ sadist; bigot; true believer; profiteer; materialist
				general	specific		
criminal/ sadist; violent; bigot; true believer; careerist; obedient follower; professional; conformist; disciplined; bureaucratic; comradely; compromised; fearful; doubter; captive participant	X	–	low-level	X	X	–	fanatic/ bigot; violent; ideological; devote warrior; true believer; profiteer; materialist; comradely; compromised; fearful; captive participant

(Glossary: X = required – = not-required ---- = non-existing category)

4.1. *Regarding Top-Level Perpetrators "Intent to Destroy" Means Knowledge and Purpose*

Top-level perpetrators are classified in most criminological studies as criminal masterminds that occupy high positions in the state apparatus and have strong and direct influence over subordinates and the public. Dictators, explains Kressel, have the ability to mix threats, manipulation, persuasion, and bribes to change a person politically and psychologically. Direct control or indirect influence over the media, schools, police, military, and other institutions and organizations over time can result in the transformation of souls and of supporters into "mindless pawns".[53] Masterminds thus influence the personality structures of their followers and delineate the goals and performance of the destructive policy which forms the legitimizing basis of the individual acts.[54] Furthermore, as Bandura puts it, "language shapes thought patterns on which actions are based."[55] This connection is crucial for understanding the role of the leader and of the distribution of responsibilities between him and his followers. The context "that at once influences the leader's attitudes and is shaped and influenced by the leader"[56] connects him with the physical perpetrators. Thus, the top-level perpetrator not only knows about the genocidal context of the concrete individual acts, but he shapes and prepares this context in the first place, i.e., he acts with the purpose towards the ultimate destruction of the respective group. Indeed, on the basis of the criminological typologies, it is safe to say that the top-level perpetrator is the only type of perpetrator that always acts with a destructive purpose. In other words, either he acts with genocidal purpose or there is no genocide at all. Thus, the twofold knowledge and purpose requirement is indispensable for his responsibility.

4.2. *As to Mid-Level Perpetrators the Knowledge-Based Approach is Applicable*

Mid-level perpetrators do not always act with purpose in genocidal contexts. A careerist or a professional, situated at the mid-level of the state apparatus, may be aware of the genocidal context and thus of the supporting nature of his conduct but he may not possess the purpose-based intent to destroy the respective group himself. In fact, he is not so much pursuing the destruction of the group but his own career in the system. Mid-level perpetrators are not necessarily involved in the objectives of the genocidal campaign. Their participation in such a campaign and even the achievement of their personal goals exist independent of the purpose to destroy. Kressel, taking the example of Rudolf Hos, demonstrates how difficult it is to draw the line between purpose and knowledge in the case of mid-level perpetrators. Hos was the chief administrator of the Auschwitz concentration camp. In his memories, Kressel argues, Höß

> 'maintains that throughout his life he strongly valued obedience and authority, but he was no sadist. He had a human heart. He was not evil. He even shot a guard, once, for abusing a prisoner against his orders. Hoess assures us he had nothing in particular against the

53 Kressel 1996: 200–201.

54 See Vest 2002: 108 ('An der Festlegung der Ziele wirken nur die *Entscheidungstrager.*' ['Exclusively *decision makers* set the objectives']). See also Paul 2008: 258.

55 Bandura 1999: 195.

56 Post 2004: 13. See for the socio-psychological background of this analysis Brewster-Smith 1968: 23, *passim*.

> Jews. He was no less, and no more, than a patriot – rendering a necessary service to his country.'[57]

So the question arises whether Höß really pursued the destruction of the Jews as a group. Did he understand this purpose as part of his job? Did he individually desire the destruction of the group or did he merely want to serve his country? These questions show how difficult it is to separate personal (individual) from state (collective) goals in the case of mid-level perpetrators. In most cases, midlevel perpetrators will at best act with knowledge of the genocidal campaign surrounding their individual acts and, in any case, this is hard enough to prove. If one were to additionally require purpose on their part there would hardly be any mid-level genocidaire.

A further issue regarding mid-level perpetrators concerns their role in society. Mid-level perpetrators are usually, but not always, state agents. They may be bureaucrats ("the Eichmann type") but could also only be profiteers. Take the director of a company who uses members of the persecuted group as "slave workers" ("the industrialist type") or the owner of a radio station who incites to genocide. Both know what they are doing and that they are acting within the framework of a genocidal policy but they do not necessarily act with a purpose of destruction. They make use of the top-level perpetrators' purpose for economic, commercial purposes (the industrialist) or they reproduce it by means of the mass media. Thus, mid-level perpetrators, regardless of whether they are state agents, profit from the genocidal purpose of the masterminds when they take opportunistic advantage of it by aligning themselves with the official genocidal policy. In other words, while mid-level perpetrators normally do not share the purpose-based intent to destroy, they are aware of its existence and the corresponding genocidal campaign, i.e., they know that their activity promotes and furthers this campaign. It is for this reason that they deserve to be punished as principals in a genocidal enterprise. To require, apart from genocidal knowledge, also genocidal purpose from them would ignore the criminologically explained reality of their genocidal conduct.[58]

---

57 Kressel 1996: 123.

58 This is also recognized by legal scholars, see e.g. Vest 2002: 108 ('Die *praktische Umsetzung* und Durchfuhrung der Entscheidung [über die Ziele] erfolgt dagegen innerhalb des von dieser Fuhrungsclique gesteckten Rahmens, so dass es auf die individuellen Ziele der einzelnen Akteure überhaupt nicht mehr ankommen kann. Es muss deshalb folgerichtig genügen, dass der einzelne bewussterweise in diesem *ihm bekannten kollektiven Muster* der ganzen oder teilweisen Zerstörung einer geschützten Gruppe agiert.'). In the same vein Schabas 2009: 252 ('Individual off enders need not participate in devising the plan. If they commit acts of genocide with knowledge of the plan, then the requirements of the Convention are met.').

4.3. Regarding the Low-Level Perpetrators it is Necessary to Distinguish Between State Agents and Private Actors. While the Former are Normally Informed About the Genocidal (State) Plan, the Latter are Not

Compared to the mid-level perpetrators, the low-level perpetrators are even less likely to act with purpose and they will certainly possess less knowledge as to the genocidal campaign. This also means that the purpose requirement cannot be reasonably demanded either.[59] As to the knowledge requirement, a distinction between low-level state agents and private actors becomes of crucial importance. In the case of the former it can be expected that they are aware of the genocidal state policy, at least in a general sense of acting within the framework of a genocidal policy. They act upon orders and obey as "instruments" for the implementation of this policy. Their knowledge may be inferred from the genocidal state policy implemented through the said orders and the fact that they are part of the genocidal state apparatus. If low-level state agents know about the context, they necessary know that their official task is part of and contribution to the state plan.

In contrast, private actors will normally not possess this knowledge and it cannot be inferred from the State policy since they are not part of the State. Even if they know by hearsay, they may lack the specific knowledge as to how their concrete acts connect to the collective genocidal conduct. In this sense one may distinguish between general and specific knowledge: The former alone – a kind of general idea of the genocidal context or policy – does not suffice;[60] rather, it must be complemented by a kind of specific knowledge linking the specific, individual acts to the concrete genocidal campaign, i.e., a particular mental connection between the individual act of the private perpetrator and the collective state crime is required. Given that the private actor does not receive formal orders which link his concrete conduct to the collective genocidal campaign, such a link can only be construed by way of this specific knowledge requirement.[61] An example of the possible lack of this link is offered by Daoud Hari in his memoir as translator in Darfur when remembering the answer of a Janjaweed Arab boy about why he attacked a village:

---

59 See Vest 2002: 108 and Paul 2008: 258.

60 59 In the same vein see Schabas 2009: 250, when criticizing that the Appeals Chamber of the International Criminal Tribunal for the Ex-Yugoslavia (*Prosecutor v. Krstić*, Case No. IT-98– 33-A, Judgment, 19 April 2004, para. 137; *Prosecutor v. Blagojević*, Case No. IT-02–60-A, Judgment, 9 May 2007, para. 123) 'has focused on evidence of State policy' rather than seriously inquired the direct perpetrators' acts which could imputed to the State in question and who 'had killed members of the groups or committed one of the other acts with genocidal intent at the personal level a la Jelisić'.

61 The distinction between low-level private actors and state agents is also supported by the first writings on genocide, see Lemkin (1944: 93), stating: 'The liability of persons who *order* genocide practices, as well as of persons who *execute* such orders, should be provided expressly by the criminal codes of the respective countries.' The liability of those low-level perpetrators who do not receive formally any orders and who do not belong to the state structure is in fact the most difficult to determine.

> 'We were told by the government soldiers that these people were going to attack our village and kill our families if we did not attack them first. They would give us money if we did this. [...] Our families need this money, and we had to protect them.'[62]

It is clear that this boy had not the slightest idea that he was acting within the context of a genocidal policy and therefore he could not have had specific knowledge without having received the respective official information. Thus, he could, at best, possess a very general knowledge but never a specific one linking his acts to a concrete genocidal campaign. To qualify him then as a genocidaire would not correspond to his mental state when carrying out the said acts.

Smeulers argues that "within a period of collective violence all individuals have to make a choice: they either go along with or they set themselves apart from it."[63] At the first glance, this idea seems to suggest a very simple binary choice pro or contra (genocidal) violence which would certainly be too simplistic for the purposes of imputation in criminal law. Yet, Smeulers herself makes later clear that things are more complicated and dynamic, arguing for the possibility of an inevitable transformation of individuals through continuous and escalating decisions.[64] Given the many different forms of participation and the complexity of human relations, many grey areas where the actor's participation does not result from a clear pro or contra choice exist.[65] The spectrum of an individual's participation in the genocidal policy ranges from acts even prohibited by the genocidal state (e.g., excessive acts going beyond the genocidal plan) to the commission of crimes under coercion.[66]

Apart from that, the quite probable ignorance of a private actor as to the genocidal state policy (if this policy is not made public) entails a certain "neutrality" of his conduct with regard to this policy. In other words, while his act certainly constitutes an assault on the members of the respective group, it does not necessarily impose a

62 Hari 2008: 95.

63 Smeulers 2008: 238.

64 See Smeulers 2008: 238 illustrating this escalating commitment by the example of the Milgram experiment and stating: 'Probably without being fully aware of the consequences people within the period prior to the collective violence, are confronted with all kinds of small and seemingly insignificant decisions that make them go along. These same decisions however compromise them into going along further and further and step by step they get deeper and deeper involved. Within a period of collective violence, many people slowly progress on a continuum of destructiveness, often without being really aware of it. This process can also be described as a pattern of escalating commitment. People get caught up by it. Slowly, inevitably.'

65 See Shaw 2007: passim and Jamieson 1998: 136.

66 Jager 1967: 76 et seq.

negative identity on the victim[67] or even "dehumanize" it.[68] The genocidal policy or context could, therefore, not so much be understood as an element of the offence but as an "objective point of reference of genocidal intent".[69]

5. Conclusion: the Structure of the Genocide Offence in Light of the Criminological Findings

The criminological findings on genocide suggest that the threefold distinction between top-, mid- and low-level perpetrators must be complemented by a further distinction between state agents and non-state (private) actors. Only the former may possess genocidal knowledge as a consequence of their official functions and duties while the latter can only be classified as genocidaire if they are specifically aware of the connection of their acts to the overall genocidal policy (i.e., a specific knowledge requirement). This distinction gains particular importance with regard to low-level perpetrators. Apart from that, criminological theories confirm the threefold classification by adding more refined typologies to the three levels. These theories make therefore a compelling case for a differentiated interpretation of the "intent to destroy" requirement in the sense of a purpose- and knowledge-based approach by applying the stricter purpose concept only to the top-level perpetrators. In the result, the top-level perpetrators, being the masterminds of a genocidal policy, possess a purpose-based and knowledge-based intent. Their purpose is to shape the overall genocidal context and is followed by the mid- and low-level perpetrators in varying degrees depending on the circumstances of each case. Mid- and low-level perpetrators need not necessarily share this genocidal purpose but must be aware of its existence and the ensuing genocidal policy. In the case of low-level private actors this awareness cannot be simply inferred from the genocidal state policy (as in the case of low-level state agents) nor from their essential involvement in the state plans (as in the case of mid-level private actors) but requires a specific knowledge in terms of a link of their concrete acts to the overall genocidal policy. Only then can a banalization of the genocide crime be avoided and their qualification as "genocidaire" justified.

---

67 See on the notion of negative group identity as explanation for genocide Simon 1996: 243–256; see also Afflitto 2000: 80 and 84 applying this concept to the analysis of genocidal victimization in Rwanda.

68 See Kelman 1973; see also Delmas-Marty 2009: 8, who also stresses the meaning of "depersonalization (*depersonnalisation*)" in genocide. I do not neglect that "dehumanization" or "depersonalization" processes are a common social component in the dynamic of genocides. However, I do not agree with the idea that these collective processes are also present in each individual perpetrator when he decides to kill, rape or steel. On the dehumanization (Dehumanisierung) of the victim and other types of neutralization see Jager 1989: 191 et seq.

69 Kres 2009: 305.

6. References

Adalian, R.P. (2009). The Armenian genocide, in: Totten & Parsons (2009), 55–92.

Ambos, K. (2009). What does "intent to destroy" in genocide mean? International Review of the Red Cross 91, 833–858.

Ambos, K. (2008). Internationales Strafrecht, 2nd ed., Munchen.

Afflitto, F.M. (2000). Victimization, survival and the impunity of forced exile: a case study from the Rwandan genocide, Crime, Law & Social Change 34, 77–97.

Arendt, H. (1964). Eichmann in Jerusalem: Ein Bericht von der Banalitat des Bosen, Munchen: Piper.

Bandura, A. (1999). Moral disengagement in the perpetration of inhumanities, Personality and Social Psychology Review 3 (3), 193–209.

Bassiouni, M.C. & P. Manikas (1996). The law of the International Criminal Tribunal for the Former Yugoslavia, Irvington-on-Hudson: Transnational publishers.

Brannigan, (1998). Criminology and the Holocaust, Crime & Delinquency 44(2), 257– 276.

Brewster-Smith, M. (1968). A map for the analysis of personality and politics, Journal of Social Issues 24 (3), 15–28.

Crelinsten, R.D. (1993). In their own words: the world of the torturer, in: Crelinsten, R.D. & Schmid, A.P. (eds.), The politics of pain: torturers and their masters, Leiden: COMT, 39–72.

Day, L.E. & M. Vandiver (2000). Criminology and genocide studies: notes on what might have been and what still could be, Crime, Law & Social Change 34, 43–59.

Delmas-Marty, M. (2009). Violence and massacres – towards a criminal law of Inhumanity?, Journal of International Criminal Justice 7, 5–16.

Drost, P.N. (1959). The crime of state, vol. 2: genocide, Leyden: A.W. Sythoff .

Friedrichs, D.O. (2000). The crime of the century? The case for the Holocaust, Crime, Law & Social Change 34, 21–41.

Gil Gil, A. (1999). Derecho penal internacional: especial consideracion del delito de genocidio, Madrid: Tecnos.

Greenawalt, A. (1999). Rethinking genocidal intent: the case for a knowledge-based interpretation, Columbia Law Review 99 (8), 2259–2294.

Gupta, D.K. (2001). Path to collective madness – a study in social order and political pathology, Westport: Praeger.

Hagan, J. & W. Rymond-Richmond (2009). Darfur and the crime of genocide, New York: Cambridge University Press.

Hari, D. (2008). The translator. A tribesman's memoir of Darfur, London: Penguin.

Haritos-Fatouras, M. (1993). The official torturer: a learning model for obedience to the authority of violence, in: R.D. Crelinsten & A.P. Schmid (eds.), The politics of pain: torturers and their masters, Leiden: COMT, 141–159.

Hilberg, R. (1992). Tater, Opfer, Zuschauer: die Vernichtung der Juden 1933 – 1945 (transl. from English by Holl, H.G.), Frankfurt am Main: Fischer.

Jager, H. (1967). Verbrechen unter totalitarer Herrschaft , Olten/Freiburg i.Br.: Walter- Verlag.

Jager, H. (1985). Individuelle Zurechnung kollektiven Verhaltens, Zur strafrechtlichkriminologischen Bedeutung der Gruppendynamik, Frankfurt a.M.: Alfred Metzner.

Jager, H. (1989). Makrokriminalitat, Studien zur Kriminologie kollektiver Gewalt, Frankfurt a.M.: Suhrkamp.

Jamieson, R. (1998). Towards a criminology of war in Europe, in: V. Ruggiero, N. Smith & I. Taylor (eds.), The new European criminology, London: Routledge, 480–506.

Jamieson, R. (1999). Genocide and the social production of immorality, Theoretica Criminology 3(2), 131–146.

Kelman, H.C. (1973). Violence without moral restraint: reflections on the dehumanization of victims and victimizers, Journal of Social Sciences 29, 25–61.

Kres, C. (2005). The Darfur report and genocidal intent, Journal of International Criminal Justice 3, 562–578.

Kres, C. (2009). The crime of genocide and contextual elements. A comment on the ICC pretrial Chamber's decision in the Al Bashir Case, Journal of International Criminal Justice 7, 283–296.

Kressel, N.J. (1996). Mass hate: the global rise of genocide and terror, New York: Plenum Press.

La Rosa, A.-M. & C. Wuerzner (2008). Armed groups, sanctions and the implementation of international humanitarian law, International Review of the Red Cross 90, 327–341.

LeBlanc, L.J. (1991). The United States and the genocide convention, Durham/London: Duke University Press.

Lemkin, R. (1944). Axis rule in occupied Europe: laws of occupation, analysis of government, proposals for redress, Washington: Carnegie Endowment for International Peace.

Lemarchand, R. (2009). The 1994 Rwanda genocide, in: Totten & Parsons (2009), 483–504.

Mann, M. (2005). The dark side of democracy: explaining ethnic cleansing, New York: Cambridge University Press.

Neubacher, F. (2005). Kriminologische Grundlagen einer internationalen Strafgerichtsbarkeit, Tubingen: Mohr Siebeck.

Niewyk, D. L. (2009). Holocaust: the genocide of the Jews, in: Totten & Parsons (2009), 129–161.

Paul, A. (2008). Kritische Analyse und Reformvorschlag zu Art. II Genozidkonvention, Heidelberg: Springer.

Post, J.M. (2004). Leaders and their followers in a dangerous world – the psychology of political behavior, Ithaca [et al.]: Cornell University Press.

Ratner, S.R., J.S. Abrams & J.L. Bischoff (2009). Accountability for human rights atrocities in international law. Beyond the Nuremberg legacy, 3rd ed., New York: Oxford University Press.

Schabas, W.A. (2009). Genocide in international law. The crime of crimes, 2nd ed., New York: Cambridge University Press.

Shaw, M. (2007). What is genocide?, Cornwall: Polity.

Simon, T.W. (1996). Defining genocide, Wisconsin International Law Journal 15, 243–256.

Smeulers, A. (2004). What transforms ordinary people into gross human rights violators? in: S.C. arey & S.C. Poe (eds.), Understanding human rights violations: new systematic studies, Alsdershot [et al.]: Ashgate, 239–256.

Smeulers, A. (2008). Perpetrators of international crimes: towards a typology, in: A. Smeulers & R. Haveman (eds.). Supranational criminology: towards a criminology of international crimes, Antwerpen [et al.]: Intersentia, 233–264.

Staub, E. (1989). The roots of evil: the origins of genocide and other group violence, Cambridge [et al.]: Cambridge University Press.

Steiner, J.M. (2000). The role margin as the site for moral and social intelligence: The case of Germany and National Socialism, Crime, Law & Social Change 34, 61–75.

Totten, S. & W.S. Parsons (eds.) (2009). Century of genocide: critical essays and eyewitness accounts, 3rd ed., New York & London: Routledge,

Verhoeven, J. (1991). Le crime de genocide. Originalite et ambiguite, Revue belge de droit international 1, vol XXIV, 5–26.

Vest, H. (2002). Genozid durch organisatorische Machtapparate: An der Grenze von individueller und kollektiver Verantwortlichkeit, Baden-Baden: Nomos.

Welzer, H. (2005). Tater – wie aus ganz normalen Menschen Massenmorder werden, Frankfurt am Main: Fischer.

Woolford, A. (2006). Making genocide unthinkable: three guidelines for a critical criminology of genocide, Critical Criminology 14 (1), 87–106.

Yacoubian, G.S. (Jr.) (2000). The (in)significance of genocidal behavior to the discipline of criminology, Crime, Law & Social Change 34, 7–19.

7. Defending the 'Undefendable'? Taking Judicial Notice of Genocide

Göran Sluiter and Koen Vriend

1. Introduction

The position of the defense, consisting of the accused and his defense counsel, in genocide trials is incomparable to the position of the defense in any other criminal trial. Genocide trials are complex cases which involve by definition a great amount of factual allegations of the most serious nature and which—with a few exceptions—generally take place at international criminal tribunals. Furthermore, because genocide cases are difficult to prove, the accusation of genocide is always combined with an accusation of crimes against humanity and/or war crimes.

In the face of massive accusations the defense is fighting an uphill battle. Generally, a fundamental reassurance in respect to his position is the absolute and unconditional burden of proof on the Prosecutor. As a result, the defense should be in a position to react to the Prosecution and should not primarily be worried that the innocence of the accused must be demonstrated; rather, it is for the Prosecutor to prove beyond a reasonable doubt that the accused is guilty of the crimes charged.

While nobody will disagree with this fundamental notion of the presumption of innocence and corresponding burden of proof, the case law of the ad hoc Tribunals demonstrates certain exceptions. We are especially concerned here with the phenomenon of taking judicial notice of adjudicated facts and facts of common knowledge, which is of increasing importance in the practice of the ad hoc Tribunals. This practice was triggered by an interest in not having to repeatedly establish elements in the indictment which have already been adjudicated. To put it simply, when there are, for example, a number of cases dealing with crimes committed against detainees in the Omarska camp, is it really necessary to bring evidence in each of these cases that the conditions in this camp were poor, that the Bosnian Serbs were in control of this camp, that there was an armed conflict going on, that the treatment of prisoners in the camp was related to that conflict etc.? In the interests of expediting proceedings one may be tempted to find no objection in taking judicial notice of such (recurring) facts, which do not go to the heart of the individual criminal responsibility of the accused. An additional factor may also be that it is regarded as simply 'not done' to question such horrible events like the Rwandan genocide or the

H.G. van der Wilt, J. Vervliet et al., *(eds.)* The Genocide Convention: The Legacy of 60 Years.

ISBN 978 9004 15328 8. pp. 81-93.

massacre in Srebrenica. But what about the position of the defense and the fundamental principles underlying the criminal process? In light of both these issues, the thesis proposed here is that taking judicial notice of material elements in the indictment should be approached with more caution than has been done by the ad hoc Tribunals thus far. The issue may be simplified, as we will do here, by submitting the question of whether judicial notice of genocide can be taken, and when this is done, whether the defense is not put in an indefensible position.

In order to address these questions we will first give a brief outline of the position of the defense in international criminal proceedings (2). Next we will provide an overview of the practice of judicial notice in international criminal law, as it has developed in the law and practice of the ad hoc Tribunals (3). At the center of this paper is a critical analysis of the ICTR Karemera decision, where the appeals chamber took judicial notice of genocide (4). We end with some concluding observations (5).

2. The Position of the Defense in International Criminal Proceedings

If one takes a defense perspective on judicial notice, a few words need to be said first about the position of the defense in international criminal proceedings generally. This paper does, however, not allow for a detailed analysis.[1]

To understand the position of the defense at international criminal proceedings, two matters must be borne in mind. First, criminal proceedings at the international level are predominantly of an adversarial nature.[2] This implies that the proceedings are dominated by the parties and that they carry the responsibility for collecting their own evidence and developing their own case strategy. In respect of fact-finding, the Judges are generally passive. Compared to its role in inquisitorial systems, the defense in adversarial systems has to be far more active from an early stage. The defense cannot simply sit back and react to the evidence presented by the Prosecutor but must be very active in finding its own witnesses and other evidence. Furthermore, the defense must also critically challenge evidence presented by the Prosecutor; cross-examination is an important tool for the defense, requiring special skills which inquisitorial defense counsel rarely possess.

The bottom line is that in inquisitorial systems the defense can generally rely on a prosecution service which is supposed to objectively establish the facts and a bench which actively engages in fact-finding, both pre-trial and at trial. These are such significant safeguards that even in event of a defense's poor performance, positive results and even acquittals are possible.[3] Conversely, in adversarial systems, the

1 Others have done this and we can recommend the recent book by J. Temminck Tuinstra, *Defence Counsel in International Criminal Law* (The Hague: T.M.C. Asser Press, 2009).

2 Cp. A. Zahar and G. Sluiter, *International Criminal Law – A Critical Introduction* (Oxford: Oxford University Press 2008), 37–45.

3 The objective role of the Prosecutor and the active fact-finding role for the judges in inquisitorial systems also goes a long way in explaining why trials in the accused's absence are allowed, and can still produce a positive outcome for the accused.

defense can clearly not count on an objective prosecutor and active judicial fact-finding. Thus, the defense has, especially in adversarial proceedings, an enormous responsibility.

A second vital contextual factor regarding the position of the defense in international criminal proceedings relates to the organizational structure of international criminal tribunals. International criminal tribunals are not part of a State structure, but are set up as or by an international organization.[4] This creates difficulties, because organs and functions are put together within a single organization, whereas at the national level there exists a far more complex system, including separation of and checks and balances between different organs, actors and institutions involved in the administration of criminal justice.

The most important contemporary international criminal tribunals, the ICTY, ICTR and ICC, are composed of three main organs, the Prosecutor, the judiciary ('Chambers') and the Registrar. The defense has only a very limited position in the organizational structure.[5] It exceeds the scope of this paper to discuss whether the absence of the defense in the organizational structure of international criminal tribunals is justifiable and if not how the situation can be improved.[6] Yet, it can be concluded that the absence of the defense as a separate organ of international criminal tribunals negatively impacts upon its position in criminal proceedings in a number of ways.[7] The overarching issue is of course that compared to the Prosecutor, the defense is structurally disadvantaged, which raises the question of whether equality of arms is sufficiently protected. In concrete terms, the defense is not attributed powers under the Statute and does not enjoy immunities in the course of investigations. Furthermore, and very importantly, there is no duty for States to assist the defense in its preparation of the case, whereas this duty exists in relation to the Prosecutor.

It follows that the defense's position in international criminal proceedings is precarious as a result of both the nature of these proceedings and the institutional framework. Below, when we explore the phenomenon of judicial notice, these are factors that must continue to be borne in mind.

3. Overview of the Practice of Judicial Notice in International Criminal Law

The taking of judicial notice of adjudicated facts and facts of common knowledge is clearly an invention unique to international criminal tribunals. As was already mentioned, the possibilities available at the ICTY and ICTR are unknown to national

4 The ICTY and ICTR were both set up as subsidiary organs to the United Nations, although the ICC was set up as a new and independent international organization.

5 At the ICTY and ICTR there is no separate defense office; it exists at the ICC, but only under the authority of the Registrar.

6 See Temminck Tuinstra, *supra* note 1.

7 In more detail, see Zahar/Sluiter, *supra* note 2, 60–68.

jurisdictions.[8] Without any solid basis in general principles of criminal procedure, there is reason to critically explore this invention.

The analysis should first have regard to the Statute and Rules. There is nothing on judicial notice in the Statute, but Judges made use of the power delegated to them to develop the procedural law by adopting a set of Rules of Procedure and Evidence. The latter contain one provision on judicial notice. Rule 94, common to the ICTY, ICTR and SCSL RPE reads:

> (A) A Trial Chamber shall not require proof of facts of common knowledge but shall take judicial notice thereof.
>
> (B) At the request of a party or proprio motu, a Trial Chamber, after hearing the parties, may decide to take judicial notice of adjudicated facts, or documentary evidence from other proceedings from the Tribunal relating to matters at issue in the current proceedings.

Trial Chambers are obliged to take judicial notice of facts of common knowledge and have discretion to take judicial notice of adjudicated facts and documentary evidence. Trial Chambers of both the ICTY and ICTR have used this provision extensively.

The legal effect of judicial notice is "to establish a well-founded presumption for the accuracy of the evidence, which therefore does not have to be proved again at trial, but which, subject to that presumption, may be challenged at that trial."[9] Judicial notice thus functions as a tool to shorten the evidentiary process. Another important argument in favor of judicial notice, derived from domestic law, is that it promotes the uniformity of judgments.[10]

The accused, often confronted with a considerable number of judicially noticed facts, may rebut those facts in court proceedings. As was already mentioned, this is a violation of the presumption of innocence: it should be for the Prosecutor to prove the criminal responsibility of the accused and not for the accused to prove his innocence by rebutting judicially noticed facts.

Rule 94 (B), a judge made provision, is an example of the sui generis character of the proceedings before the ad hoc tribunals.[11] To take judicial notice of facts of common knowledge (Rule 94 (A)) is not revolutionary, every criminal law system allows for judges not to demand solid evidence of facts that no one would seriously dispute.

---

8 See O-Gon Kwon, "The Challenge of an International Criminal Trial as Seen from the Bench," *Journal of International Criminal Justice* 5 (2007), 369.

9 *Prosecutor v. Milutinović et al.*, Decision on Prosecution Motion to Admit Documentary Evidence, 10 October 2006, Case No.: IT-05-87-T para. 15.

10 R. Cross, C. Tapper, *Cross on Evidence* (London: Butterworths , 6th ed. , 1985) 70.

11 Article 15 ICTY Statute: "The judges of the International Tribunal shall adopt rules of procedure and evidence for the conduct of the pre-trial phase of the proceedings, trials and appeals, the admission of evidence, the protection of victims and witnesses and other appropriate matters." In the same manner: article 14 ICTR Statute. Article 14 SCSL Statute declares the ICTR RPE applicable to the SCSL proceedings.

3.1 *Facts of Common Knowledge*

Facts of common knowledge are typically general facts of history, geography and the laws of nature.[12] Some well-known examples derived from UK case law are: "the streets of London are full of traffic," "cats are kept for private purposes" and "the life of a criminal is an unhappy one."[13] Dutch courts took judicial notice of the fact that "drug related crimes are regularly committed at the Zeedijk in Amsterdam" and "intense emotions can be fatal for elderly."[14]

Whereas the ad hoc tribunals are under an obligation to take judicial notice of such facts, the ICC Statute provides for discretion for the Trial Chamber to take judicial notice of such facts: "The Court shall not require proof of facts of common knowledge but *may* take judicial notice of them."[15] Both the ICC Statute and the ICC RPE are silent on judicial notice of adjudicated facts and documentary evidence.

The legal effect of taking judicial notice of facts of common knowledge is to end the evidentiary process. In contrast with adjudicated facts and documentary evidence, facts of common knowledge that have been judicially noticed cannot, by definition, be challenged anymore by the defense.[16]

3.2 *Adjudicated Facts*

The ICTY in particular has often dealt with the use of judicial notice. In the 2003 Krajišnik decision on judicial notice, the Trial Chamber presented an 8 pronged test to determine whether an adjudicated fact can be judicially noticed.

> (...) the Chamber finds that, for a fact to be capable of admission under Rule 94 (B), it should be truly adjudicated in previous judgements in the sense that:
> (i) it is distinct, concrete and identifiable;
> (ii) it is restricted to factual findings and does not include legal characterizations;
> (iii) it was contested at trial and forms part of a judgement which has either not been appealed or has been finally settled on appeal; or

12 *Prosecutor v. Semanza*, Judgment, Case No.: ICTR-97-20-A, 20 May 2005, para. 194.

13 Tapper, *Cross on Evidence*, 63; A. Keane, *The Modern Law of Evidence* (Oxford: Abingdon, 1985) 494.

14 G.J.M. Corstens, *Het Nederlands strafprocesrecht* (Deventer: Kluwer, 6e druk, 2008) 668.

15 Article 69 (6) ICC Statute. Emphasis added.

16 *Prosecutor v. Semanza*, Decision on the Prosecutor's Motion for Judicial Notice and Presumptions of Facts Pursuant to Rules 93 and 54, Case No.: ICTR-97-20-I, 3 November 2000, para. 41. In the same manner: *Prosecutor v. Krajišnik*, Decision on Prosecution Motion for Judicial Notice of Adjudicated Facts and for Admission of Written Statements of Witnesses Pursuant to Rule 92*bis*, Case No.: IT-00-39-PT, 28 February 2003, para.16. *Prosecutor v. Norman et al.*, Fofana – Decision on Appeal against 'Decision on Prosecution's Motion for Judicial Notice and Admission of Evidence,' Case No: SCSL-04-14-AR73, 16 May 2005, (Separate Opinion by Justice Robertson) 5.

(iv) it was contested at trial and now forms part of a judgement which is under appeal, but falls within issues which are not in dispute during the appeal;
(v) it does not attest to criminal responsibility of the Accused;
(vi) it is not the subject of (reasonable) dispute between the Parties in the present case;
(vii) it is not based on plea agreements in previous cases; and
(viii) it does not impact on the right of the Accused to a fair trial.[17]

For several years this Krajišnik decision served as a precedent for both ICTY and ICTR decisions. Gradually, some of the above criteria were altered or even deleted from the list. For example, the criterion that facts must be restricted to factual findings is only formally adhered to. In Karadžić, judicial notice was taken of facts containing terms such as "attack" and "civilians."[18] Those terms stem from international humanitarian law and are, arguably, legal findings with serious consequences attached to them. The Karadžić Trial Chamber noted that although certain terms can be used in both a legal and non-legal context those terms are not to be regarded as legal, deference being accorded to the context in which the fact was presented.[19] It is doubtful, though, whether there is truth in that observation: if terms have both a legal and non-legal aspect, why not use synonyms instead and leave it to the Trial Chamber to attach legal conclusions to factual findings?

The criteria the Krajišnik Trial Chamber presented in its decision are derived from previous cases before the ICTY, without citing any external authoritative source, such as international case law or scholarly literature.[20] This means that besides Rule 94 as such, the criteria to determine whether to take judicial notice are also exclusively judge-made.

3.3 Documentary Evidence

In contrast with adjudicated facts, there is international precedent for taking judicial notice of documentary evidence. The Charter of the International Military Tribunal at Nuremberg states:

17 *Prosecutor v. Krajišnik,* Decision on Prosecution Motions for Judicial Notice of Adjudicated Facts and for Admission of Written Statements of Witnesses Pursuant to Rule 92*bis*, Case No.: IT-00-39-PT, 28 February 2003, para. 15.

18 *Prosecutor v. Karadžić,* Decision on Third Prosecution Motion for Judicial Notice of Adjudicated Facts, Case No.: IT-95-5/18-PT, 9 July 2009, Facts 1609 and 1647.

19 *Prosecutor v. Karadžić,* Decision on Third Prosecution Motion for Judicial Notice of Adjudicated Facts, Case No.: IT-95-5/18-PT, 9 July 2009, paras. 40-45.

20 The Trial Chamber summed up in § 14 that it had sought recourse to the rulings in *Simić, Sikirica, Kvočka, Kupreskic, Milošević,* and *Ljubičić.. Prosecutor v. Krajišnik,* Decision on Prosecution Motions for Judicial Notice of Adjudicated Facts and for Admission of Written Statements of Witnesses Pursuant to Rule 92bis, Case No.: IT-00-39-PT, 28th February 2003.

> The Tribunal shall not require proof of facts of common knowledge but shall take judicial notice thereof. It shall also take judicial notice of official governmental documents and reports of the United Nations, including the acts and documents of the committees set up in the various Allied countries for the investigation of war crimes, and the records and findings of military or other tribunals of any of the United Nations.[21]

Surprisingly, the Nuremberg Tribunal admitted only one official governmental report into evidence.[22] It is instructive to compare the Nuremberg Charter with the Charter of the International Military Tribunal for the Far East (the 'Tokyo Tribunal'). Where the Nuremberg Charter does not make a distinction between taking judicial notice of the existence and the veracity of the document in question, the Tokyo Charter does:

> The Tribunal shall neither require proof, of facts of common knowledge, nor of the authenticity of official government documents and reports of any nation nor of the proceedings, records, and findings of military or other agencies of any of the United Nations.[23]

The distinction between the existence or authenticity on the one hand and the veracity of documents on the other is fundamental and can also be discerned in present day proceedings.

The ICTR in Bizimungu stated that:

> Thus, by taking judicial notice of the above-listed documents [from bodies and organs of the UN, KV], the Chamber merely relieves the Prosecutor of his formal burden of establishing the authenticity and existence of such documents. However, the Trial Chamber will decline to take judicial notice of the veracity of the statements and conclusions of such documents.[24]

This position had already been accepted by the ICTR in the 2000 Semanza decision on judicial notice.[25] Thus, the ICTR, at least in its early interlocutory decisions, makes a clear distinction between the existence and the reliability of documentary evidence. It follows that this is detrimental to the Prosecutor, because he still has to formally prove the facts contained in the judicially noticed documents. The ICTY, on the other hand, allows for judicially noticing facts contained in documentary evidence. The Milutinović et al. Trial Chamber explicitly ruled that by taking judicial

21 Article 21 Charter IMT at Nuremberg.

22 R. May, M. Wierda, *International Criminal Evidence* (New York: Transnational Publishers , 2002) 136.

23 Article 13 (c) (5) (d) IMTFE.

24 *Prosecutor v. Bizimungu,* Decision on Prosecution's Motion for Judicial Notice Pursuant to Rules 73, 89 and 94, Case No.: ICTR-99-50 I, 2 December 2003, para. 39.

25 *Prosecutor v. Semanza,* Decision on the Prosecutor's Motion for Judicial Notice and Presumptions of Facts Pursuant to Rule 94 and 54, Case No.: ICTR-97-20-I, 3 November 2000, para. 38.

notice of documentary evidence, judicial notice is taken of the existence, authenticity and the content of the documents.[26]

In its most recent decision on documentary evidence, the ICTY Trial Chamber in Karadžić ruled that judicial notice of documentary evidence is permitted when the documents referred to have been submitted into evidence in previous cases. In other words, when the documents in question have been scrutinized by both parties during the original court proceedings, the Trial Chamber may take judicial notice of them in subsequent proceedings.[27] It is noted that the accused in the subsequent proceedings still has the possibility of rebutting the judicially noticed documentary evidence. To act otherwise would be to deprive the accused of his fundamental right to question the evidence against him, particularly where the accused believes he raises new objections against the documentary evidence which have not been raised in the original proceedings.[28]

Trial Chambers may also take judicial notice of facts based on documentary evidence, although the distinction between adjudicated facts and documentary evidence becomes somewhat blurred. In our view, facts that have been established by a Trial Chamber referring to documentary evidence should be judicially noticed as adjudicated facts instead of documentary evidence.

It is important to note here, that the Nuremberg and Tokyo Tribunal articles on documentary evidence were originally intended to cover UN documents and official documents of member states. In Karadžić and in other cases before the ad hoc tribunals, documentary evidence also includes facts derived from expert reports and forensic material.

4. The Karemera Decision: Taking Judicial Notice of Genocide

One of the most controversial decisions on judicial notice was handed down by the ICTR Appeals Chamber in the Karemera et al. case. In its 2006 decision on interlocutory appeal, the Appeals Chamber ruled on the motion of the Prosecution to take judicial notice of the following: "Between 6 April 1994 and 17 July 1994, there was a genocide in Rwanda against the Tutsi ethnic group." The Appeals Chamber deemed this a fact of common knowledge and stated that: "The fact of the Rwandan genocide is a part of world history, a fact as certain as any other, a classic instance of a 'fact of common knowledge.'"[29]

26 *Prosecutor v. Milutinović et al.*, Decision on Prosecution Motion to Admit Documentary Evidence, Case No.: IT-05-87-T, 10 October 2006, para. 31.

27 *Prosecutor v. Karadžić,* Decision of Third Prosecution Motion for Judicial Notice of Adjudicated Facts, Case No.: IT-95-5/18-PT, 9 July 2009, para. 14.

28 A similar argument was raised in *Prosecutor v. Šešelj,* Decision on the Prosecution Motion to take Judicial Notice of Facts under Rule 94 (B) of the Rules of Procedure and Evidence, Case No.: IT-03-67-T, 10 December 2007, para. 6.

29 *Prosecutor v. Karemera et al.*, Decision on Prosecutor's Interlocutory Appeal of Decision on Judicial Notice, Case No.: ICTR-98-44AR74 (C), 16 June 2006, para. 33.

This ruling of the Appeals Chamber has serious consequences. First, according to the wording of Rule 94 (A), Trial Chambers are now under an obligation to take judicial notice of this fact. Second, to take judicial notice of 'genocide' is to take judicial notice of a legal term, explicitly forbidden under the Krajišnik criteria. It is worthwhile to consider here the sources the Appeals Chamber refers to in determining whether a genocide occurred. They include: scholarly articles and books (by non-legal scholars), media reports, U.N. reports and resolutions, national court decisions, government and NGO reports.[30] The Appeals Chamber also referred to ICTR case law.[31] This raises another problem: based on what definitions did those reports, books and articles conclude that a genocide occurred in Rwanda? It was not based on the legal definition as described in the ICTR Statute, but on historical or sociological ones.[32] It has been argued that the general concept of genocide and the legal definition of it are closely interconnected and to regard genocide in Rwanda as a fact of common knowledge is therefore allowed.[33] There is truth in this observation, but within criminal proceedings it is the prerogative of the judges to conclude that certain events amount to the legal definition of genocide.

The Appeals Chamber deviates from the criteria set out in Krajišnik by judicially noticing a legal term. It is remarkable that the Appeals Chamber judicially noticed the Rwandan genocide as a fact of common knowledge and not as an adjudicated fact (which was possible, because the ICTR Trial Chamber and Appeals Chamber had already ruled that genocide had occurred in Rwanda).[34] Judicially noticing facts under Rule 94 (B) leaves open the possibility for the defense to rebut the judicially noticed facts, which is an important safeguard for the fair trial rights of the accused—particularly the presumption of innocence. Facts judicially noticed under Rule 94 (A) cannot be challenged by the defense.

It follows that the Karemera decision has serious consequences for those facing charges of genocide. But the Appeals Chamber noted that also in the case of charges of crimes against humanity the reasoning of the Karemera Appeals Chamber is

30 Ibid., para. 34.

31 Ibid.

32 Instructive is K. Jonassohn, K. Solveig Bjornson, *Genocide and Gross Human Rights Violations in Comparative Perspectives* (New Brunswick: Transaction, 1998). In the first chapter on the question 'what is genocide' the authors observe: "(...) the definition of genocide contained in the United Nations Convention on Genocide, adopted in December 1948, was quite unsatisfactory for one very simple reason: none of the major victim groups of those genocides that have occurred since its adoption fall within its restrictive specifications."

33 R. Mamiya, "Taking Judicial Notice of Genocide? The Problematic Law and policy of the *Karemera* Decision," *Wisconsin International Law Journal* 25, vol. 1 (2007).

34 *Prosecutor v. Akayeshu*, Judgment, Case No.: ICTR-96-4-T, 2 September 1998; *Prosecutor v. Kayishema & Ruzindana*, Judgment, Case No.: ICTR-95-1-T, 21 May 1999; *Prosecutor v. Musema*, Judgment and Sentence, Case No.: ICTR-96-13-A, 27 January 2000; *Prosecutor v. Kayishema & Ruzindana*, Judgment (Reasons), Case No.: ICTR-95-1-A, 1 June 2001,; *Prosecutor v. Semanza*, Judgment and Sentence, Case No.: ICTR-97-20-T, 15 May 2003.

helpful for the Prosecutor. Judicially noticing genocide, according to the Appeals Chamber, "may also provide relevant context for other charges against the Accused, such as crimes against humanity."[35]

One can only speculate why the Appeals Chamber has labeled genocide as a fact of common knowledge which is clearly a legal term and has extremely serious implications for the rights of the accused.

One explanation could be that the ICTR courtroom should not be used as a public forum for genocide deniers, namely those who question the existence of the Rwanda genocide. As numerous legal and non-legal articles and books on recent Rwandan history have argued, the atrocities committed in the spring and summer of 1994 are among the most heinous of acts.

Nevertheless, in criminal proceedings the defense should feel free to question all the evidence pertaining to the crimes allegedly committed by the accused, even when that implies questioning the occurrence of genocide as such. It is a fundamental right of any accused, and one that is protected by various international treaties, to have counsel to represent him in court and to let that counsel put forward any argument that is within the limits set by the Statute, the Rules of Procedure and Evidence, Code of Conduct and the directions of the presiding judge.[36]

Additionally, this Decision deprives the defense of not only challenging that an enormous number of people were killed—a ridiculous position, but one that the Prosecution should disprove on the basis of the evidence—but also rules out, for example, the potential for the defense to make the argument that there was no intent to destroy in whole the Tutsi ethnic group, but that the intent was essentially to win the war with the RPF. We are definitely not claiming that this argument has merit, but it is something that the accused should be entitled to raise—at the very least. Maybe it should not be regarded as a rebuttable adjudicated fact, but at least it is by far outside of the realm of facts of common knowledge. This is a vital legal issue—namely whether efforts towards war could in some way negate genocidal intent.

As pointed out by the Karemera Trial Chamber, to judicially notice a nationwide genocidal campaign is, perhaps surprisingly, irrelevant in individual proceedings before the Tribunal:

> it does not matter whether genocide occurred in Rwanda or not, the Prosecutor must still prove the criminal responsibility of the Accused for the counts he has charged in the Indictment. Taking judicial notice of such a fact as common knowledge does not have any impact on the Prosecution's case against the Accused, because that is not a fact to be proved.[37]

---

35 *Prosecutor v. Karemera et al.*, Decision on Prosecutor's Interlocutory Appeal of Decision on Judicial Notice, 15 May 2003,Case No.: ICTR-98-44AR74 (C), 15 May 2003, paras. 37-8.

36 See for example Rule 44 (B) ICTR RPE. Article 6 ECHR, Article 14 ICCPR.

37 *Prosecutor v. Karemera et al.*, Decision on Prosecution Motion for Judicial Notice, Case No.: ICTR-98-44-R94, 9 November 2005, para. 7.

This finding of the Trial Chamber was set aside by the Appeals Chamber, but it remains to be seen whether noticing the genocide in Rwanda as a fact of common knowledge will expedite proceedings currently pending before the Tribunal. From a substantive criminal law perspective, the Trial Chamber was right to conclude that in individual cases it is irrelevant whether or not genocide occurred in Rwanda in determining the individual responsibility of the accused.[38] The Prosecutor has to prove that (1) the accused committed any of the forbidden acts listed under Article 2 (2) (a-e) ICTR Statute; (2) that the victims were members of one of the protected groups; and (3) that the accused acted specifically in order to destroy the protected group (the dolus specialis or special intent). It follows, as the Trial Chamber correctly observed, that it is irrelevant whether a nationwide genocidal campaign was going on:

> it is simply not a fact to be proven to have the accused convicted. From a substantive criminal law perspective the ruling of the Appeals Chamber, thus, does not lessen the burden of proof on the Prosecutor. As noted by Kirsch, 'individual criminal responsibility for genocide cannot be determined by simply referring to the existence of a system of genocide or a genocidal campaign on its own.[39]

This view is not shared by the Appeals Chamber. The Appeals Chamber ruled that it is of "obvious relevance" to the prosecution to have genocide judicially noticed, because it "provides the context for understanding the individual's actions."[40] From the wording of Article 2 of the ICTR Statute on genocide, it follows that context is not a fact that has to be proven to convict the accused on charges of genocide.

To judicially notice genocide as a fact of common knowledge might be a way of trying to silence genocide deniers. This motive may seem a very legitimate one, but an international criminal tribunal is not created to deliver politically desirable statements. Furthermore, whereas genocide denial regarding the Holocaust is a criminal offence in certain jurisdictions, any defense pleading that would take serious risks by denying the Rwandan genocide has to our knowledge not been criminalized in any way, making no legal impediments for the defense at the ICTR to raise this, or at least to have the Prosecutor prove it.

First and foremost, the judges of the Tribunal have to determine the individual criminal responsibility of the accused. To attribute other functions to an essentially

38 See for example: Kevin Jon Heller, "Prosecutor v. Karemera, Ngirumpatse & Nzirorera. Case no. ICTR-98-44-AR73(C). Decision on Prosecutor's Interlocutory Appeal of Decision on Judicial Notice," *The American Journal of International Law* 101, no. 1 (2007) 157-163.

39 Stefan Kirsch, "The two notions of genocide: distinguishing macro phenomena and individual misconduct," *42 Creighton L. Rev. 347* 2009 at 347. Kirsch offers an instructive overview of the different concepts of genocide (referred to by him as 'social' and 'legal')

40 *Prosecutor v. Karemera et al.*, Decision on Prosecutor's Interlocutory Appeal of Decision on Judicial Notice, Case No.: ICTR-98-44-AR73(C), 16 June 2006, para. 36.

legal institution is to ask more than judges can, and should deliver. Commenting on the Nuremberg trials, Hannah Arendt observed that:

> The purpose of a trial is to render justice, and nothing else; even the noblest of ulterior purposes – 'the making of a record of the Hitler regime which would withstand the test of history,' as Robert G. Storey, executive trial counsel at Nuremberg, formulated the supposed higher aims of the Nuremberg Trial – can only detract from the law's main business: to weigh the charges brought against the accused, to render judgment, and to mete out due punishment.[41]

The ICTR has convicted over 20 persons on counts of genocide and it is likely that more will follow suit. In the light of the foregoing, it is questionable what the Karemera decision adds to the jurisprudence of the ICTR. The decision is detrimental to the fair trial rights of the accused (in particular the presumption of innocence and the right of equality of arms) and it presents a finding which could have easily been deducted from other trial and appeal judgments. The mandate of the ICTR, as stipulated UNSC Resolution 955 (1994), is limited to the prosecution of persons responsible for genocide and other serious violations of international humanitarian law.[42] The Tribunal was not created to provide for an accurate historical record, although its judgments will certainly help historians and social scientists to do so. To judicially notice the genocide in Rwanda as a fact of common knowledge is detrimental to the fair trial rights of the accused and, therefore, the Appeals Chamber should have limited itself to determining the individual criminal responsibility of Karemera et al.

From the perspective of public opinion the ICTR Appeals Chamber Decision does not seem like sound policy to us. We are all aware that the ICTR is critically viewed by Rwandans of Hutu ethnicity, and the fact that there has not yet been any trial of RPF members and/or leaders only aggravates this. Taking judicial notice of genocide as a fact of common knowledge may be seen as strengthening the authority of this fact, intending to end all discussion on this. But in our view the far more powerful tool is the repetitious submission of evidence proving the occurrence of evidence. It is likely that opponents to the ICTR, part of the public opinion, consider ending the discussion in this way as a sign of weakness.

5. Concluding Observations

International criminal tribunals have significant difficulty in effectively managing complex trials, such as genocide trials. It is logical that solutions are envisaged which could lead to shorter and better managed trials. But it is not a proper solution that trials are shortened by structurally taking judicial notice of large numbers of disputed facts. It strengthens the impression that the accused is defending an indefensible case. The phenomenon of judicial notice shifts the burden of proof—or even removes

41 H. Arendt, *Eichmann in Jerusalem. A report on the banality of evil* (London: Faber and Faber, 1963) 232.

42 UNSC Resolution 955 (1994).

certain 'facts' from the fact-finding process altogether—to the defense. This is generally inconsistent with the accused's entitlement to the presumption of innocence. What is more, it is particularly damaging in a system where the defense is in a situation of structural inequality of arms vis-à-vis the Prosecutor and where the defense carries the sole responsibility for collection of exculpatory evidence. It is quite painful that there is little room in international criminal law for these difficulties of the defense and how they are exacerbated by the phenomenon of judicial notice.

But it is not only the position of the defense that concerns us. The Karemera decision, where judicial notice of genocide was taken, demonstrates the slippery slope we're on. Not only is it inappropriate to take judicial notice of a legal term such as genocide, but it may damage the authority of international criminal tribunals. Although a bit more burdensome—but we submit there is no convincing proof that trials will last much longer without judicial notice—the repetitious presentation of evidence will only strengthen the authority and quality of fact-finding. Trying to put an end to discussions, as was done by taking judicial notice of genocide, may be fuel for the fire of public opinion, which is hostile towards international criminal justice. Right or wrong, it may give the impression that there is not enough rather than overwhelming evidence. If the latter is the case, just present it.

Victims

8. Compensating Victims of Genocide

Liesbeth Zegveld

1. Reparation and the Genocide Convention

When genocide has been committed, the existence of large numbers of victims is a fact. These victims will seek redress and they should be enabled to do so.

The drafters of the Genocide Convention had redress and reparation for victims of genocide in mind—indeed, reparation for victims of genocide was included in a draft of the Genocide Convention.[1] The draft article read:

> When genocide is committed in a country by the government ... or by sections of the population ... the state shall grant to the survivors ... redress of a nature and in an amount to be determined by the United Nations.[2]

At the end of the day, however, the proposed article was left out.[3] It was believed that redress and compensation should be part of the jurisdiction of an eventual genocide court.[4] It was agreed back in 1947 that such a court "shall also be authorized to assess damages on behalf of persons found to have sustained losses or injuries as a result of the violation of this Convention by any High Contracting Party."[5] In view of these intentions, the lack of jurisdiction of the International Criminal Tribunal for the Former Yugoslavia (ICTY) and the International Criminal Tribunal for Rwanda

1 William A. Schabas, *Genocide in International Law* (2000), 400.

2 Article XIII: "When genocide is committed in a country by the government in power or by sections of the population, and if the government fails to resist it successfully, the state shall grant to the survivors of the human group that is a victim of genocide redress of a nature and in an amount to be determined by the United Nations." United Nations, Doc. E/447 (1947), 5-13. The Netherlands agreed: "The principle of awarding an indemnity in cases where this can be done, seems reasonable.": United Nations, Doc. E/623/Add.3 (1948).

3 Schabas, Genocide in International Law, see n 1, 400.

4 Ibid., 401.

5 United Nations, Doc A/401 (1947), Article VII.

H.G. van der Wilt, J. Vervliet et al., *(eds.)* The Genocide Convention: The Legacy of 60 Years.
Copyright 2012 Koninklijke Brill NV. ISBN 978 9004 15328 8. pp. 97-104.

(ICTR) to deal with compensation for victims is quite surprising. Both ad hoc tribunals have convicted persons for genocide, and the ICTR has been established for the explicit purpose of prosecuting persons responsible for the genocide in Rwanda in 1994.[6] But the victims of these genocides have themselves been denied a role before these tribunals—they only serve as witnesses and cannot claim compensation against those convicted of genocide.

The International Criminal Court (ICC) makes up for this failure. This court is competent to try perpetrators of genocide and also widely opens its doors to victims. The ICC may award reparations to the benefit of individual victims,[7] and it may do so directly against a convicted person.[8]

The Statute of the ICC (the Statute) is the first embodiment of the right of victims to reparations. As such, it is facing a whole range of questions which arise when dealing with compensation claims made by genocide victims. One such question is how the ICC will deal with the massive volume of compensation claims. One of the main reasons why legal avenues for victims to claim compensation are often opposed is the mass nature of the violations. The fear is that thousands or millions of individuals will file a claim, which would result in unacceptable delays and a colossal increase in costs for both claimants and defendants.

I believe this fear is real,[9] and that the question of how the ICC can deal with the massive volume of compensation claims is legitimate. The ICC already has to deal with large numbers of victims and many more are knocking at its door. Implementation of victims' rights poses for the Court a huge question flowing from the massive volume of victims' claims.

2. Mass Claims Procedures

So far, the answer to the massive volume of victims' compensation claims has been the establishment of the so-called "mass claims procedures".[10] Mass claims procedures—as distinguished from ordinary court procedures, such as those before the

---

6 United Nations, Doc. S/RES/955 (1994), para. 1:

> Decides hereby, having received the request of the Government of Rwanda (S/1994/1115), to establish an international tribunal for the sole purpose of prosecuting persons responsible for genocide and other serious violations of International Humanitarian Law committed in the territory of Rwanda and Rwandan citizens responsible for genocide and other such violations committed in the territory of neighbouring States, between 1 January 1994 and 31 December 1994 and to this end to adopt the Statute of the International Criminal Tribunal for Rwanda annexed hereto ... .

7 United Nations, Doc. A/CONF. 183/9 (1998), Article 75, para. 1.

8 Ibid., Article 75, para. 2.

9 Liesbeth Zegveld, "*Rechtsherstel voor Slachtoffers van Schendingen van het Internationaal Humanitair Recht* [Remedies for War Victims]", 37 "*Vrede en Veiligheid* [*Peace and Justice*]" 1, 10-31 (2008). The English version was published in L. van den Herik and C Stahn eds., "*Future Perspectives on International Criminal Justice.*"

10 Another method is via lump sum agreements, which have been repeatedly concluded following international armed conflicts, to deal with large numbers of claims at once.

ICC—offer a temporary forum to a clearly defined group of victims who have all suffered losses in the same event.[11] The fundamental difference between mass claims procedures and ordinary court procedures is the large number of victims that mass claims procedures deal with. The number of cases under the United Nations Compensation Commission umbrella, for example, is 2.8 million claims.[12]

The massive volume of claims has strongly determined the nature of mass claims procedures. They deal with large groups of comparable claims simultaneously and do not, therefore, employ the same individual approach that is used in the courts.[13] Mass claims procedures have an administrative character—although individual claimants sometimes submit their own claims,[14] they do not play a leading role in the proceedings. In addition, mass claims procedures are, generally speaking, more flexible with regards to obtaining evidence and the burden of proof.[15]

As liability under international law does not now necessarily need to be established in these agreements, however, the legal relevance is limited.

11 The mechanisms stand alone and are simple to access by the victims. The outcome is binding. The Kosovo Housing and Property Claims Commission (HPCC) described the basic characteristics of a mass claim mechanism as follows: "[T]he Commission ... note[s] that ... a mass claims process can be broadly understood as a process designed to deal with a high number of claims that arise out of the same extraordinary situation or event and are filed with a decision-making body within a limited period of time, thus claimants in a mass claims process are generally in the same situation, having suffered the same or similar losses within the same period of time." HPCC/RES/7/2003 (April 11, 2003).

12 "If the number of documents one is dealing with reaches a critical mass, the application of mass claims processes cannot be excluded a priori. After all, it is the numbers that tend to make the difference between arbitration and mass claims." Veijo Heiskanen, "Virtue Out of Necessity: International Mass Claims and New Uses of Information Technology," in *Redressing Injustices Through Mass Claims Processes: Innovative Responses to Unique Challenges*, ed. Permanent Court of Arbitration (2006), 37.

13 The Eritrea-Ethiopia Claims Commission (EECC) can, in order to promote the speedy settlement of claims, accept "such methods of efficient case management and mass claims processing as it deems appropriate, such as expedited procedures for processing claims and checking claims on a sample basis for further verification only if circumstances warrant."*Agreement Between the Government of the Federal Democratic Republic of Ethiopia and the Government of the State of Eritrea* (December 12, 2000), Article 5, para. 10, http://www.pca-cpa.org/upload/files/Algiers%20Agreement.pdf.

14 In some cases through their governments, such as with the EECC and the UNCC.

15 Jacomijn J. Van Haersolte-van Hof, "Relaxed Standard of Proof," in *Redressing Injustices*, ed. Permanent Court of Arbitration, 17. Another reason for flexible demands with respect to evidence is the circumstances under which the losses have occurred, usually war, and the long period of time since they took place. Compare, for example, Article 22 of the Claims Resolution Tribunal for Dormant Accounts in Switzerland Rules, "Relaxed Standard of Proof," http://www.crt-ii.org/_crt-i/rules_procedure.html and Section 22 of the International Organization for Migration in relation to the German Forced Labour Programme, "Evidentiary Standard," http://www.compensation-for-forced-labour.org/english_home.html.

Advocates of mass claims procedures argue that, when mass compensation is at issue, the traditional individual approach is undesirable, as thousands or even millions of individual proceedings would need to be instituted.[16] Where large numbers of victims are involved, advocates of mass claims procedures argue that there is no other choice than accepting the more collective approach.[17] This argument determines the procedures used for mass claims brought by victims before the ICC.

3. Mass Claims before the ICC

How does the ICC handle the mass nature of the crimes brought before it? And how could it handle the potentially large number of claimants appearing before it? Although no criminal procedure has started as of yet, hundreds of victims have already submitted their claims to the ICC. This number is growing every day, not least because it is a stated objective of the ICC to reach as many victims as possible.[18]

The ICC takes an individual approach. According to the Rules of the ICC, a victim is a natural person who has suffered losses as a result of a crime which falls within the jurisdiction of the ICC.[19] The rules therefore refer to victims as individuals and, as such, not to groups or members of groups. The Statute does not provide for so-called "class actions", the possibility to claim compensation via a collective procedure.

At the same time, the Statute also provides mechanisms to aid the ICC in processing large numbers of victims.[20] An example of such a mechanism is that the

16 One of the reasons why a legal process to claim compensation is often closed for victims is the enormity of the violations. See, for example, commentary on *Leo Handel et al. v. Onev. Andrija Artucovic*, 601 F. Supp. 1421 (January 31, 1985), District Court, in *How Does Law Protect in War*, eds. Marco Sassoli and Antoine Bouvier (1999), 713-19.

17 This is said to be particularly so with reference to mass claims procedures. See, for example, with reference to the UNCC, the report and recommendations of the panel of commissioners concerning the fourth installation of claims for compensation for leaving Iraq or Kuwait (Category A Claims) in United Nations, Doc. S/AC.26/1995/4 (October 12, 1995), para. 9, http://www2.unog.ch/uncc/.

18 Under Rule 96 of the Rules of Procedure and Evidence (RPE) of the ICC, the clerk of the Court is obliged to generate publicity "as much as possible and in all kinds of manners," with reference to the compensation procedure of the Court, "with other victims, interested parties and interested States," the objective being to inform victims about their rights and how they can participate in the proceedings. To this end, the clerk may enter into alliances with relevant member States and request assistance from non-government organizations: United Nations, Doc. PCNICC/2000/1/Add.1 (2000).

19 Ibid., Rule 85.

20 When the Statute was being drawn up, many delegations were indeed worried that the potentially large numbers of victims would make participation practically impossible: G. Bitti and H. Friman, "Participation of Victims in the Proceedings," in *The International Criminal Court: Elements of Crimes and Rules of Procedure and Evidence*, ed. R. S. Lee (2001), 456.

rules are drawn up in such a way as to leave the ICC ample leeway for appreciation.[21] The Court can decide on the modalities for victims to participate in proceedings. In the case of large numbers of victims, it can decide on a system that will put the least pressure on the Court.[22]

To date, however, the ICC has preferred to interpret the rules more extensively than restrictively. For example, it has determined that victims may already participate in the preliminary investigation. There are no proceedings against a suspect at that stage, let alone a claim for compensation.[23]

The only requirement individuals have to fulfil to participate at the preliminary stage of a possible proceeding is to state that they have become the victim of an event which might be deemed a crime which falls within the jurisdiction of the ICC.[24] According to the Trial Chamber, participation of victims at this stage can serve to clarify facts and to punish the offender for the crimes, even if the offender has yet to be identified.[25] This and other judgments of the ICC warrant the conclusion that the ICC attaches great value to the participation of victims in proceedings.[26] This is a good thing.

---

21 Ibid.

22 Other mechanisms enabling the Court to serve large numbers of victims are collective compensation and collective representation. Rule 90 of the RPE of the ICC stipulates that the Court may demand a common legal representative for a group of victims as a condition for their participation: "Where there are a number of victims, the Chamber may, for the purposes of ensuring the effectiveness of the proceedings, request the victims or particular groups of victims, if necessary with the assistance of the Registry, to choose a common legal representative or representatives." The aim of this provision is to increase the effectiveness of the proceedings.

23 Pursuant to Article 68, para. 3 , victims are entitled to explain their viewpoints and concerns where they touch on their personal interests. This means that the Court not only decides whether the personal interests of victims are at issue, but also at which moment and in which way the victims are allowed to bring their viewpoints and concerns to the fore. In the decision of the ICC, in *Situation in the DRC,* Decision on the applications for participation in the proceedings of VPRS 1,VPRS 2, VPRS 3, VPRS 5 and VPRS 6, 1CC-01704-01/06-101, P-T Ch I (January 17, 2006), para. 50, the Court decided that the personal interests of the victims could, in principle, already be at issue during the preliminary investigation of a situation.

24 Prosecutor v. Joseph Kony, Vincent Otti, Okot Odhiambo and Dominic Ongwen, Decision on Victims' Applications for Participation a/0010/06, a/0064/06 to a/0070/06, a/0081/06 to a/0104/06 and a/0111/06 to a/0127/06, ICC-02/04-01/05, P-T Ch II (August 10, 2007), para. 83.

25 In the words of the Chamber: "The personal interests of victims are affected in general at the investigation stage, since the participation of victims at this stage can serve to clarify the facts, to punish the perpetrators of crimes and to request reparations for the harm suffered."

26 Another example is the Appeals Chamber decision of February 13, 2007 in the Prosecutor v. Lubanga, where it was established (at para. 43) that when victims participate in an appeal, they have to submit a request to that end again. According to the Appeals Chamber, Rule 86, para 8. was subordinate to Article 68, para. 3 of the statute. This was

Even so, however, it is essential to realise the latent problem posed by enormous numbers of victims. I wonder, for example, whether it would not have been better to delay the participation of victims until the actual trial of the suspect, or even until after the trial, at which time—in the case of a conviction—the victims can claim compensation. The participation of many victims at such an early stage of the preliminary criminal investigation increases the work load of the ICC considerably and delays proceedings. The risk of a lack of this awareness is a risk which mass claims procedures have already encountered: unacceptable delays in the judicial process and high costs for the ICC, the suspect and victims. It is also conceivable that the participation of large numbers of victims, if not kept on the right track, may damage the rights of the suspect to a fair and speedy trial.

4. Domestic Courts

How do domestic courts deal with mass actions of victims of genocide? The principle of victims' participation and reparation laid down in the Statute has been derived from national criminal law systems. In civil jurisdictions, such as France, Germany and the Netherlands, victims can join criminal proceedings and raise a compensation claim based on tort under domestic law. The case against the Dutch businessman, Frans Van Anraat, is an example.

Last year, Van Anraat was prosecuted for genocide. He was convicted by the District Court of The Hague for supplying chemicals to Saddam Hussein's regime in the 1980s.[27] Iraq used Van Anraat's chemical substances for chemical warfare, and 120,000 Iraqi Kurds and Iranian civilians fell victim to these bombardments.[28] The Kurdish and Iranian victims of the chemical warfare joined as civil parties in the criminal case, with the aim of obtaining compensation from Van Anraat if he were convicted.

The District Court of The Hague expressed its fear that large numbers of victims of the chemical warfare would present their claims to the Court. Its fears were understandable. The Dutch legal system is not equipped to cope with mass claims, and class actions do not exist under the Dutch legal system. Section 51a of the Dutch

the first time that the Appeals Chamber considered the way in which the victims could participate in an interim appeal. Although the Pre-Trial Chamber had already permitted victims to participate in the proceedings of this case, each victim had to submit another request for participation, explaining again how this appeal would touch them in their personal interests and why they should be able to present their point of view before the Appeals Chamber. The Appeals Chamber did not think that it was automatically bound by an earlier decision of the Pre-Trial Chamber in relation to this matter: Judgment on the Appeal of Mr. Thomas Lubanga Dyilo Against the Decision of Pre-Trial Chamber I entitled *"Décision sur la Demande de Mise en Liberté Proviso ire de Thomas Lubanga Dyilo,"* ICC-01/04-01/06-824 (February 13, 2007).

27 Criminal Case Against Van Anraat, LJN: BA4676 (May 9, 2007), Court of Justice of The Hague, www.rechtspraak.nl.

28 Abbas Foroutan, *Medical Experiences of Iraq's Chemical Warfare* (2003).

Criminal Procedure [Wetboek van Strafvordering] states that a person who has suffered direct damage as a result of a criminal offence can join in the trial to claim compensation as an injured party. This means that each individual must institute his or her own proceedings and only represents him or herself.

In the case against Van Anraat, it was decided that only fifteen victims could present a claim for compensation. This decision was prompted, inter alia, by the fear which the Court had spoken of,[29] but it meant that the other victims were left empty-handed.[30] What would have happened if more Kurds and Iranians had presented their claims against Van Anraat to the Court? Without doubt, the Court could not have refused them, but they would have weighed down the system. The rules of procedural law—for example, that every victim is allowed to make a statement to explain his or her claim and that every victim may question witnesses—are not designed for large number of victims.

5. Conclusion

When genocide has been committed, the existence of large numbers of victims is a fact. The answer to the massive volume of victims' compensation claims has been the establishment of the so-called "mass claims procedures." The establishment of mass claims procedures is a decision made by governments which, on a case-by-case basis, determine whether to do something for victims or not. There is usually no political consensus supporting mass claims procedures. This means that many victims will continue to be dependent on traditional dispute settlement procedures before ordinary courts. There are, however, very few examples of how an ordinary court in regular proceedings should deal with this.

I do not believe that large numbers of victims creates a fundamental problem. Rather, the problem to be solved is the modalities necessary for their participation. The ICC could, for example, think about a limit to the participation of victims in an investigation in situations where a suspect has not yet been identified. Both the ICC and the Netherlands could consider making "class actions" possible. The key feature of a class action is that a court, in the interests of efficiency, can declare the outcome of proceedings for one claimant applicable to all claimants who are able to present a like claim. What should be considered is the need to establish, per individual case, the circumstances which can be imputed to the victim, and a causal link between the conduct and the damage. This is not a big step: under Dutch civil law interest groups are already able to litigate for anonymous individuals. But these interest groups cannot yet claim financial compensation.

We owe it to victims seeking redress to think about solutions. The drafters of the Genocide Convention wanted redress and reparation for victims of genocide to be part of the jurisdiction of an international court. Redress for victims is an impera-

29 Participation of the claimants was limited to one or no more than two victims per place mentioned in the summons (in total this amounted to four villages in Iraq and six in Iran).

30 They did, however, have the possibility of continuing the case in civil proceedings.

tive demand of justice. It is not enough to lay responsibilities on states and to punish perpetrators—victims must be furnished with the means to obtain their rights, otherwise they are helpless from a legal point of view.

9. Why Compensation is a Mixed Blessing

Selma Leydesdorff

1. Introduction

I have been asked to discuss the advantages and disadvantages of financial compensation and to comment, as a historian, on a legal debate. Although I express concern about the human cost of the bitter compensation struggle, this does not imply a waning solidarity with those who are trying to win compensation through lawsuits and trials. Over the years, I have admired Liesbeth Zegveld, the lawyer who is the major speaker at this session, for her tenacity in defending the survivors of the Bosnian genocide. We both know well how the manipulations by the prosecutor in The Hague and the unexpected changes of judges[1] have compounded the survivors' feelings of forsakenness, loneliness and desolation. These survivors have to deal with the psychological trauma of what happened to them every day. I myself joined the victims of Srebrenica; I sat down with them and offered support when they delivered their writ of summons.[2] I say that 'I joined them,' because I am not a lawyer. I felt their loneliness, as well as the hostility from the representatives of the Dutch state, while I sat next to the two women representing the thousands who feel that they are fighting an uphill battle "against the entire world." They knew how much I, coming from a Jewish family that had to deal with compensation issues for decades after the Second World War, have concerns regarding the process of compensation. This discussion voices my concern, and I hope that it will contribute to what is primarily a juridical debate.

---

1 In December 2007 the court of The Hague changed the composition of the chambers dealing with Srebrenica. The most important change was the replacement of Judge Punt, who seemed most inclined to mediate in one of the cases (*Mustafić*). When questions were asked in Parliament, the Minister of Justice of course denied any suggestion of manipulation. The Minister did not manage to take away the suspicion. See Answer to Questions in Parliament no. 2070821930 (2008).

2 *Writ of summons (June 4, 2007) against the State of the Netherlands and the United Nations.*

H.G. van der Wilt, J. Vervliet et al., *(eds.)* The Genocide Convention: The Legacy of 60 Years.
Copyright 2012 Koninklijke Brill NV. ISBN 978 9004 15328 8. pp. 105-114.

I argue that the focus on compensation is part of a specific legal discourse, which seems to dominate the field. This discourse is centered on the indictment, and the demand for compensation places the legal trial at the center of the social reconstruction process. But in doing so, we risk neglecting the social and psychological dimensions of the victims' emotional needs and feelings of emptiness.[3] I warn against this, and argue that we need to look beyond the indictment. We tend to forget that the victims' core desire is for recognition, which goes far beyond compensation. Political philosopher Nancy Fraser described recognition as a

> reciprocal relation between subjects, in which each sees the other both as its equal and also as separate from it. This relation is constitutive for subjectivity: one becomes an individual subject only by virtue of recognizing, and being recognized by, another subject. Recognition from others is thus essential to the development of a sense of self.[4]

To be denied recognition—or to be 'misrecognized'—is to suffer both a distortion of one's relation to one's self and an injury to one's identity, because it involves reconnection to a society and a world that seem to have been lost.

We must remind ourselves that monetary compensation never restores lost social and cultural capital. It does not revalidate the right to exist as a human being, which is a crucial factor in being able to go on living. Whoever looks at the survivors' wishes after the Holocaust and its historiography, or reads the many psychological reports, will see that the absolute central desire is to return to a normal daily life and to escape the legal and administrative web. Right from the beginning, German financial compensation after World War II, although materially helpful, had the bitter taste of "blood money," as one Sinti woman called it as early as 1945 (the Sinti were among the first to receive compensation).[5]

2. To Know Where They Are

Over the years, I have studied the memories and reactions of the victims of mass atrocities—the Jews during the Second World War and the Bosniaks during the war in Bosnia-Herzegovina. I have interviewed many survivors of the Holocaust and the Srebrenica genocide.[6] I have learned that, more than anything else, the victims

3 Laurel E. Fletcher and Harvey M. Weinstein, "Violence and Social Repair: Rethinking the Contribution of Justice to Reconciliation," *Human Rights Quarterly*, 24 (2002) 601-603.

4 Nancy Fraser, "Rethinking Recognition,"*New Left Review* 3 (2000) 107-120. Nancy Fraser and Axel Honneth, *Redistribution or Recognition?* (2003).

5 Paul Őfner and Marcia Rooker, "Van het schooien om brood tot het eisen van respect, De naoorlogse behandeling van Sini en Roma," *Mensenheugenis*, ed. H. Piersma (2001) 71.

6 Selma Leydesdorff, *De Leegte Achter ons Laten, Een Geschiedenis van de Vrouwen van Srebrenica* (2008),translated into Bosnian: *PraŽninu ostaviti iza nas, Istorija žena Srebrenice* (2009). See also Nanci Adler, Selma Leydesdorff et al., *Memories of Mass Re-*

want to know what happened to their loved ones. They cannot psychologically accept the 'truth' that those innocent people were murdered. After 1945, Jews waited endlessly for the return of those who had disappeared, in many cases holding on to hope until it was no longer possible to believe that they would learn where and how their loved ones had been killed.

Max, whom I interviewed about his stay and forced labor in Auschwitz, told me about his lost brother: "There is not a day that I don't think of him." Did he expect to see him ever again? "For years I believed so, also in my dreams: He will come back, he will come back." I asked him when he was certain, and gave up hope. "It was never certain; there is just a moment when you cross that line, after many years," he answered.[7]

Safija, an elderly lady whom I interviewed in the unpleasant refugee camp of Grab Potok, told me:

> I waited till last year, hoping I would get a message they were alive. Maybe they had been transported to another country and would send a message. But when they found the body of my oldest son, I lost hope. I knew. I went to the funeral—I know where his body is resting. But regarding my younger son, I still pray to God that I'll hear he is somewhere. May God fulfil my wish, that he is somewhere, that he is alive, someplace.[8]

Suhreta knew her husband had been killed. She knows exactly where and how. She told me the story of his slow murder in such detail that I nearly had to stop the interview. But she waited in her house until confirmation came that the bodies of her husband and sons had been found.[9] And Haša, the mother of two boys who were killed, said:

> I always hope that my son will come alive. When I dream about him, I see him clearly, and then I say to myself that he will come, then that he will not come. Then I think that maybe somebody will bring a paper to confirm that he was found somewhere. But nobody will ever come back alive. Nobody.[10]

While still waiting, survivors have started to speak out and to inscribe their ordeals in the historical record through books, diaries, poems, and an interminable struggle for recognition. This is as true for the Holocaust as it is for Bosnia: memoirs, poems, and plays are published in order to remember, to keep the memory alive, and to

---

pression: Narrating Life Stories in the Aftermath of Atrocity (2009). The interviews on the Holocaust were done in the context of the Mauthausen Surviviors Documentation Project (Austria) and as part of the Former Slave and Forced Labour Project (Germany).

7 Interview Max Koker, Former Slave and Forced Labour Project.

8 Interview Safija K, Grab Potok (2004).

9 Interview Suhreta M, village near Srebrenica (2004).

10 Interview Haša Selimović, Kulina Bana, Lukavać (2006).

combat oblivion and historical amnesia.[11] To know and to remember are two sides of the same on-going process of mourning. They reflect the need and yet the inability to give these horrendous events their rightful place in history.

3. Material Goods Are Not All-important

One could argue that Srebrenica was 'only' thirteen years ago, so the pain is still acute. However, the same sharp feelings of loss were also evident among my Shoah interviewees. The loss of loved ones is more important than anything else, but poverty adds to the misery. To live in a refugee camp, to exist in unimaginable destitution without financial or psychological help, is another form of non-recognition. It permeates the whole personality; everything is experienced within a sense of total loss. Nezira, who lives in a suburb of Sarajevo, no longer cares for life:

> I cannot help crying, I think that this is the end of my life. First my father's remains were found and then my son's. My husband died … forty days had passed after his death when I buried my son. I went with my only child. There was no one to lay him in the grave. Neighbours and people—somebody—put him in the grave; I don't really know what happened.[12]

Zumra told one of my collaborators in an interview in Sarajevo:

> Not one day passes that I haven't said something about it. That means it is on my mind all the time. I can't understand. Sometimes I visit a happy family, where all the members are there together, and they have problems buying a fridge, or they need to change the curtains or something else in their house. I'm not interested in that. I don't—I don't have the power inside me to listen to that. I don't worry anymore about which dress I have on, what kind of shoes, which bag. All I worry about now is that I'm neat, that I'm not filthy, and I pray to dear Allah to keep me sane, to keep me aware and reasonable, so that I can communicate normally with people.[13]

4. Lack of Communication

People who have lost their sense of place in the world live in a chaotic nightmare; context and connections have become blurred and one's position in society has dissolved. It feels as though nothing is left. All that remains is the story of grief and loss, a story that others prefer not to hear. Societies do not know how to accommodate traumatic stories. Talking about one's past, and hence being able to present a meaningful identity, is difficult not only for Srebrenica survivors, but also for many of my interviewees from the Shoah. It is difficult enough to remember and to talk about it,

11 To give some examples for Srebrenica in English: Isnam Taljic, *The Story of Srebrenica* (2004). Nihad Nino Catic and Ljudi Beznada, *Mensen van de Wanhoop* (2007). Sadik Salimonic, *The Road of Death* (2008).

12 Interview Nezira Suljemanović, Ilidža (2005).

13 Interview Zumra Sekhomerović by Velma Sarić, Sarajevo.

but even more so when people do not want to hear the grim details. Learning about another person's humiliation is unpleasant and uncomfortable. Henny, one of the interviewees in the Forced Labour[14] project, told me:

> People could not stand my story. I became aware of that very quickly; you had to keep your mouth shut. What are you imagining, they would ask, and I was stigmatized as a person with a wild imagination ... which fortunately I am. I am grateful for that; my imagination is so rich that I am forced to speak the truth. They didn't appreciate that, so I shut up. Why should I open up? Even now after sixty years I did not tell my story to my children.[15]

5. Difficult Stories

During interviews, accounts of such catastrophes are not immediately understandable. Narratives of trauma are not straightforwardly referential; rather, they are what Cathy Caruth calls expressions of "a crisis of witnessing." She has dealt extensively with the ways trauma is sedimented in language and literature,[16] and considers any eyewitness account to be rooted in dislocations of history, which are imperative.[17] Whoever has interviewed trauma cases knows that chronology fails, lapses occur, and confusion is normal.[18] Talking about trauma often means reliving it in all of its pain, difficulty, fear, confusion, and shame.

According to Dori Laub, the American psychiatrist and founder of the Fortunoff Collection at Yale:[19]

> I will propose there is a need for tremendous libidinal investment in those interview situations: There is so much destruction recounted, so much death, so much loss, so much hopelessness, that there has to be an abundance of holding and of emotional investment in the encounter.[20]

---

14 A large oral history project, consisting of more than 800 interviews, that was supervised by the Fernuniversität Hagen. Besides the many publications it produced, see Christoph Thonfeld, 'My whole Life I have Shivered': Homecoming and New Persecution of Former Slave and Forced Laborers of Nazi Germany *Memories of Mass Represssion, Narrating Stories in the Aftermath of Atrocity*, eds. Nanci Adler, Selma Leydesdorff, et al. (2009). Natalia Timofeyeva, et al., *Hitler's Sklaven* (2008).

15 Interview Henny L, Amsterdam (2005).

16 Cathy Caruth, *Unclaimed Experience: Trauma, Narrative and History* (1996).

17 Michael G. Levine, *The Belated Witness: Literature, Testimony and the Question of Holocaust Survival* (2006).

18 Kim Lacy Rogers, Selma Leydesdorff and Graham Dawson, eds., *Trauma, The Life Stories of Survivors* (2004). See also Shoshana Felman and Dori Laub, *Testimony: Crises of Witnessing in Literature, Psychoanalysis and History* (1992). Dominick La Capra, *Writing History, Writing Trauma* (2001).

19 Besides the Shoah Visual Foundation, this is the largest audiovisual archive on genocide of the United States. Compared to the former, it is far more academic in its approach.

20 Shoshana Felman & Dori Laub, *supra* note 18, at 71.

Absolute freedom of speech is required, patience is obligatory. Answers are never given, but the desire to answer always leads to the beginnings of a new story, since one memory brings forth new memories. The narrator is often unaware of how much s/he has to tell. There is an emotional dynamic between the two who sit together, having committed themselves to the story. In this difficult process of remembering, the use of existing narration genres is a way to escape personal memories, and collective memories are redundant. This complicates any understanding of what is told. The interviewer has to continually question if the story is indeed personal, or if the language of others is being used.

By narrowing the survivors' desires down to material compensation and juridical procedures, the survivors' life stories are also reduced to the demands, format, and language of the law. In preparation for the proceedings and in court, exact information is required,[21] yet the victim struggles with something incomprehensible, something beyond any traditional concept of history.[22] The significance of remembered life stories lies not in absolute truth, but in how one remembers, how one gives meaning and representation to events. [23] Stories do not exist until they are told, and an adequate history cannot be written without including the victims' suffering and the survivors' memories. Therefore we should not dismiss them as constructions that lack factual authority, but rather regard them as ontological authenticity.[24]

This view of survivor subjectivity is not in line with how witness accounts are perceived in the public arena, where the 'true" story of what "really' happened and the exact timeline are needed. The court proceedings of the International Tribunal for the Former Yugoslavia are creating history based on eyewitness accounts, in a similar manner as to how the Nuremberg trials and other post-Holocaust trials have created history.[25] But the trials of the post-Holocaust era were never accepted as history. In all these cases, eyewitness stories create a history that needed and needs to be constructed, especially when written documentation is incomplete, destroyed, or failing.

In his groundbreaking article "Judging History," the American historian Richard Wilson[26] shows how unique the International Tribunal is. Judges need a place where they can be free from the polarized national histories that have dominated the former Yugoslavia. There is not yet a clearly established right or wrong, as was the case in the period after 1945. What has been achieved is the writing of a new

21 Several of the women whose life stories serve in the Writ of Summons of the Survivors of Srebrenica were interviewed by me at another time. They sometimes seemed to be different persons, although the "facts" they talked about were the same.

22 Francois Davoine and Jean-Max Gaudilliere, *History Beyond Trauma* (2004) 253.

23 James E. Young, *Writing and Rewriting the Holocaust: Narrative and the Consequences of Interpretation* (1990).

24 Id. at 22.

25 Leon Goldensohn, *Nuremberg Interviews, An American Psychiatrist's Conversations with the Defendants and Witnesses* (2004).

26 Richard Wilson, "Judging History: The Historical Record of the International Criminal Tribunal for the Former Yugoslavia," *Human Rights Quarterly*, 27, no. 3 (2005) 908-42.

history based on evidence and accountability, which was extracted from accounts that are tailored to that purpose. The proceedings and convictions are now part of the authoritative collective memories, but in the process, individual suffering and its recognition were silenced. Srebrenica 'became; a genocide after the Kristić verdict; and after the eyewitnesses told their stories, they disappeared into the masses. "Bosnian Muslims" is always plural, as is "women, children, and the elderly." "They" have become anonymous, a people without history.[27]

While the law is busy establishing its truth, and stories are told in order to get proof, survivors must frame their stories according to the demands of the judges. The survivors are looking for a different truth, one that has been denied, yet often they assume the court proceedings will help them to find it. Answers to the many questions that haunt them (often framed by the words 'Search for Justice and Truth') are more important to them than material compensation.

One example is the testimony of Kada Hotić in the Orić case.[28] She clearly wanted to tell about the stream of refugees from Bratunac to Srebrenica. Bratunac was conquered in 1992. It was a massacre. Suddenly neighbor turned against neighbor, and there was unprecedented violence. Refugees from there felt betrayed by friends and she wanted to explain what happened. The judge, however, was only interested in how the local population of Srebrenica had raided the area surrounding the town in 1993-94. The accused at that trial was supposedly the leader of those raids, in which many had been killed. The court wanted details from 1993-94, but Kada Hotić's mind was focused on an earlier period (1992). The end result was chaos.

6. Juridical Past and Historical Past

Both legal discourse and historical discourse try to understand the history of an epoch and its causality, but their outcomes are different.[29] As a historian, I researched the daily life of Srebrenica during the siege (1992-1995). At first, most information came from official reports and from the International Tribunal. The first type of information tended to meet the demands of the commission,[30] and the second type the demands of the law. Both gave a specific image of the town under siege, an image that was filtered through the lens of knowing that the people there would be slaughtered. Their common task was to discover who was accountable and to assign responsibility; the picture that emerges is one of people who were bound to die. But the people living there were not aware that they were going to be killed. Another perspective shows a town that was vibrant and full of people who strongly believed they would survive, because they were protected by the United Nations. There were

27 ICTY Case No: IT-98-33-A, Judgement: Apr. 19, 2004.

28 ICTY IT 03-68, Apr. 26, 2006, pp. 9680ff.

29 See also Carlo Ginzburg, *History, Rhetoric and Proof* (1999).

30 Despite these remarks, I think that the research done by Ger Duijzings in the larger context of the official report on Srebrenica by the Netherlands Institute on War Documentation on Srebrenica under siege (2002) is excellent.

sharp divisions between population groups, with an upper class of endogenous inhabitants and masses of newcomers. In the end, of course, they were all miserable.

Again, the historical comparison with the Holocaust is obvious. Most people in the Jewish ghettos of occupied Poland were not aware that they were going to be killed. That awareness took a long time to develop. People kept decency and cultural life alive as long as possible. This was true for the agency of the Jews in the ghettos and it was also true for the besieged town of Srebrenica. The same pattern was found in the siege of Sarajevo, which has been studied by anthropologists.[31] Sabra told me about her efforts with a group of women to save Srebrenica's library.[32] How does one unearth this part of history from beneath the layers and layers of accusations of atrocities? Where does one tell about it? Is it still possible to witness that history? Whoever sits down with the survivors and really takes the time to listen carefully will hear it, but only if priority is given to the story.

7. The Need for a Different Truth

For survivors, truth can be defined as "knowledge about the fate of loved ones." When survivors use the word 'justice,' they often mean that they want to know who was responsible and why events happened as they did.

When describing the first actions for 'Justice and Truth' by her organisation (The Mothers of Srebrenica and Žepa), Zumra told how the Bosnian authorities wanted them to stop behaving like widows. The women had stopped traffic in the town and on one of the highways to the sea. The authorities were angry:

> When we came to Sarajevo County, they told us: 'We don't deal with those things. We have more important things to do.' So we stopped traffic, and we got bad criticism from the government. They said: 'What do you want, do you know what you are doing, what it means to stop traffic? People have to go to work, to school.' Our prime minister was Silajdžić. He told us, 'Death comes every day.' But he knew where his parents were buried. We don't know where our families are buried, we don't know where they are—They say we lie. But we only tell the truth; we fight for justice. Nothing else.[33]

During another interview, Zumra said:

> We organized the first protest in front of the International Red Cross in Tuzla. We requested that the Red Cross help us to find out where our missing ones are, as we had waited for two months and hadn't heard anything about them. A crowd of 5,000 men and women gathered in front of the International Red Cross. We waited for someone from the International Red Cross to talk to us, to clarify. We were hoping that their people who

31 Ivana Maček, 'Imitation of Life:' Negotiating Normality in Sarajevo under Siege," *The New Bosnia Mosaic: Identities, Memories and Moral Claims in Post-War Society*, eds. Xavier Bougarel et al. (2007).

32 Interview Sabra Kolenivić, Sarajevo (2004).

33 Interview Zumra Sekhomerović by Velma Sarić, Sarajevo (2004).

> went out in the field, that they had seen something, that we could get some information. However, after they saw us gathered in large numbers, no one had the decency to show up and to talk to this mass of people. All these people—hurt, with all that pain, not knowing, expecting and searching, with all that dissatisfaction—started to behave out of control, no one could control us. Women got angry, picked up stones, and stoned the International Red Cross premises.[34]

It was another moment of non-recognition.

Suhra corroborated Zumra's story:

> I must tell you the truth, we organized many meetings, and we caused chaos in Tuzla. We even threw stones at the Red Cross and the cantonal government, hoping that something would improve. We thought that if anybody had been captured, he would be released then. We wanted to attract the attention of the world.[35]

8. Is It Possible to Really Listen?

People prefer to go on with life, and so societies go on. Grief is disturbing, so stories of trauma are avoided. In his work on the Fosse Ardeantini in Rome where hundreds of citizens were killed in 1944,[36] the oral historian Alessandro Portelli demonstrated clearly that citizens did not want to be reminded of all the grief after the war. Life went on. When a mourning woman entered a shop, she was served first. One might think this was out of respect for a widow in black. In fact, the other customers did not want to see such women any longer. Those who reminded the others by publicly mourning and wearing black were ostracized. To my knowledge, there is no society that has a public place for daily mourning, for the ordinary expression of bewilderment. There was no place for Jews in the world after 1945 unless they shut up. Public mourning was limited to a few moments of formal commemoration.

9. To Reconnect?

If legal language and the demands of law become the dominant narrative for framing eyewitness accounts of genocide, we risk erasing a representation of how deeply lives have been disrupted. We erase the fragmentations, the silences, the dislocations. By not allowing the full truth of the stories in all their layered and unfinished forms, by dismissing them as outbursts of emotion, we deny their mediated authenticity and the way they might reconfigure or even remake the world for those who have lost their place in it. In turn, we dislocate the meaning and place assigned to an event. In this entwinement between the legal truth and the victim's need to speak out, material compensation is merely one of many ways to reclaim a place in the world.

---

34 Interview Kada Hotić and Zumra Sekhomerović, Sarajevo (2004).

35 Interview Šuhra Sinanović, Ilias (2005).

36 Alessandro Portelli, *The Order has been Carried Out: History, Memory and Meaning of a Nazi Massacre in Rome* (2003).

To tell and to speak are at least as important as all those other things, such as depolarized education systems, promotion of tolerance, stronger independent media, the challenging of dominant national narratives, the privileging of other voices (e.g., women's groups), truth-and-reconciliation commissions, places for mourning, and finally the prosecution of the criminals. International institutions have made the last of these the most visible. Institutionalizing pain is not the way to express anger and hope, and to overcome a lack of context. The law can be a beginning for reconnection, but let there be no mistake: compensation can never be more than a partial response to the survivors' needs.

The desire to be recognized must be acknowledged in ways other than compensation. It has to do with behavior—including the manner in which compensation is given, with empathy and humanity.

In Giorgio Bassani's A Plaque in Via Mazzini (1952), a man returns to Ferrara. People know he has seen the German concentration camps and they are afraid to interact with him. The man is totally isolated and cannot settle down. In the end he disappears again, for the second time with an unknown destination. No one knew what happened. Some felt ashamed, but some did not.

10. Some Measure of Justice. The Holocaust Era Restitution Campaign of the 1990s *

Michael Marrus

1. Introduction

The restitution agreements discussed in this book may be likened to the "laws" in the famous quip attributed to Otto von Bismarck, the nineteenth-century Iron Chancellor of Imperial Germany: "Laws are like sausages," Bismarck is supposed to have said, "it is best not to see them in the making." The "laws," in this case, were outcomes of startling revelations, charges and countercharges, politics, campaigning, public and private threats, and litigation, followed by many months of arduous negotiations—in one important instance through the courts, in another with contending parties brought together by governments, and in still another with private industrial and organizational representatives working together. Different somewhat from other instances, restitution of works of art, which will be considered in the next chapter, could involve variations on all these pathways to resolution, and at least as much acrimony and notoriety, even if fought on a smaller scale. In every case, these settlements purported to achieve "some measure of justice" for survivors of the Holocaust or, in some cases, their heirs. To this day there remain disagreements over the extent that they managed to do so and about the processes by which these settlements were reached. By no means is everyone happy with what was achieved. But there were settlements, and I think there is a consensus, even among the defendants, that something positive was achieved. Instrumental in reaching this result were concepts and procedures of American civil law, often articulated in the idiom of human rights. This chapter examines the pathways to resolution and gives some sense of why, to many at least, and notwithstanding the high moral purpose, these were unmistakably sausagelike, unappealing at close scrutiny.

* Reprinted with permission and previously published in: Michael Marrus, "Restitution in the 1990s" (Chapter 1), in: "Some Measure of Justice. The Holocaust Era Restitution Campaign of the 1990s", pp. 10-35, The University of Wisconsin Press, 2009.

H.G. van der Wilt, J. Vervliet et al., *(eds.)* The Genocide Convention: The Legacy of 60 Years.

Swiss and Other Banks

The engine of the American restitution campaign, which drove the issue forward from the mid-1990s, was the affair of the Swiss banks, the global controversy begun in 1996 when the leadership of the World Jewish Congress decided to contest the issue of dormant accounts, originally held by Jews who became Holocaust victims, on which there had never been proper postwar reporting or appropriate restitution.[1] To be sure, this was not the first time the Swiss banking community heard accusations about Holocaust-era accounts. Nor was this the first time that plaintiffs had sought to use civil courts in the United States to seek justice for the Holocaust. But the matter had remained largely invisible, beneath the radar of international publicity and public controversy. American courts had been unreceptive. Their reasoning was that without legislative direction it was not their business to reach back over several decades to right wrongs committed in faraway countries in circumstances that were on a scale and complexity ill suited to the application of tort law.[2] It should be added that the Swiss were scarcely responsive through this same period. It was only in the mid-1990s that this question emerged, full-blown, in the glare of American political, legal, and social contention. Within a short time, as one analyst puts it, the Swiss banks issue "came to symbolize how justice was denied to Holocaust survivors."[3]

Early revelations came in the spring of 1995 from Israeli historian and journalist Itamar Levin, deputy editor of an Israeli business newspaper, Globes, and a student of Holocaust history. Levin disrupted the phlegmatic world of Swiss inquiries into long-standing accusations of mishandling Jewish accounts with a series of articles on how the banks had mistreated heirs of deceased Holocaust victims and had wrongfully retained heirless accounts.[4] His reports documented obstacles set by the bankers in the way of accessing Holocaust-era accounts, most notoriously the cynical requirement of death certificates for account holders who had been murdered in Auschwitz, Treblinka, Majdanek, and other camps. And the amounts were potentially huge: from nearly 300 million Swiss francs said to have been owed in 1946, Levin calculated, on the basis of interest and changes in currency values, a total of

---

1 Particularly useful on the subject of the Swiss banks is the official Web site of the Swiss Banks Settlement: *In re Holocaust Victim Assets Litigation*, United States District Court for the Eastern District of New York, Judge Edward R. Korman Presiding (CV-96–4849), available at http://www.swissbankclaims.com/, last accessed September 24, 2008.

2 See the comments by Shari C. Reig, "The Swiss Banks Holocaust Settlement" (2007), available at http://www.redress.org/PeacePalace/HolcaustSettlementSR.pdf, last accessed June 10, 2008.

3 Regula Ludi, "The Swiss Case," Centre for European Studies Working Paper Series No. 80, *Historians as Trouble-Shooters: Officially Commissioned Surveys of Holocaust Legacies in France and Switzerland* (n.d.), available at http://www.ciaonet.org/wps/luro2/luro2.pdf, last accessed April 29, 2008.

4 Itamar Levin, *The Last Deposit: Swiss Banks and Holocaust Victims' Accounts*, trans. Natasha Dornberg (Westport, Conn.: Praeger, 1999), 99–104. See also Ronald W. Zweig, *German Reparations and the Jewish World: A History of the Claims Conference* (2nd ed., London: Frank Cass, 2001), 4–5.

6.4 billion Swiss francs.[5] The international press carried the story first in 1995: London's Jewish Chronicle relayed the charges and noteworthy articles appeared in U.S. publications, including the Wall Street Journal and the New York Times.[6] Newsweek and Time gave prominent place to the issue two years later. The latter introduced its cover story on the issue with an image of emaciated survivors with a foreground of gold bars in the shape of a swastika. According to Time, while the "proximate cause" of the crusade against the Swiss bankers was money, "the soul-searing intent of the men and women who set the hunt in motion was to peel back the veil time had cast over the evils of Nazism and expose the truth."[7] Israeli leaders, including the prime minister at the time, Yitzhak Rabin, seized upon the matter, as did the flamboyant and energetic Rabbi Israel Singer, deputy to Seagram liquor magnate Edgar Bronfman at the head of the World Jewish Congress.[8] Within a short time, restitution became a global issue. "In the course of 1995–7," writes one participant, "Western media was flooded with information on stolen Jewish property which had not been returned. The phenomenon itself was amazing: material on confiscation of property, bank deposits and gold transactions, which would usually be suitable for historical journals, found its way onto the front pages of national newspapers, capturing international media interest with extraordinary intensity. It was as if the facts had been revealed for the first time, and material which in the past had been the basis of Hollywood action movies, suddenly appeared to be historic reality."[9]

Within little over a year of Levin's report, lawyers filed three class action lawsuits in a federal court in Brooklyn against the three major Swiss banks—Credit Suisse, the Union Bank of Switzerland (UBS), and the Swiss Bank Corporation—claiming tens

5 Hans J. Halbheer, "To Our American Friends: Switzerland in the Second World War," American Swiss Foundation, available at http://www.americanswiss.org/content/, last accessed June 9, 2008.

6 Peter Gumbel, "Secret Legacies," *Wall Street Journal*, June 21, 1995; Nathaniel C. Nash, "Swiss Raise Hopes of Tracing Lost War Deposits," *New York Times*, August 3, 1995.

7 Johanna McGeary, "Echoes of the Holocaust," *Time*, February 24, 1997.

8 "Israeli Media Attitudes toward the Shoah: An Interview with Yair Sheleg," Jerusalem Center for Public Affairs (2003), available at http://www.jcpa.org/phas/phas-sheleg.htm, last accessed April 29, 2008. According to Itamar Levin, Singer, whose wife's family came from Switzerland, first became interested in the Swiss issue in 1993 while working for the World Jewish Restitution Organization, which he had helped to found the previous year, under the umbrella of the World Jewish Congress, to seek restitution of Jewish properties from all European countries except Germany and Austria (Levin, *Last Deposit*, 96). According to another report, Singer's first encounter with the issue came the next year when he read Paul Erdman's novel *The Swiss Account*, with its allusion to Allen Dulles's intelligence-gathering activity in wartime Switzerland and a U.S. intelligence operation to track down Nazi gold in that country. See McGeary, "Echoes of the Holocaust."

9 Avi Beker, "Introduction: Unmasking National Myths," in Avi Beker, ed., *The Plunder of Jewish Property during the Holocaust: Confronting European History* (Houndmills, Basingstoke: Palgrave, 2001), 10. Cf. Isabel Vincent, *Hitler's Silent Partners: Swiss Banks, Nazi Gold, and the Pursuit of Justice* (Toronto: Knopf, 1997), 232–33 and passim.

of millions of dollars in damages and restitution and involving more than two dozen different law firms. A battle that would last for many months, which would extend to wartime forced and slave labor as well as insurance, which would reach into several countries and many different areas of wrongdoing during the Holocaust, and which was backed by some two million claimants around the world, had effectively begun.[10]

To the Swiss, these lawsuits did not come completely out of the blue. As historian Regula Ludi has shown, the Swiss had their own reasons, in the mid-1990s, to rethink the patriotic memories of the wartime period, with their celebrations of Swiss armed neutrality, heroic resistance to Nazism, and principled services to humanitarianism.[11] Such views were in some quarters seen as outdated, out of keeping with more recent concerns for minorities and global preoccupations with human rights. While still widely held, traditional Swiss patriotic views were also contentious by this time. Other, more critical perspectives existed, and they could not help but spill over onto matters related to the Holocaust. There was even some rethinking in high places. In 1995, even before the Swiss banking scandal broke, Swiss Confederation president Kaspar Villiger apologized to the country's Jewish community for its treatment of Jewish refugees during the war and its refusal to accept more into the country.[12]

Historical interpretations were not permitted to evolve at a leisurely pace, however—assuming that is what they would have done. Rather, the Swiss were abruptly called to account in the contestations of high-stakes American litigation. To the lawyers for the plaintiffs, seeking what they understood as belated justice for the Holocaust meant fitting an unfathomable historic catastrophe more than half a century old into menacing legal threats and fierce accusations. And so rather than following a meandering path of historical revision, the Swiss enlisted historical interpretation, just as did their opponents, in a great class action struggle that unfolded in the United States.

Pressure mounted as attention focused on the litigation and the related issue of unreturned gold looted from the central banks of Nazi-conquered European countries, including gold that had been taken from the Jews. Among the latter was even gold that had been pried loose from the teeth of the murdered Jews in the death camps and that had disappeared into the Swiss bank vaults. Early on, Singer and

10 The estimate of the number of claimants comes from the calculations of Peter van der Auweraert, "Holocaust Reparations Claims Fifty Years After: The Swiss Banks Litigation," *Nordic Journal of International Law* 71 (2002): 561 and n. 13.

11 On "patriotic memories" see Pierre Lagrou, *The Legacy of Nazi Occupation: Patriotic Memory and National Recovery in Western Europe, 1945–1965* (Cambridge: Cambridge University Press, 2000).

12 Stuart E. Eizenstat, *Imperfect Justice: Looted Assets, Slave Labor, and the Unfinished Business of World War II* (New York: Public Affairs, 2003), 48; Regula Ludi, "Waging War on Wartime Memory: Recent Swiss Debates on the Legacy of the Holocaust and the Nazi Era," *Jewish Social Studies* 10 (2004): 134. According to Ludi, Villiger's apology "signaled a change in official images of the past, which no longer relied exclusively on recollections of resistance and achievements of military defense" (ibid.). See also Nathaniel Nash, "Swiss Raise Hopes of Tracing Lost War Deposits," *New York Times*, August 3, 1995.

Bronfman recruited the New York Republican firebrand Senator Alfonse D'Amato, chairman of the Senate Banking Committee. An enthusiastic champion of his Jewish constituents, D'Amato was running for reelection and resourcefully seized upon the issue. Amid charges that the banks held many hundreds of millions of dollars in Holocaust accounts, D'Amato's banking committee began to hold hearings on the matter.[13] Researchers from his office went to work—not infrequently going over ground that had been covered by academic researchers years before but that was little known to the wider public. "Toward the end of 1996," writes Isabel Vincent, D'Amato's investigators were feeding sensational stories "to an eager international press corps on an almost daily basis."[14] Later, when the campaign against the Swiss banks had intensified, he publicly urged banking authorities to block a proposed merger of two of the banks involved in the litigation, the Swiss Bank Corporation and the Union Bank of Switzerland, "pending the outcome of a thorough investigation [into] ... the disposition of assets of Holocaust victims and their heirs, and their record of collaboration with the Nazis."[15] At a Democratic fund-raising luncheon at his apartment in April 1996, Bronfman, a major supporter of the administration, buttonholed Hillary Rodham Clinton and gained an appointment with President Clinton the next day. The Clintons were both, thereafter, onboard.[16]

Carried along by the momentum of litigation, increasing political support, and growing antipathy toward the Swiss, popular appreciations of the scale of the wrongdoing magnified significantly. Representatives of forty-one nations met at the London Gold Conference in December 1997 to discuss outstanding wartime issues, putting even more pressure on the Swiss. The more critics heard about the Swiss story, the more outraged they became. "This is the greatest robbery in the history of mankind," announced Elan Steinberg, one of Bronfman's deputies at the World Jewish Congress.[17] Steinberg, the aggressive champion of the campaign on a day-to-day

13 United States Congress, Senate Committee on Banking, Housing, and Urban Affairs, *Hearings before the U.S. Senate Committee on Banking, Housing, and Urban Affairs* (Washington, D.C.: U.S. G.P.O. 1996), April 23, 1996.

14 Vincent, *Hitler's Silent Partners*, 239–40.

15 Alfonse M. D'Amato to Alan Greenspan, February 5, 1998, available at http://www.senate.gov/comm/banking_housing_and_urban_affairs/general/corresp/0205fed.htm, last accessed April 30, 2008. New York governor George E. Pataki similarly threw his weight behind this effort. According to his press release: "Before these two institutions are given the chance to launch a new era in their respective histories, they must convince New York's bank regulators and the Federal Reserve's Board of Governors that they're doing everything in their power to rectify a great injustice from the past." "Governor Pataki Joins Senator D'Amato to Oppose Swiss Banks Merger," March 24, 1998, available at http://www.claims.state.ny.us/pr980324.htm, last accessed May 13, 2008.

16 John Authers and Richard Wolffe, *The Victim's Fortune: Inside the Epic Battle over the Debts of the Holocaust* (New York: Perennial, 2002), 16 and passim; and McGeary, "Echoes of the Holocaust."

17 Quoted in Tom Bower, *Nazi Gold: The Full Story of the Fifty-Year Swiss-Nazi Conspiracy to Steal Billions from Europe's Jews and Holocaust Survivors* (New York: HarperCollins, 1997), 310.

basis, became a force to be reckoned with. "We know that a lot of people don't agree with our tactics," he told one interviewer, "but so what? It's not our responsibility to be nice to the Swiss and get them off the hook. We represent the Jewish people, and we are trying to achieve truth and justice for those who have been victimized for more than fifty years."[18]

As the campaign intensified, accusations broadened from the restitution of dormant accounts to include a wide range of wrongs against victims of the Holocaust. As law professor Michael Bazyler notes, "because the Swiss banks were accused in these lawsuits not only of wrongfully keeping … deposited funds but also of earning money by trading with the Nazis in goods made by slave labor and in possessions looted from the victims (including gold), the beneficiaries of the Swiss banks had to include victims of these Nazi policies as well."[19] Assembling a formidable case, the plaintiffs presented claims to the court that were enough to make any Swiss banker blanch: "breach of contract, breach of fiduciary duty, conversion, conspiracy, unjust enrichment, conspiracy to violate international law, complicity in violations of international law, negligence and violations of Swiss Federal Banking Law and the Swiss Code of Obligations." These involved not only demands for restitution and compensation but also damages under the Alien Tort Claims Act of 1789, according to which aliens could sue in American courts for a tort committed in violation of the "law of nations." Put simply, the plaintiffs sought to use American courts to seek compensation for Holocaust-era violations of human rights.[20] Reinforcing their claim, Israel Singer increased the pressure. During the autumn of 1997 there was talk of a boycott, regulatory pressure from New York City officials, and calls to block the proposed merger between the Swiss Bank Corporation and the Union Bank of Switzerland. Secretary of State Madeleine Albright added her voice, urging that the Swiss parliament follow the example of the United States in discovering "the truth about the Holocaust and events related to it." And Congress, too, sprang into action. From mid1996 to 2001 the Senate and House of Representatives held some fourteen separate hearings on Holocaust-related restitution matters.[21]

18 Vincent, *Hitler's Silent Partners*, 180.

19 Michael J. Bazyler, *Holocaust Justice: The Battle for Restitution in America's Courts* (New York: New York University Press, 2003), 31.

20 Auweraert, "Holocaust Reparations Claims," 568; Anthony J. Sebok, "Mass Restitution Litigation in the United States," in David Dyzenhaus and Mayo Moran, eds., *Calling Power to Account: Law, Reparations, and the Chinese Canadian Head Tax Case* (Toronto: University of Toronto Press, 2005), 359; Rudolf Dolzer, "The Settlement of War-Related Claims: Does International Law Recognize a Victim's Private Right of Action? Lessons after 1945," *Berkeley Journal of International Law* 20 (2002): 298.

21 Authers and Wolffe, *Victim's Fortune*, 14–20; Greg Bradsher, "Research, Restitution, and Remembrance: The Federal Government and Holocaust-Era Assets," lecture at B'nai Israel Synagogue, April 20, 2001, available at http://www.archives.gov/research/holocaust/articles-and-papers/federal-government-and-holocaust-assets-1996-2001.html, last accessed July 22, 2008; David Rohde, "Judge Weighs Fate of Suit Filed by Jews against Swiss," *New York Times*, August 1, 1997.

Sensing early in the day that they had a major public relations disaster on their hands, the Swiss responded with three initiatives. First, an agreement between the Swiss Bankers Association and the major Jewish organizations established an international committee of experts, headed by Paul Volcker, the former head of the United States Reserve Bank, with a twofold mandate: "(a) to identify accounts in Swiss banks of victims of Nazi persecution that have lain dormant since World War II or have otherwise not been made available to those victims or their heirs; and (b) to assess the treatment of the accounts of the victims of Nazi persecution by the Swiss banks." The Volcker Committee's audit, it was later acknowledged by an American court, was "likely the most extensive audit in history, employing five of the largest accounting firms in the world at a cost of hundreds of millions of dollars to the defendants."[22] Second, as a gesture of goodwill while the dispute was being resolved, the Swiss government established a $200 million humanitarian fund (later raised to $400 million) for needy Holocaust survivors, administered by Swiss and Jewish authorities. And third, the Swiss parliament established ablue-ribbon international investigative commission, headed by a respected historian from Zurich, Jean-François Bergier, to examine Switzerland's role during the Second World War. The commission enjoyed a broad mandate and exceptionally good working conditions. And its report, ultimately released in final form in March 2002, proved devastating to the Swiss banks' case.[23]

Long before that happened, in the familiar scenario with lawsuits of this scale, the parties eventually found their way to negotiation and settlement, assisted and pushed and prodded by Judge Edward R. Korman, Chief Judge of the United States District Court in Brooklyn, before whom the various lawsuits had been consolidated in March 1997, and assisted at critical junctures by Stuart Eizenstat, the delegate of the Clinton administration who was to play a vital role in subsequent restitution negotiations. An experienced civil servant who had served as American ambassador to the European Union, Eizenstat came to the issue from service as a special envoy of the American government on property recovery issues in Central and Eastern Europe in the mid-1990s. Later, he prepared two stinging reports on wartime collaboration with the Nazis: the first on looted Nazi gold deposited in Swiss banks and retained thereafter, including that which had belonged to murdered Jews, and the second on neutral governments' wartime involvement with the Nazis operating through Swiss channels.

The Swiss banks situation was complicated by, among other things, deep divisions among the plaintiffs' attorneys about how to proceed with the case. Some of the latter opted for a wider set of claims against the Swiss, including their involvement in slave labor, their assisting the Germans in looting Jews' assets, and their

22 Independent Committee of Eminent Persons, *Report on Dormant Accounts of Victims of Nazi Persecution in Swiss Banks*, December 1999, 1–2, available at http://www.crt-ii.org/ICEP/ICEP_Report_ToC.pdf, last accessed April 30, 2008; and *In re Holocaust Victim Assets Litigation*, 105F.Supp.2d, 151.

23 See the Web site of the Independent Commission of Experts (ICE)–Second World War, available at http://www.uek.ch/en/index.htm, last accessed April 30, 2008.

restrictive refugee policies. Others focused more narrowly for the restitution of bank accounts.[24] Following the Swiss banks affair, and with the blessing of the American government, Eizenstat helped bring the contending parties together on related restitution issues concerning other banks, German industry, insurance, and art—urging accommodation, identifying common ground, and shaping an outcome acceptable to the interests of the United States.

Eizenstat struggled to circumvent litigation and challenged the lawyers constantly—sometimes in extreme frustration. "Lawyers are lawyers the world over," he complained in his memoir on the restitution campaign. While full of sympathy for the plaintiffs' cause, he saw his role as promoting compromise among the contending parties and bringing as much calm as he could to the roiling legal waters.[25] For a time, in the summer of 1998, the talks broke down and at that point Judge Korman had a decisive impact. Many felt, however, that Eizenstat's involvement was essential for settlement. The New York Times even published an editorial praising his efforts, referring to him as "a long-serving American Government official who has brought a rare degree of energy and attention to these difficult matters."[26]

Judge Korman, before whom the Swiss banks parties came as litigants, used the authority of his office and the courts to clarify legal issues and to postpone ruling on some procedural matters, thereby pressuring the parties to settle and in the end to hammer out an agreement—which in this case he was responsible for administering. In Eizenstat's view, "it took Korman and the threat of sanctions to get the banks over the top."[27] Committed to righting the record of the history of the affair, Korman was a distinguished jurist who was appointed under President Ronald Reagan and who had worked with and respected Burt Neuborne, a New York University law professor and one of the lead counsel for the plaintiffs. Neuborne, in turn, thought Korman's handling of the negotiations "masterful" and, like many others on the plaintiffs' side, believed that he was the indispensable impresario of the final settlement. Critical of the Volcker Committee for what he felt was too indulgent a view of the Swiss banks, Korman preferred what he felt was the harsher judgment of the Bergier Commission. He was, therefore, not a disengaged arbiter, but he was widely believed to be fair.

Following a colorfully recounted dinner with the lawyers of both sides in August 1998, hosted by Korman at the famous Gage & Tollner steak house in Brooklyn near his courthouse, the judge brought the two sides to what eventually became a Settlement Agreement.[28] "The judge basically told us—and he was only half joking—that

24 See especially Jane Schapiro, *Inside a Class Action: The Holocaust and the Swiss Banks* (Madison: University of Wisconsin Press, 2003).

25 Eizenstat, *Imperfect Justice*, 231.

26 "A Distinguished Public Servant," *New York Times*, January 19, 1999.

27 Julia Collins, "Taking on the Unfinished Business of the Twentieth Century," *Harvard Law Bulletin*, Summer 1999, available at http://www.law.harvard.edu/news/bulletin/backissues/summer99/index.html, last accessed May 21, 2008.

28 For descriptions, see Authers and Wolffe, *Victim's Fortune*, 94–99; Susan Orenstein, "Gold Warriors: The Inside Story of the Historic $1.25 Billion Settlement between Holo-

no one would leave the room until there was a deal," recalled one participant.[29] And so there was, ensuring that the matter would not come to trial, following the pattern of virtually all class action lawsuits.[30] The Swiss banks (Credit Suisse and the Union Bank of Switzerland) agreed to establish a Settlement Fund of $1.25 billion for the compensation and relief of several categories of plaintiffs. As agreed to in a distribution plan under the auspices of a Special Master of the court, Judah Gribetz, five categories of claims were identified: a Deposited Assets Class to which the bulk of the money would go, made up of those with unresolved Swiss bank accounts; a Slave Labor Class I, made up of those forced to work for German companies whose profits were sheltered in Switzerland; a Slave Labor Class II, made up of those forced to work for Swiss-controlled companies in Germany; a Refugee Class, made up of those who had been mistreated as refugees by Switzerland; and a Looted Assets Class, made up of those whose property was looted by the Nazis and disposed of by Swiss institutions.[31] The plaintiffs agreed to dismiss all their claims, and Eizenstat found a way to reassure the Swiss through an "all Switzerland" release that precluded subsequent litigation.

To the initiated, what was remarkable about the settlement was that the substance of the wrongdoing was never definitively resolved in court. To be sure, Judge Korman was hardly silent on matters of substance. Evenhanded before the settlement was reached in August 1998, he took public exception, several years later, to what he believed was a continuing whitewashing of Swiss wrongdoing during and after the war. Korman continued to spar with the Swiss over the implementation of the settlement, vigorously challenging the bankers on their interpretation of the historical record.[32] However, the judge's decisions on procedural issues were no substitute for a final resolution in court. "Except for the Volcker audits, conducted inde-

caust Victims and the Swiss Banks," *American Lawyer* (September 1998): 63–64; Eizenstat, *Imperfect Justice*, 168–70.

29 Richard Z. Chesnoff, *Pack of Thieves: How Hitler and Europe Plundered the Jews and Committed the Greatest Theft in History* (New York: Doubleday, 1999), 271.

30 The Swiss government was not a party to the agreement, which was concluded with the Credit Suisse and the Union Bank of Switzerland, the largest and most important of the Swiss banks. The other defendant, the Swiss Banking Corporation, had been allowed to merge in 1998 with the Union Bank of Switzerland.

31 Shari C. Reig, "The Swiss Banks Holocaust Settlement," paper presented at the Conference on Reparations for Victims of Genocide, Crimes against Humanity and War Crimes: Systems in Place and Systems in the Making, the Peace Palace, The Hague, the Netherlands, March 1–2, 2007, available at http://www.redress.org/PeacePalace/HolcaustSettlementSR.pdf, last accessed April 30, 2008. Shari Reig was the Deputy Special Master for the administration of the distribution of the settlement under Judah Gribetz.

32 *In re Holocaust Victim Assets Litigation*, 302F.Supp.2d 59 (E.D.N.Y., 2004); Edward Korman, "Rewriting the Holocaust History of the Swiss Banks: A Growing Scandal," in Michael J. Bazyler and Roger P. Alford, eds., *Holocaust Restitution: Perspectives on the Litigation and Its Legacy* (New York: New York University Press, 2006), 115–32, especially 117; Burt Neuborne, "A Tale of Two Cities: Administering the Holocaust Settlements in Brooklyn and Berlin," in Bazyler and Alford, *Holocaust Restitution*, 77. See

pendently from the lawsuits," writes Eizenstat, "the evidentiary essence of the legal process that could have lent legitimacy to the massive settlement was utterly lacking. Not one shred of traditional legal discovery was made. Instead, external pressures and the intervention of the U.S. government compensated for the serious flaws in the legal cases."[33]

To the lawyers and much of the public, however, the settlement was momentous: not only because of its considerable magnitude—$1.25 billion—but also because of the pathway that it opened for other lawsuits then being contemplated or even under way. "By settling the litigation, UBS and Credit Suisse had set a precedent for the rest of Europe's corporate establishment," write John Authers and Richard Wolffe. "They had also provided the perfect tactical template for the Jewish advocates. The deadly matrix of strategies used against the Swiss—lawsuits backed by high-pitched public relations, governmental pressure, and threats of sanctions—could be used again and again."[34]

Many of the lawyers involved with the Swiss banks went to the courts in the late 1990s with subsequently filed lawsuits against German, Austrian, French, Belgian, and even British and American banks. Their claims had to do with so-called "Aryanized accounts"—deposited money and valuables that had been confiscated by the banks, acting under Nazi directives or general policy, together with other acts of alleged complicity with the wartime persecution and attendant profiteering at the Jews' expense. Sometimes the banks involved were the direct successors of wartime banking houses. But sometimes, too, the relationship was cloudy. Institutions such as the German Deutsche Bank or the Austrian Creditanstalt were familiar to all students of banking history in Germany and Austria, for example, and their complicity with Nazi persecution fit people's general understanding. But this was hardly the case with the American Wells Fargo & Company. A claim against the latter appeared when Wells Fargo acquired a Belgian bank in 1996 and balked at paying obligations under a settlement reached with some twenty-two different banks in Belgium.[35] Other cases, against Barclay's Bank, Chase Manhattan, and J.P. Morgan, arose because of the activity of their Paris branches during the wartime occupation of France.

Associated with almost all these claims were not only the wartime robberies but also their cover-up—hiding or destroying evidence both in the postwar period and

---

also William Glaberson, "Judge Accuses Swiss Banks of Stonewalling," *New York Times*, February 21, 2004.

33 Eizenstat, *Imperfect Justice*, 177. Eizenstat cites Korman's own view of the ultimate resolution: "As crucial as Judge Korman was to the settlement, even he admitted that the courts are too cumbersome for the efficient dispatch of cases with this kind of diplomatic and political weight: 'This should have been done as a government-to-government agreement. Litigation was the least desirable way to deal with it.'" Ibid.

34 Authers and Wolffe, *Victim's Fortune*, 105.

35 Michael J. Bazyler and Amber L. Fitzgerald, "Trading with the Enemy: Holocaust Restitution, the United States Government, and American Industry," *Brooklyn Journal of International Law* 28 (2003): 699, n. 48.

subsequently, as highlighted in one egregious case in January 1997 when a Swiss security guard and subsequent whistleblower, Christoph Meili, caught a Zurich branch of the Union Bank of Switzerland red-handed, in the dead of night, shredding some relevant wartime documents.[36] As we shall see, these charges led to some painful encounters, both in Congress and the court of public opinion. The Swiss banks affair involved some of the most flagrant instances of what Judge Korman later found to be "decades of improper behavior"—hiding the existence of bank accounts of Holocaust survivors, stonewalling on claims, destroying records, and deceiving external agencies seeking to discover the truth.[37] The case of the French banks was also important because of the symbolic significance of bringing the proud French bankers and the French government to account before American courts, legislators, and the wider American society, and also because of the legal precedents deployed when a federal judge allowed the case to go forward. As with the Swiss banks, eventually these lawsuits were settled, mostly in early 2001, at the end of the Clinton administration and through the Herculean efforts of Stuart Eizenstat.[38]

2. Slave and Forced Labor

Throughout the 1990s, the largest Nazi-era claims by far were those filed against German corporations on behalf of Jewish and non-Jewish wartime survivors who had been dragooned into wartime labor for private corporations in the Third Reich. As historians have come to appreciate, the employment, often under duress and in terrible conditions, of as many as twelve million Europeans was one of the fundamental policies of the Third Reich and an essential requirement of its war making and imperial strategy during the Second World War.[39] "Employment of foreign forced laborers was not only limited to large-scale enterprises," according to the leading German authority, Ulrich Herbert. "It was applied throughout the whole economy; from the small farm and locksmith's shop with just six workers, to the national railway system, the local authority districts, the big armament companies and also many private households."[40] In all, the Nazi regime employed foreign workers in virtually every walk of life, from farms to churches to heavy industry and concentration camps. In the late summer of 1944 these numbered close to eight million and represented one-quarter of the workers in the entire German economy. This was, it has been noted, "the largest use of foreign forced labor since the end of slavery in

36 See the description in Authers and Wolffe, *Victim's Fortune*, 32–36.

37 *In re Holocaust Victim Assets Litigation*, 105F.Supp.2d, 139, 152 (E.D.N.Y., 2000); *In re Holocaust Victim Assets Litigation*, 302F.Supp.2d, 39 (E.D.N.Y., 2004).

38 Bazyler, *Holocaust Justice*, chap. 4.

39 Mark Spoerer, *Zwangsarbeit unter dem Hakenkreuz* (Stuttgart: Deutsche Verlags-Anstalt, 2001); Ulrich Herbert, *Hitler's Foreign Workers* (Cambridge: Cambridge University Press, 1997).

40 "Final Compensation Pending for Former Nazi Forced Laborers," *Deutsche Welle*, October 27, 2007, available at http://www.redress.org/PeacePalace/HolcaustSettlementSR.pdf, last accessed May 5, 2008).

the nineteenth century."[41] In the case of Jews, the term "slavery" is to some degree a misnomer, as their veteran advocate Benjamin B. Ferencz pointed out years ago: Jews were regularly employed simply as another means of mass murder; they were supposed to be worked to death, with the products of their labor squeezed out of the victims as a by-product of the murderous process.[42] As to the many hundreds of thousands of surviving workers, most had never received any reparation whatsoever.[43]

Beginning in March 1998 with a spectacular lawsuit against the American automotive giant Ford and its German subsidiary, lawyers went to courts in five different states, from New York to California, to win compensation and damages for the use of their clients' wartime labor.[44] The defendants included familiar pillars of German industry—Siemens, Daimler Benz, Volkswagen, Degussa, Hugo Boss, Bayer, Hoechst, and so on. The claims were astronomic, amounting to some $37 billion at the beginning of the process.[45] Significantly, 80 percent of the claimants represented in the various classes were non-Jews, coming from the various East European nationalities that had never been compensated by their home governments for their wartime labor and suffering at the hands of the Germans. For a time the defendant companies, including some prominent American firms such as Ford, sued because of their relationship with their wartime German branches, put up a stout defense, mainly arguing, along with procedural challenges, that the claims should have been made against the German government, representing the regime that had been responsible for the persecution of Jews and other peoples of Europe. In the months that followed there were legal ups and downs, political pressures, and political intervention on both sides of the Atlantic—from Bill Clinton in the United States and the German chancellor Gerhard Schröder, whose Social Democrats had favored restitu-

41 Ulrich Herbert, "Forced Laborers in the Third Reich: An Overview," *International Labor and Working Class History* 58 (2000): 193.

42 Benjamin B. Ferencz's classic account is: *Less than Slaves: Jewish Forced Labor and the Quest for Compensation* (Cambridge, Mass.: Harvard University Press, 1979). On this point see 17–30 and passim. See also Christopher R. Browning, *Nazi Policy, Jewish Workers, German Killers* (New York: Cambridge University Press, 2000).

43 "Of the hundreds of German firms that used concentration camp inmates, the number that paid anything to camp survivors could be counted on the fingers of one hand. Less than 15,000 Jews received any share of the combined total of under $13 million paid by the few German companies. Even the severe hardship cases of those who had survived work for I.G. Farben at Auschwitz got no more than $1,700 each. Krupp's Jewish slaves and those who toiled for Siemens had to settle for $825. The AEG/Telefunken slaves each received no more than $500, and the Jews who worked for Rheinmetall received even less." Ferencz, *Less than Slaves*, 188. See also Herbert, "Forced Laborers in the Third Reich," 207–15.

44 See Keith Bradsher, "Suit Charges Ford Profited by Nazi-Era Forced Labor," *New York Times*, March 5, 1998.

45 John Authers, "Making Good Again: German Compensation for Forced and Slave Laborers," in Pablo De Greiff, ed., *The Handbook of Reparations* (Oxford: Oxford University Press, 2006), 431.

tion in the federal election and triumphed over the more recalcitrant Helmut Kohl's conservative Christian Democrats in October 1998. Unlike the case with the Swiss banks in which governments maintained an arm's length, Washington and Berlin urgently pressed for a resolution and involved themselves in the process, which soon extended to other governments as well—those of Eastern Europe as well as Israel, representing their citizen-claimants.

Negotiations began in early 1999 and, in addition to the litigants and victims' groups, involved no fewer than eight sovereign governments—those of Germany, the United States, Israel, the Czech Republic, Poland, Russia, Belarus, and Ukraine. After close to a year of arduous deliberations, the logic of settlement prevailed. The agreement reached with German industry at the end of 1999, amounting to DM 10 billion or about $5.2 billion in all, made an important distinction between two classes of plaintiff: a smaller class, the slave laborers, mainly Jews who had toiled in concentration camps and who were intended to be worked to death, and the much larger class of forced laborers, mostly Slavic people who had worked elsewhere for the German war machine under a variety of conditions, ranging from the most cruel to the relatively favorable. The former, said to number some 240,000, received a token payment of $7,800 per worker, and the latter, of whom there were about 1.2 million still alive, $2,600 each. The settlement was wide-ranging, extending also to some life insurance obligations as well as claims of some business owners who had not previously been compensated for wartime robberies. A German Foundation Fund, referred to as "Remembrance, Responsibility and Future," was to take charge of the process of compensation at the German end and was to conduct educational and commemorative programs about the Nazi persecution. Remarkably, the lawyers, the victims' groups, the Anglo-American lead negotiators (Eizenstat for the United States and Count Otto Lambsdorff for Germany), and the diplomatic representatives all managed to agree. To the industrialists, in addition to winning back a measure of goodwill in the United States, the prize was "legal peace"—the dismissal of the existing lawsuits and the promised intervention of the American government to prevent such cases from going forward in the future. This last, although not easy given American constitutional restraints, was eventually achieved.[46] To the victims, the result was a no doubt symbolic, but nevertheless tangible, recognition of their sufferings that was long overdue.[47] And from the German government, in line with a series of important declarations that extended back to those of Konrad Adenauer, there was an apology by German President Johannes Rau before an assembly of survivors: "I pay tribute to all those who were subjected to slave and forced labor under German rule and, in the name of the German people, beg forgiveness. We will not forget their suffering."[48]

46 Bazyler, *Holocaust Justice*, chap. 2; Anthony J. Sebok, "Unsettling the Holocaust (Part I)," August 28, 2000, available at http://writ.news.findlaw.com/sebok/20000828.html, last accessed September 18, 2008.

47 Sebok, "Mass Restitution," 364.

48 "Statement by President Johannes Rau on the Agreement on the Level of Foundation Funding for the Compensation of the Victims of Forced Labor," December 19, 1999,

3. Insurance

Claims against European insurance companies, amounting originally to billions of dollars, proved to be more complicated, more contentious, and more difficult to resolve than the slave and forced labor cases, possibly because, at least when viewed in general terms, the wrongdoing was less clear cut and more difficult to measure than the confiscation of bank accounts or the human rights violations of German industry. Prior to the Holocaust, Jews may have owned as much as $2.5 billion in insurance policies, used at the time as a convenient vehicle for savings and investment.[49] This money was placed in literally dozens of companies headquartered in several European countries. These included the Allianz AG, headquartered in Munich and the second-largest insurance company in the world, and the giant, Italian-based Assicurazioni Generali S.p.A., known as Generali, founded by Jewish merchants in Trieste in the nineteenth century and headed, until recently, by a survivor of Auschwitz.[50] But there were also smaller concerns, the names of which were usually unknown to the more than ninety thousand claimants who eventually sought compensation for Holocaust-era losses.[51]

First filed in the spring of 1997 and eventually consolidated in New York before Judge Michael Mukasey (later U.S. Attorney General under President George W. Bush), the class action suits against the insurers alleged that the companies had colluded with the Nazis to confiscate the policies of Jews and facilitate their persecution and that they had covered up their wrongdoing after the war and blocked appropriate restitution through legalistic, bureaucratic, and other subterfuges. The insurers offered several responses. Many claimed that they had no choice but to operate under Nazi directives and that they had often done their best to preserve the interests of their clients. As to prewar accounts for which they claimed to lack evidence or responsibility, they usually explained this by their wartime and postwar situation: some claimed that their records had been destroyed during the war; some companies had merged with others; some had been nationalized by the Soviet-dominated countries of Eastern Europe; and some insisted that claims had been resolved in earlier agreements between Germany and global reparations agreements of earlier times. Some of the original insurers, it was noted, had simply gone out of business.

German Embassy, Washington, D.C., available at http://www.germany.info/relaunch/politics/speeches/121799.html, last accessed July 22, 2008.

49 Bazyler, *Holocaust Justice*, 110.

50 Ibid., 113. Generali was the insurance company for which Franz Kafka worked briefly in Prague. Sander L. Gilman, *Franz Kafka* (London: Reaktion Books, 2005), 42; Authers and Wolffe, *The Victim's Fortune*, 108–9.

51 See Lawrence S. Eagleburger and M. Diane Koken, *Finding Claimants and Paying Them: The Creation and Workings of the International Commission on Holocaust Era Insurance Claims* (2007), available at http://www.icheic.org/pdf/ICHEIC%20Legacy%20Document.pdf, last accessed May 6, 2007.

The companies did, however, acknowledge that they had no alternative but to address outstanding claims.[52]

For a time it looked like the insurance companies were on the same road to settlement as the Swiss banks. Pressure came from state regulators and on occasion legislators, highly susceptible to opinion on the state level where the industry was regulated. On the companies' side, insurance associations tried to make their members' case. In August 1998, six major European insurers reached agreement with U.S. insurance regulators, the Claims Conference, the World Jewish Restitution Organization, and the Israelis to constitute the International Commission on Holocaust-Era Insurance Claims (ICHEIC, pronounced "eye-check") to facilitate the resolution of claims.[53] It appointed as its chairman Lawrence Eagleburger, a veteran State Department official, diplomat, and experienced negotiator who had been Secretary of State under George H. W. Bush. Pointedly, ICHEIC left the lawyers outside this process—a decision that appealed to the insurers and the Jewish organizations and that was supported by Eizenstat but was later blamed for the delays and foraresolution not satisfactory to many claimants.[54] In a radical departure from the path taken with the banks and German corporations, ICHEIC agreed to work by consensus, to the extent possible. Discussion proceeded slowly, however, and the two sides skirmished. Several states, notably California, passed laws to require the insurers to disclose information about unpaid Holocaust accounts. The companies sought to have those laws invalidated. In its Garamendi decision, in 2003, the U.S. Supreme Court did so, finding California's statute in conflict with the right of the federal government to conduct foreign policy.[55]

ICHEIC began to implement its claims process for policies of Nazi persecutees in February 2000, promising to do justice to account holders without cost to the claimants and agreeing to use relaxed standards of proof for policyholders in well-defined cases. Notably, the process was to be inclusive not only of policies issued by the participating companies but also of all prewar and wartime insurance, including nonparticipating companies and companies no longer in existence—a breathtaking commitment by present-day insurers. Determining valid recipients was not easy. ICHEIC published the names of some 500,000 potential policyholders; 90,000 applied before a deadline of March 2004. Both the process of identifying possible claimants and assessing claims drew criticism. Critics also blamed ICHEIC for its allegedly expensive overhead, its lack of transparency, its occasionally stringent rulings, and its unwillingness to publish more complete prewar and wartime lists of policyholders. Most of all, critics complained that the process was moving at a snail's

52 Lawrence Kill and Linda Gerstel, "Holocaust-Era Insurance Claims: Legislative, Judicial, and Executive Remedies," in Bazyler and Alford, *Holocaust Restitution*, 241.

53 See the official ICHEIC Web site, The International Commission on Holocaust Era Insurance Claims, available at http://www.icheic.org/, last accessed September 24, 2008.

54 See Bazyler, *Holocaust Justice*, 162–66.

55 *American Insurance Association v. Garamendi*, 539 U.S. 396 (2003).

pace.[56] At one point, Eagleburger stormed out of a meeting with representatives of the European companies and resigned from his chairmanship of ICHEIC, charging that the commission was making insufficient progress on the seventy-nine thousand claims it had received to that point. Returning to his post the next day, he continued to struggle with the insurers. In 2001, after two years of battering from both sides, Eagleburger expressed his frustration to a largely Jewish audience: "I have negotiated at one point or another in my life with the North Vietnamese, with the Soviet Union; you name it, I've met with them. I don't think I've found any of them more difficult or more frustrating than have been the companies."[57] For their part, the companies defended the confidentiality and professionalism of their policies, although they insisted on operating from a head office in London, outside the reach of U.S. regulatory authority and litigation subpoena power.

Rejecting the "rough justice" approach of the German corporations on slave and forced labor, ICHEIC sought a much more precise determination about what was owed. As Eagleburger explained in ICHEIC's final report, "there was no instruction manual" for spreading the word, in many languages, to people around the world, and for identifying valid policyholders among tens of thousands of claimants. Adjudicators "were constantly juggling the need for speedy resolution (particularly given the advanced age of the survivors) with the importance, intricacies, and need for fairness and justice of the issues being discussed." But as he freely admitted, the commission "sacrificed time efficiencies for process effectiveness."[58] Clearly, not everyone was satisfied with the balance struck.

But in the end there was restitution, through a process that was unprecedented. In their final accounting, ICHEIC announced awards on insurance policies to more than forty-eight thousand survivors of the Holocaust and their heirs around the world, amounting to over $306 million. Elaborating, ICHEIC noted that among those who received payments totaling nearly $100 million were eight thousand claimants who had not been able to name a specific insurance company; in addition, the commission designated $30 million for East European claimants for cases in which "policies had been written by companies that had been nationalized or liquidated after the war and for which no present day successor could be identified."

56 See Sidney Zabludoff, "ICHEIC: Excellent Concept but Inept Implementation," in Bazyler and Alford, *Holocaust Restitution*, 260–67; Charles E. Boyle, "Holocaust Insurance Claims Panel Faces Recriminations over Delays," *Insurance Journal*, February 11, 2002, available at http://www.insurancejournal.com/magazines/west/2002/02/11/features/21936.htm, last accessed June 6, 2008; and "Holocaust and Insurance: Too Late, Too Slow, Too Expensive," *Economist*, August 2, 2003. But cf. the positive evaluation by Roman Kent in his statement to the U.S. Senate Foreign Relations Subcommittee on International Operations and Organizations, Democracy and Human Rights, Hearing on "Holocaust Era Insurance Restitution after ICHEIC," May 6, 2008, available at http://www.senate.gov/~foreign/testimony/2008/KentTestimony080506p.pdf, last accessed June 30, 2008.

57 Authers and Wolffe, *Victim's Fortune*, 265.

58 Eagleburger and Koken, *Finding Claimants and Paying Them*, 20.

Thirty-one thousand persons also received "humanitarian awards" totaling $31 million, in cases "that contained a high level of anecdotal information regarding insurance but could not be matched against any company records." And finally, ICHEIC contributed $169 million to various humanitarian programs for Holocaust survivors, supporting welfare, health services, and other social programs.[59] Roman Kent, a member of ICHEIC and chairman of the American Gathering of Holocaust Survivors, presented both the positive and the negative. "Survivors had waited too long for insurance companies to address the theft of thousands of policies," he said, in a less than enthusiastic commentary. Still, he added, "the ICHEIC process has, at last, provided some small acknowledgement of this theft and restored what is possible for those survivors and their family members who are still alive."[60]

4. An American Campaign

The story that I have told to this point cannot be properly understood without reference to a critical element of its context—the overheated atmosphere of American high-stakes, class action litigation. Extensively questioned and even detested by some in the United States, mass litigation of this sort, in which lawsuits are brought on behalf of a large group of plaintiffs, was alien, though not unfamiliar, to most of the seasoned business leaders in these contests and deeply unappreciated by European academic and practicing jurists.[61] Put simply, to many Europeans the practice of U.S. civil litigation was "justice run amuck."[62] Begun with consumer-related

---

59 Ibid., 49–50, and Eagleburger's transmittal letter of June 18, 2000, available at http://www.icheic.org/pdf/Chairman%20Eagleburger%20Cover%20Letter.pdf, last accessed June 6, 2007. See also International Commission on Holocaust Era Insurance Claims (ICHEIC), *Lessons Learned: A Report on Best Practices, June 2007*, available at http://www.icheic.org/pdf/ICHEIC%20Best%20Practices%20Paper.pdf, last accessed May 6, 2008.

60 "ICHEIC Announces Successful Completion of Holocaust Era Insurance Claims Process (March 20, 2007)," ICHEIC Final Press Release, available at http://www.icheic.org/pdf/FINAL%20ICHEIC%20PRESS%20RELEASE%203-20-07.pdf, last accessed June 6, 2008.

61 Stuart Eizenstat provides a useful definition appropriate for this context: "Class action suits are specifically recognized in the Federal Rules of Civil Procedure and by most states of the Union. These suits permit a few individuals to bring a case on behalf of hundreds, thousands, or even millions of others who have supposedly suffered similar injuries and who can recover if the suit is successful, even though they may know nothing about the case or even about the potential injury. Class actions are often legal platforms to raise politically sensitive issues. The principal attraction is that large numbers of people may have legitimate claims—often small ones individually—and could never gain redress any other way. The suits are an increasingly effective way to hold companies publicly responsible for mass injuries." Eizenstat, *Imperfect Justice*, 75–76.

62 Charles E. Boyle, "Holocaust Insurance Claims Panel Faces Recriminations over Delays," *Insurance Journal*, February 11, 2002, available at http://www.insurancejournal.com/magazines/west/2002/02/11/features/21936.htm, last accessed June 6, 2008.

litigation and reaching spectacular heights with settlements for injuries caused by tobacco, asbestos, and pollution, this kind of lawsuit has extended widely into other fields, stimulated by the ingenuity, resolve, and combativeness of plaintiffs' counsel. For an introductory guide to this culture I can do no better than to refer to a set of guidelines crafted for a professional journal by one of the most energetic of these legal gladiators, Morris A. Ratner, a very bright young San Francisco lawyer who represented plaintiffs in the Swiss banks and German corporations cases and who worked closely with the veteran Michael Hausfeld, a widely respected lead attorney in the Swiss banks and German corporations cases.[63]

As Ratner freely admits, central to this high-powered system is the arrangement of contingency fees, by which lawyers are paid only when there is a favorable outcome and through an agreed percentage of the settlement that must be approved by the court. Structured in this way, contingency fees mean that attorneys' already robust competitive urges are fueled by economic necessity—and in some cases, it must be said, by the attraction of huge earnings in the event of gigantic settlements. "Lawyers pursuing human rights or individual class action cases on a contingency basis cannot afford to select the wrong cases, or to posture those cases in an unfavorable manner," Ratner candidly indicates.[64] Put more bluntly, aggression is practically built into the system. Up against defendants with generally deep pockets, and sometimes expending millions of dollars both to wage these legal battles and comply with the ground rules for them, plaintiffs' lawyers can often not afford to lose—or to soften the arguments made on behalf of their clients. At the same time, plaintiffs' counsel, often portrayed as pit bulls in the fight, can see themselves as underdogs. "Wielding greater resources," Ratner observes, defendants "are usually capable of purchasing big-firm legal representation, accompanied by the large volume of offensive legal work often intended to delay proceedings, bury plaintiffs' counsel in paper, and scare over-burdened courts into dismissing or limiting victims' claims."

"The case law is riddled with the legal equivalent of train wrecks, where victims' claims have been dismissed on numerous grounds," Ratner notes. "Conversely, there is also a danger in victims' advocates' being too timid, and failing to creatively use the judicial system to obtain justice, even in tough cases." Need one add, selecting defendants does not derive from a careful weighing of historical responsibility. Facing countless legal hurdles, the lawyers must identify defendants over whom the courts will accept jurisdiction and who will ultimately make the investment of legal talent, time, and money worthwhile. "For example," notes Ratner, "in the Nazi-era slave labor litigation, plaintiffs sued only a fraction of the German companies that were involved in the use of slave labor during the Holocaust; plaintiffs sued those

63 Morris A. Ratner, "Factors Impacting the Selection and Positioning of Human Rights Class Actions in United States Courts: A Practical Overview," *New York University Annual Survey of American Law* 58 (2003): 623–50; Authers and Wolffe, *Victim's Fortune*, 39–40.

64 Ratner, "Selection and Positioning of Human Rights Class Actions," 623.

companies that they believed had sufficient contact with the United States to justify an exercise of personal jurisdiction by the court over those defendants."[65]

After describing the formidable legal challenges, Ratner goes on to outline the importance of "government contacts and support" in the resolution of these battles. Cooperation with government enabled the plaintiffs to apply "the maximum pressure," notably in the Swiss banks case by Senator Alfonse D'Amato. "Victims' advocates' relationships with the United States State Department, banking committees in New York, insurance commissioners and other public figures also played prominently in the dynamics that ultimately prompted the settlement of the Nazi-era litigation," he noted.[66] Similarly, "media coverage" was a crucial part of the overall strategy "to complement the political activities and grass roots activism." Lawyers had to be prudent, however, and Ratner recommends against showboating: "counsel should be wary of becoming the target of media attention which risks the inevitable anti-lawyer, anti-legal fees type of coverage that plagued the Holocaust cases."[67]

The operatic contest suggested in Ratner's advice to his colleagues was in fact staged during the Holocaust-era litigation, negotiation, and settlement in the late 1990s. From the Olympian heights of the German philosophical tradition, Hannah Arendt once noted the inadequacy of "juristic concepts" to deal with matters such as genocide and the Holocaust.[68] For participants in the struggles against the Swiss and other banks and corporations, however, the restitution campaign of the 1990s had precious little to do with "juristic concepts." Elan Steinberg of the World Jewish Congress put it brutally. "Why did it work?" he asked. "Because we beat their brains out. It's like Pharaoh. This is punishment."[69] Robert A. Swift, a litigator who acted for the plaintiffs in the Swiss banks case and in later suits suggested more elegantly that the outcome "may owe more to political, diplomatic and media pressure than to the likelihood of a court verdict"—although he insisted that nothing could have

65 Ibid., 626. As Ratner freely admits, "Often, the parties most directly responsible for torture, genocide, mass conversion of assets, and other international law violations are not susceptible to suit in a United States court." Reasonably enough, he notes, "corporations doing business in the United States ... are the easiest entities to bring to justice in United States courts." Ibid., 629. Ratner further notes that the defendants must often be chosen *before* a careful investigation of the facts: "Although the advice to conduct historical research prior to filing seems relatively obvious and mundane, lawyers often file prior to having completed a factual investigation, such that the complaint must be revised and the class must be redefined during the course of the litigation. Although not ideal, this is sometimes unavoidable, either because information is not readily available or because the plaintiffs are aged or infirm and need quick relief. Any research, especially interviews of potential witnesses, must be conducted within applicable ethical constraints." Ibid., 625, n. 5.

66 Ibid., 646–47.

67 Ibid., 648.

68 Hannah Arendt, *Eichmann in Jerusalem: A Report on the Banality of Evil* (New York: Viking, 1965), 292.

69 Authers and Wolffe, *Victim's Fortune*, 382.

happened without "credible, triable and quantifiable claims" being presented.[70] Burt Neuborne, recently referred to as "one of the nation's leading public interest lawyers," allowed that "the litigation was as much about politics as it was about law." Indeed, it was "an untidy mixture of law, politics and raw emotion."[71] Whatever their emphasis, both plaintiffs and defendants would have agreed: it was impossible to ignore the public pressure, the bluster, and the various kinds of collective mobilization utilized to promote final agreement.

How people reacted to this depended in part on their views of lawyers and the American practice of tort law, not to mention the substantive issues of restitution for the Holocaust. In my view, we should at least accept that there were reasonable grounds to feel uncomfortable about the process. Occasionally, when negotiations became especially heated, the word "blackmail" passed the lips of defendants or their representatives. Although such charges are hardly unusual in litigation, this prompted furious objections and insinuations of corporate greed and wrongdoing. What I think one should keep in mind about this part of the restitution campaign is that it was part and parcel of a legal culture that is widely contested, that has both strong defenders and critics, and that marks a particular moment in the American legal tradition.[72]

During the campaign itself, it is important to note, not all the proponents of restitution felt comfortable with the aggressive posture of the litigators. Stuart Eizenstat, who had a ringside seat in the battles of the lawyers, saw the lawsuits as the perhaps unavoidable catalysts for the real process—negotiation among representative groups, facilitated also by diplomatic engagement. "The lawsuits were simply a vehicle for a titanic political struggle, which was messy, sometimes unseemly, and constantly frustrating," was his summation. The lawyers could be outrageous; he decried "their often infantile, ego-driven maneuvers, quarrels, and manipulations, peppered with accusatory words like 'scandalous, double-crossed, poisonous, evil,' and worse"—although he conceded that without them there would have been no settlements.[73] The litigators "hijacked the Swiss bank dispute"; they were "a witches brew of egos and mutual jealousies, greatly complicating my responsibility to keep the Swiss affair from careening out of diplomatic control and … impeding my ability to develop a coherent bargaining unit with which the Swiss could deal."[74] His preference for resolving the disputes, and his own personal expertise, was diplomacy—the

70 Robert A. Swift, "Holocaust Litigation and Human Rights Jurisprudence," in Bazyler and Alford, *Holocaust Restitution*, 53.

71 Burt Neuborne, "Holocaust Reparations Litigation: Lessons for the Slavery Reparations Movement," *New York University Annual Survey of American Law* 58 (2003): 619; Joel Siegel, "Getting His Due," *New York Magazine*, October 2, 2006.

72 See Richard O. Falk, "Armageddon through Aggregation? The Use and Abuse of Class Actions in International Dispute Resolution," *Michigan State University/Detroit College of Law Journal of International Law* 10 (2001): 205–38.

73 Eizenstat, *Imperfect Justice*, 226, 340–42.

74 Ibid., 75.

value of which was, in his estimation, one of the major lessons of the entire Holocaust restitution movement.[75]

The public posture of the plaintiffs' lawyers was of course part of the negotiating process. Referred to by one journalist as "the attack dog of the class action world," Michael Hausfeld, of Cohen, Milstein, Hausfeld and Toll, was known as the "most feared lawyer in Washington, D.C.," according to an article posted on the firm's own Web site; the celebrated Melvyn Weiss, referred to by Forbes as "Mr. Class Action," framed a newspaper article in his office referring to himself as the "Crocodile Lawyer."[76] Paul Volcker, whose pivotal investigation set the framework for the Swiss banks settlement, "despised the class-action lawyers" according to Eizenstat, "seeing them as greedy egomaniacs more interested in burnishing their shingles than serving their long-suffering clients."[77] At the World Jewish Congress, Singer and Steinberg harbored deep suspicions about the lawyers, in one view disliking them for stealing the Jewish organization's show.[78] Seeking mediation, Eizenstat "felt like the manager of an insane asylum; if the inmates had not actually taken it over, they certainly had been let out of their rooms."[79] The most outrageous personality, according to almost everyone, was an energetic personal injury specialist named Edward Fagan who emerged as the advocate for tens of thousands of survivors and other claimants and whose signature strategy was a media appearance alongside Holocaust victims, together with demonstrations, prayer vigils, and a disruptive, attention-grabbing unwillingness to defer to his more experienced colleagues.[80]

As the contests widened, aggression was not limited to the fight between the two sides. By the time the Swiss banks affair moved close to a settlement, according to one well-informed observer, "not only were the two sides not talking to each other—neither were some of the plaintiffs' lawyers."[81] Prior to the final discussions, the claimants' attorneys fought furiously with one another to sign up the most clients and to gain the upper hand in strategy. By the autumn of 1998 these battles were reaching a boiling point. The New York Times headlined one story "Jewish Groups Fight for Spoils of Swiss Case." As the report described, "competing lawyers from the United States barnstormed across Europe soliciting clients, publicly castigating each other and privately maneuvering to oust their adversaries."[82] Two main factions emerged, one headed by Michael Hausfeld and Melvyn Weiss, two lions of the

75 Ibid., 366.

76 Drew Cullen, "IBM Escapes Holocaust Suit," *The Register*, March 30, 2001; Robert Lenzner and Emily Lambert, "Mr. Class Action," *Forbes*, February 16, 2004.

77 Eizenstat, *Imperfect Justice*, 116–18.

78 Ibid., 118–19.

79 Ibid., 153.

80 Ibid., 77; Barry Meier, "An Avenger's Path," *New York Times*, September 8, 2000; "Metro Views: An Endeavor Cloaked in Sanctity," *Jerusalem Post*, February 4, 2008.

81 Orenstein, "Gold Warriors," 64.

82 Barry Meier, "Jewish Groups Fight for Spoils of Swiss Case," *New York Times*, November 29, 1998.

class action world, and the other by Edward Fagan, a loose cannon whose stylistic vulgarity went hand in hand with his inexperience in this scale of class action litigation. "The two teams were spending their time denigrating each other, their ability, parentage, ethnic heritage, you name it," according to Burt Neuborne. European Jewish leaders were often aghast as the class action lawyers came to town: not only were these quarrelsome outsiders signing up local claimants, they claimed to speak for masses of survivors, confronting local and national institutions. Antisemitism, some said, would be the inevitable result.[83]

Congressional hearings were an occasion for politicians to enter the fray. Survivors of the Holocaust made emotional appeals. Meetings of banking and insurance regulators offered platforms for new interventions. Along with the politicians, public officials joined their accusations. New players appeared: Alan Hevesi, the chief financial officer of New York City emerged as an important force, orchestrating regulatory challenges to the Swiss banks. In California, flanked by the state's governor Gray Davis, the state's insurance commissioner Chuck Quackenbush, a prominent Republican, took on the insurance companies: "We come to send a message," he told them. "You can pay now or we guarantee you will pay more later."[84] Campaigns against the banks, corporations, and insurance companies involved petitions, full-page advertisements in newspapers, and threats of punishing sanctions. Pension fund managers threatened the Swiss with a boycott on the scale of the divestment campaign against the apartheid regime in South Africa.[85] Insults were common. According to Eizenstat, the worst came with negotiations over money: These were "like a boxing match, with many rounds but few rules, certainly not those of the Marquis of Queensberry. There were rabbit punches, low blows, and verbal insults on all sides. It took us months to move from the opening round to the final round

83 This seems likely to have been the reason behind Simon Wiesenthal's warning "against too harsh an attitude toward" the Swiss. See David Rohde, "Judge Weighs Fate of Suit Filed by Jews against Swiss," *New York Times*, August 1, 1997, cited in a report from Agence France-Press, July 31, 1997.

84 Bazyler, *Holocaust Justice*, 137.

85 John Authers, "Stories: The Road to Restitution," FT.com, August 15, 2008, available at http://www.ft.com/cms/s/0/bdc94ee-68d0-11dd-ae5-0000779fd18c.html, accessed September 16, 2008. Speaking of sanctions, Bazyler notes that these threats of boycott were not only opposed by the Swiss, who filed diplomatic protests with Washington, but also the Clinton administration: "All during the movement, the federal government urged the state and local governments not to impose sanctions. The most vocal critic of the sanctions was Stuart Eizenstat, Clinton's 'point man' on the Holocaust restitution issues. Eizenstat argued that the sanctions were counterproductive, but time and time again, he was wrong. The sanctions worked and became a much-used tool in the claims against subsequent defendants in the Holocaust restitution movement. Sanctions were either used or threatened against Austrian and French banks, European insurance companies, and German firms. In each instance, they worked magnificently either to invigorate long-ignored World War II claims or to break impasses over stalled negotiations." Bazyler, *Holocaust Justice*, 22.

about money, and each negotiating session featured the pounding of heavyweight prizefighters."[86]

5. Reactions

To the litigators who argued on behalf of the plaintiffs and to those who favored Holocaust restitution, the settlements were a triumph of American jurisprudence and a fitting conclusion of a historic campaign. At amoment of satisfaction in Berlin in July 2000, celebrating the culmination of negotiations with the German government and corporations, Stuart Eizenstat was exceptionally generous to the representatives of the Holocaust survivors, particularly given what we have already seen of his harsh views on the matter: "It was American lawyers, through the lawsuits they brought in U.S. courts, who placed the long-forgotten wrongs by German companies during the Nazi era on the international agenda. It was their research and their work which highlighted these old injustices and forced us to confront them. Without question, we would not be here without them." And he added with regard to their remuneration—the object of no little contention: "The legal fees they will receive are far less than would normally be received for such a large settlement and represent only about one percent of the total [settlement]. This is eminently reasonable given their contribution."[87] Judge Korman's similarly generous assessment of American counsel, particularly the more junior among them, prompted a historical reflection when he chastised senior Swiss judges for being insufficiently generous to survivor claimants: "It's because of young Americans that every mess in Europe was cleaned up in this century," he lectured his Swiss counterparts.[88]

"The real hero of this story is the American justice system," wrote Michael Bazyler. "The unique features of the American system of justice are precisely those factors that made the United States the only forum in the world where Holocaust claims could be heard today."[89] Melvyn Weiss, later to fall afoul of the justice system himself as we shall see, also believed that the outcome was a tribute to American law. "The litigation against Swiss banks, German industry, and others reinforces my strong belief in the precious role of the American legal system as a significant cornerstone of modern society," he wrote. The settlements demonstrated "the vital role of America's legal system in protecting and, indeed, safeguarding human rights and the rule of law." He even added a warning to those who wanted to trim the sails of litigators like himself: "Any attempt to constrict access to the American court system, or otherwise limit the efficacy of the class action device should be resisted as an

86 Eizenstat, *Imperfect Justice*, 140.

87 "Remarks of Stuart E. Eizenstat, Deputy Secretary of the Treasury, Special Representative of the President and Secretary of State for Holocaust Issues, 12th and Concluding Plenary on the German Foundation, Berlin, Germany, July 17, 2000," available at http://germany.usembassy.gov/germany/img/assets/8497/eizenstat071700.pdf, last accessed May 12, 2008. On the subject of fees, see chapter 5.

88 Authers and Wolffe, *Victim's Fortune*, 364.

89 Bazyler, *Holocaust Justice*, xii–xiii, emphasis in original.

attack on a cornerstone of American greatness."[90] American greatness was similarly on the mind of Burt Neuborne as he contemplated the link between the outcome of the Holocaust-era litigation and "the astonishing success of our economic and political models":

Measured by prosperity, freedom, innovation, tolerance and the simultaneous achievement of social mobility and political stability, the American experiment is a remarkable success. It is so successful that no major economic player on the world stage can hope to succeed without participating vigorously in our market and reaping the benefit of our economic prosperity. But that market, and the resulting prosperity, did not spring up by accident. Our success flows from a social and political commitment to fairness and the values of decency that find their expression in the American respect for the rule of law—a virtually unique legal system that provides a genuinely level playing field for a poor Holocaust survivor seeking to confront a corporate giant. In short, I believe that we are prosperous in large part because we have enjoyed—and dispensed—the blessings of "Equal Justice under Law" and have built a legal system that provides the weak with a fair chance of victory, at least sometimes.

To be sure, Neuborne conceded, it would have been better to have litigated these cases in Europe, where the crimes occurred. However, "the legal systems of Switzerland and Germany are so stacked in favor of defendants and so hostile to the claims set forth in the Holocaust cases that it would have been suicidal to litigate in those forums." Those countries simply lacked the legal machinery by which to resolve such claims. In both Germany and Switzerland, "class actions are perceived as a symptom of American madness. The mindset of the judiciary is timid and rigidly locked into the status quo. In short, the European courtroom is not currently a level playing field; it is a fortress for the powerful. Until European justice evolves into a level playing field, lawyers have no choice but to resort to an American courtroom as the only game in town."[91]

In the debate on the role of the United States in the resolution of these disputes, no one denies the special receptivity of American courts and the American public environment for Holocaust-related claims. However, both American critics and many Europeans have challenged the moral and legal claims that I have noted here. In fairness, it should be stressed that such criticisms make sense when applied to class actions in general, rather than to anything particular to the Holocaust-related suits. Europeans often see the United States as a "litigation-driven society," of which multiparty lawsuits are a primary expression. "A prevailing view amongst European experts," according to one analyst, "is that the U.S. style class action can simply be used to leverage large sums of money from a corporation to claimant attorneys through contingency fees 'earned' in return for settling a large number of claims

---

90 Melvyn I. Weiss, "A Litigator's Postscript to the Swiss Banks and Holocaust Litigation Settlements: How Justice Was Served," in Bazyler and Alford, *Holocaust Restitution*, 111–12.

91 Burt Neuborne, "Preliminary Reflections on Aspects of Holocaust-Era Litigation in American Courts," *Washington University Law Quarterly* 80 (2002): 831–32.

sometimes of speculative value."[92] Particularly irksome in the view of these commentators is that none of the Holocaust restitution contests have ultimately been resolved on the merits of the case. In the end, the defendants simply calculated that it was cheaper to settle than to continue. Owen Pell, a counsel for the defendants, noted that his clients simply had drawn the obvious conclusion: "Companies have learned you don't judge a lawsuit by its merits… . You judge it by the potential public relations damage."[93] To critics, this result is "one of the last steps along this path toward the lawsuit as a business deal."[94]

Companies and their lawyers, one should add, were not only discomfited by the mobilization outside the courts; they were not too happy with what happened inside them as well. It is not hard to see, just beneath the surface, the unease of those who come from the civil law jurisdictions when plunged into the heated arena of adversarial justice. On occasion, lawyers for the plaintiffs ventured forth with barely a legal leg to stand on: in some cases this was fully in keeping with an Anglo-American "tradition of tort suits that go against the current of law and that welcome 'justice as struggle'"; but for the Europeans, as University of Pittsburgh legal academic Vivian Curran notes, "courts which hear tort actions are neither the best equipped nor the best accepted for adjudicating issues of public and historical importance."[95] As well, the Europeans could be extremely uneasy with American lawyers pressing for "rough justice"—broad agreement on liability, without laboring over individual cases. In the Swiss and French banks case, for example, the bankers' instincts were to resolve each and every claim, however long it took, to as precise a degree as possible. The Americans preferred a negotiated settlement resolved around the bargaining table. "It didn't sound like justice," was the reaction of a member of the French delegation upon hearing the American plan.[96] "The class action suit is unknown here in Germany," reported historian Gerald Feldman as he tried to understand the reactions of the Allianz, the insurance company that engaged him to assist their case, "and the adversarial system employed in American civil law makes it possible for lawyers to make broad charges, insinuate all kinds of misbehavior, and present very shallow and even implausible arguments. Their purpose is [to] open up every conceivable area to discovery and force the opponent to disgorge information that

92 Christopher Hodges, "Multi-Party Actions: A European Approach," *Duke Journal of Comparative and International Law* 11 (2001): 343.

93 Allen C. Guelzo, "Reparations Then and Now," *First Things*, June/July 2002, available at http://www.firstthings.com/article.php3?id_article=2038, last accessed May 13, 2008.

94 Samuel P. Baumgartner, "Human Rights and Civil Litigation in United States Courts: The Holocaust-Era Cases," *University of Washington Law Quarterly* 80 (2002): 842.

95 Vivian Grosswald Curran, "Globalization, Legal Transnationalization and Crimes against Humanity: The Lipietz Case," Legal Studies Research Paper Series, Working Paper No. Year-Number 2008-03, February 2008, 4–5, available at http://papers.ssrn.com/s013/papers.cfm?abstract_id=1087425, last accessed May 13, 2008.

96 Authers and Wolffe, *Victim's Fortune*, 154. On "rough justice," see also Eizenstat, *Imperfect Justice*, 137–38.

will improve the plaintiff 's case."[97] And behind that, the major goal was, as always, to settle, and to do so on the best possible terms for the claimants.

The problem here, from the perspective of those unaccustomed to or uncomfortable with resolution through the rough-and-tumble of the American system, is that such outcomes arguably undermine the rule of law. In the words of Samuel Baumgartner, an academic with both Swiss and American legal experience, the result is "a litigation system in which power (including judicial power), money (who has it and who does not), and tactics seem to be more important in the outcome of litigation than a finding of who is right and who is wrong."[98] What for Bazyler, Neuborne, Weiss, and others is the admirable reach of the American courts in calling others to account as well as a leveling of the judicial playing field is for many Europeans an unwarranted mobilization of political and economic power, the imposition of a lex americana or an exercise of judicial imperialism.[99] Defendants and their publics resent American sponsorship of a "courthouse for the world," practicing what has been termed "the blackmail of oppressive aggregation."[100] "Imagine how we would feel," asks Joseph G. Finnerty, a lawyer for the defendants in a class action suit, "if courts in another part of the world decided they had jurisdiction over alleged actions by America, in America, against other Americans. We would be affronted, and rightly so."[101]

Finally, in response to American claims about bringing the Europeans to a reluctant acknowledgment of their wartime pasts, critics have pointed to the allegedly lackluster results of the United States' ownefforts to organize restitution for its own shortcomings during the Holocaust—not to mention other cases of extreme violence in the American past. "Having held other countries up to the harsh light of history,"

---

97 Gerald D. Feldman, "The Business History of the 'Third Reich' and the Responsibilities of the Historian: Gold, Insurance, 'Aryanization,' and Forced Labor," an Occasional Paper of the Center for German and European Studies at the University of California, Berkeley (January 1999): n.p., republished in a revised version in Norbert Frei, Dirk van Laak, Michael Stolleis, eds., *Geschichte vor Gericht. Historiker, Richter und die Suche nach Gerechtigkeit* (Munich: Beck, 2000),103–29.

98 Samuel P. Baumgartner, "Class Actions and Group Litigation in Switzerland," *Northwestern Journal of International & Business Law* 27 (2007): 316.

99 Baumgartner, "Human Rights and Civil Litigation in United States Courts," 845. For the general context of this perspective, with particular reference to Switzerland, see Wolfgang Wiegand, "The Reception of American Law in Europe," *American Journal of Comparative Law* 39 (1991): 229–48. See also Siobhan Morrissey, "Vive les class actions: Europe Is Showing More Interest in Legal Mechanisms That Have Come under Fire in the United States," *ABA Journal*, September 15, 2005, available at http://abajournal.com/magazine/vive_les_class_actions/, last accessed July 20, 2008.

100 Falk, "Armageddon through Aggregation," 228.

101 Adam Liptak, "Class-Action Firms Extend Reach to Global Rights Cases," *New York Times*, June 3, 2007. See also idem, "Foreign Courts Wary of U.S. Punitive Damages," *New York Times*, March 26, 2008; and John Y. Gotanda, "Charting Developments concerning Punitive Damages: Is the Tide Changing?" *Columbia Journal of Transnational Law* 45 (2007): 507–28.

observes Stuart Eizenstat, "we have a special responsibility to hold ourselves to the highest standard."[102] But this has not always been realized. Notably, a proposal to establish a fund for needy Holocaust survivors to be supported by American corporations that had been sued or threatened with litigation failed to attract support or indeed any private donors.[103] Also, the Presidential Advisory Commission on Holocaust Assets (PCHA), the Clinton administration effort to assess United States dealings in Holocaust-era assets, ended in what was widely seen as disappointment. Between 1998 and 2001 a panel of experts chaired by Edgar Bronfman labored away to produce a report that, in the views of many at least, failed to get to the bottom of American responsibilities and to promote American-sponsored restitution.[104] In Bazyler's judgment, PCHA's "track record has been poor."[105] According to an account in the New York Times, "objections to the panel's work were so strong that some staff members said they contemplated writing a minority report." "We didn't do as good a job as we could have," Bronfman admitted, referring particularly to American involvement in looted art. Lack of time, too narrow a mandate, and insufficient documentary evidence were cited as reasons for the failure to meet expectations. According to Gerald Feldman, the commission "had some good scholarship but didn't do anything with it."[106]

Rosner v. United States was a high-profile lawsuit over alleged American wrongdoing concerning property stolen from Holocaust victims.[107] At issue was the famous Hungarian Gold Train, a Hungarian fascist transport of Jewish valuables seized before Hungarian Jewish deportations and allegedly pocketed by some American soldiers at the end of the war.[108] Finally settled in September 2005, the issue of the Gold Train, which had been the object of investigations by PCHA, much publicity, and a book by the Israeli historian Ronald Zweig, was finally put to rest with a settlement mediated by the Justice Department. After protracted negotiations the

102 Stuart E. Eizenstat, "The Unfinished Business of the Unfinished Business of World War II," in Bazyler and Alford, *Holocaust Restitution*, 311.

103 Bazyler and Fitzgerald, "Trading with the Enemy," 742–48.

104 See "Plunder and Restitution: Findings and Recommendations of the Presidential Advisory Commission on Holocaust Assets in the United States and Staff Report," December 2000, available at http://www.pcha.gov/PlunderRestitution.html/html/Home_Contents.html, last accessed May 12, 2008.

105 Bazyler and Fitzgerald, "Trading with the Enemy," 749. However, see the replies to his critics by Kenneth Klothen, former executive director of PCHA, in ibid., 797–810.

106 Ralph Blumenthal, "Panel on Nazi Art Theft Fell Short, Experts Say," *New York Times*, March 3, 2003.

107 *Rosner et al. v. United States*, Case No. 01-1859-CIV-SEITZ (S.D.Fla).

108 Ronald W. Zweig, *The Gold Train: The Destruction of the Jews and the Second World War's Most Terrible Robbery* (New York: Allen Lane, 2002). See the official Web site, "The Hungarian Gold Train Settlement, U.S. District Judge Patricia Seitz," available at http://www.hungariangoldtrain.org/index_en.asp, last accessed September 4, 2008. See also Gábor Kádár, *Self-financing Genocide: The Gold Train, the Becher Case and the Wealth of Hungarian Jews* (Budapest: Central European University Press, 2004).

Americans agreed to the payment of some $4.5 million a year for five years to some sixty thousand needy Hungarian Holocaust survivors around the world—and this without admitting the theft or even that any law had been broken. Had the United States set an example to others for the resolution of such disputes? Some thought not.[109] Attempting to penetrate the fog of rhetoric associated with the Gold Train—the vastly inflated mythology of "Jewish gold," claiming billions of dollars worth of disappeared assets, the hyperbolic accusations of theft and greed, and the dark allegations of reparations withheld—Zweig struggled admirably to bring the affair down to earth. A Hollywood film appeared on the Gold Train not long after the war. In Zweig's view, "When the story of the Hungarian Gold Train resurfaced in the 1990s it was strongly influenced by these images of drama and excitement skillfully created on film. In the popular reconstruction of the past, Hollywood is more important than history."[110] So thought some about the class action lawsuits.

109 See "Justice for 'Gold Train' Victims," *New York Times*, August 9, 2004; "The Hungarian Gold Train Settlement. U.S. District Judge Patricia Seitz," available at http://www.hungariangoldtrain.org/index_en.asp, last accessed September 4, 2008. Eizenstat's judgment is not complimentary: "Instead of acting as we had urged other governments and their companies to act, instead of seeking a neutral examination of the facts found by our presidential commission, the Justice Department moved to dismiss the case on the basis of the statute of limitations, the sovereign immunity of the United States, and the inappropriateness of the federal court system as a proper forum. These were the kinds of defenses made by the foreign governments with whom I dealt." Eizenstat, "Unfinished Business of World War II," 312.

110 Zweig, *Gold Train*, 4.

Denial

11. On the Outlawing of Genocide Denial *

Johannes Houwink ten Cate

1. Introduction

This article, originally a lecture on the topic for the CEJI ("A Jewish Contribution to an Inclusive Europe"), constitutes a contribution to the discussion on the European Union (EU) Framework Decision on combating racism and xenophobia, which was published on April 20. According to this decision, "Public [dis]approval, denial or gross trivialization of genocide, crimes against humanity and war crimes will be criminalized if the crime is directed against a group of persons because of their race, colour, religion, descent, or national or ethnic origin." It is the combination of genocide denial and other forms of denial with the racist or xenophobic agitation that is criminalized, not the denial of genocide in itself.

The discussion of this topic will not subside for the time being, because the European Parliament has to be consulted. The Council will subsequently assess the observations of the Parliament before the Framework Decision is formally adopted. The provisions of this Framework Decision do not apply directly; rather, member states must implement them into their national law.[1]

Since 1989 I have worked as a historian of the Holocaust, and since 2002 I have had a chair at the University of Amsterdam in the field of Holocaust and genocide studies. This is a chair in the Faculty of the Humanities. It is not in the Faculty of Law. I do hope, however, that I am aware of some of the legal issues concerning genocide and genocide denial, but please do not expect too much of me in that field.

* In honor of my friend, Hans Warendorf (b. 1934), with whom I have discussed most of the topics outlined in this text.

1 "News Alert of the German Presidency," *Common Criminal Provisions against Racism and Xenophobia*, April 20, 2007; "Maximumstraf in EU voor aanzetten tot haat of geweld," ("Maximum punishment in EU for incitement to hate or violence") *De Volkskrant*, April 20, 2007.

H.G. van der Wilt, J. Vervliet et al., *(eds.)* The Genocide Convention: The Legacy of 60 Years.
 ISBN 978 9004 15328 8. pp. 145-158.

As you know, history does not deal with the past in its entirety. Historians are not antiquarians.[2] We do not collect facts like a botanist would collect plants or seeds. We select historical phenomena for our research because we think that they are interesting to ourselves and to others as well.

The pursuit of history, to quote Johan Huizinga, by far the best Dutch historian of the twentieth century, is the mental form in which a society accounts for its past.[3] The selection process of the historian thus takes places in a given social environment.

To drive this point home: history is like a wishing well. The sounds we hear from the well are our own sounds. Because society expects from us, the historians, that we deal in hard facts, and that we present our findings as such. But, in reality, there are but very few facts that are not subject to interpretation in one way or another.

2. What Constitutes Genocide?

So, to give you one last practical example: some historians have labeled the twentieth century the "century of genocide," and on good grounds, for many millions have died as a consequence of genocide. But I would not argue with a colleague from another field, who maintains that the twentieth century was, rather, the century of free elections, of the liberation of women, of the expansion of higher education, or of the EU for that matter. All these phenomena were typical of the twentieth century as well.

It has now become commonplace to view genocide as the general phenomenon and the Holocaust as one particular genocide, amongst others.

I do have to stress, however, that this view does not have a long tradition. A quarter of a century ago the historical position that was taken by most of my colleagues was that the Holocaust was unique. Nothing could compare with the Holocaust, the premeditated and highly industrialized murder of the Jews in Europe. During the 1980s German historians and philosophers such as Jürgen Habermas engaged in a fierce debate, the so-called Historikerstreit, which was all about this question: whether the Holocaust was unique. This debate ended in a clear victory for those historians and philosophers who considered that the Holocaust was unique.[4]

How much has changed? Now, no more than twenty years later, the number of scholars who maintain that the Holocaust is unique is very small indeed.[5] They are fighting a lost battle, and they know it. A more frequently held view is that the

---

2 M. Bloch, *Apologie pour l'Histoire ou Metier d'historien* (Paris, 2004), 63. I thank my colleague, Dr. Joel S. Fishman (Jerusalem), for this footnote.

3 In 1926 Huizinga wrote that "geschiedenis de geestelijke vorm is waarin een cultuur zich rekenschap geeft van haar verleden" ("history is the mental form in which a society accounts for its past")

4 The best single book on this topic is Charles S. Maier, *The Unmasterable Past: History, Holocaust, and German Nationalism* (Cambridge: Mass., 1988).

5 For an exceptional standpoint, see: S.T. Katz, *The Holocaust in Historical Context: The Holocaust and Mass Death before the Modern Age* (New York, 1994).

Holocaust, while not unique, is "singular" (Christian Meier)[6] or "unprecedented" (Yehuda Bauer).[7]

This last word, "unprecedented," was originally coined by Raul Hilberg for the death camps of Treblinka, Belzec and Sobibor, because the Nazi combination of gas with concentration camps was without precedent. "Never before in history had people been killed on an assembly-line basis."[8] Recent developments have changed this historical perspective as well, and now very many of my colleagues would agree with the German scholar Christian Meier that it is not the Holocaust that is unique. What is unique is the intensity with which we still remember the Holocaust.[9]

History is the history of bloodshed, and history is traditionally written by the victorious powers, not by the vanquished. Entire peoples and entire civilizations have vanished from the face of the earth, and only the names of the victorious powers (Persians, Greeks, Romans, Portuguese, Spaniards, Dutchmen etc) come to our minds. Those who have lost, those who were wiped out, are very frequently forgotten. As a policy, genocidal policies can be highly effective.

Not many youngsters who grow up in Adana, in Turkey, know that their city was to a large extent built by Greeks. The Kurdified third-generation Bulgarians who now populate Diyarbekir, in Eastern Turkey, live in houses built by Armenian Christians, but they are unaware of this. During the Cold War, the memory of the Holocaust was successfully repressed in the Eastern Bloc, to give you another example. Bosnian schoolchildren of Serbian descent are not taught that Srebrenica was a genocide, but rather that there was a civil war, and that the Muslim population of Srebrenica is to be blamed for a defeat of its own making.

One of the reasons why the vanquished are forgotten is because survivors usually flee from the regions of their destruction, if they can. In some cases there are no survivors. The Incas and Aztecs perished as a result of the flu and the common cold, which their Spanish masters infected them with while telling their contemporaries that these peoples, who sacrificed their children to their Gods, were not human anyway.

If there are survivors, they stay clear of the sites of their destruction. The majority of Polish survivors left Poland after 1946. Vienna is a provincial town, since the Jews were thrown out in 1938. The Jews, the highly assimilated German Jews that is, did not return to Germany after the Holocaust. The Armenians have not returned to Turkey. The widows of Srebrenica remain in Tuzla.

Survivors of genocide and ethnic cleansing leave—not to return.[10] They adapt to their new surroundings. They assimilate and then they vanish. Only if they have no other option, if their poverty forces them to, do survivors live together with the ex-

---

6 C Meier, *Vierzig Jahre nach Auschwitz. Deutsche Geschichtserinnerung heute* (München, 2. Auflage, 1990), 47-51.

7 Y. Bauer, *Rethinking the Holocaust,* (New Haven/London, 2001).

8 R. Hilberg, *The Destruction of the European Jews, Vol. III* (New York/London, 1985), 863.

9 Katz, *Holocaust in Historical Context,* see n. 6.

10 N. Naimark, *Fires of Hatred: Ethnic Cleansing in Twentieth-century Europe* (Cambridge: Mass., 2001), 184.

ecutioners of their families, as was the case in Rwanda and Cambodia, for instance. In some exceptional cases, survivors of genocide manage to catch the public eye. If they promote themselves as spokespersons for a lost culture, they are usually more effective than in their role as genocide victims.

The Holocaust is unique because it still figures so prominently in the European collective memory of the twentieth century. Perhaps this is an understatement. Perhaps Europe has but very few collective memories. European history is the history of the European wars. One of the very few memories that unite Europeans is the memory of National Socialism, the Third Reich of Adolf Hitler, and the killing of the Jews. This memory has remained, because post-war generations made a conscious effort to remember it. I think that the German expression Erinnerungsarbeit, the labor of remembrance, is apt. The need to remember the Holocaust, in Eastern as well as in Western Europe, is enshrined in the Stockholm Declaration (2000) and in a new international organization, The Task Force for Holocaust Education, Remembrance and Research, which now counts twenty-four member states. In my view, this example proves that states do take sides in historical debates.[11] Holocaust education is an obligatory part of the high school curriculum in a many European states, and in the most densely populated states of the United States (US) as well.

Now, in my modest opinion, civilizations are not unlike school children. They remember the events which are of some use to them. In my view nobody phrased the importance of the unprecedented Holocaust better than Sir Isaiah Berlin. According to Berlin, in the post-Holocaust era awareness of the necessity of a moral law is no longer sustained by belief in reason, but by the memory of horror. To quote the biographer of Berlin, Michael Ignatieff, "the Holocaust demonstrates both the prudential necessity of human rights and their ultimate fragility."[12]

I have just mentioned Rwanda and Srebrenica. I think that these—legally acknowledged—genocides have dealt a devastating blow to the belief that the Holocaust was unique. Perhaps it is useful to let me explain why the impact of Rwanda, and up to a point Srebrenica as well, has been so huge.

These events occurred in a highly optimistic period of European and world history, after the fall of the Wall. The fall of the Iron Curtain opened huge opportunities for the creation of a new world order, in very much the same way that the defeat of Hitler's Germany and of Imperial Japan in 1945 created such an opportunity. The aftermath of the Second World War resulted in the creation of the United Nations (UN), the Universal Declaration of Human Rights, the Genocide Convention and the International Military Tribunal of Nuremberg. The aftermath of the Cold War resulted in the international tribunals and in UN peacekeeping missions at the beginning of the 1990s, which were essentially arrogant and pedantic. These peacekeeping missions ended in total failure in Rwanda in 1994 and in Srebrenica in 1995.[13]

---

11 For more information see the website of the Task Force (www.holocausttaskforce.org).

12 M. Ignatieff, *Human Rights as Politics and Idolatry* (Princeton/Oxford, 2001), 81.

13 M. Ignatieff, *The Warrior's Honor: Ethnic War and the Modern Conscience* (London, 1998), 89-105.

After Rwanda it was difficult to maintain that the Holocaust was unique. In fact, during the last decade the number of historical massive human rights abuses and mass killings has increased enormously, because politicians, parliaments, historians, and other scholars have decided to change their verdicts, as it were. Awareness of the Armenian genocide[14] has increased, thanks to American and French politicians and European institutions. This genocide was recognized by the US House of Representatives on September 12, 1984, by the European Parliament on June 18, 1987, and by the Council of Europe on April 24, 1998. The French Parliament passed a law of recognition on January 29, 2001 and a law on denial of the Armenian genocide on October 12, 2006.

The German Cabinet Minister for Development, Madame H. Wieczorek-Zeul, acknowledged that the killing of the Hereros in Namibia constituted a genocide in August 2004, one century after the fact. The US Secretary of State, Colin Powell, said in the US Senate that the killings in Darfur constituted a genocide on September 9, 2004. In the parliament of Ukraine, the former allies of Mr. Yuschenko recently passed a law concerning the manmade famine by Stalin in Ukraine in the 1930s, labeling the "Holodomor" a genocide on November 28, 2006 to be precise, in a move that angered Russia. The Polish Parliament agreed with this point of view some weeks later.[15]

Sometimes politicians head the genocide trail. In other cases legal experts do, and sometimes, not always, they follow the politicians. The International Criminal Tribunal for Rwanda (ICTR) has ruled that Rwanda was a genocide, the International Criminal Tribunal for the Former Yugoslavia (ICTY) has considered Srebrenica a genocide,[16] and so did the International Court of Justice (ICJ), very recently.[17] Undoubtedly, the Cambodia Extraordinary Chambers will consider the killings of Vietnamese, Buddhist Monks, and the Cham by the Khmer Rouge as cases of genocide.[18]

14 The most important recent book on the Armenian genocide is: T. Akcam, *A Shameful Act: The Armenian Genocide and the Question of Turkish Responsibility* (New York, 2006).

15 Because all of this can easily be found on the internet, I have refrained from writing footnotes. Furthermore, the political dimensions of these decisions and laws can be best evaluated by reading them on the internet.

16 See the websites of the ICTR and the ICTY (www.icty.org; www.unictr.org; www.icj-cji.org). One of the best contributions on the topic is: M. Mennecke and E. Markusen, "The International Criminal Tribunal for the Former Yugoslavia and the Crime of Genocide," in *Genocide: Cases, Comparisons and Contemporary Debates*, ed. S. L. B. Jensen (Copenhagen, 2003), 293-359.

17 Case Concerning the Application of the Convention on the Prevention and the Punishment of the Crime of Genocide [Bosnia vs. Serbia], International Court of Justice, February 26, 2007, para. 297.

18 See: B. Kiernan, *The Pol Pot Regime. Race, Power and Genocide in Cambodia under the Khmer Rouge, 1975-1979* (New Haven/London, 2002, 2nd Edition), 456-465.

And in other cases, those of Bangladesh (1971), East Timor (1975-1979), or the famine under Chairman Mao, historians and/or social scientists plea for the verdict of genocide.[19] I have colleagues who refer to slavery in America as the 'Black Holocaust'. In Australia, the Aborigines now refer to themselves as Kooris and believe that they are the victims of genocide.[20] German right-wingers sometimes label the ferocious attack on Dresden, which took place in February 1945, as a genocide. This label has also been applied when "referring to racial integration, methadone maintenance programs, certain features of the medical treatment of Irish Catholics, and the closing of synagogues in the Soviet Union."[21]

In my view we have now reached a point in the spread of the concept of genocide, and in the political use and misuse of that concept, where we have to make an effort to make some distinctions. The word genocide was invented by a Polish-Jewish legal expert by the name of Raphael Lemkin. It is a combination of two words: the Greek word genos (in Dutch and German: volk or Volk) and the Latin word cidere (which means "to kill").[22] The criminality of genocide is laid down in the UN Genocide Convention of 1948 (which was implemented by the Dutch government in 1964). This treaty outlaws genocide, however, it was primarily drafted as an instrument to punish perpetrators of genocide.

I will now quote from the Convention of 1948, which is verbally repeated in the other core legal texts, such as the Rome Statute of the International Criminal Court and the rules on grave breaches of international humanitarian law, the International Crimes Act, which became law in the Dutch state on June 19, 2003:

> Anyone who intentionally commits any of the following acts with the intent to destroy, in whole or in part, a national, ethnic, racial or religious group: killing members of the group, causing serious bodily or mental harm to members of the group; deliberately inflicting on the group conditions calculated to bring about its physical destruction in whole or in part; imposing measures intended to prevent births within the group; forcibly transferring children of the group to another group is guilty of genocide and liable to life imprisonment [or to a prison term not exceeding twenty years].[23]

Genocide, in the view of the ICJ, is all about genocidal intent to destroy the members of a group—a national, ethnic, racial, or religious group, as such—in whole or in part, because of the positive characteristics of that group, the intent being the main thing (and not the result). Naturally, "great care must be taken in finding in the facts a sufficiently clear manifestation of that intent."

---

19 See the contested Wikipedia-article: "Genocide" http://en.wikipedia.org/wiki/Genocide.

20 A. Grosser, *Verbrechen und Erinnerung* (München, 1993), 55-65.

21 Mennecke and Markusen, "The ICTY," 296.

22 S. Power, *A Problem from Hell: America and the Age of Genocide* (London, 2003), 17-70.

23 Rules on grave breaches of international humanitarian law (International Crimes Act). See the website of the Dutch Ministry of Foreign Affairs (www.minbuza.nl).

If a political group is destroyed (say the Kulaks, the richer farmers in Stalin's Russia), this is not genocide. As the ICJ recently pointed out, negative characteristics (i.e. non-Serbs or non-Allies for that matter, in the case of Dresden) are not sufficient. Thus, the attack on Dresden in this view was a war crime, during an inhumane war fought by the Allies to topple a genocidal regime.[24] The victims have a common positive identity. If they do not, the crime committed against them does not constitute genocide.

This genocidal intent (dolus specialis) has to be specific and direct, as both the ICJ and the ICTY have ruled. This rules out ethnic cleansing (the intent of which is removal, not destruction)[25] and manmade famines, because these famines lack directness. The purpose of slavery is exploitation, not destruction. Slavery, in fact, is all about keeping people alive. The killing of the Hereros was, in my view, a war crime as well, in the context of a colonial war.

On the basis of these legal criteria, the number of genocides that have been recognized as such is limited. I hope that I can make this statement of fact, without being guilty of genocide denial in numerous other cases. Casting doubt upon claims of genocide in itself, in my mind, is not criminal. I do it all the time.

In some cases, casting doubt can produce something good. In 1977, before he had denied the Holocaust, the British historian David Irving went on American television, live. In that broadcast he provocatively promised to pay anyone US$10,000 who could show him a document signed by Hitler, in which Hitler ordered the destruction of the Jews. This led to a highly valuable scientific debate, which lasted more than ten years, on decision making processes in the context of the Holocaust.[26] I will not bore you with the outcome, but please do believe me when I state that scholars need debates, and that provocations can be useful.

I think, however, that legal verdicts are of the essence in determining what constitutes genocide. The Prosecutors of the ICTR and the ICTY have proven genocides in Rwanda and Srebrenica. The ICJ has found that Srebrenica was a genocide. A local Swiss Court in Lausanne has found a Turkish politician guilty of denial of the Armenian Genocide.[27] So this short list consists of the Holocaust, Rwanda, Srebrenica, and, perhaps, if we take the local Swiss Court seriously, the Armenian Genocide. I do think that the quality of the judges in international courts is impressive, if we com-

24 F. Taylor, *Dresden: Tuesday, February 13, 1945* (London, 2004). In my view, the counterargument that all wars are inhumane is not convincing. Some types of warfare are more inhumane than others. There are just wars. For this last view, see M. Walzer, *Just and Unjust Wars: A Moral Argument with Historical Illustrations* (New York, 1977, 3rd edition).

25 International Court of Justice, *Case Concerning the Application*, paras. s187-188, 189, 190 and 193. Some other legal experts, however, see this as a *dolus generalis.*

26 Two excellent contributions are: P. Longerich, *Politik der Vernichtung: eine Gesamtdarstellung der Nationalsozialistischen Judenverfolgung* (München/Zürich, 1998) and C.R. Browning, *Nazi Policy, Jewish Workers, German Killers* (Cambridge, 2000), 26-57.

27 See http://www.swissinfo.ch/eng/Home/Archive/Cabinet_rebukes_justice_minister.html?cid=5509272 accessed March 10, 2007 and Article 261bis of the Swiss penal code.

pare these international courts to national courts. The procedures of international courts tend to be the most transparent of legal procedures.

I think that this process of judicial discussions has had an enormous influence. Perhaps EU proposals to outlaw genocide denial could have a similar and equally beneficial influence.

I am certainly not a propagandist of international criminal law per se, in all aspects that is. I am aware—along with the legal expert Lawrence Douglas—of some of the drawbacks, in particular in so far as they concern the concept of national sovereignty (the state usually being the prosecutor of crimes, not the defendant, as was the case with Hitler's Third Reich in Nuremberg up to a point). And I seriously doubt whether the rights of the defendant are still sufficiently protected; whether tribunals do not go too far, especially in their acceptance of a wide range of types of evidence. And perhaps prosecutors are pushing things too far if they use a concept like "joint criminal enterprise" (which enables judges to convict a defendant for crimes he has not committed in person).[28]

All of that being said, I think that recent experiences with these tribunals have been positive, even if some political and other leaders consider them too costly and too time consuming. But these considerations are also practical in nature.[29] I think one of the most important advantages of the tribunals is their pedagogical use, as the case against Adolf Eichmann in Jerusalem has dramatically shown. These court cases can do what nobody else can: they can bring the crime and the victims together in the dramatic setting of a court. In creating this directness they can create media explosions. The ICTY case against Slobodan Milosevic has very much proven that these cases are high risk enterprises, for the very same reasons. Eichmann, in comparison, was a very simple defendant to deal with.[30] He did not put up much of a fight. In my view it is highly unlikely that the ICTY would have considered Milosevic, had he lived, guilty of the genocidal event in Srebrenica. And this would have been a terrible defeat for Mrs. Carla del Ponte and a huge victory for Mr. Milosevic.

I do not think that court cases against the perpetrators of genocide are useful in a deterrent sense. Perpetrators of genocide kill for ideological reasons. They believe in all sincerity that they give orders to kill the internal enemies of their state. They truly think that they are acting in self-defense, that killing the enemy inside is not a breach of the law, but rather that killing this enemy is a moral imperative.[31]

---

28 This is a direct echo of remarks made by Lawrence Douglas during the Yad Vashem International Conference, December 19-21, 2006, *Justice and the Holocaust: Post World War II Trials, Representations, Awareness and Memory.*

29 Staunch defenders of truth and reconciliation commissions, such as ICTJ (International Centre for Transitional Justice) founder Alex Boraine, are keen on making this point. For an example, see: N. Adler ed., *Genocide and Accountability. Three Public Lectures by Simone Veil, Geoffrey Nice and Alex Boraine* (Amsterdam, 2004).

30 During their panel session at the Yad Vashem International Conference (see n. 30) my impression was that Lawrence Douglas and Michael J. Bazyler agreed on this.

31 O. Bartov, *Mirrors of Destruction: War, Genocide and Modern Identity* (New York, 2000), 152-165.

Now, because a strict legal definition has been interpreted in the sense of specific genocidal intent by both the ICTY and the ICJ, I think that it is possible and perhaps even wise to discuss whether it is possible to outlaw the denial of genocide, in light of the existence and successful promotion of Holocaust education, and in light of the educational use of international tribunals.

3. Outlawing Genocide Denial?

Please allow me to devote the rest of my contribution to this topic to the question of how, perhaps, to outlaw genocide denial? I will not repeat the different arguments against such a law. In my view, my countryman, A. L. J. Janssens of the Law Faculty of Groningen University, has addressed these questions in an admirable way, in an article which can easily be found on the internet. I will merely summarize his criticism of a Dutch draft law. I think the criticism is fivefold:

1. According to Dutch law, there is nothing much wrong with insulting fellow human beings provided there is no damage done to one's dignity in a social sense. Judges can evaluate that social damage; they can evaluate whether an insult involves contempt or discrimination. They cannot, however, assess the psychological impact of an insult. They are judges, not psychoanalysts.
2. Janssens asks what actual damage denial does. In his view, the damage is done in particular in Germany and in Austria, i.e. in states where the now dominant political culture is closely connected to acceptance of the Holocaust.
3. The third point is that of freedom of expression and/or speech.
4. The fourth point is that Janssens doubts whether such a legal project would prove effective. He does not believe that a law on denial would work as a deterrent.
5. The fifth point deals with the question of what we do with other genocides, or rather with alleged genocides. Janssens does not believe that judges, as paid agents of states, should be responsible for rulings which would state that crime A (for instance, the Holocaust) constituted a genocide, whereas crime B (for instance, the Allied bombing of Dresden) is not to be considered a genocide.[32]

As a citizen of the Dutch democracy, I am in full agreement with Janssens, in particular when he defends freedom of expression and speech. Democratic states allow their citizens to speak their minds. Non-democratic states tend to do away with freedom of speech.

Many Holocaust deniers, by the way, do not discriminate against Jews, even if the act of Holocaust denial is immoral and offensive. The point is made by Janssens, but perhaps more adequately by Richard J. Evans, the principal witness for the defense in the most famous Holocaust court case since the Eichmann trial—the libel suit against Penguin Books UK and Deborah Lipstadt, brought before the High Court in London in 2000 by David Irving.

32 A. L. J. Janssens, *De loochenaars van Auschwitz; de ongewenstheid van strafbaarstelling.* See http://rechten.eldoc.ub.rug.nl.

Evans, in summarizing earlier work on Holocaust denial, wrote that:

> In reducing them all to a lowest common denominator, it seemed clear that Holocaust denial involved the minimum following beliefs:
>
> (a) The number of Jews killed by the Nazis was far less than 6 million; it amounted to only a few hundred thousand, and was thus similar to, or less than, the number of German civilians killed in Allied bombing raids.
>
> (b) Gas Chambers were not used to kill large numbers of Jews at any time.
>
> (c) Neither Hitler nor the Nazi leadership in general had a program of exterminating Europe's Jews; all they wished to do was to deport them to Eastern Europe.
>
> (d) 'The Holocaust' was a myth invented by Allied propaganda during the war and sustained since then by Jews who wished to use it to gain political and financial support for the state of Israel or for themselves. The supposed evidence for the Nazi's wartime mass murder of millions of Jews by gassing and other means was fabricated after the war.[33]

Evidently, although "a good deal of [the deniers] can be linked to racial hatred and anti-Semitic animosity,"[34] the purpose of deniers is often to blame the Allies for the death of (German) civilians and to exculpate Hitler and the rest of the Nazi leadership.

Because Evans concedes in a footnote that not all Holocaust deniers permanently agree with the statement under (d), it is in my view—following Janssens—very likely that a law which combines, in a strict way, Holocaust denial with discrimination or incitement of racism and/or xenophobia as a prerequisite for punishment, would not regard very many of those who deny the Holocaust as guilty.

As far as the ability of judges to decide what constitutes genocide and what does not is concerned, I beg to differ with Janssens. I think the Framework Decision at hand deals with this problem by focusing on verdicts by courts, and I have already said that I think this is wise. There is, furthermore, no doubt that national courts which reside in the more than 100 different states that have ratified the Rome Statute of the International Criminal Court (ICC) could turn out verdicts on genocide in the future.[35] The court case in The Hague against a war merchant, a Dutch national named Van Anraat, who sold chemicals used for the production of poisonous gas to Saddam Hussein, is a case in point, and so naturally is the court case against Saddam Hussein itself.

In its judgment on Van Anraat, The Hague Court of Appeal noted:

> Nevertheless, the Court deems that a final judicial judgment regarding the important as well as internationally significant question whether certain actions by certain persons as mentioned in the charges should be designated as genocide, deserves a better motivated

33 R. J. Evans, *Lying about Hitler: History, Holocaust and the David Irving Trial* (New York, 2001), 110, 283.

34 Ibid, 109.

35 See the url of the ICC: www.icc-cpi.int.

judgment (which should be based on conclusive evidence) than the one on which the Court was able to establish its observation.[36]

Here, a national court noted that it found it difficult to decide whether certain actions constituted genocide. And indeed it is, if we take into account that The Hague Court of Appeal had to evaluate crimes which took place many years ago and thousands of miles away.

Now, I think that there is a case to be made for outlawing genocide denial, provided that this punishable denial involves denial of the verdicts of the ICTY, ICTR and the ICJ, and denial of future verdicts of the ICC and national courts as well.

The truth of the matter is that the perpetrators of genocide very often go unpunished. German courts did make an effort to punish the perpetrators of the Holocaust, but of the 200,000 perpetrators less than 5,000 were punished. This is two and a half per cent.[37] This percentage illustrates that perpetrators are usually not punished, whereas (as I said earlier) the victims of genocide tend to vanish from the face of the earth. This forms the background of my proposal.

The second background of my proposal is that—contrary to popular belief—freedom of speech in an absolute sense does not exist anywhere in the civilized world. As Dr. Janssens demonstrated in an admirable book, which he wrote in a joint effort with Prof. A. J. Nieuwenhuis of the University of Amsterdam, the Dutch case makes it clear that the distribution of pornographic images of children is what he calls a "crime of expression"; many states have, to give another example, outlawed lese-majesté and incitement of racial hatred because this incitement threatens public order.[38]

I would like to make this point in a non-legal way, by trying to describe what the motives behind genocide awareness and genocide denial are.

As I said earlier, genocide awareness historically speaking is a recent invention. Or, to put it in another way, a direct connection between human rights abuses and the awareness of these abuses simply does not exist in the public sphere. The Portuguese, to give an example of this, were far more important slave traders than the Dutch, but that does not seem to worry them. The Dutch did not trade that many slaves, but because our society is inhabited by descendants of slaves, the slave trade is a cause for concern for the Dutch.

In contrast to the reaction of the Portuguese stands the reaction of one of the dukes of Alva, a Spanish duke who nowadays stills feels guilty about the actions of the former dukes in the Netherlands in 1580. He invites scholars to his castle on a regular basis and, before the scholars discuss the wrongdoings of his predecessors, he duly apologies for these wrongdoings.

36 See LJN: AX6406, District Court of The Hague, December 23, 2005, 09/751003-04, English translation, www.rechtspraak.nl; LJN: BA6734, The Hague Court of Appeal, May 9, 2007, 2200050906-2, English translation, www.rechtspraak.nl.

37 For figures, see the website of Dr. Dick de Mildt, http://www1.jur.uva.nl/junsv/.

38 A. L. J. Janssens, in A. J. Nieuwenhuis, *Uitingsdelicten* (Deventer, 2008).

You can easily imagine what the life of genocide scholars would be like if everybody behaved in this highly laudable way. Unfortunately, genocide awareness by perpetrators is highly exceptional because the perpetrators feel that they were doing the right thing—that is, protecting the best interests of their states by killing dangerous opposition to national interests.

Perhaps the true problem of genocide denial is not that individuals deny a particular genocide. The problem more generally, as many victims know from their firsthand experience, is that perpetrators are frequently in denial. Serbia, the Republica Srpska and the current government of Turkey are no exceptions.

The continuity of political regimes makes it difficult to concede that genocide has taken place. As a product of Vichy, Francois Mitterand found it difficult to admit that the French state was partly responsible for the anti-Jewish policies of the Vichy government.[39] Jacques Chirac in France and Gunnar Persson in Sweden could admit part responsibility because they personally were not connected to the previous political elites, in the same way as Konrad Adenauer or Willy Brandt were not connected to the political elite of the Third Reich.

Awareness of genocide usually occurs only after a drastic political change. A change of regime does not in itself, however, create a situation in which genocide or other grave abuses of human rights are acknowledged. Two examples may suffice.

The current government of Turkey strongly identifies with Atatürk—not with the government that ordered the deportations of the Armenians in 1915-1917—and nevertheless finds it difficult to recognize this genocide.

After 1945, many European states that had been liberated by the American and British forces prosecuted war crimes. But the crimes that were punished were the crimes committed by the German army and the Waffen-SS. These often concerned the executions of civilians. The involvement of Dutch, French or Belgian prominent civil servants in the persecution and mass arrests of Jews during Nazi occupation was, on the other hand, not often punished.[40] Very often the police chiefs responsible were even not fired, but stayed in office. In this respect, the Polish and Ukrainian examples and experiences of today resemble those of Western Europe after 1945.

No state has ever suffered such a loss of international credibility because of gross human rights abuses as Germany. Awareness of genocide is up to a point political justice, the use of justice for political ends that is.[41] One of the most convincing ways to argue that a former regime was criminal in nature is to maintain that it committed genocide.

The German Federal Republic which succeeded the Third Reich of Adolf Hitler—and that is my point—promoted Holocaust awareness because it could do so without compromising itself. The same is essentially true in Iraq, because the current Iraqi government also views itself as a liberated state, and not merely a vanquished power.

39 For France, see: E. Conan and H. Rousso, *Vichy, un passé qui ne passe pas,* Paris, 1994.

40 For an example, see: Klaus-Dietmar Henke/ Hans Woller, *Politische Sauberung in Europa,* Stuttgart 1998.

41 The classical work on this topic is: O. Kirchheimer, *Politische Justiz: Verwendung juristischer Verfahrensmöglichkeiten zu politischen Zwecken,* Frankfurt am Main, 1981.

Perpetrator states do not admit genocide, unless there is foreign pressure as well. Even the most willing and the most cooperative of defendants, the simultaneously vanquished and liberated Federal Republic of Germany that is, had to be persuaded to admit guilt.[42]

History, in my view, has also demonstrated that Holocaust awareness, or genocide awareness for that matter, need not depend upon perpetrators. Holocaust awareness and its promotion were characteristics of the part of the world which was called the Free West during the Cold War. In that period, Holocaust awareness was effectively limited to the Free West.

It was not a coincidence that the first free parliament of the German Democratic Republic acknowledged the Holocaust.[43] Since the fall of the Wall, Holocaust education has become obligatory in large parts of eastern Europe, thanks also to the Task Force. I do not think that this has to lead to a reduction in freedom of speech or freedom of expression.

4. Summary

So let me now sum up and conclude.

History is full of massive abuses of human rights. Most of them are forgotten. Awareness of such abuses is exceptional. This is strictly a post-Second World War phenomenon. As a lesson in political morality, the unprecedented Holocaust demonstrates both the prudential necessity of human rights and their ultimate fragility.

Outlawing genocide denial will result in an increase of foreign pressure on perpetrators, such as Serbia, the Republika Srpska and Turkey.

In my view, the outlawing of genocide denial is sound, provided that courts first establish that there was a case of genocide (and genocidal intent).

The verdicts of international tribunals would be preferable to rulings of national courts. In the future, decisions that might be given under the Rome Statute of the International Criminal Court (ICC) could give rise to more verdicts on genocide than national courts. Recent developments—for instance the conviction of Dutch war merchant Van Anraat in The Hague to a seventeen-year prison term (currently on appeal)—do point in that direction.

Such verdicts will intensify public debates on genocide and other gross abuses of human rights. Such debates are needed by historians who cannot fulfill their tasks without such debates. History, after all, is about accounting for the past.

I fail to see why freedom of speech and expression should be at stake when denial of genocide will constitute a criminal offence. Freedom of speech and expression are limited in civilized states, as my example of the illegality of child pornography has shown. Many governments promote Holocaust education as part of their educational policies and encourage other governments to do the same. This means that states are not neutral, as far as the past is concerned, and that they do take sides, without effectively limiting or impeding freedom of speech and expression.

42 Meier, *Vierzig Jahre*, 64, 53.

43 Grosser, *Verbrechen und Erinnerung*, 279.

5. Outlook

On the other hand, if only non-democratic states limit freedom of speech and expression, this could be a reason not to punish genocide denial by law. There are certainly ways to alleviate the plight of survivors other than by punishing the denial of genocide as a criminal offence. Survivors could find it gratifying if perpetrators of genocide were punished.

For survivors and their dependents it would be beneficial if there was an official international institution which could establish whether certain events constituted genocide. Such a public law institution would best be established by the international community, and would create the possibility for officially acknowledging historical genocides in cases where there are no defendants to be put in the dock.

In my view, the recent verdict of the ICJ in the case of Bosnia v. Serbia, which held that Srebrenica was a genocide, was essentially such a historical ruling. If a court can pass a verdict on genocidal events which took place more than a decade ago (or, as German courts have frequently done, on events which happened up to fifty years ago), evidently the difference between rulings on actual genocides and rulings on historical genocides is not a matter of principle.

A decision of such a public law institution, certifying that an event constituted genocide, could be especially useful if the denial of genocide by individuals or by perpetrators is to be outlawed. It would also assist national courts who try perpetrators and accomplices of genocide, in cases where the means and expertise for establishing whether genocide has taken place are lacking. This would reduce the workload of courts up to a point, as they would still need to judge the culpability of individual perpetrators and their accomplices.

A public law institution which could establish genocide could arrive at its decisions in a way comparable to that of the international tribunals and the ICJ, as the new International Criminal Court in The Hague will be doing shortly.

If such a public law institution is established, the perpetrator—or perhaps a "perpetrator state"—could refute that it had genocidal intent. In such cases this would probably give rise to plea bargaining by perpetrator states. Such plea bargaining is, in my view, what the Serbian legal team did in the recent ICJ case.

If states consider it to be their more or less universal duty to try perpetrators of genocide, perhaps they will also consider it their more or less universal moral obligation to worry about the victims of genocide as well.

The states that establish a public law institution could also form a fund, out of which compensation could be paid, perhaps in particular to those who live in third-world states. Now victims have to make do with truth and reconciliation commissions, essentially because the state cannot afford to compensate them. Lower administrative tribunals could deal with the division of the funds later on, and perhaps use them to fund remembrance and educational purposes.

Such an institution could be an offshoot of the International Criminal Court in The Hague, which has created a department under the leadership of Madame la Ministre Simone Veil, to watch over the interests of victims.

12. *Les Fleurs du Mal*, The Need to Confront Holocaust Distortion

Hagen Fleischer

> Hitler was blamed for something that did not actually take place. Later the history of mankind will blame him for not ridding Europe of the Jews, though he could have ... This time there will be no kind German Nazis to gather up the Jews and send them to Madagascar, but Knights of the White Apocalypse. I imagine them galloping, swords unsheathed, on blond steeds of death.
>
> K. Plevris, Greek holocaust denier[1]

> There is something a little ironic about being banged up for the crime of 'denying' the Holocaust by the very people who started it. Such was the fate of David Irving.
>
> Rod Liddle, "They've made a martyr out of this Holocaust denier," *Sunday Times* (London), Dec. 24, 2006.

In 1986 the prominent German historian Ernst Nolte raised the issue of the unique nature of Nazi crimes. His assertion that Nazism, and in consequence the Holocaust, should be interpreted as a defensive reaction to, or even as a replica of, Bolshevism triggered the famous Historikerstreit: the fiercest dispute ever to shake German academia over how to put the Nazi era in context. The Nolte camp lost this battle, but soon began preparing the ground for a return to the fray after revisionism was supposedly justified in 1989/90 by the implosion of state Communism. In contrast with the growing distance in time from the actual events, the Holocaust discourse intensified, becoming even more emotional, obtaining a quasi-sacred dimension, which has not happened with any other genocide. The unique status of the Holocaust makes it the focus of multifarious distortion.

---

1 Konstantinos Plevris, Oi Evraioi, oli i alitheia [*The Jews, the Whole Truth*] (2006) 852, 872.

H.G. van der Wilt, J. Vervliet et al., *(eds.)* The Genocide Convention: The Legacy of 60 Years.
 ISBN 978 9004 15328 8. pp. 159-170.

During the Cold War there were two competing camps using WW II as the legitimate paradigm for distinguishing good from evil. Both camps conveniently identified 'good' with their own past and present actions. In the 1990s, however, the West assumed a virtual monopoly on interpretation, particularly so in 1999 when it used the "Holocaust analogy" for Kosovo.[2] After equating Slobodan Milošević with Hitler and Serbian concentration camps with Auschwitz, it was easy to claim the need to deal with 'equivalent situations' in equivalent ways. President Bill Clinton urged the American Society of Newspaper Editors: "We must follow the example of the WW II generation, by standing up to aggression and hate."[3] Later, George W. Bush would clumsily attempt to repeat this performance in reference to Afghanistan and Iraq. His visit to Auschwitz on the eve of D-Day, the anniversary of the Allied landing at Normandy, where he 'apologized' for the U.S. leadership during WW II not bombing the German death machinery in Auschwitz, was "choreographed to serve immediate policy objectives." The President invoked Nazi horrors as a "reminder" that evil must be fought, assuming that he and his alliance embodied "good."[4] His (and his entourage's) murky and opportunistic references to WW II—"History proves we're doing fine"[5]—reduced history to political ammunition. Indeed, whenever hard-liners and right-wing tabloids on both sides of the Atlantic equate topical enemies with Hitler & Co. they almost always depict military action against the regimes they despise as "morally just" as WW II. [6] The controversial bestselling author Daniel J. Goldhagen, even invoked the concept of "denazification" when advocating that the Serbs and Iraqis be re-educated as the Allies had successfully re-educated the Germans after 1945.[7]

A recent survey on Holocaust trivialization listed as outstanding examples that "U.S. presidents were compared to Hitler and the actions of the United States and its allies in Iraq and Afghanistan were compared to those of Nazi Germany."[8] Distortion the other way round, however, when such comparisons were made by U.S. presidents against others, was much more dangerous since it was used to justify large scale military operations. There is also the aspect of the proliferation of Holocaust analogies backfiring on Washington in that other victimized populations, in

2 *Benjamin R. Bates, "Circulation of the World War II / Holocaust analogy in the 1999 Kosovo intervention: Articulating a vocabulary for international conflict," J. Language & Politics, 8, no. 1 (2009) 28-51.*

3 Washington Post, April 16, 1999.

4 World Socialist, June 5, 2003; cf. NYT, June 1, 2003.

5 Washington Post, July 20, 2003.

6 Washington Times, Jan. 7, 2003; Hagen Fleischer, "The past beneath the Present, The Resurgence of WWII Public History after the Collapse of Communism," Historein, 4 (2004) 95-96.

7 Quotes in Hagen Fleischer, *Oi Polemoi Tis Mnimis* (2008) 340.

8 Manfred Gerstenfeld, "Holocaust Trivialization," Post-Holocaust & Anti-Semitism, 68 (2008) http://www.jcpa.org/JCPA/Templates/ShowPage.asp?DRIT=3&DBID=1&LNGID=1&TMID=111&FID=624&PID=0&IID=2199&TTL=Holocaust_Trivialization.

particular African Americans and Native Americans, began claiming compensation for the 'black' and 'red' holocausts committed against them by white America.

The Germans have to face up to the moral and material consequences of other, rival 'holocausts' as well, the most serious being the genocide of the Roma (Gypsies) and the mass murder of handicapped people hidden beneath the euphemism 'euthanasia.' The recently coined term 'Gay Holocaust' has little historical foundation, but the Herero people of Namibia are more justified in their claim that the large-scale extermination of their forefathers by the Kaiser's troops should be recognized as the first Holocaust of the 20th century. On the other hand, many organized Sudeten Germans expelled from Czechoslovakia or victims of Allied carpet bombing also refer to their suffering as 'genocide.' All these groups complain about the selective division of memories and of a hierarchy of victims established by political lobbying.[9]

There is less sympathy for the suffering of the Jews in countries such as Russia, Poland, and Greece, where the majority population also suffered heavily under German occupation, or in the Baltic countries, where dark memories of Communist rule endure. In these countries there is something of a competition in claiming victimization, in which groups contend that commemorating primarily Jewish victims diminishes non-Jewish suffering. The balance, of course, tips both ways. In Greece, for example, some Jews take offense when the plural "Greek Holocausts" is used to describe, on the www.greekholocausts.gr website, massacres committed by German troops in Kalavryta, Distomo, and other "martyr villages". Other Greeks, Gentiles, while reminding that "Holocaust" is a Greek word, take offense at use of the "monopolistic" capital 'H' for Holocaust and the "Jews' lion's share in indemnification" supposedly resulting from this.[10] It should be possible, by using the Hebrew term Shoah for the genocide of the Jews, to reduce such tensions in Greece, and opportunities for trivialization, in general.

Greece has so-called 'special relations' with the Arab world, because, since the state of Israel was founded, any resurgence of tensions in the Middle East has tended to bring hidden prejudices to the surface. In Greece, as elsewhere, the frequent escalations—with much of the responsibility borne by the Jerusalem government and its calculated over-reactions to the provocations by radical Palestinian groups—intensified anti-Israeli feelings within large segments of the population. These feelings were expressed mainly in the mass media, but also by well-known intellectuals and prominent individuals from all political positions and several social organizations. Numerous mainstream papers depicted Israel as a 'Nazi state.' Rabidly 'anti-Zionist' and latently anti-Semitic statements and cartoons, often on front pages, equated the Star of David with the Swastika and depicted the Palestinians as victims of a 'new Auschwitz' or of a modern crucifixion. Instances of 'Holocaust inversion,' portraying Jews as Nazis, were not limited to Greece. During the Lebanon war, the most prominent example was the cartoon in the biggest Socialist Norwegian paper depicting

9 Fleischer, *Oi Polemoi*, 93, 225-228, 321-323, 545.

10 *See, e.g.*: K. Konstantinidis, *letter to the editor*, Elevtherotypia (Sept. 22, 1997).

the Israeli prime minister as trigger-happy SS criminal Amon Göth, widely known from Schindler's List.[11]

These critics were strange bedfellows with Holocaust deniers asserting that the Nakhba, the plight of the Palestinians from 1948 up to now, was and is much worse than whatever had happened to the Jews—meaning that the latter or, almost identically, 'the Zionists,' are the real villains. In this they were joined by 'soft' deniers, who avoid outright Holocaust denial for fear of legal action. Instead, they trivialize the Holocaust by questioning or denying important aspects: its scope, its original intentions, and its mechanisms (in particular the existence of gas chambers).

In contrast to Holocaust denial, no legal consequences seem feasible for "grossly trivializing" the Shoah (or any other genocide)—since trivialization, with its large swath of manifestations and intentions, is difficult even to define.[12] Its practitioners frequently select a single aspect that superficially resembles a component of the genocide as the basis for abusive comparison. Unlike other people who distort the Holocaust, most trivializers who are not closet deniers do not target Jews but act out of thoughtlessness.

Since Nazi Germany remains the archetype of a destructive, genocidal regime, any political entity in conflict with another political entity may compare its opponent with Hitler; almost any major crime or transgression may be denounced as a Holocaust. With the growing distance in time from WW II and the waning of knowledge about the true extent of the unprecedented horrors committed then, Hitler has become a metaphor for evil, a secularized version of the devil. All over the world, politicians increasingly discredit adversaries, unpopular regimes, ideologies, or practices by identifying them with stereotypical images from the Nazi past—obliterating meanings and proportions. Examples given above illustrate trivialization at the top level of world politics, where the offenders usually insist on their manipulative analogies. In contrast, entities who indulge in 'low-level' trivialization in order to impress the public are often led to apologies by public criticism.

Abusive 'metaphoric' Holocaust imagery was used in the dispute between Euro-zealots and Euro-adversaries. It was used by environmentalists and animal rights activists to promote their causes against global warming or inhumane conditions for animal breeding and slaughtering, the latter coining the slogan "The Holocaust on your plate." The higher Catholic clergy, from the Archbishop of Cologne to the late Pope John Paul II, accused governments that have legalized abortion of having killed more innocent children than Herod, Stalin, or Hitler. The Irish president Mary McAleese, representing her country at the sixtieth anniversary of the liberation of Auschwitz, compared the fate of the Jews with that of her Catholic brethren in British-held Northern Ireland. Several hard-line anti-smoke-campaigns have attempted to shock a broader public by using the term "Tobacco Holocaust." Recently we en-

---

11 Dagbladet, 10.7.2006. Others, such as the Canadian prime minister Stephen Harper, went the other way round comparing Hezbollah with the SS. *The Gazette* (Montreal), 23.8.2006.

12 Even Roberto Benigni's masterpiece *Life Is Beautiful* could be censored by zealot bureaucrats as gross trivialization.

countered the opposite extreme. In response to increased anti-smoking measures in Europe, some smokers have been wearing T-shirts with a yellow Star of David containing the word "smoker" (instead of "Jew") to indicate that they were the victims of a new Holocaust.[13] All these perpetrators' beat a partial or total retreat due to public criticism.

Even Jews, who should know better, have misused the metaphor of the greatest crime against humanity. Moshe Kantor, President of the European Jewish Congress, while referring to the dangers of Holocaust trivialization, at the same time stressed the need to oppose assimilation by European Jewry, otherwise "sooner or later we will come to a final solution [sic] without any Holocaust."[14] Other Jewish leaders have denounced "the holocaust of assimilation" and intermarriage as "Silent (or White) Holocaust."[15] (The term White Holocaust otherwise appears in hate sites as being perpetrated by Jews against the "White Race".)[16] In the 1990's, one of the last survivors of the Warsaw ghetto uprising called the Serbian war against Bosnia "Hitler's recent victory" —a term later widely used, in contradiction, by Greek and other pro-Serbian analysts after NATO began bombing Yugoslavia.[17]

In Germany, too, the 1999 NATO bombing of Serbia brought about a reversal of the pre-1990 national consensus that the uniqueness of Nazi war crimes permanently ruled out any German military involvement abroad. Suddenly, the media and politicians, including most Social Democrats, turned their moral position upside down and justified their support of NATO intervention by calling upon what they called Germany's historic obligation to forestall "another Auschwitz," by which they meant that Serbian ethnic cleansing was taking on genocidal dimensions.

Since 2002, another distinct break occurred in Germany when large books paying unusual homage to several aspects of German suffering in WW II skyrocketed up the bestseller lists. In particular, Jörg Friedrich's book Fire[18] about the Allied carpet bombing of German towns used terminology hitherto associated with the Holocaust: ordinary Germans were suffocated, "gassed," and "annihilated" in basements, which—because of premeditated Allied bombing tactics—worked not as shelters but as "gas chambers" or "crematoria." The message to the public was clear. "No other people" had suffered as much as the Germans. Friedrich's narrative lopsidedly focuses on attacks by the Allied military against German civilians and avoids putting any of these attacks within the context of German crimes. A reference to Auschwitz stresses an error committed by the Allies, i.e. the Anglo-American decision not to bomb the railways leading there. Although Friedrich is no Holocaust denier, he provided arguments to German neo-Nazis who gratefully adopted (and developed) his assaults upon "war criminal Churchill" and the "Allied bombing holocaust."

13 Quotations in: Fleischer, *Oi Polemoi*, 333-334.

14 Jerusalem Post, Jan. 29, 2008.

15 Gerstenfeld, *supra* note 8.

16 E.g.: http://www.israelect.com/reference/WillieMartin/White_Holocaust.htm.

17 Quotations in Fleischer, "The past beneath the Present," 95.

18 Quotations in Fleischer, "The past beneath the Present," 60-65.

In the 'new' nationalist states of east central Europe there is little interest in the 'Final Solution.' Previously, Communist historiography had listed millions of murdered Jews—from Babi Yar to Auschwitz—merely as national victims, without any reference to their Jewish identity, the very reason they were killed. Few things have changed in this respect. The focus is again on national victimhood, albeit this time caused by Communist rule. Concerning the large-scale annihilation of the pre-war Jewish minorities, the mainstream societies in east central Europe continue to hover between denial and comparative trivialization.[19] The new national remembrance cultures are characterized by a suspicious paucity of references to native involvement in the genocide. This suggests intentions to skim over the shadier aspects of the pre-Communist era, such as the fervent anti-Semitism inextricably bound up with pre-war nationalism in most of these states. In some countries with a significant record of collaboration with the Nazi "New Order," the ruling elites refute or hush up any association with such aspects of their past. In June 2003, the Romanian government issued a blunt denial of their country's involvement in the Holocaust. Four days later, after heavy protests and ridicule from abroad, Bucharest admitted having played a role in the genocide. But this move aimed at the country's image abroad and had little effect on domestic discourse.

The situation in the Baltic countries seems even worse. For instance, in Latvia few people remember that during the first two months after the German invasion 35,000 Jews were slaughtered, many of them 'spontaneously,' without German involvement. Instead, academic and, in particular, public history refers to another 'forgotten Holocaust,' meaning the persecution of the Baltic people by the Soviet regime and its 'Jewish henchmen,' adopting the Nazi slogan of Judaeo-Bolshevism. Baltic nationalists, some in high positions, equate the Holocaust with the loss of lives to Red Terror—promoting the concept of 'two genocides' and emphasizing that priority should be given to the 'forgotten one' committed by Soviets (and Jews) against the Baltic people. However, the desire of almost all ex-Communist states to join Western economic, political, and military alliances was used by the West as leverage to remind them that admission was not possible without a certain amount of common cultural advancement, including more objectivity in dealing with their own war history.[20]

Several strategies are used to sanitize Fascism and distort the Holocaust. People doing this describe themselves as 'revisionists,' thereby usurping the rich tradition of genuine revisionist, non-conformist, historians in many countries contributing to our knowledge. Challenging and revising dominant interpretations is the historian's first duty, but this must not include remaking history by denying and deconstructing incontestable historical facts.

By this reasoning, several European states led by Germany demanded to criminalize Holocaust denial as an attempt to rehabilitate Nazism and racial crime. They were opposed by Britain, some Nordic countries, and Berlusconi's Italy. In April 2007, after six years of argument and under a German presidency, the justice minis-

---

19 Michael Shafir, *Between Denial And 'Comparative Triviliazation': Holocaust Negationism in Post-Communist East Central Europe*, (2002).

20 Fleischer, "The past beneath the Present,"75.

ters of all 27 EU countries agreed to impose jail sentences of between one and three years for: "publicly condoning, denying or grossly trivializing crimes of genocide, crimes against humanity and war crimes ... when the conduct is carried out in a manner likely to incite to violence or hatred against" groups based on color, race, or ethnic origin. Despite considerable political pressure from interested parties, no specific reference to the Holocaust, the Armenian genocide, or the "Stalinist Holocaust" was made.[21] This framework decision left considerable discretion to member states and national parliaments as to how the decision would be implemented. At that time Holocaust denial already had been made a criminal offense in fourteen European states, although in different ways and with varying penalties.[22]

The decision taken by the 27 ministers had few enthusiastic supporters. Some Jewish and anti-racist groups criticized the proposed legislation for being "perhaps worse than none," since this "minimalist compromise" had been "watered down to the point of rendering it toothless."[23] Liberal and leftist intellectuals protested against what they perceived as a state's monopoly upon historical truth, an infringement of the constitutional right of free speech and the "freedom of history and teaching" [sic]—"official anti-fascism" used as an instrument of legitimization by former East European regimes, leading to a "nanny state and its memory police."[24] Although their intentions differed, their wording largely coincided with the spurious argumentation of Holocaust deniers.[25]

The argument that freedom of speech must be granted without reservations to even the worst enemies of that particular freedom sounds 'fair' but can be suicidal. The Weimar Republic had an outstanding democratic constitution that collapsed precisely because of the unrestrained freedom of propaganda granted to the Nazi conspiracy. The flowers of evil, with their poisonous outgrowth particularly dangerous to adolescents, should not be pampered and should not be treated as a protected species for ecologically political reasons.

Even democratic countries necessarily must place some limits upon 'free expression.' The U.S., in spite of its famous First Amendment, has banned the wearing of Ku Klux Klan hoods and the burning of crosses. In all countries there are laws against various excesses of free expression, such as blasphemy, hardcore porn, per-

21 The Guardian (Apr. 20, 2007).

22 However, in late 2007 the constitutional court in Spain overturned the anti-denial legislation after a legal appeal brought by a leading neo-Nazi. In Spain now Holocaust denial is not subject to sanction. Only *justifying* the Holocaust and publicly endorsing it is still punishable.

23 *http://zionism-israel.com/israel_news/2007/05/europe-adopts-watered-down-holocaust.html.*

24 *See*, e.g., Timothy G. Ash, "The Freedom of historical debate is under attack by the memory police," Guardian (Oct. 16, 2008). Luigi Cajani, "Europe moves to censor historians," *http://www.uni-leipzig.de/~eniugh/congress/documents/paper%20luigi%20cajani.pdf.*

25 Cf., e.g.,: "thought police," "mind control," "crimethink," in www.australianfreepress.org, passim.

jury, or libel. Gross slander of both individuals and legal entities is punishable by law. Calling the murder of six millions Jews a lie is—apart from justifying Nazi hubris—an outrageous offense against the victims' dignity, a second assassination, in fact, this time of their memory. In consequence, Holocaust denial has nothing to do with freedom of historical research and debate. It neither contributes to knowledge nor reinterprets historical facts, but perverts both. No core value of democracy is endangered here. The dispute is about an excess of speech that is not a legitimate part of public discourse but extreme anti-Semitism disguised as revisionism. In refusing an application by the famous denier Roger Garaudy, the European Court of Human Rights ruled:

> Denying crimes against humanity is one of the most acute forms of racial defamation towards the Jews and of incitement to hatred of them. The denial or revision of historical facts of this type call in question the values underpinning the fight against racism and anti-Semitism and are capable of seriously disturbing public order. Such acts adversely affect the rights of others and are incompatible with democracy and human rights.[26]

With the exception of Islamist deniers, most 'Holocaust revisionists' are neo-Nazis from all over the planet. This becomes clear by comparing them with those who deny the genocidal character of other ('consanguineous') mass scale crimes, particularly the descending generations of perpetrator nations, as is the case with Turkey downgrading the Armenian genocide to 'events.' Only Holocaust deniers support each other on an international level. They disguise facts in order to rehabilitate Nazism and its record, since remembrance of the Holocaust is the main obstacle to their preaching of anti-Semitism and nationalistic xenophobia, the same messages proclaimed by the Nazis. Exonerating Nazi Germany of responsibility for WW II dovetails with blaming the Jews for its outbreak. Most deniers, then, describe the "Holohoax"[27] as the prime example of how Jews manipulate history and its public discourse for their own benefit. In this argumentation the Jewish state appears delegitimized as having been established on false pretenses. This is the reason most neo-Nazi deniers meet with radical Islamists, considering or at least implying that destruction of Israel would be legitimate. It is within this context that European right-wing extremism takes advantage of gaps in hate speech legislation while building their networks with strongholds in those states where no adequate legal responses exist—from Spain to Eastern Europe, from the U.S. to Iran.

It is difficult to prove whether or not false information is disseminated 'knowingly.' Similarly, it is often hard for a court to interpret the limitations of 'acceptable' speech and to decide whether transgressions are 'likely' to incite racial hatred or violence, a decision that could make the difference between freedom and jail. The line between tolerable expression of denial and its (outlawed) consequences is indistinct,

26 Decision June 24, 2003, IV, www.echr.coe.int/Eng/InformationNotes/INFONOTEN054.htm.

27 E.g. http://www.biblebelievers.org.au/holohoax.htm, http://www.judenfrei.org/holocaust-hoax.

thin and permeable, as the following examples show. In most countries, Anne Frank is the archetype victim of Nazi genocide because we can comprehend the cruel fate that came to this one teenage girl,[28] whereas we cannot grasp the enormity of the murder of six million largely anonymous victims. This is the reason anti-Semitic hate speech defames Anne's diary as a hoax constructed by 'world Jewry.' The public burning of this diary in an East German town[29] was a powerful reminder of Nazi book burning in May of 1933. Then and now, young pyromaniacs were less guilty than the adults who instigated them.

Self-styled revisionists from all ages and all countries praise the regime in Teheran, which has promoted denial to state policy and combined it with the idea of wiping the Jewish state off the map. For the time being, activists (the younger ones) in Greece and elsewhere must be content with vandalizing monuments and graveyards. Evidently, propaganda becomes particularly dangerous when it focuses on youth[30] with catch phrase like "real history resisting official history." By mail or in person, deniers in many countries distribute their material to schools.

In Greece, prominent foreign Holocaust-deniers have had their books translated and promoted by mainstream publishers. Their Athenian audiences were not limited to the extreme Right but included respected figures from the middle-of-the-road or the 'anti-Zionist' Left. Such was the late Vasilis Rafailidis, who followed Garaudy in calling the Nazi gas chambers a "gigantic lie" and the Holocaust a scam since the Jews were "very alive and kicking."[31] In 2003, David Irving, the guru of neo-Nazi "revisionism," was extolled as a "mystic of truth" in the Athens War Museum by Vyron Polydoras, a leading figure of the New Democracy party now in power.[32] In all cases, there was a remarkable response by young extremists.

Anti-Semitic newspapers in Greece have incited their readers to prevent Holocaust lectures at schools while praising "those brave students" who "kicked Jewish propagandists out" of a high school in Thessalonica.[33] The most prominent Greek denier, lawyer and would-be historian Kostas Plevris, has expressed his intention to punish "pro-Semitic" teachers as "national traitors" and "distorters of history" who "ought to be hanged—and if the state cannot do it, Greeks will be found to execute the traitors."[34] Plevris, who openly claims to be an ardent admirer of Hitler, the SS, and "morally superior" Nazism, was the first and only denier convicted in Greece. In December 2007, he was given a suspended sentence of fourteen months imprisonment because his 1,400 page tome of anti-Jewish rant was judged to instigate ra-

28 Remember, in (black-and-white) *Schindler's List*, the uniquely colourized image of the little girl in the red coat.

29 *Tageszeitung* (Berlin), Feb. 26, 2007.

30 Lynne Lamberg, "Hate-Group Web Sites Target Children, Teens," *Psychiatric News* (Feb. 2, 2001).

31 E.g., his series of articles in large circulation Ethnos (Oct. 21-Nov. 1, 1996).

32 He has since recanted, claiming that he had not been properly informed.

33 Fleischer, *Oi Polemoi*, 453.

34 Plevris, *Oi Evraioi*, 95

cial hatred. Even then, both public prosecutors had argued for his release, endorsing Plevris's claim that he was entitled to freely express a different opinion on the subject of his "scholarly" research![35] This position was strengthened when, in March 2009, the appeals court acquitted Plevris on the grounds of the free speech. This decision seriously damaged Greece's image worldwide,[36] meeting with enthusiastic approval only from neo-Nazi electronic and print media.

In fact, the appeals court ignored neo-Fascist graffiti and pamphlets asking the public to "liberate Greece from Jewish occupation" and tear down any monument referring to the Holocaust "scam."[37] Neo-Fascist activists may now refer to the acquittal of Plevris who explicitly calls for action[38]:

> The time for retaliation has come. ... Every Greek, every person who is aware of the subversion carried out by Jewish Zionism, should act on his own as an individual and mobilize himself against Jews ... taking whatever action is necessary.[39]

The same "activists" may stress that the court in effect permitted Plevris to propagate his "opinion" that the Jews were criminals and parasites, a non-white "subhuman" race, and that the Nazis were (only!) to be criticized for having left their good work half-done.[40] The book in dispute can be downloaded from the internet, where the author has several fan clubs (on facebook, etc.).

Many Liberals maintain that, instead of restrictive legislation, "strength of argument, widespread outcry and ridicule will defeat the Holocaust-deniers." According to this argument "de facto social censorship" will "self-regulate such 'excesses' of free speech by ostracizing, ridiculing, and shunning those who propagate them."[41] Unfortunately, however, that deniers' premises are demonstrably wrong, malicious,

35 Elevtherotypia, Dec. 5, 2007.

36 C. Schlötzer, "Judenhass in Griechenland. Triumph des Rassisten," Sűddeutsche Zeitung (March 30, 2009).

37 Hagen Fleischer, "Griechenland: Das bestrittene Phänomen" in Vorurteil und Rassenhass, eds. Hermann Graml et al. (2001) 222. The leader of the German neo-Nazi NPD was even more outspoken when he admitted his desire to destroy the Berlin memorial for the "so-called" Holocaust to use its 2,711 concrete steles in constructing "appropriate foundations for the chancellery of the new Reich" (Fleischer, *Oi Polemoi*, 454).

38 Questions still surround the investigation by Italian authorities about neo-Fascist Italian terrorists cooperating with the military junta in Athens (1967-1974). Six Greek "contacts" were identified: Plevris and five of his followers.

39 Plevris, *Oi Evraioi*, 139, 269.

40 *Id.*, passim. He comments (1075) on a photo of Auschwitz: "They are right to maintain the camp in good condition since nobody knows what might happen in the future." *See also* above (motto 1).

41 Chris Huhne, "Holocaust denial and a case that shows flaws in the EU," Independent (Oct. 24, 2008); Jens F. Laurson and George A. Pieler, "Europe's Choice. Freedom to deny or denial of freedom?" (May 28, 2007) http://www.reason.com/news/printer/120405.html.

or foolish, does not prevent them from spreading. We must not discount the effect skilled deniers with pretensions to academic seriousness can have, especially upon the young. Many academic teachers have had unpleasant experiences with students who prepared essays by 'Googling' for information on the internet. Hate has gone high tech. The biggest anti-Semitic hate-site, "Jew Watch," specializing in "revisionist education," boasts that in 2008 "it achieved 5 million hits," ranking "up to 10 times higher" than the U.S. Holocaust Museum's website: "Why? Our visitors learn more. We offer more. We study & archive the truth."[42] Holocaust deniers have constructed their own fictional universe of mystic counter-reality, allegedly under deadly threat from the real universe, which has fallen prey to Jewish conspiracy. A functional dialogue with the champions of counter-reality is impossible.

Just as there are limits to the desirable and necessary dialogue among different ideological currents, there must be moral and practical limits as well for a dialogue between 'interpretations' of history – especially when one side is not interested in contributing to a better understanding of the past but relies on ignoring, decontextualizing, and manipulating source material, often to the point of outright falsification. Even though historians no longer reduce history to sheer facts and events, they certainly can not reduce history to arbitrary 'interpretation,' removing it from its factual foundation. Discussion of all the aspects of WW II and the Jewish genocide are legitimate, including the question of whether or not the latter is 'unique'. Whether or not WW II or the genocide actually took place, however, are issues beyond discussion.

The strategic issue is how to make Holocaust denial unacceptable in word and deed, how to silence deniers without giving them the publicity they primarily seek[43] and then the opportunity to pose as persecuted martyrs to the notion of freespeech. There is no definite solution. Social censorship, mentioned above, should be applied rigorously. Academia and the media should refuse deniers a platform. For all the legislative measures still needed for some cases, we must avoid any exaggerated legal response. There can be no question about persecution of drunken prattle or of the socially deranged who seek publicity by being 'criminalized.' When persecution is restricted to clear-cut, high-profile, cases, it should be possible to protect both freedom of academic speech and freedom from hate speech (and action). An unwavering demonstration that there will be no safe havens for extremists propagating a return to Nazi practices in word and deed, is particularly needed in the countries that spawned the Holocaust or lost many of their citizens to it. The geographical-historical context in which statements are made is often of crucial importance.[44]

Repeatedly, pressure on regimes or other political entities that sponsor Holocaust denial have been successful. The frequency of denial and other neo-Nazi activities decreased after David Irving was tried and sentenced but increased after his "triumphant" release, when he was invited to speak in several places, from Budapest to

42 http://www.americancivilrightsreview.com/jewwatch.htm, http://jewwatch.com/.

43 "Irving gets just what he wanted – his name in the headlines," Scotsman (Feb. 23, 2006).

44 *See*, e.g., Deborah Lipstadt, "Denial should be defeated by facts, not laws," (July 16, 2007) http://www.spiked-online.com/index.php?/site/article/3609/.

the sophisticated Oxford Union debating society.[45] Other examples show the same correlation.[46] Obviously deniers, flagrant spreaders of hate, must be brought to trial where their web of lies can be shredded. Having them publicly exposed and convicted is more important than putting them in prison, just as is the case with the remaining aged war criminals still living around the world.

45 Rafael Medoff and Alex Grobman, "Holocaust Denial: a Global Survey - 2007," http://www.wymaninstitute.org/articles/HolocaustDenial2007.pdf.

46 See, e.g., Michael Whine, "Expanding Holocaust Denial and Legislation against it,", Jewish Political Studies Review, 20, nos. 1-2 (2008), available at: http://www.jcpa.org/JCPA/Templates/ShowPage.asp?DRIT=5&DBID=1&LNGID=1&TMID=111&FID=625&PID=0&IID=2202&TTL=Expanding_Holocaust_Denial_and_Legislation_Against_It.

Countries

13. The United States and the Genocide Convention: The Sovereignty Package in Perspective

Lawrence LeBlanc

1. Introduction

Representatives of the United States were involved in drafting the Genocide Convention (the Convention) during most of the stages it passed through on its way to eventual adoption by the United Nations General Assembly in 1948. Soon thereafter, in June 1949, President Harry S. Truman requested the Senate's advice and consent to the ratification of the Convention. Almost forty years later, in February 1986, the Senate adopted a resolution of ratification. Subsequently, in October 1988, the Congress adopted implementing legislation for the Convention and President Ronald Reagan deposited the United States' instrument of ratification at the United Nations.

The resolution of ratification reflected a compromise to overcome the objections of the most outspoken critics of the Convention. Known as the Lugar-Helms-Hatch Sovereignty Package (see Appendix), the resolution consisted of understandings indicating how the United States interpreted the meanings of various words and phrases contained in the Convention; and two reservations—one to the dispute resolution clause, which would allow the International Court of Justice (ICJ) to settle disputes among the parties to the Convention; the other affirming the supremacy of the US Constitution over the provisions of the Genocide Convention. The sweeping terms of the sovereignty package make it unique among the instruments of ratification deposited by states parties to the Convention, and close allies of the United States strongly objected to its terms. Nonetheless, they remain in effect.

The purpose of this paper is to put the sovereignty package into historical perspective and to weigh the implications it has had for the United States' subsequent ratification of human rights treaties. Since ratifying the Genocide Convention, the United States has ratified the Convention against Torture, the International Covenant on Civil and Political Rights, the Convention on the Elimination of All Forms of Racial Discrimination, and two protocols to the Convention on the Rights of the Child. As we will see, the resolutions of ratification adopted for these treaties reflect the precedent that was set in the case of the Genocide Convention.

H.G. van der Wilt, J. Vervliet et al., *(eds.)* The Genocide Convention: The Legacy of 60 Years.
Copyright 2012 Koninklijke Brill NV. ISBN 978 9004 15328 8. pp. 173-186.

2. The Cold War, Domestic Politics, and the Genocide Convention Debate

President Truman most probably expected swift ratification of the Genocide Convention when he asked the Senate to give its advice and consent to ratification in 1949. Indeed, in view of the horrendous nature of the crime of genocide,[1] why would a treaty that aimed to prevent it and punish perpetrators not be ratified quickly? Moreover, the Convention enjoyed broad support. In addition to President Truman, the State Department, prominent senators active in foreign affairs, and numerous civic groups and organizations supported its ratification.[2] A subcommittee of the Senate Committee on Foreign Relations held hearings on the Convention in 1950 and favorably reported it to the full committee. However, because of opposition to ratification among some influential senators, including Senator Tom Connally (D-TX), who chaired the Committee on Foreign Relations at that time,[3] and the American Bar Association (ABA), the full committee did not recommend ratification to the Senate as a whole. The ABA changed its position to favor ratification in the mid 1970s, but by then it had done tremendous damage to the Convention and its standing in the Senate.[4]

The debate over the Genocide Convention had stirred up a hornets' nest of issues related to perceived threats to the sovereignty of the United States through the early work of the United Nations on human rights. In the early 1950s, these concerns gave rise to a proposal to amend the United States Constitution to restrict presidential discretion in the treaty-making process. The proposed Bricker Amendment, named for Senator John Bricker (R-OH), was intended to accomplish that objective. President Dwight Eisenhower successfully opposed the adoption of the Bricker Amendment, but at a significant price—his administration would not push for the ratification of any human rights instruments or the Genocide Convention.[5] No further

1 Helen Fein, *Human Rights and Wrongs: Slavery, Terror, Genocide* (2007); Matthew Lippman, "Genocide: The Crime of the Century; the Jurisprudence of Death at the Dawn of the New Millennium," 23 *H. J. INT'L L.*, 3; John Quigley, *The Genocide Convention: An International Law Analysis* (2006); William A. Schabas, "Genocide in International Law" (2000); "Origins of the Genocide Convention: From Nuremberg to Paris," 40 *C.W.R. J. INT'L L.*, 1-2.

2 Lawrence J. LeBlanc, *The United States and The Genocide Convention 4-7* (1991); John Cooper, *Raphael Lemkin and the Struggle for the Genocide Convention 189-208* (2008).

3 *Hearings on the Genocide Convention before a Subcomm. of the Senate Comm. on Foreign Relations,* 81st Cong., 2d Sess. (1950); *Executive Sessions of the Senate Foreign Relations Committee, Historical Series* (1977).

4 See Phillips, "The Genocide Convention: Its Effects on our Legal System," 35 *A.B.A.J.* 623 (1949); Phillips and Deutsch, "Pitfalls of the Genocide Convention," 56 *A.B.A.J.* 641 (1970); Bitker, "Genocide Revisited," 56 *A.B.A.J.* 71 (1970); Goldberg and Gardner, "Time to Act on the Genocide Convention," 58 *A.B.A.J.* 141 (1972) and "Resolution," 62 *A.B.A.J.* 475-76 (1976).

5 Natalie Kaufman, *Human Rights Treaties and the Senate: A History of Opposition* (1990); Duane Tananbaum, *The Bricker Amendment Controversy: A Test of Eisenhower Political Leadership* (1988); Frank Holman, *Story of the Bricker Amendment* (1954).

action was taken on the Convention until the 1970s, during the administrations of presidents Richard Nixon and Jimmy Carter. In response to their requests, Senate hearings were held in 1970, 1971, and 1977,[6] and on several occasions the committees that held the hearings recommended ratification subject to understandings aimed at clarifying the meanings of words and phrases contained in the Convention. But the Senate actually debated ratification only once during this period, in 1973-74, and a resolution of ratification could not be adopted because of a filibuster. Another filibuster prevented ratification later, in 1984.[7]

Through all of these failed attempts, the debates revealed sharp disagreements among proponents and opponents of ratification that were grounded in Cold War politics and domestic politics. The issues concerned the basic definition of genocide established by the Convention, and some others related to the implementation of the Convention. What is remarkable about the debates that ranged over almost forty years is that they changed very little in substance and ferocity until shortly before the adoption of the sovereignty package in 1986.

The definition of the crime of genocide that was the cause of so much controversy in the United States is contained in Article II of the Convention. It provides:

> In the present Convention, genocide means any of the following acts committed with intent to destroy, in whole or in part, a national, ethnical, racial or religious group, as such:
> (a) Killing members of the group;
> (b) Causing serious bodily or mental harm to members of the group;
> (c) Deliberately inflicting on the group conditions of life calculated to bring about its physical destruction in whole or in part;
> (d) Imposing measures intended to prevent births within the group;
> (e) Forcibly transferring children of the group to another group.

Some critics of Article II focused specifically on the potential implications of its terms for domestic law and politics. For example, they quibbled over such words and phrases as the intent to destroy a group "in whole or in part." What did a part of a group mean? Would only one person constitute a part of a group? Or was a part of a group more than one? Did the perpetrators of genocide have to have the intent to destroy an entire group, even if they only succeeded in destroying a part of it? What did "mental harm" mean? Questions of this sort were raised over and over again beginning with the first hearings on the Convention in 1950.[8] The representatives

6 *Hearings on the Genocide Convention before a Subcomm. of the Senate Comm. on Foreign Relations,* 91st Cong., 2d Sess. (1970); *Hearings on the Genocide Convention before a Subcomm. of the Senate Comm. on Foreign Relations,* 92nd Cong., 1st Sess. (1971); *Hearings on the Genocide Convention before the Senate Comm. on Foreign Relations,* 95th Cong., 2nd Sess. (1977).

7 *Hearings on the Genocide Convention before the Senate Comm. on Foreign Relations,* 99th Cong., 1st Sess. (1985).

8 *1950 Senate Hearings,* see n. 3.

of the ABA were especially outspoken in this regard,[9] and their opposition carried a great deal of weight among southern conservative senators.

The ABA and the southern senators feared that the Genocide Convention might be invoked within the United States by opponents of segregationist practices and laws. Specifically, they feared that the Convention could be interpreted as applying to lynchings of black Americans, or that racial segregation could be considered genocidal under the terms of the Convention. Although proponents of ratification argued that the Convention was intended to deal with crimes such as those committed by the Nazis during World War II, not racial segregation in the southern part of the United States, the opponents held steadfastly to their positions. It did not help the cause of ratification when a radical black activist, William Patterson, presented a petition to the United Nations in December 1951, claiming that genocide was being committed in the United States. Nothing came of his petition, but Senator Tom Connally and others saw the submission of the petition itself as sufficient proof that the Genocide Convention could become an instrument in the domestic civil rights struggle.[10]

Additional concerns about the terms of Article II reflected a preoccupation with Cold War politics. Article II is not open-ended: it specifically mentions national, ethnic, racial, and religious groups as objects of protection.[11] In the earliest stages of drafting the Convention, political groups were also covered. But the word "political" was later dropped because of Soviet opposition. Critics attacked this decision, claiming that it created a loophole in the Convention that would benefit the Soviet Union and other totalitarian states which might persecute a national group, for example, but claim that they were really taking measures against subversive political opponents of the state.[12]

But many drafters of the Convention supported the Soviet viewpoint on political groups for good reasons. They argued that political groups were not stable, or not as stable as national, ethnic, racial, or religious groups. For this reason, the drafters of the Convention put attacks against political groups aside, to let them be seen more as "politicide" rather than genocide.[13] The issue is not completely settled, and some argue that the Convention should be amended to protect political groups.[14]

---

9 LeBlanc, *United States and the Genocide Convention,* see n. 2, 40-56.

10 Cooper, *Raphael Lemkin*see n. 2, 205-06.

11 Cooper, *Raphael Lemkin,* see n. 2, 209-14; Schabas, *Genocide in International Law*see n. 1, 102-50;

12 *1950 Senate Hearings,* see n. 3, 194; *1971 Senate Hearings,* see n. 6, 54; LeBlanc, "The United Nations Genocide Convention and Political Groups: Should the United States Propose an Amendment?," 13 *Yale J. INT'L L.* 268-295 (1988)

13 Fein, *Human Rights and Wrongs,* see n. 1, 126-32; Harff and Gurr, "Toward Empirical Theory of Genocides and Politicides: Identification and Measurement of Cases Since 1945," 37 *I.S.Q.* 359-371 (1988); Harff and Gurr, "Conceptual and Policy Issues in Early Warning Research: An Overview," 4 J. *Ethno-Devel* (1994).

14 LeBlanc, *The United Nations Genocide Convention,* see n. 12; Schabas, *Genocide and International Law,* see n. 1, 102-50; Van Schaak, "Crime of Political Genocide: Repairing the Genocide Convention's Blind Spot," 106 *Yale J. INT'L L* (1997).

There was another consideration. During the drafting stage, the United States supported a provision regarding an international criminal court in Article VI, whereas the Soviet Union opposed it. Towards the end of the negotiations, the United States' representatives agreed to a compromise whereby a provision regarding the creation of an international criminal court was adopted in Article VI in exchange for dropping political groups from Article II.[15] The United States' representatives believed that the international criminal court significantly strengthened the Convention.

The clash between the proponents and opponents of ratification gave rise to efforts to reach a compromise that would open the way for ratification of the Convention. This compromise was to ratify the Convention conditionally, that is, subject to understandings regarding specific provisions in the Convention that were of special concern to the opponents. Thus, on four occasions in the 1970s and in 1984, a proposed resolution of ratification included three understandings and a declaration to the effect that the United States would not deposit its instrument of ratification until after the implementing legislation had been adopted. This declaration was to make clear that the Genocide Convention was a non-self-executing treaty. It is arguable that the Convention is a non-self-executing treaty under the terms of Articles V and III, but the opponents of ratification were never prepared to leave a stone unturned and therefore insisted on the declaration. The United States could, of course, ratify self-executing treaties. But the question of whether or not a treaty is self-executing or non-self-executing is a matter of great practical consequence, as the very recent dispute between the United States and Mexico regarding noncompliance by the United States with the Vienna Convention on Consular Relations of 1963 shows.[16]

3. Nicaragua, the ICJ, and the Sovereignty Package

The tenor of the debates over the ratification of the Genocide Convention by the United States changed dramatically in the mid-1980s. Although President Ronald Reagan's administration had shown no interest in the Convention during his first term, he endorsed ratification towards the end of his 1984 campaign for re-election at a speech to the Jewish organization B'nai B'rith. The timing of the endorsement as well as the venue provoked cynicism in the Senate, especially among Democrats who wondered how it was that a review of the treaty which had allegedly started at the beginning of the Reagan administration in 1981 had taken so long and been mysteriously completed at such an opportune time.[17] But the real significance of President Reagan's endorsement was, of course, that he had undermined the position of the most outspoken critics of the Convention, especially Senator Jesse Helms (R-NC), the senior Republican on the Senate Committee on Foreign Relations. No one could argue that President Reagan would willingly take steps to undermine the sovereignty

15 LeBlanc, *United States and the Genocide Convention,* see n. 2, 61-7.

16 Mexico v. United States of America (2004) ICJ, Summary of the Judgment of March 31, 2004.

17 *Hearings on the Genocide Convention before the Senate Comm. on Foreign Relations,* 98th Cong., 2nd Sess. (1984).

of the United States, or that he was somehow in league with liberal internationalists who favored a stronger United Nations. Now even Senator Helms seemed to favor ratification, but only in a manner consistent with the United States Constitution.[18]

But the ICJ would deliver the ammunition that opponents of the Convention, such as Senator Helms, needed to gut the treaty. In April 1984, Nicaragua instituted proceedings against the United States alleging that the conduct of military and paramilitary activities in and against Nicaragua were in violation of international law.[19] Despite vigorous protest by the United States, in part on the ground that the dispute between Nicaragua and the United States was wholly political, the court went on to claim that it had jurisdiction to hear the case, and, ultimately, to find that the United States had violated international customary and treaty law in actions it had taken against Nicaragua.[20] But the court's claim that it had jurisdiction in the case was alone sufficient to send shockwaves through the Senate. Prior to the Genocide Convention, the United States had ratified some seventy treaties that contained dispute resolution clauses allowing for ICJ jurisdiction. Nicaragua demonstrated that the acceptance of such clauses could work to the disadvantage of the United States. Therefore, the opponents of ratification now concentrated on drafting a resolution of ratification that would protect the "sovereignty" of the United States, broadly understood. Indeed, as they claimed in floor debate, the resolution was a "true" sovereignty package and reduced the Convention to a "mere symbol" of opposition to genocide. Even then, eleven Republican senators, including Helms, voted against it.[21]

The sovereignty package contains a declaration to the effect that the United States would not deposit its instrument of ratification at the United Nations until Congress had adopted implementing legislation. The clear intention of this declaration was to say that the United States did not consider the Genocide Convention to be a self-executing treaty, even though, as suggested earlier, this seems clear in the terms of the Convention itself. The implementing legislation, the Genocide Convention Implementation Act, was adopted in 1988, and, as we shall see later, it was modified in 2007.

Two of the understandings in the sovereignty package concern specific words and phrases that appear in Article II of the Convention. One asserts that there must be a "specific [emphasis added] intent to destroy, in whole or in substantial part, a national, ethnical, racial, or religious group as such;" another states that the United States understands the term "mental harm" in Article II(b) to mean "permanent impairment of mental faculties through drugs, torture, or similar techniques." A third understanding applies to the international criminal court referred to in Article VI of the Convention and states that the United States "declares that it reserves the right to effect its participation in any such tribunal only by a treaty entered into specifically for that purpose with the advice and consent of the Senate." This un-

18 Ibid., 1.

19 Nicaragua v. United States of America (1984) ICJ (hereinafter referred to as *Nicaragua*), Jurisdiction and Admissibility, Judgment of November 26, 1984.

20 Nicaragua v. United States of America (1986) ICJ, Merits, Judgment of 27 June 1986.

21 132 Cong. Rec. S1369 (daily ed. 19 February 1986).

derstanding effectively blocked—or at least clearly indicated the Senate's intention to block—a president from using an executive agreement to accept a statute of an international criminal court that might come into existence in accordance with the terms of Article VI. The recent experience of the United States with the statute of the International Criminal Court, established in 2002, suggests that even if such a tribunal is established by a treaty requiring Senate advice and consent, a presidential request for the ratification of such a treaty is likely to be met with intense hostility.

The terms of the Genocide Convention Implementation Act of 1988[22] reiterated the substance of the understandings included in the sovereignty package: the requirement of specific intent, the meaning of mental harm, and the grounds on which US courts could exercise jurisdiction in cases of alleged genocide. As regards the latter, adopted in 1988, the implementing legislation embraced only the territorial and nationality principles under which US courts could exercise jurisdiction. In short, the offense had to be committed in the United States or the offender had to be a national of the United States, even if the act had been committed abroad. Obviously, this meant that in cases such as the Rwanda genocide, persons who had allegedly committed the crimes and later entered the United States or were found in the United States could not have been tried in the United States because they were not nationals of the United States, or the acts had not been committed in the United States. Put another way, under the terms of the Genocide Convention Implementation Act of 1988 the United States could have become a safe haven for persons who had committed genocide abroad. In December 2007, however, under the leadership of Senator Richard Durbin (D-IL), chair of the Subcommittee on Human Rights and the Law of the Senate Committee on Foreign Relations, the Genocide Accountability Act was passed; it allows US courts to exercise jurisdiction under the territorial or nationality principles, as had been established in 1988, but also if (1) the "alleged offender is an alien lawfully admitted for permanent residence in the United States;" (2) the alleged offender is a "stateless person whose habitual residence is in the United States;" or (3) if after the offense had occurred "the alleged offender is brought into, or found in, the United States, even if that conduct occurred outside the United States."[23] The adoption of this legislation is a novel way to get around understandings or reservations in resolutions of ratification.

Finally, the sovereignty package contains two reservations. One is a reservation to Article IX of the Convention and states that "before any dispute to which the United States is a party may be submitted to the jurisdiction of the International Court of Justice ..., the specific consent of the United States is required in each case."[24]

---

22 1988 U.S. Code *Title 18: Crimes and Criminal Procedure: Chapter 50A – Genocide, Section 1091.*

23 2007 U.S. Code *Title 18: Crimes and Criminal Procedure: Chapter 50A – Genocide, Section 1091.* (Amended by the Genocide Convention Accountability Act, 2007; citation is to Legal Information Institute, Cornell University Law School.)

24 On Article IX see De Weese, "The Failure of the International Court of Justice to Effectively Enforce the Genocide Convention," 26 *DEN. J. INT'L L. & POL.* (1998); Quigley, *Genocide Convention*, see n. 1; Schabas, *Genocide and International Law*, see n. 1, 418-446.

Clearly, this reservation indicated the hostility of the most outspoken opponents of ratification towards the ICJ, for having declared that it had jurisdiction in the case of Nicaragua. But the reservation marked a departure from past practices of the United States. The second reservation affirms the supremacy of the US Constitution—as interpreted by the United States—over all provisions of the Genocide Convention. It states that "nothing in the Convention requires or authorizes legislation or other action by the United States of America prohibited by the Constitution of the United States as interpreted by the United States."

Both of the reservations are significant, but for different reasons. It is arguable that any reservation to the dispute resolution clause in Article IX, for example, obviates the need for any other reservation or understanding, whether or not it is a true understanding or a reservation cloaked as an understanding. If a party to the Convention wanted to object to any policy or practice of the United States as being inconsistent with the interpretation, application, or fulfillment of the Convention, it would have to try to negotiate a solution. It would have great difficulty elevating the disagreement to the level of a dispute and taking the case to the ICJ under Article IX, because the United States could simply refuse to go to court. Indeed, if reservations of this sort are permissible, they amount to an ultimate defense mechanism and no other reservation is required. The entire Soviet bloc (excluding Yugoslavia) evidently used reservations to Article IX in this way, but then became exposed to external challenges regarding their compliance with their obligations under the Convention when they withdrew their reservations in the late 1980s and early 1990s.[25] The reservation also makes it impossible for the United States to bring charges to the ICJ against another party to the Convention who may not have made a reservation to Article IX. Under the doctrine of reciprocity, the other state could invoke the US reservation and decline to go to court. The second reservation, regarding the supremacy of the US Constitution over the terms of the Genocide Convention, throws into question the depth of the United States' commitment to joining with other states in combating the crime of genocide.

Other parties to the Genocide Convention were free, in accordance with the established rules of treaty law, to object to the terms of the sovereignty package. Objections were soon forthcoming, but only to the two reservations, not to any of the understandings. It is significant that the practices of the objecting states have varied, raising questions about the effectiveness of some rules of treaty law.

States most closely aligned with the United States have been the most likely to object to the US reservations. Denmark, Finland, Greece, Ireland, Italy, the Netherlands, Norway, Mexico, Spain, Sweden, and the United Kingdom all objected to the constitutional supremacy reservation. In substance, the basis for their objections were essentially the same, namely, that the reservation created uncertainty about the extent of the United States' commitment to the Convention, and that it was not acceptable because it is a generally recognized rule of international law that no state

25 *Multilateral Treaties Deposited with the Secretary-General: Chapter IV Human Rights, No. 1, The Genocide Convention* (2008). Updated periodically online at http://treaties.un.org/Pages/Home.aspx?lang=en.

can invoke provisions of its domestic law as reasons for not living up to its international obligations.[26]

Only four states (Greece, Mexico, the Netherlands, and the United Kingdom) have objected to the United States' reservation to the jurisdiction of the ICJ in Article IX, all on the ground that it was incompatible with the object and purpose of the Convention. According to the Vienna Convention on the Law of Treaties, the effect of an objection depends on the intentions of the objecting state, which could range from simply voicing an objection to indicating that the reservation is so offensive that the objecting state does not consider itself in treaty relations with the reserving state. Greece and the United Kingdom simply indicated that they objected to the United States' reservation to Article IX, but neither indicated that any specific consequences flowed from their objection. Mexico also objected to the US reservation, stating that it "should be considered invalid because it is not in keeping with the object and purpose of the Convention," but it did not consider its objection "as preventing the entry into force" of the Convention between Mexico and the United States.

Only the Netherlands, which has consistently objected to reservations to Article IX on the ground that they are incompatible with the object and purpose of the Convention, carried its objection to its logical conclusion and stated that it would not consider itself in treaty relations with the United States until the reservation is withdrawn. The Netherlands has been very consistent in this practice, objecting to all reservations to Article IX. At the same time, it has also recognized itself in treaty relations with all states that have withdrawn their reservations to Article IX, as it did in the case of the Soviet bloc states.[27]

While the practice of the Netherlands regarding reservations to Article IX is commendable, it is extremely rare. Most commonly, states do not object to reservations made to the Genocide Convention. Moreover, there is little consistency among states that do object. Some object to the reservations of some states but not to those of others, even if the reservations are practically indistinguishable in substance. The practice of allowing states to ratify multilateral treaties with reservations was intended to increase acceptance of the treaties among states, but it remains unclear, on the basis of practice regarding reservations to the Genocide Convention, if this practice has actually produced better results than the alternatives: permitting no reservations whatsoever, or allowing states parties to block the participation of others who proposed to join with unacceptable reservations.

4. The United States Practice Following the Adoption of the Sovereignty Package

Since the adoption of the sovereignty package in 1986, the United States has ratified a number of human rights treaties. All of these instruments were ratified conditionally, in some cases with a combination of reservations and understandings. The

26 Ibid.

27 Ibid.

Convention against Torture provides one of the most interesting examples of how the resolution of ratification for the Genocide Convention has set a precedent. The General Assembly adopted the Convention against Torture in December 1984. It was signed on behalf of the United States in April 1988, and ratified in October 1994 subject to two reservations, five understandings, and one declaration.[28] The declaration follows the Genocide Convention sovereignty package and declares that all of the substantive provisions of the Convention against Torture (Articles 1 through 16) are non-self-executing. The understandings all concern specific aspects of the substantive articles of the Convention and indicate what they are understood to mean so far as the United States is concerned. The reservations mimic the reservations to the Genocide Convention in some respects. One asserts the supremacy of the US Constitution in applying the Convention against Torture, at least so far as it relates to the prevention of cruel, inhuman, or degrading treatment or punishment. According to the reservation, the United States considers itself bound by this obligation only insofar as cruel, inhuman, or degrading treatment or punishment are understood to be prohibited by the fifth, eighth, and fourteenth amendments to the US Constitution. The second reservation applies to the dispute resolution clause in Article 30 of the Convention against Torture. According to Article 30(1), disputes between parties concerning the interpretation or application of the Convention that cannot be settled through negotiation "shall, at the request of one of them, be submitted to arbitration." If the parties cannot agree to the procedures for arbitration, any one of them "may refer the dispute to the ICJ by request in conformity with the Statute of the Court." The United States made a reservation to the terms of Article 30.

Only a few parties to the Convention against Torture have objected to the United States' conditions of ratification. In fact, only three of them have objected, all to the constitutional reservation. Finland, the Netherlands, and Sweden objected on the grounds that the reservation was incompatible with the object and purpose of the Convention, and that the United States could not invoke the provisions of domestic law as an excuse for failing to live up to an international obligation. The Netherlands' objection was the most precise in this regard. It stated that the obligation to prevent cruel, inhuman, or degrading treatment or punishment specified in Article 16 of the Convention against Torture was essential to the object and purpose of the Convention. The Netherlands went on to say that the US understandings had "no impact" on the obligations of the United States. But neither the Netherlands nor Finland and Sweden found the constitutional reservation or any of the understandings so offensive that they did not consider themselves in treaty relations with the United States. To the contrary, the Netherlands specifically indicated that its objections did not preclude the entry into force of the Convention between the Netherlands and the United States.[29]

28 *Multilateral Treaties Deposited with the Secretary-General: Chapter IV Human Rights, No. 9, Convention against Torture and Other Cruel, Inhuman or Degrading Treatment or Punishment* (2008). Updated periodically online at http://treaties.un.org/Pages/Home.aspx?lang=en.

29 Ibid.

The attacks against the United States on September 11, 2001 have brought the Convention against Torture to the forefront in the debate within the United States regarding the treatment of persons captured in the Afghan and Iraq wars. Critics point to what they perceive as flagrant violations of the United States' obligations under the terms of the Convention Against Torture, and argue, among other things, that the United States has adopted extremely narrow definitions of terms like cruel, inhuman, and degrading treatment or punishment; that its conditions of ratification are actually opposed to the plain meaning of the terms of the Convention. Defenders of the Bush administration point to the narrowness of the US interpretations of those terms and argue that the plain meaning of the terms of the Convention against Torture are much too broad to be acceptable. In short, according to the administration, the United States is not in violation of its obligations under the Convention.[30] Even prior to the September 11 attacks, in May 2000, the Committee against Torture, when considering the United States' periodic report, urged the United States to withdraw its conditions of ratification.[31] But, as recently as 2005, the United States refused to withdraw any of its conditions.[32]

The United States' resolutions of ratification to the other human rights instruments follow very much in the footsteps of its resolution on the Convention against Torture. The resolutions of ratification for the International Covenant on Civil and Political Rights[33] and the Convention on the Elimination of All Forms of Racial Discrimination both declare that all the substantive articles of the treaties are non-self-executing.[34] The resolutions of ratification for the two Optional Protocols to the Convention on the Rights of the Child declare that by ratifying the protocols the United States has not assumed any obligations under the terms of the Convention itself, which the United States has not ratified.[35] For both the International Covenant on Civil and Political Rights and the Convention on the Elimination of All Forms of

30 A.C.L.U., *Extraterritorial Applications of the Convention Against Torture: The Failure of the United States to Comply with the Convention Against Torture* (2008), available online at http://www.aclu.org/safefree/torture/A.pdf.

31 United Nations, Doc. A/55/44, C.A.T. *Concluding Observations Concerning the United States* (2000).

32 U.S. Dept. of State, *Second Periodic Report of the United States of America to the Committee Against Torture* (2005), available online at http://www.state.gov/g/drl/rls/45738.htm

33 *Multilateral Treaties Deposited with the Secretary-General: Chapter IV Human Rights, No. 4, International Covenant on Civil and Political Rights* (2008), updated periodically online at http://treaties.un.org/Pages/Home.aspx?lang=en.

34 *Multilateral Treaties Deposited with the Secretary-General: Chapter IV Human Rights, No. 2, International Convention on the Elimination of All Forms of Racial Discrimination* (2008), updated periodically online at http://treaties.un.org/Pages/Home.aspx?lang=en.

35 *Multilateral Treaties Deposited with the Secretary-General: Chapter IV Human Rights, No.11b, Optional Protocol to the Convention on the Rights of the Child on the Involvement of Children in Armed Conflict* (2008), updated periodically online at http://treaties.un.org/Pages/Home.aspx?lang=en; *Multilateral Treaties Deposited with the Secretary-General: Chapter IV Human Rights, No.11c, Optional Protocol to the Convention on the*

Racial Discrimination, the resolutions of ratification contain extensive provisions in the form of reservations and understandings that condition the United States' obligations in a manner consistent with the provisions of the US Constitution. In the case of the Convention on the Elimination of All Forms of Racial Discrimination, the United States made a reservation to the dispute resolution clause in Article 22 of the Convention stating that "before any dispute to which the United States is a party may be submitted to the International Court of Justice" for resolution, "the specific consent of the United States is required in each case."

Most of the objections to the US conditions of ratification to these four instruments have concerned the conditions specified in the resolution of ratification for the Covenant on Civil and Political Rights. The objecting states are, again, historical US allies: Belgium, Denmark, Finland, France, the Federal Republic of Germany, Italy, the Netherlands, Norway, Portugal, Spain, and Sweden. Some of them took issue with the labels used by the United States for its conditions of ratification, claiming that some of the "understandings" were in reality "reservations," and that the reservations were incompatible with the object and purpose of the Covenant. Some statements that were labeled as "reservations" were also found to be incompatible. But none of the objecting states indicated that they were not in treaty relations with the United States because of the unacceptable understandings or reservations. In fact, most indicated that their objections did not constitute an obstacle to the entry into force of the Covenant between them and the United States.[36]

5. Conclusions

The forty-year period following the adoption of the Genocide Convention—culminating in the adoption of a resolution of ratification by the United States Senate in 1986 and the creation of implementing legislation by the United States Congress in 1988—was characterized by sporadic and exceedingly contentious debate over a variety of issues related to the definition of the crime of genocide, and the measures that could be taken to prevent the crime and punish the perpetrators. The Convention always seemed to enjoy broad support, but the opponents of ratification seemed to always have the upper hand in the debate. They were able to force the proponents on the defensive, dominate the debate, and engage in filibusters to block ratification. A variety of domestic political and Cold War issues were raised repeatedly, and, even if without merit, were couched in ways that rallied opponents around the US Constitution and national sovereignty. The constitutional requirement that two-thirds of the one hundred senators present and voting must vote in favor of a resolution of ratification for it to be adopted is difficult to achieve, but it is especially difficult, if not impossible, to achieve in cases where the subject matter is as controversial as the Genocide Convention.

Rights of the Child on the Sale of Children, Child Prostitution and Child Pornography (2008), updated periodically online at http://treaties.un.org/Pages/Home.aspx?lang=en.

36 See n. 33.

As we have seen, as horrendous as the crime of genocide is, the earliest debate on the ratification of the Convention reflected a profound suspicion of the evolving work of the United Nations on human rights, which could lead to meddling in the internal affairs of the United States on such sensitive issues as racial discrimination, and the effect that the emerging Cold War would have on the safety and security of the United States. As irrational as these concerns may have been, they were presented in an alarmist way and had a tremendous impact on the conduct of the debate. President Ronald Reagan's endorsement of ratification in 1984 was crucial to the outcome because it undermined the position of the most outspoken critics of the Convention, who were all fellow conservative Republicans. But while the president's endorsement resulted in ratification, it was under circumstances that were dictated by the opponents of ratification in the form of the sovereignty package.

The terms of the sovereignty package were designed to specifically fit the Genocide Convention, but they have had a lasting impact. This can be seen in instruments of ratification adopted by the United States for several human rights instruments. These instruments contain conditions that affirm the supremacy of the US Constitution over the provisions of the treaties, and, where appropriate, reserve the United States' position on dispute resolution clauses. Although some parties to the Genocide Convention and the other treaties have objected to the United States' conditions of ratification, the practice among states in this regard varies considerably and is woefully inconsistent, raising questions about the effectiveness of treaty law in the new millennium.

6. Appendix: Resolution of Ratification (Lugar-Helms-Hatch Sovereignty Package), adopted February 19, 1986

Resolved (two-thirds of the Senators present concurring therein), That the Senate advise and consent to the ratification of the International Convention on the Prevention and Punishment of the Crime of Genocide, adopted unanimously by the General Assembly of the United Nations in Paris on December 9, 1948, and signed on behalf of the United States on December 11, 1948 (Executive O, Eighty-first Congress, first session), Provided that:

I. The Senate's advice and consent is subject to the following reservations:
   (1) That with reference to Article IX of the Convention, before any dispute to which the United States is a party may be submitted to the jurisdiction of the International Court of Justice under this article, the specific consent of the United States is required in each case.
   (2) That nothing in the Convention requires or authorizes legislation or other action by the United States of America prohibited by the Constitution of the United States as interpreted by the United States.

II. The Senate's advice and consent is subject to the following understandings, which shall apply to the obligations of the United States under this Convention:
   (1) That the term "intent to destroy, in whole or in part, a national ethnical, racial, or religious group as such" appearing in Article II means the spe-

cific intent to destroy, in whole or in substantial part, a national, ethnical, racial, or religious group by the acts specified in Article II.

(2) That the term "mental harm" in Article II (b) means permanent impairment of mental faculties through drugs, torture, or similar techniques.

(3) That the pledge to grant extradition in accordance with a state's laws and treaties in force found in Article VII extends only to acts which are criminal under the laws of both the requesting and the requested state and nothing in Article VI affects the right of any state to bring to trial before its own tribunals any of its nationals for acts committed outside a state.

(4) That acts in the course of armed conflicts committed without the specific intent required by Article II are not sufficient to constitute genocide as defined by this Convention.

(5) That with regard to the reference to an international penal tribunal in Article VI of the Convention, the United States declares that it reserves the right to effect its participation in any such tribunal only by a treaty entered into specifically for that purpose with the advice and consent of the Senate.

III. The Senate's advice and consent is subject to the following declaration: That the President will not deposit the instrument of ratification until after the implementing legislation referred to in Article V has been enacted.

14. The Soviet Perspective on the Drafting of the UN Genocide Convention[1]

Anton Weiss-Wendt

1. The Genocide Convention and the Cold War

This article provides a Soviet perspective on the United Nations (UN) Genocide Convention, by placing the drafting process into the broader context of the Cold War. I argue that the Soviet position towards the definition of genocide hardened as the division of the postwar world into two warring camps became a reality in 1947. As far as the implementation of the Genocide Convention was concerned, somewhat ironically, the Soviet Union and the United States came to exercise similar views. The ideological adversaries worked hard to install safeguards that would make it difficult, if not utterly impossible, to use the Genocide Convention as legal blackmail. In effect, these efforts had rendered the Genocide Convention dysfunctional.[2]

I start with the premise that, the failure to apply the Genocide Convention was mainly due to the ideological confrontation between the Soviet Bloc and the West. To put it differently, the Genocide Convention could be used in international and national courts only after the end of the Cold War. As I went along with my research, however, I realized that the Cold War was more than just an unintended after-effect. The wording of the Genocide Convention, enunciated by the highest international body on December 9, 1948, breathes politics. This observation makes me shift the focus away from the legal debates surrounding the Genocide Convention and into the realm of high politics. Looking from the perspective of Soviet-American relations, the Genocide Convention is a noteworthy document. The Genocide Convention was one of the first significant documents of international law negotiated within

1 This article is part of ongoing research and therefore should not be considered as the author's definitive treatment of the subject. A slightly different version of this article previously appeared in *Rafał Lemkin: A Hero of Humanity*, eds. Agnieszka Bieńczyk-Missala and Sławomir Dębski (Warsaw: Polish Institute of International Affairs, 2010), 179–93.

2 The first ever conviction on charges of genocide was handed down by the International Criminal Tribunal for Rwanda in the case of Jean-Paul Akayesu in 1998, that is, fifty years after the Genocide Convention was adopted.

H.G. van der Wilt, J. Vervliet et al., *(eds.)* The Genocide Convention: The Legacy of 60 Years.
Copyright 2012 Koninklijke Brill NV. ISBN 978 9004 15328 8. pp. 187-197.

the pluralistic environment of the UN. For the Soviet Union, which broke away from self-imposed political isolation only during the war years, multilateral debates on the Genocide Convention proved to be a major test in diplomacy. Soviet conduct in the conference room reflected the attitude of Stalin's regime towards the UN, which was in turn influenced by both communist ideology and a more pragmatic approach to international politics adopted during the Second World War. The opprobrium that the word genocide entails inevitably played out at the negotiation table, shaping the positions of the sides involved in the drafting process. And yet, I contend that postwar geopolitics contributed the most to making the Genocide Convention a dead letter.

The questions that I ask are most relevant to the history of the Cold War and comparative genocide studies. Scholars working in either field, however, have paid surprisingly little attention, if any, to the historical and political context of the Genocide Convention. While genocide scholars—in the beginning predominantly political and social scientists—have been bogged down in interpretations and definitions of genocide, historians of the Cold War have passed over the protracted discussions at the UN as a mere illustration of decisions taken at the highest political level. This explains why, for example, the most comprehensive account of the Soviet record at the UN was published over a half a century ago.[3] One of the foremost experts on the Cold War, Melvyn Leffler, in his recent synthesis of postwar history does not mention even once the International Military Tribunal at Nuremberg, the Genocide Convention, the Universal Declaration of Human Rights, or international law for that matter. Grand in design and execution, his 586-page study barely makes any references to the UN.[4] Another example would be Leo Kuper, lawyer by profession and a pioneer of comparative genocide studies. Writing in 1981, Kuper did not detect any Marxist analysis in the arguments presented by a Soviet delegate during the drafting process. He found it surprising, wondering about the lost possibility for the Soviets, who could have tried to weave the Marxist theory of class struggle as a driving force in history into a theory of genocide.[5] In fact the Soviets did apply Marxist analysis, if only out of habit, when they spoke of the "scientific definition of genocide."

---

3 Alexander Dallin, *The Soviet Union at the United Nations* (London: Methuen &Co, 1962). Trained as a historian, Dallin is probably best known for his book on German occupation policies in Russia, published in 1957. Much less known are his studies commissioned by the US military that paint scenarios of a potential military confrontation between the USSR and the United States, based on patterns of collective behavior of the Soviet people in Nazi-occupied territories. See: Alexander Dallin, *Reactions to the German Occupation of Soviet Russia* (Maxwell Air Force Base, Ala: Human Resources Research Institute, 1952); Alexander Dallin, *Odessa, 1941-1944: A Case Study of Soviet Territory Under Foreign Rule* (Santa Monica: U.S. Air Force Project Rand, 1957).

4 Melvyn P. Leffler, *For the Soul of Mankind: The United States, The Soviet Union, and the Cold War* (New York: Hill and Wang, 2007).

5 Leo Kuper, *Genocide: Its Political Use in the Twentieth Century* (New Haven: Yale University Press, 1981), 47.

By placing the drafting process at the UN into its historical and political context I seek to correct several popular misconceptions about the resultant Genocide Convention. Even though Nazi policies of mass murder in 1939-45 did serve as a catalyst for the debates—indeed, for the very creation of the word genocide—the drafters never conceived of a genocide treaty as an ultimate evil index, or as a measuring stick for past atrocities. As regards discussions surrounding the Genocide Convention, specific historical precedents were rarely mentioned in the deliberations of a respective subcommittee or at General Assembly meetings. For example, virtually nothing had been said about the destruction of the Ottoman Armenians, a subject that had an impact on Raphael Lemkin's early ideas on genocide. Neither was Stalinist terror mentioned by name, aside from random remarks by a United Kingdom (UK) delegate at the General Assembly. Even then, he referred to recent mass deportations of whole nations and slave labor camps, but not the man-made famine of 1932-33 or political purges of 1936-38.

The Genocide Convention was a forward-looking document, not to be applied retroactively. Evidently, any piece of legislation is at the same time a compromise and an act of political will. In that respect, the Genocide Convention was more politics than any other comparable document of international law, for example, the Universal Declaration of Human Rights. This explains why two important elements of the Genocide Convention, protection of political groups and the preventive function, were deliberately left unresolved.

The function of prevention is developed the least within the framework of the Genocide Convention. This is not to say that the participating states were not concerned with prevention. It is just that they had a different idea of prevention, namely, to ensure that their state or any of its citizens could never be brought to (international) justice. Hence, the safeguard mechanisms incorporated into the body of the Convention make it difficult to implement, let alone help to prevent genocide. One of the most contentious issues is the exclusion of political groups among those protected by the Genocide Convention. It has been conventional wisdom to put the blame on the Soviet Union. Scholar after scholar, particularly those who consider ethnic deportations of the 1930s and 1940s and the famine of 1932-33 instances of genocide, refer to the Soviet resolve at the UN to see political groups stricken out of the final draft of the Genocide Convention.[6] This contention is built on a circular

6 Helen Fein, "On Preventing Genocide", in *Genocide and Human Rights: A Global Anthology* (Lanham, MD: University Press of America, 1982), 270; Lyman Legters, "The Soviet Gulag: Is It Genocidal?", in *Toward the Understanding and Prevention of Genocide*, ed. Israel Charny (Boulder, CO: Westview Press, 1984), 63–65; Helen Fein, "Scenarios of Genocide: Models of Genocide and Critical Responses" in *Toward the Understanding and Prevention of Genocide*, ed. Israel Charny (Boulder, CO: Westview Press, 1984), 40; Leo Kuper, "The Genocidal State: An Overview", in *State Violence and Ethnicity*, ed. Pierre van den Berghe (Niwot, CO: University Press of Colorado, 1990), 23–29; Kurt Jonassohn, *Genocide and Gross Human Rights Violations in Comparative Perspective* (New Brunswick, NJ: Transaction Publishers, 1998), 56–57; Stéphane Courtois, "Introduction: The Crimes of Communism", in *The Black Book of Communism: Crimes, Terror, Repression*, ed. Stéphane Courtois et al. (Cambridge, MA: Harvard University

logic. The Soviet Union was eager to eliminate political groups from the wording of the Genocide Convention, allegedly because it was aware that killing group members on the basis of their political affiliation constitutes genocide, and that the use of mass terror against its own citizens was, therefore, genocide.

Remarkably, historians have only recently joined in the debate on the applicability of genocide based on the political or social identification of victims. Paying more attention to the evidence on the ground, a number of students of Soviet and German history have placed Stalinist crimes into a category other than genocide.[7] The evidence emerging from the 1947-48 deliberations corroborates the marginality of political groups in conceptualizing genocide on the one hand, and their exploitation for the specific ideological purposes by both Moscow and Washington on the other. Not having political groups listed alongside with racial, national, religious, and ethnic groups—protected under the letter of the Genocide Convention—preserved the option of interfering in each other's affairs by means of armed groups styled as legitimate opposition.

Press, 1999), 8–10, 16; Otto Pohl, "Stalin's Genocide Against the 'Repressed Peoples'", in *Journal of Genocide Research*, V2 N2 (2000), 271–72, 289; Barbara Harff, "No Lessons learned From the Holocaust: Assessing Risks of Genocide and Political Mass Murder Since 1955", in *American Political Science Review*, V97 N1 (February 2003): 58; Robert Gellately and Ben Kiernan, "The Study of Mass Murder and Genocide," in *The Specter of Genocide: Mass Murder in Historical Perspective* , ed. Robert Gellately and Ben Kiernan (Cambridge: Cambridge University Press, 2003), 18; Eric Weitz, *A Century of Genocide: Utopias of Race and Nation* (Princeton: Princeton University Press, 2003), 10; Norman Naimark, "Totalitarian States and the History of Genocide" in *Telos* N136 (Fall 2006): 17–19; Norman Naimark, *Stalin's Genocides* (Princeton: Princeton University Press, 2010).

7 Barbara Green, "Stalinist Terror and the Question of Genocide: The Great Famine," in *Is the Holocaust Unique: Perspectives on Comparative Genocide* ed. Alan Rosenbaum (Boulder, CO: Westview Press, 1998), 155–57; Ian Kershaw and Moshe Lewin, "Afterthoughts," in *Stalinism and Nazism: Dictatorships in Comparison*, eds. Ian Kershaw and Moshe Lewin (Cambridge: Cambridge University Press, 1997), 354–55; Nicolas Werth, "A State Against Its People: Violence, repression, and terror in the Soviet Union," in *The Black Book of Communism: Crimes, Terror, Repression*, ed. Stéphane Courtois et al. (Cambridge, MA: Harvard University Press, 1999), 262–68; Robert Thurston, "Stalinism in Context and Perspective: Sources of Permission to Hate in Europe," in *Enlightenment and Genocide: Contradictions of Modernity*, eds. James Kaye and Bo Stråth (Bern: Peter Lang, 2000), 202; Amir Weiner, "Nothing But Certainty." in *Slavic Review*, V61 N1 (Spring 2002): 45; Amir Weiner, "When Memory Counts: War, Genocide, and Postwar Soviet Jewry", in *Landscaping the Human Garden: Twentieth-Century Population Management in a Comparative Framework*, ed. Amir Weiner (Stanford: Stanford University Press, 2003), 175, 225; Michael Mann, *The Dark Side of Democracy: Explaining Ethnic Cleansing* (Cambridge: Cambridge University Press, 2005), 17; Nicolas Werth, "The Crimes of the Stalinist Regime: Outline for an Inventory and Classification", in *The Historiography of Genocide*, ed. Dan Stone (Basingstoke: Palgrave, 2008), 409-415. In consideration of the totality of the actions of Stalinist regimes against the Ukrainian peasants in 1932-33, however, Werth is ready to classify the Great Famine as genocide.

The fear that the Genocide Convention could be used as political leverage against the United States and the Soviet Union respectively proved justified. The representatives of the so-called captive nations eagerly incorporated genocide into their lexicon. The suppression of democracy in East Central Europe, the final round of Stalinist deportations in 1949, and the anti-Semitic campaign of the early 1950s—these and other instances of gross human rights violations took on a new life under the heading of genocide. Taken aback, Moscow retaliated. The main target of Soviet attacks was segregationist policies in the American South. At different times, the Korean War, wars of decolonization, and later the Vietnam War were all labeled as genocidal. The Soviet invasion of Afghanistan presented one last opportunity to level an accusation of genocide before the Cold War was over.

The Cold War had compromised the Genocide Convention before it could even be applied once. It did not happen to the Universal Declaration of Human Rights, however, precisely because it was an affirmation of intent rather than a binding treaty. Drafted simultaneously, the latter by far overshadowed the former in terms of fundamental value and popular knowledge. More concrete and less controversial than genocide, human rights have enjoyed universal support and the resolve to implement them worldwide. In the end, it was the longing for the rights and freedoms listed in the Universal Declaration rather than the prospect of punishment built into the Genocide Convention that brought down the Soviet colossus.

2. The Soviet Union at the UN: The Early Years

Many of the politicians who gathered at San Francisco in 1945 assumed that the world could be divided between the great powers on the basis of each minding its own business and neither interfering unduly with the hegemony of the other.[8] The Soviets believed that Big Two, Big Three, Big Four, or Big Five diplomacy would prevent the UN from turning into a debating society instead of a powerful and efficient enforcer of their will. Contemporaneous American analyses grasped fairly well the dilemmas that the Soviets faced in their dealings with the UN. Soviet fear and suspicion of the Western world was a powerful element in postwar international affairs. The Russians were acutely distrustful of the outside world. According to Leninist analysis, the capitalist West would sooner or later run into one of its cyclical crises, which may lead to fascism, imperialism, and war. In such a war, the United States and Britain would be pitted against the Soviet Union. The first prerequisite of Soviet cooperation with the UN, wrote a former member of the US War Department in 1946, would therefore be an assurance against a Western Bloc capable of marginalizing the Soviet Union politically and economically. The second prerequisite was an acknowledgement of a security zone in the form of friendly nations around its far-flung borders.[9] Nevertheless, the Soviet Union initially appeared to be coopera-

8 Robert H. Hadow, "Ideological Conflicts Within U.N.," in *The ANNALS of the American Academy of Political and Social Science*, N252 (1947): 16.

9 Louis E. Brown, "Will the Soviet Union Co-operate With the United Nations?" in *The ANNALS of the American Academy of Political and Social Science*, N246 (1946): 46.

tive—having made several important concessions at San Francisco—and agreed to establish the UN headquarters in New York City. None of it would have been possible had the Soviets anticipated the antagonisms that later developed.

The atmosphere of conflict had dominated the life of the UN since its first assembly in early 1946. Instead of being an organ established to preserve the peace made by the great powers, the UN, as one analyst wrote, had become a battleground between certain governments unable to make peace. The use of the UN as a locus for justifying national acts by both sides in the conflict forewarned eventual disruption. To put the blame on "only one rogue government, the Soviet Union," as Assistant Secretary of State Dean Rusk had done, is to ignore the dynamics of postwar international relations. Actually, a great many Americans sought to push the Communists out and convert the UN into a military alliance against them.[10]

The veto power had been an issue of contention from the very beginning. Although the Anglo-Saxon nations fought tooth and nail against the veto, without its acceptance the Charter of San Francisco could not have been signed. The Soviet delegation was reacting to the perceived hostile moves of Western governments rather than advancing an aggressive policy designed to subvert the UN. Until the process of decolonization sent scores of Third World countries into the General Assembly, the Soviet Union and its satellites found themselves constantly on the defensive on the UN floor. Inexperience negotiating within a multilateral setting, particularly during the first postwar years, further hampered Soviet efforts at the UN, and the veto power, exercised excessively by the Soviet delegation, was useless when it came to drafting the Genocide Convention.

3. Soviet Objections

The Soviets had several objections to the Genocide Convention. To begin with, they disapproved of its very existence, arguing that the Nuremberg principles had covered all the provisions of the proposed genocide treaty. The UK delegation held a similar view, suggesting that the best thing to do would be to request the International Law Commission to codify the Nuremberg principles. The British maintained that a large number of member states would prefer that solution to drafting a separate convention.[11] A tactical restraint on ideology had assisted the Soviets in having the Nuremberg Tribunal, for the most part, organized and run according to their own script. The concept of crimes against humanity and crimes against peace—which placed all responsibility upon a state proclaimed as an aggressor, that is, Nazi Germany—had effectively granted the Soviet Union immunity for crimes as grievous as the ethnic deportation of whole nations in 1941-44 or the mass execution of Polish officers at

10 D. F. Fleming, "The United States in the United Nations," in *The ANNALS of the American Academy of Political and Social Science*, N278 (1951): 73, 82.

11 Davies (UK), UN official records, General Assembly, 2nd session, 1947, American Jewish Archives, Lemkin Papers, Ms 60, Box 4, Series 7.

Katyn in 1941.[12] This reason alone was enough to make the Soviets want to use the Nuremberg principles as a benchmark.

However, there was more to it than just political expedience. As an American ally that had endured huge losses at the hands of the Nazis—US Secretary of State James Byrnes reminded us—the Soviet Union enjoyed a "tremendous deposit of good will" at the end of the Great War.[13] The Soviet experience in the Second World War was a defining moment in the country's history. The Great Patriotic War, as it was known in the Soviet Union, became a new founding myth, replacing such historical markers as the Bolshevik Revolution, the Civil War, crash industrialization, and mass industrialization. Although the human cost was as high, or even higher, the noble cause—fighting against Nazi German aggression—made the sacrifice worthwhile. More importantly, the Second World War was one of the rare moments when the Stalinist regime had enjoyed the genuine support of the (Russian) population.[14] The victory over Nazi Germany, which communist authorities attributed to the superior organization of the Soviet people, was attained in Berlin, signed into a treaty in Potsdam, but pronounced in Nuremberg. The International Criminal Tribunal at Nuremberg came to symbolize the ultimate victory of good over evil. But if genocide was the crime of all crimes, then it had to be directly linked to Nazism, and by extension to the Nuremberg proceedings. In short, Soviet attempts to incorporate the Nuremberg Charter into the wording of the Genocide Convention were not intended to affirm Soviet dominance, but rather to ascertain its status as a country that had played a major role in defeating Nazi Germany.

Among other issues pertinent to the genocide treaty, the Soviet delegation was particularly concerned with procedure and an international criminal court. The Soviet Union tried to amend Article VIII by inserting a requirement for all alleged cases of genocide to be submitted to the Security Council. The Soviets were once again on the defensive, trying to ensure their control as a permanent member of the Council over potential hostile moves of the West. The Soviets continually objected to establishing an international criminal court, holding on to the principle of sovereignty and non-interference in the internal affairs of states. The court would most likely be used as a means of interference—as the Ukrainian representative at the UN Sixth Committee argued—and would simultaneously violate the Nuremberg Charter. The most the Soviets were willing to concede was ad hoc international tribunals set up after the Nuremberg model.[15] Soviet opposition was grounded in political rather than legal arguments. The meeting of a special committee of the General Assembly in Geneva in August 1951 was expected to set up a court with international

12 Telford Taylor, *The Anatomy of the Nuremberg Trial: A Personal Memoir* (New York: Alfred A. Knopf, 1992), 639.

13 James F. Byrnes, "Agreements With Russia: Analysis of Factors That May Bring War or Peace," in *American Bar Association Journal*, V34 (November 1948): 980.

14 Amir Weiner, *Making Sense of War: The Second World War and the Fate of the Bolshevik Revolution* (Princeton, NJ: Princeton University Press, 2001), 7, 19, 171.

15 UN, Department of Public Information, Press Release November 24, 1954, American Jewish Archives, Lemkin Papers, Ms 60, Box 4, Series 3.

criminal jurisdiction. Once the court was functioning, some authors warned, there would be nothing to prevent the UN from indicting Soviet leaders for crimes committed in the Baltic States (see below).[16] Naturally, that was a rather unappealing prospect for the Kremlin.

4. The World Comes Apart, 1947

In the period 1945-47 the dominant view in Soviet foreign policy was that the wartime grand alliance had to be preserved, at least to a certain extent. This outlook was informed by several political and ideological convictions. Moscow counted on internal contradictions within the capitalist system on the one hand, and on the international standing of the USSR—particularly after its expansion into Eastern Europe—on the other. The Soviets believed that they had a common interest with the West in peace and commerce, and specifically in containing Germany. A series of political setbacks experienced in 1947, however, made the Soviets reconsider their foreign doctrine. It began with the proclamation of the Truman Doctrine in March and the discontinuation of allied negotiations on the future of Germany at the Council of Foreign Ministers conference in Moscow in April. The launch of the Marshall Plan on June 5 and its subsequent rejection by the Soviet Union was, in the words of Geoffrey Roberts, "a major precipitating factor in the Soviet declaration of the Cold War and the radical turn in Moscow's ideological and political policy in autumn 1947." In September 1947, the Deputy Foreign Minister Andrei Vyshinsky spoke of the Marshall Plan at the UN. According to Vyshinski, the Marshall Plan was designed as an offshoot of the Truman Doctrine to split Europe into two camps. Thus, by mid-1947 Stalin's regime had made a full circle, effectively reclaiming an ideological vision of the world circa 1939. The proposition that capitalism had changed in nature as a result of the war was abandoned. A return to Marxist-Leninist ideological orthodoxy internally, and the acceptance of a hawkish interpretation of the long-term agenda of the United States, inevitably made Soviet foreign policy take a more militant stance in 1947-48. The choice made by the Soviet Union in the fall of 1947, not unlike that by the United States, was to abandon diplomacy and the search for agreement. Instead, both superpowers sought to gather strength by protecting their own interests.[17]

Among the many conflict zones, Greece was a tipping point leading to the outbreak of the Cold War. The establishment of a UN Commission of Investigation in Greece further accentuated the significance of that particular Balkan country within the geopolitical context of the postwar era. The Greek Civil War seemed to furnish evidence of an aggressive Soviet move to extend its control over nations critical to US security. Indeed, by late 1946 Greece remained the only country in the Balkans outside Soviet hegemony. The US government conceived of a new policy aimed at preventing the Greek Communists from coming to power. The UN Commission

16 William Attwood and Seymour Freidin, "Why Stalin Must Be Tried for Murder," in *Collier's*, June 30, 1951.

17 Geoffrey Roberts, "Moscow and the Marshall Plan: Politics, Ideology and the Onset of the Cold War, 1947," in *Europa-Asia Studies*, V46 N8 (1994): 1371–82.

was set up in December 1946 in response to a complaint submitted by Greece to the Security Council, in which it accused Yugoslavia, Bulgaria, and Albania of assisting the Communist guerillas, fomenting civil strife, and threatening its territorial integrity. The new US Secretary of State George Marshall agreed to participate, suggesting that the whole issue would otherwise play into Soviet hands. The Americans and the British were convinced that the guerillas were taking orders from Moscow, which was not true. Soviet consent to the establishment of the Commission was prompted by a desire to weaken the British as well as to keep the Yugoslav Communists and their Greek clients in check. During the summer months of 1947 the Security Council had maneuvered itself into a dead end over the Greece problem. The pattern had been set, with the United States tabling draft resolutions thwarted by the Soviet veto, and vice versa. Finally, on October 21 the General Assembly accepted the resolution (by forty votes to six, with eleven abstentions) establishing the UN Special Committee on the Balkans. The Communist countries rendered the Committee obsolete, however, by having refused to recognize its legitimacy.[18]

The Greek Civil War assumed a potent ideological dimension, exploited by the great powers in advancement of their strategic interests. Stalin was following events rather than leading them, and he lost. Stalin capitalized on the Communist insurgency in order to expand Soviet influence in Greece as well as to curb Tito's ambitions. However, he did not intend to escalate the Civil War, which might have jeopardized the long-term objectives of Soviet foreign policy. The Anglo-American Bloc interpreted Stalin's pragmatism as a deliberate calculation to get the upper hand in Greece by proxy. This suspicion precipitated the Truman Doctrine, that is, the steadfast policy of moral and material opposition to Communism. The Soviet stance at the UN had been weakened too. Despite frequent references to the UN Charter, whenever it was opportune the Soviets overlooked a provision that forbade meddling with the internal affairs of member states. The non-interference clause offered a legal justification for the Anglo-American position vis-à-vis the UN Commission of Investigation in Greece. The handling of the Greek Civil War by the UN created a precedent, which had a bearing on the Soviet position towards the Genocide Convention.

5. Political Groups Omitted

In late November 1947 a political bomb went off: the Lithuanian legation in Washington D.C. submitted to the UN an appeal that charged the Soviet authorities with genocide against the Lithuanian nation. The appeal spoke of the perpetual threat to the Lithuanian people posed through mass arrests, killings, and deportations, and called upon the international body to intervene against enslavement and extermination, in accordance with the fundamental rights guaranteed by the UN Charter. The commentary in The New York Times reminded of a common Soviet practice to

18 Thanasis Sfikas, "Britain, the United States, and the Soviet Union in the United Nations Commission of Investigation in Greece, January-May 1947," in *Contemporary European History*, V2 N3 (1993): 244–60.

transfer hostile populations from the strategic border areas, naming specifically the Chechens, the Ingush, and the Crimean Tartars. The inhabitants of the three Baltic States, who had been fighting against the Russian rule, were eventually to expect the same fate. The charges of genocide had been raised before in unofficial reports and had found significant support among the Lithuanians fighting for the freedom of their country, including those in the armed resistance movement. On November 25, representatives of the former Baltic governments launched a formal appeal to the General Assembly. They asked the President of the Assembly Osvaldo Aranha to circulate among the delegates the 34-page document filled with the evidence of Soviet genocide. The General Assembly was encouraged to take action towards liberating the Baltic countries from Soviet control.[19]

The joint Baltic appeal posed a problem for the UN. Although the Genocide Convention was yet under discussion in the UN committees, the resolution from December 1946, which had declared genocide an international crime, imposed upon the General Assembly the duty to act on it. At the very least, speculated The New York Times, the Assembly seemed to be under an obligation to investigate the charges. Although Russia would surely refuse to cooperate, the Greek precedent provided for an investigation on the basis of whatever evidence was available. What the Assembly could not afford, wrote the newspaper, was "to turn its back and look the other way when the spokesmen of small nations appeal for a hearing on life-or-death charges of this kind."[20] This kind of discussion could not but have sounded the alarm for the Soviets. The provisions of the Genocide Convention had not been agreed upon yet, but the Soviet Union felt the brunt of it already. The most ominous aspect appeared to be the connection between anti-Soviet insurgence and charges of genocide. Would that imply that by hunting down and killing members of the resistance the Soviet Union had placed its head under the blade of international law? From the viewpoint of the Soviet delegation at the UN, this whole episode had enforced only one conclusion: to do anything possible to ensure that the Genocide Convention could never be used against the Soviet Union. Ideally, Soviet representatives would work hard to put the Americans and the British on the defensive by means of the Genocide Convention.

Several Latin American delegations joined in the opposition against including political groups. One of the delegates eloquently explained his position:

> On our continent," he said in camera, "we are always having a revolution. Then we dance a rumba and forget it. But if this treaty includes political groups, the loser of the revolution can claim before the world that the winner violated the genocide pact and must be punished.[21]

19 *The New York Times*, November 22 and 25, 1947; *Novoe Russkoe Slovo*, November 26, 1947.

20 *The New York Times*, November 22, 1947.

21 Herbert Yahraes, "He Gave a Name to the World's Most Horrible Crime," in *Collier's*, March 3, 1951.

Although not a revolution by any standards, the extension of Soviet influence into Eastern Europe suggested a similar scenario. The first action undertaken in all of these countries was neutralizing and, if necessary, eliminating political opposition. This explains why the Soviets were less than thrilled if stifling the opposition would be classified as genocide. Let me illustrate this using the example of a clause in Article II of the Genocide Convention, the clause that dealt with the forced transfer of children. Clause E referred to such practices as those of the Ottoman Sultans, who carried off Christian children and made them Muslims and slaves. All such acts, however, must be carried out with intent to destroy a group in whole or in part. For that reason, the alleged relocation of children for re-education by the Communist guerillas in the Greek Civil War did not constitute genocide. The intention was to destroy the ascendant political group rather than the Greek national group. If the word political had been retained in Article II to designate one of the protected groups, however, this and similar acts might have been classified as genocide.[22] And that was exactly what the Soviets, and increasingly more so the Americans, wanted to avoid. Both governments wanted to have a free hand at sponsoring insurgent groups—invariably identified as "opposition" or "liberation" movements—without being afraid of an international sanction. One of the earlier commentators on the Genocide Convention, Nehemiah Robinson, indicated as early as 1960 that the main reason behind the exclusion of political groups from the final draft was because, in the opposite case, the UN might be able to intervene in the domestic strife of a country.[23]

6. Postscript

The United States was among the first to sign the Convention, on December 11, 1948. The Soviet Union, Belorussian SSR, and Ukrainian SSR (with reservations with respect to Articles IX and XII) followed a year later, on December 16, 1949. They became the thirty-third, thirty-sixth, and thirty-seventh signatories to the Convention. As regards Article IX, the Soviet Union did not consider as binding the provision that referred disputes between the contracting parties to the International Criminal Court. With regard to Article XII, the Soviets insisted that the Genocide Convention should extend to dependent territories, including trust territories. The Soviet Union, Belorussian SSR, and Ukrainian SSR deposited their instruments of ratification on May 3, August 11, and November 15, 1954, respectively. Past that date, the prospect of US ratification all but dissipated. As soon as the United States ratified the Genocide Convention in November 1988, the Soviet Union withdrew its reservations. The Cold War was over.

22 Richard Gilliam, "The Genocide Convention and Racial Relations," unpublished paper, no date [between 1951 and 1953], American Jewish Archives, Lemkin Papers, Ms 60, Box 4, Series 6.

23 Nehemiah Robinson, *The Genocide Convention: A Commentary* (New York: World Jewish Congress, 1960), 59.

Archives

15. Truths, Memories and Histories in the Archives of the International Criminal Tribunal for the Former Yugoslavia[1]

Eric Ketelaar

1. Introduction

In 1993, the United Nations (hereinafter UN) Security Council established the International Criminal Tribunal for the Prosecution of Persons Responsible for Serious Violations of International Humanitarian Law Committed in the Territory of the Former Yugoslavia since 1991 (hereinafter ICTY) "for the sole purpose of prosecuting persons responsible for serious violations of international humanitarian law committed in the territory of the former Yugoslavia."[2] The central purpose of the ICTY, as of any criminal court, is the deterrence of, and retribution for serious wrongdoing.[3] But from the start, expectations of what the Tribunal could achieve went beyond the primary judicial goal of establishing the truth about and a historical record of what happened, contributing to healing individuals' and communities'

1 This is a slightly different version of my paper, "Truths, Memories, and Histories in the Archives of the ICTR and the ICTY," presented at the conference "60 Years Genocide Convention," organized by the Amsterdam Center for Holocaust and Genocide Studies, the Amsterdam Center for International Law and the Peace Palace Library, The Hague, 8 December 2008. Another version was published as E. Ketelaar, "A living archive, shared by communities of records", in *Community archives. The shaping of memory*, eds. J. A. Bastian and B. Alexander (London, Facet 2009) 109-132.

2 United Nations Security Council (1993) *Resolution 827*, http://www.icty.org/x/file/Legal%20Library/Statute/statute_827_1993_en.pdf [accessed 22 June 2011]; M.C. Bassiouni, and P. Manikas, *The Law of the International Criminal Tribunal for the Former Yugoslavia* (Irvington N.Y, Transnational, 1996) 1-36 and 199-236; M.P. Scharf, *Balkan Justice: the story behind the first international war crimes trial since Nuremberg* (Durham N.C., Carolina Academic Press 1997); G.J. Bass, *Stay the Hand of Vengeance: the politics of war crimes tribunals* (Princeton and Oxford, Princeton University Press 2000).

3 M. Osiel, *Mass Atrocity, Collective Memory, and the Law* (New Brunswick, Transaction 1997).

H.G. van der Wilt, J. Vervliet et al., *(eds.)* The Genocide Convention: The Legacy of 60 Years.
 ISBN 978 9004 15328 8. pp. 201-221.

traumas, and to reconciliation.[4] Connected with the diverse expectations of the outcomes of the Tribunal's work are expectations of the role the Tribunal's archives can play. Anticipations are mounting as the ICTY's work is near completion and decisions about the legacy of the Tribunal are imminent.

In this essay, I explore the potentials of the ICTY archives in establishing truth, engaging with history and practicing memory – all of which may help communities in the former Yugoslavia and elsewhere to not only come grips with their own past but to also acknowledge a past shared with neighboring ethnic and political communities. [5] I will argue that these expectations can only be met by a living archive as a place of contestation allowing for what Hayden White has called different kinds of discourse about "what happened and what is to be done"—the archive not merely as a storage technique but primarily as a force for delegitimizing mystified and traditionalised memories.[6]

Media in Bosnia and Herzegovina, Republika Srpska, Serbia, and Croatia brought the archives of the ICTY into the limelight with headlines like: "Sarajevo joins race for ICTY archive";[7] "Discussion on the fate of ICTY archive"[8]; "Fighting for the Hague documents"[9]; "BiH, Serbia, Croatia all lobby to take over ICTY archives".[10] The headlines also attest to contesting views on the fate of the archives, which vary by region in the former Yugoslavia.[11] Even within one region there are competing views. The mayor of Sarajevo reportedly claimed that the ICTY archives contain "the only established version of the truth, unlike the three versions that currently exist" in Bosnia and Herzegovina.[12]

4 S. Power, "Stopping Genocide and Securing 'Justice:' learning by doing," *Social Research*, 69 (2002) 1099-1106.

5 I refrain from dealing with "memoricide": eradicating communities' identities by destroying their archives. See J. Kolanovic, "Archives en temps de guerre: l'expérience de la Croatie," *Archivum*, 42 (1996) 173-180; M. Kovacevic, "War Damage Suffered by the State Archives of Bosnia and Herzegovina," *Archivum*, 42 (1996) 181-186; A.J. Riedlmayer, "Crimes of War, Crimes of Peace: destruction of libraries during and after the Balkan wars of the 1990s," *Library Trends*, 56 (2007) 107-132.

6 H. White, "Catastrophe, Communal Memory and Mythic Discourse: the uses of myth in the reconstruction of society," in *Myth and Memory in the Construction of Community: historical patterns in Europe and beyond*, ed. B. Stråth (Bruxelles and New York, P.I.E.-Peter Lang: 2000) 55.

7 "Sarajevo Joins Race For ICTY Archive," *Dnevni avaz*, (20 November 2007).

8 "Discussion on the Fate Of ICTY Archive," *Nezavisne novine*, (24 November 2007).

9 "Fighting for the Hague Documents," *Nedeljni Telegraf*, (19 March 2008), 5.

10 "The archive material of the Tribunal is of crucial importance, our history will be written based on it," *Vecernji list* (25 March 2008).

11 The territory of the former Yugoslavia comprises the states of Bosnia and Herzegovina (consisting of two entities: the Federation of Bosnia and Herzegovina and Republika Srpska), Croatia, Kosovo, Republic of Macedonia, Montenegro, Serbia, and Slovenia.

12 S. Škuletić, "Sarajevo Major: The City of Sarajevo will Request the ICTY Archives On Its Own," *Dnevni avaz Dnevni avaz*, 5 (2008); P.B. Miller, "Contested Memories: the

Since its establishment the Tribunal has indicted 161 persons. As of June 2011, proceedings against 125 have been concluded. Proceedings are on-going with regard to thirty-six accused, and one (Hadžić) is still at large.[13] In 2003, the Security Council called on the ICTY to take all possible measures to complete the work. It is now estimated that all trials and appeals will be concluded in 2012. A key component of the ICTY completion strategy concerns the appropriate disposition of its archives.

In 2005, I submitted to the registrar of the ICTY a report called "The Legacy of the United Nations International Criminal Tribunal for the former Yugoslavia (ICTY): Justice, Reconciliation, and Memory," based on research carried out between September 2004 and July 2005.[14] Concurrently, the United States Institute of Peace and the National Peace Foundation sponsored Trudy Huskamp Peterson to undertake a comparative review of the temporary international tribunals and the records they create.[15] While my report focuses on the measures to be taken with regard to the ICTY records in the framework of the Tribunal's completion strategy, Peterson's report offers a conceptual framework for creating a central international judicial archive under UN auspices, with standards to select, preserve, and manage the records of temporary international criminal courts.

I reconnected with the ICTY archives when I was appointed as a member of the Advisory Committee on the Archives of the UN Tribunals for the former Yugoslavia and Rwanda (ACA), established by the registrars of the two Tribunals in October 2007.[16] The ACA was mandated to provide an independent comparative analysis of

Bosnian genocide in Serb and Muslim minds," *Journal of Genocide Research*, 8 (2006) 311-324.

13 www.icty.org (Accessed 22 June 2011).

14 E. Ketelaar, *The Legacy of the United Nations International Criminal Tribunal for the former Yugoslavia (ICTY): justice, reconciliation, and memory* (Amsterdam, University of Amsterdam: 2005) (unpublished). I was assisted by postgraduate students enrolled in the Master of Archival Science program of the University of Amsterdam: Ernestine Baake, Esther Balkestein, Jelle Bosma, Marie-Christine Engels, Kees Fluyt, Wim Mastenbroek, and Natasja Pels. I presented some of the results of this research to the Second International Conference on the History of Records and Archives (ICHORA2) in Amsterdam, 1-3 September 2005.

15 T.H. Peterson, *Temporary Courts, Permanent Records* (Washington DC, United States Institute of Peace: 2006), http://www.usip.org/files/resources/sr170.pdf [accessed 22 June 2011]; see also T.H. Peterson, *Final Acts: a guide to preserving the records of truth commissions* (Woodrow Wilson Center Press and The Johns Hopkins University Press, Washington DC and Baltimore 2005) http://www.wilsoncenter.org/press/peterson_finalacts.pdf [accessed 22 June 2011].

16 The other members of ACA were Justice Richard Goldstone, former Chief Prosecutor of the ICTY and the ICTR (chair), Saliou Mbaye, former national archivist of Senegal, Judge Mohamed Othman, a member of the Tanzanian High Court, former Prosecutor at the East Timor UN Administration, and former Chief of Prosecutions at the ICTR, and Cecile Aptel, former staff member of both the ICTY and ICTR. I have benefited greatly from the insights and fellowship of the ACA. I also want to record my gratitude to Hans Holthuis, registrar of the ICTY and his staff for their invaluable assistance and

the potential locations for the archives of each of the Tribunals and to examine related issues concerning those archives. The ACA submitted its report to the registrars in September 2008.[17]

2. ICTY Archives

The ICTY archives comprise video and audio recordings, 2,200 gigabytes of electronic material, artifacts, and 1,449 meters of paper records. [18] Nearly eighty-two percent of the paper records exist in both paper and digital format. The bulk (seventy percent) are the substantive records of the Office of the Prosecutor (OTP). These include records and material obtained in the course of investigations, such as witnesses' statements and other evidence. All over the former Yugoslavia, the OTP seized documents by the truckload, and from various sources tons of documents, photographs, intercepts of telecommunications, and videos were received.[19] They are from public and private provenances and include records of military and civil government agencies in and outside the former Yugoslavia, personal correspondence, audiovisual items, diaries, and other similar material. In most cases, the originals have been returned to the owner or provider, leaving a copy in the archives of the Tribunal.

A second category are the judicial records comprising all court files and records obtained or generated by the Tribunal in support of and during the indictment phase, the pretrial, trial, and appeal procedures, as well as procedures relating to the

---

support to my research. The views expressed in the present paper are those of the author in his personal capacity and do not necessarily represent the views of the United Nations.

17 Unlike my 2005 study and the ACA report the present paper does not deal with the current management and the future location of the ICTY archives. Those and other issues are dealt with in the Report of the Secretary-General of the United Nations "on the administrative and budgetary aspects of the options for possible locations for the archives of the International Tribunal for the Former Yugoslavia and the International Criminal Tribunal for Rwanda and the seat of the residual mechanism(s) for the Tribunals," 21 May 2009 http://icty.org/x/file/About/Reports%20and%20Publications/CompletionStrategy/090521_sg_report_residual_mechanism.pdf [accessed 22 June 2011] and in Resolution 1966 (2010) of the UN Security Council, 22 December 2010 http://www.icty.org/x/file/About/Reports%20and%20Publications/ResidualMechanism/101222_sc_res1966_residualmechanism_en.pdf [accessed 22 June 2011].

18 The term archives applies, according to the UN administrative instruction ST/AI/326 of 28 December 1984, "to those records to be permanently preserved for their administrative, legal, historical or informational value." Records are, following the definition in that instruction, "all documentary materials, regardless of physical type, received or originated" by the Tribunal: http://archives.un.org/unarms/doc/AI_326_UN_Archives_.pdf [accessed 22 June 2011]. I have updated some figures from Peterson, *Temporary Courts* on the basis of information provided by ICTY staff, as of November 2007/August 2008. See also the figures in the Report of the Secretary-General (2009), referred to in the preceding footnote.

19 J. Hagan, *Justice in the Balkans: prosecuting war crimes in the Hague tribunal* (Chicago, University of Chicago Press: 2003).

transfer of cases. These include English and French transcripts and the audio-visual recordings of the proceedings, evidence tendered in court, motions, decisions, and all other documents and relevant correspondence created by the judges and the parties.

Other types of records that relate to the judicial process, but are not part of the official case files, are records of meetings; general correspondence files; records concerning the privileges and immunities of the Tribunal; agreements with the host country, with other states, and with intergovernmental organizations; correspondence with individual states in order to help enforce sentences and the relocation of witnesses; press files; publications by the Tribunal; and, lastly, the Tribunal's website (www.icty.org), which is, among other things, an archive from which the public can download the public version of transcripts, etc. In 2008, the website recorded more than one million page hits each month for the English site and close to one million each month for the Bosnian/Croatian/Serbian site.

The administrative records include records concerning human resources, procurement, finance, and other administrative support functions. Judges, the prosecutor, the registrar, and members of staff will have kept working papers. To the extent that they relate to the conduct of the Tribunal's activities, they have value as part of the ICTY's legacy.[20] This applies equally to the records created and received by the defense counsel and not submitted to the Tribunal.

The ICTY's Judicial Database (JDB) provides electronic access to court records in most of the Tribunal's cases.[21] The JDB includes court filings, judgments, decisions, exhibits (but not three dimensional artifacts), transcripts, and statistical information needed for registered users (usually from the OTP and the defense counsel) to conduct legal research. The database has to be separately accessed for public records, and confidential material may only be accessed with the appropriate security access. The JDB is a legal research tool and not designed to function as a database of archival records.

As early as 1994, the judges instructed the registrar to make and preserve "a full and accurate record of all proceedings, including audio recordings, transcripts and, when deemed necessary by the Trial Chamber, video recordings".[22] All courtroom sessions have been recorded on video (with audio track) and audio. The complete

20 J.L. Sax, *Playing Darts with a Rembrandt: public and private rights in cultural treasures* (Ann Arbor, University of Michigan Press: 1999).

21 D. Pimentel, "Technology in a War Crimes Tribunal: recent experiences at the ICTY," *William and Mary Bill of Rights Journal*, 12 (2004) 715-729; Peterson, *Temporary Courts, Permanent Records.*

22 United Nations International Criminal Tribunal for the former Yugoslavia (2006) *ICTY Rules of Procedure and Evidence*, http://www.icty.org/x/file/Legal%20Library/Rules_procedure_evidence/IT032Rev45_en.pdf [accessed 22 June 2011] rule 81; P. Mason, *Report on the Impact of Electronic Media Coverage of Court Proceedings at the International Criminal Tribunal for the former Yugoslavia* (The Hague and Southampton, Centre for Media and Justice at the Southampton Institute: 2000); Peterson, *Temporary Courts, Permanent Records*; S. Haufek, *Reconciliation and the Expansive Archive: cultural memory and the legacy of the International Criminal Tribunal for the former*

video contains all confidential material (for example testimonies by witnesses whose identity has to be kept secret), while a redacted version contains only public material. The audiovisual record of the proceedings is more comprehensive than the official transcripts. The transcripts exist in two versions, in English and French, while the audiovisual record contains Bosnian, Croatian, and Serbian as spoken by defendants and witnesses. Moreover, in the transcripts 'the entire visual content of the footage of atrocities committed throughout the region is in most instances reduced to two words: "videotape played". [23]

Legally, the records created and received by the Tribunal are the property of the UN. However, they do not belong to the Tribunal; they constitute a legacy, a "joint heritage," shared by a number of "communities of records".[24] These communities consist of different stakeholders (to be identified in the following section), each with a right to know from the ICTY archives.

Stakeholders

The stakeholders with a concern in the ICTY archives occupy different spatial and temporal positions, depending on the degree of their involvement in the core business of the Tribunal. The interests of stakeholders change over time. Some will not have an immediate interest; others' interests may gradually increase or decrease.

The first category of stakeholders comprises those who now or in the near future have an interest in the primary legal business of the ICTY, viz., to bring to justice persons responsible for serious violations of international humanitarian law committed in the territory of the former Yugoslavia since 1991. This goal will not be reached upon completion of the Tribunal's mandate in 2012. Part of the completion strategy is to transfer to competent national jurisdictions (inside and outside the former Yugoslavia) those cases involving the accused of intermediate and lower rank .[25] For domestic courts, prosecutors, and defence counsel, the ICTY records will continue to be active records. [26]

Yugoslavia. Master's thesis (unpublished) (Amsterdam, University of Amsterdam, Department of Media Studies: 2006).

23 H. Lennon, "A Witness to Atrocity: film as evidence in international war crimes tribunals," in *Holocaust and the Moving Image: representations in film and television since 1933*, eds. T. Gaggith, and J. Newman (London, Wallflower Press: 2005) 65-73.

24 E. Ketelaar, "Sharing: collected memories in communities of records," *Archives and Manuscripts*, 33 (2005) 44-61.

25 D. Raab, "Evaluating the ICTY and its Completion Strategy: efforts to achieve accountability for war crimes and their tribunals," *Journal of International Criminal Justice*, 3 (2005) 82-102.

26 According to Rule 11bis (D) of the ICTY Rules of Procedure and Evidence, when a case is referred to another court, "the Prosecutor shall provide to the authorities of the State concerned all of the information relating to the case which the Prosecutor considers appropriate and, in particular, the material supporting the indictment" : United Nations International Criminal Tribunal for the former Yugoslavia (2006) ICTY Rules of Procedure and Evidence, http://www.icty.org/x/file/Legal%20Library/Rules_procedure_evidence/IT032Rev45_en.pdf [accessed 22 June 2011].

Fifteen states have so far agreed to enforce the Tribunal's sentences. The judicial authorities in these countries need to have access to the medical files and other records concerning convicts, which were created by the ICTY. The Tribunal retains certain supervisory responsibilities,[27] which (upon completion of the Tribunal's mandate) have to be transferred to a successor agency. That successor agency will need access to the relevant records. Other stakeholders with an interest in ICTY's archives, because they were involved in the core legal business of the Tribunal, are the United Nations, former ICTY staff and defense counsel, governments in the region, indicted and convicted persons, and witnesses.

Slightly more distant from the core legal business of the Tribunal, but nevertheless with an interest in the primary values of the Tribunal's records are victims and their relatives, many of whom live outside the former Yugoslavia;[28] victims' groups and other nongovernmental organizations; the media; the International Criminal Tribunal for Rwanda; the International Criminal Court; and other criminal justice organizations.[29] Scholarly researchers (in law, history, political science, etc.) intersect this first category of stakeholders as well as the second, which comprises all those who were not directly involved in the trials before the Tribunal but whose interest in the Tribunal's archives will develop over time.[30] The ICTY archives have a significant secondary value for several reasons, analogous to the arguments recently proposed by Bruce Montgomery with regard to the archives of human rights organizations:

1. The archival record is important for historical accountability, which will be 'used by researchers, prosecutors, and victims alike with the aim of analyzing and making known the dimensions of particular human rights violations;'
2. The archival evidence 'is important for the memory of the thousands of victims and survivors of human rights abuses, their relatives, and others who must individually confront the truth of what transpired. Retaining the memory of victims and survivors is also important to preserve at least some semblance of identity for those who suffered extreme depredations...;'
3. Archival records of human rights abuses will likely assume new and critical importance as this evidence becomes pivotal in the adjudication of cases. Post-

27 D. Tolbert, "Reflections on the ICTY Registry," *Journal of International Criminal Justice*, 2 (2004) 480-485; Peterson, *Temporary Courts, Permanent Records.*

28 L. Huttunen, "'Home' and Ethnicity in the Context of War: hesitant diasporas of Bosnian refugees," *European Journal of Cultural* Studies, 8 (2005) 177-195.

29 Peterson, *Temporary Courts, Permanent Records*; T. A. Adami and M. Hunt, "Genocidal Archives: the African context – genocide in Rwanda," *Journal of the Society of Archivists*, 26 (2005) 105-121.

30 The archives of the International Military Tribunal and the US Nuremberg Military Tribunals are, some 60 years since their creation, used very rarely by lawyers and professional historians, but mostly by private individuals interested in a relative who testified or served in some capacity with the court, or people who are a relative of a victim of Nazi aggression etc. (T.K. Nenninger (US National Archives and Records Administration), personal communication to E. Balkestein, University of Amsterdam, March 15, 2005).

authoritarian governments can only be helped if they confront the crimes of the past and end impunity with the aim of building new democratic societies based on the rule of law.[31]

3. Truths

In February 2007, the Humanitarian Law Center in Belgrade, along with its partners the Research and Documentation Center in Sarajevo and Documenta Center for Dealing with the Past in Zagreb, jointly organized a forum called Establishing the Truth about War Crimes and Conflicts. The conference agreed that the ICTY archives will play a very significant role in truth-telling and truth-seeking. During the conference, however, representatives of victims' organizations expressed their disapproval of its title "claiming that victims are the only rightful owners of the truth".[32] What did they mean by 'the truth?'

Four notions of truth were used by the South African Truth and Reconciliation Commission: factual or forensic truth; personal or narrative truth; social or 'dialogue' truth, and healing and restorative truth.[33] Richard Wilson proposes to categorize these into two truth paradigms: forensic truth and narrative truth.[34] The former is "the familiar legal or scientific notion of bringing to light factual, corroborated evidence, of obtaining accurate information through reliable (impartial, objective) procedures".[35] As an ICTY president wrote, establishing the truth in the courtroom of the ICTY means that the atrocities in former Yugoslavia will become "facts established by law.".[36] However, defendants, witnesses, prosecutors, and judges tell, hear, and record something that counts as true in a particular case, a particular trial, within the legal context.[37] The legal forum is not interested in anything but the fo-

31 B.P. Montgomery, "Fact-Finding by Human Rights Non-Governmental Organizations: challenges, strategies, and the shaping of archival evidence," *Archivaria*, 58 (2004) 23.

32 Documenta center for dealing with the past, *Conclusions from International Conference "Establishing the Truth about War Crimes and Conflicts," Second Regional Forum on Transitional Justice* (2007) http://www.documenta.hr/eng/index.php?option=content&task=view&id=29&Itemid= [accessed 4 July 2008].

33 Truth and Reconciliation Commission of South Africa, *Report, vol. 1* (1998) http://www.doj.gov.za/trc/report/ [accessed 22 June 2011]; A.R. Chapman and P. Ball, "The Truth of Truth Commissions: comparative lessons from Haiti, South Africa, and Guatemala," *Human Rights Quarterly*, 23 (2001) 1-43.

34 R. Wilson, *The Politics of Truth and Reconciliation in South Africa: Legitimizing the Post apartheid State* (Cambridge, Cambridge University Press: 2001).

35 Truth and Reconciliation Commission of South Africa, *Report*, 111.

36 C. Jorda, "The Major Hurdles and Accomplishments of the ICTY: what the ICC can learn from them," *Journal of International Criminal Justice*, 2 (2004) 572-584, 577.

37 J. Edkins, *Trauma and the Memory of Politics* (Cambridge, Cambridge University Press: 2003); Montgomery, "Fact-Finding by Human Rights Non-Governmental Organizations."

rensic truth. It cannot "move beyond categorising through abstractions that are necessarily reductions in the scope of possible categorisations of persons and events."[38]

This 'legal myopia' continues to cause misunderstanding and frustration to victims who want to tell their truth, but for whom only a legal forum is accessible. They are "tools in the prosecutors' case, confined in their testimony to only those fragments of their experience that meet the legal standard of relevant evidence".[39] One can only guess what many of the thousands of witnesses before the ICTY may have endured.[40] One of the Tribunal's fundamental contributions to international humanitarian law is its jurisprudence on sexual slavery and rape.[41] However, as a former senior trial attorney regretfully remarked, "the priority in the case seemed to be on legal theory rather than on the more immediate purpose of illustrating and showing how, and explaining why, sexual assault is used as a weapon of terror".[42] On the other hand, for many witnesses giving testimony gave "a little bit of dignity".[43] Also, several of ICTY's judgments contain a narrative explaining the origins and contexts of the conflict, thereby providing a broader picture of which the particular case forms only a part.[44] Still, the rules of the legal procedure generally prevent

38 E.A. Christodoulidis, "Truth and Reconciliation as Risks," *Social Legal Studies*, 9 (2000) 179–204.

39 M. Minow, "The Hope for Healing: what can truth commissions do?" in *Truth v. Justice*, eds. R. Rotberg and D. Thompson (Princeton and Oxford, Princeton University Press: 2000) 238; see also D.L. Hafner and E.B.L. King, "Beyond Traditional Notions of Transitional Justice: how trials, truth commissions, and other tools for accountability can and should work together," *Boston College International and Comparative Law Review*, 30, no. 1 (2007)104; M. Dembour and E. Haslam, "Silencing Hearings? Victim-witnesses at war crimes trials," *European Journal of International Law*, 15, (2004) 151-177; W.J. Booth, "Communities of Memory: on identity, memory, and debt," *American Political Science Review*, 93 (1999) 249-263.

40 M. Klarin, "The Tribunal's Four Battles," *Journal of International Criminal Justice*, 2 (2004) 546-557; E. Stover, "Witnesses and the Promise of Justice in The Hague," in *My Neighbor, My Enemy: justice and community in the aftermath of mass atrocity*, eds. E. Stover and H.M. Weinstein (Cambridge, Cambridge University Press: 2004) 104-20; E. Stover, *The Witnesses: war crimes and the promise of justice in The Hague*, (Pittsburgh, University of Pennsylvania Press: 2005); S. Leydesdorff, De leegte achter ons laten. Een geschiedenis van de vrouwen van Srebrenica (Amsterdam, Bert Bakker: 2008).

41 G. Niemann, "The Life and Times of a Senior Trial Attorney at the ICTY from 1994 to 2000," *Journal of International Criminal Justice*, 2 (2004) 435-445; P.M. Wald, "Punishment of War Crimes by International Tribunals," *Social Research*, 69 (2002) 1119-1134; P.M. Wald, "ICTY Judicial Proceedings: an appraisal from within," *Journal of International Criminal Justice*, 2 (2004) 466-473.

42 M. Schrag, "Lessons Learned from ICTY Experience," *Journal of International Criminal Justice*, 2 (2004) 427-34, 431.

43 A. Sachs, "Archives, Truth, and Reconciliation," *Archivaria*, 62 (2006) 1-14, here 12; see also R.J. Goldstone, *For Humanity: reflections of a war crimes investigator* (New Haven Conn., Yale University Press: 2000) 65-66.

44 G. Robertson, *Crimes Against Humanity: the struggle for global justice*, 3rd ed, (New York and London,The New Press: 2006) 394-418.

the ICTY (or any court) from providing an all-encompassing narrative framework, involving bystanders within and outside the region, and "the complex interactions among ideologies, leaders, mass frustrations, historic and invented lines of hatred, and acts of brutality".[45]

Narrative truth includes the categories of personal, social, and healing (or restorative) truth, emphasizing narrative, subjective dimensions of truth. Narrative truth does not strive at factual truth, but attempts to explain why, according to the narrator, things happened and to give meaning to these events, both to the individual narrator and to society.[46] Currently, civil society groups in the former Yugoslavia and international actors are focusing on forensic truth, while there are few attempts to heal and reach reconciliation through story telling or involving communities on the local level.[47] While forensic truth can be shared, narrative truth will always be contested. As Michael Ignatieff argued in his renowned piece Articles of Faith:

> Truth is related to identity. What you believe to be true depends, in some measure, on who you believe yourself to be. And who you believe yourself to be is mostly defined in terms of who you are not. To be a Serb is first and foremost not to be a Croat or a Muslim. Even people who fought to maintain a moral space between their personal and their national identities are now unable to conceive that one day Zagreb, Belgrade and Sarajevo might share a common version of the history of the conflict.[48]

It is clear that the truth that victims claim as being their monopoly[49]—as is the truth claimed by aggressors and bystanders—will be at odds with the forensic truth contained in the ICTY archives. Moreover, "the idea of accessible court records that speak for themselves…is problematic".[50] Indeed, records do not speak for themselves; their 'tacit narratives' echo the user's interests, hopes, and fears.[51] It is the autonomous responsibility of the user to determine what information he or she gets out

45 Minow, "The Hope for Healing: what can truth commissions do?," 238; see also M. Minow, *Between Vengeance and Forgiveness: facing history after genocide and mass violence* (Boston, Beacon Press: 1998) 40; J. Balint, "Law's Constitutive Possibilities: reconstruction and reconciliation in the wake of genocide and state crime", in *Lethe's Law: justice, law and ethics in reconciliation*, eds. E. Christodoulides and S. Veitch (Oxford and Portland, Hart Publishing: 2001) 136

46 A. Wieviorka, "The Witness in History," *Poetics Today*, 27, no. 2 (2006) 385-396.

47 N. Zupan, "Facing the Past and Transitional Justice in Countries of Former Yugoslavia" in *Peacebuilding and Civil Society in Bosnia-Herzegovina: ten years after Dayton*, ed. M. Fischer (Berlin, Lit Verlag: 2006) 327-42.

48 M. Ignatieff, "Articles of Faith," *Index on Censorship*, 5 (1996) 110-122, 114.

49 E. Jelin, "The Politics of Memory: the human rights movements and the construction of democracy in Argentina," *Latin American Perspectives*, 21, no. 2 (1994) 38-58.

50 Minow, *Between Vengeance and Forgiveness*, 125.

51 E. Ketelaar, "Tacit Narratives: the meanings of archives," *Archival Science*, 1 (2001) 143-155.

of the archives.[52] This empowers the user to re-create in his or her own way what is found in the records that were created by the Tribunal. That is why archives are never closed and never complete: every individual and every generation are allowed their own interpretation of the archive, to reinvent and to reconstruct its view on and narrative of the past.[53] That is to say (in Hanna Arendt's words), it has

> the right to write its own history. We admit no more than that it has the right to rearrange the facts in accordance with its own perspective; we don't admit the right to touch the factual matter itself.[54]

That factual matter is – if one has to choose between the four truths – ultimately the truth. The selectivity and the 'constructedness' of the criminal trial may have frustrated survivors and their families, either present in the courtroom, or left behind where the atrocities were still fresh in the memories of the land and of the people. However, once the selectivity and 'constructedness' are frozen in the Tribunal's records, they are no longer an obstacle for telling your story, your truth, and storing your myth in what Hayden White calls the communal traditionalized memory.[55]

A number of socio-psychological studies affirm that it takes a long time (twenty to thirty years) before individuals and communities are ready to revisit and to reconstruct their past. Apparently, and for different reasons, they need some distance in time.[56] As Jeffrey Olick contends, the only collectivity "that can be healed and can learn the lessons of history and make something of them, is the next generation."[57] We should therefore not be surprised when society's immediate use of the Tribunal's archives turns out to be rather limited. Over time, both the current generation and their children will (re)discover the possibilities of the archives as sources of history.

---

52 A. Menne-Haritz, "Access - The Reformulation of an Archival Paradigm," *Archival Science*, 1 (2001) 57–82; P. Macpherson, "Theory, Standards and Implicit Assumptions: public access to post-current government records," *Archives and Manuscripts*, 30 (2002) 6-17.

53 This reasoning resembles James Booth's argument that we have some measure of choice in determining how our understanding of the past will be shaped: W.J. Booth, *Communities of Memory: on witness, identity, and justice* (Ithaca and London: Cornell University Press: 2006) 182.

54 H. Arendt, "Truth and Politics," in *Between Past and Future: eight exercises in political thought* (Hammondsworth, Penguin Books: 1977) 238-39; Wieviorka, "The Witness in History," 396: "Each person has the right to fashion his or her own history, to put together what he or she remembers and what he or she forgets in his or her own way. [...] Each person has an absolute right to his or her memory, which is nothing other than his or her identity, his or her very being. But this right can come into conflict with an imperative of the historian's profession, the imperative of an obstinate quest for the truth."

55 White, "Catastrophe, Communal Memory and Mythic Discourse," 53.

56 J.W. Pennebaker, D. Paez and B. Rimé, eds., *Collective Memory of Political Events: social psychological perspectives* (Mahwah NJ, Lawrence Erlbaum: 1997) 103-127.

57 J.K. Olick, *The Politics of Regret: on collective memory and historical responsibility* (New York, Routledge: 2007) 148.

4. Histories

It is not only the victims and their families who have to come to grips with the past; their communities and society at large have to acknowledge it as well. What Elizabeth Jelin maintains for post-totalitarian Argentina is true for the former Yugoslavia too: "Only when the incorporation of historical events becomes an active and dynamic process can it feed into the construction of a democratic culture and collective identity."[58] What function in this process would the ICTY archives have as a historical record?

The expectation that the ICTY would establish a historical record can be traced back[59] to the words of Robert Jackson, the chief prosecutor at the Nuremberg trial, who said that the prosecution had documented from German sources the aggressions, persecutions, and atrocities "with such authenticity and in such detail that here can be no responsible denial of these crimes in the future and no tradition of martyrdom of the Nazi leaders can arise among informed people."[60] Jackson's words were echoed by the ICTY's first president, Antonio Cassese, who observed that the Tribunal "has established a record of events that will go down in history and may not be impugned in future."[61] The ICTY cites in its Krstić judgment the words of Nuremberg prosecutor Telford Taylor who said that it is "important that these incredible events be established by clear and public proof, so that no one can ever doubt that they were fact and not fable...."[62] The objective is not so much creating a record contributing to historiography, but to prevent denial. As Ruti Teitel wrote, "The ICTY's responsibility should be to forge and disseminate a record that limits the possibility

58 Jelin, "The Politics of Memory," 53.

59 J.B. Allcock, ed., *The International Criminal Tribunal for the Former Yugoslavia. Report by the Scholars' Initiative. Research Group 10*, http://www.cla.purdue.edu/academic/history/facstaff/ingrao/si/scholars.htm [accessed 22 June 2011].

60 M.B. Harmon and F. Gaynor, "Prosecuting Massive Crimes with Primitive Tools: three difficulties encountered by prosecutors in international criminal proceedings," *Journal of International Criminal Justice*, 2 (2004) 403-426, 404.

61 A. Cassese, "The ICTY: a Living and Vital Reality," *Journal of International Criminal Justice*, 2 (2004) 585-597, 597; M.P.Scharf, *Balkan Justice: the story behind the first international war crimes trial since Nuremberg* (Carolina Academic Press: 1997) 215: "While there are various means to achieve an historic record of abuses after a war, the most authoritative rendering is possible only through the crucible of a trial that accords full due process."

62 United Nations International Criminal Tribunal for the former Yugoslavia (2001) Judgment IT-98-33-T, http://www.icty.org/x/cases/krstic/tjug/en/krs-tj010802e.pdf [accessed 22 June 2011] para. 95; The ICTY continues in asserting that "It is therefore imperative to document these "incredible events" in detail. However, the central issue in this case is the role that one man, General Krstić, played in the criminal acts and whether he is legally responsible for conduct that amounts to war crimes, crimes against humanity or genocide."

of historical denial."[63] However, she also argues that a court that tries to go beyond individual accountability to assess the historical reality at large risks "sacrificing individual rights to the societal interest in establishing a historical record."[64]

Indeed, the findings of any trial can be nothing more than a contribution to creating a larger historical record because the focus is on specific crimes and perpetrators, not on wider historical events.[65] A trial has to be selective, focusing on the indicted individual or individuals, on their accountability for crimes committed by them or because of them. As the Israeli court in the Eichmann case stated very clearly:

> The desire was felt—readily understandable in itself—to give, within the limits of this trial, a comprehensive and exhaustive historical account of the events of the catastrophe... [But] the Court ... must not allow itself to be enticed to stray into provinces which are outside its sphere. The judicial process has ways of its own ... whatever the subject-matter of the trial .... The Court does not possess the facilities required for investigating general questions of the kind referred to above.[66]

Can one expect from the ICTY that, within the limits of the judicial process, it investigates the historical, political, sociological, and economic causes that led to the conflict in former Yugoslavia?[67] The Tribunal, in its first judgment (in the Tadić case) devoted some forty-eight pages (out of 285) "to say something in a preliminary way about the relevant historical, geographic, administrative and military setting about

63 R.G. Teitel, Justice Seeks an Exit Strategy, *Taipei Times* (2005) http://www.globalpolicy.org/intljustice/tribunals/yugo/2005/0107justiceexit.htm [accessed 5 July 2008]; see also D.F. Orentlicher, *Shrinking the Space for Denial: the impact of the ICTY in Serbia* (New York, Open Society Institute: 2008) http://www.soros.org/initiatives/justice/focus/international_justice/articles_publications/publications/serbia_20080520/serbia_20080501.pdf [accessed 22 June 2011].

64 R.G. Teitel, *Transitional Justice* (Oxford University Press: 2000) 76; see also R. Zacklin, "The Failings of Ad Hoc International Tribunals," *Journal of International Criminal Justice*, 2 (2004) 541-545.

65 B.N. Schiff, "Do Truth Commissions Promote Accountability or Impunity? The case of the South African Truth and Reconciliation Commission," in *Post-conflict Justice*, ed. M.C. Bassiouni (Ardsley N.Y., Transnational Publishers: 2002) 325-343.

66 Osiel, *Mass Atrocity, Collective Memory, and the Law*, 80-81; see also F. Bayard, ed., *Le génocide des Juifs entre procès et histoire 1943-2000* (Bruxelles, Complexe : 2000). Lawrence Douglas, while conceding that didactic trials as the Eichmann trial "are not well equipped to render history in its complexity", and not denying "that history and law are governed by differing epistemological and evidentiary conventions", warns against over-exaggerating the differences: L. Douglas, "History and Memory in the Courtroom: reflections on perpetrator trials," in, *The Nuremberg Trials: international criminal law since 1945*, eds. H.R. Reginbogin, and C.J.M. Safferling (München, Saur: 2006) 95-104, 98, 101.

67 S. Basic, "Bosnian Society on the Path to Justice, Truth and Reconciliation," in *Peacebuilding and Civil Society in Bosnia-Herzegovina: ten years after Dayton*, ed. M. Fischer, 2nd ed (Berlin, Lit Verlag: 2007).

which evidence was received".[68] In a later judgment (in the Krstić case), the judges were more negative about their role as history writers:

> The Trial Chamber leaves it to historians and social psychologists to plumb the depths of this episode of the Balkan conflict and to probe for deep-seated causes. The task at hand is a more modest one: to find, from the evidence presented during the trial, what happened during that period of about nine days and, ultimately, whether the defendant in this case, General Krstić, was criminally responsible, under the tenets of international law, for his participation in them. The Trial Chamber cannot permit itself the indulgence of expressing how it feels about what happened in Srebrenica, or even how individuals as well as national and international groups not the subject of this case contributed to the tragedy. This defendant, like all others, deserves individualised consideration and can be convicted only if the evidence presented in court shows, beyond a reasonable doubt, that he is guilty.[69]

Nevertheless, the ICTY has been praised because it was able to put its judgments in a broader historical context. Richard Wilson commends the ICTY judgments in the Tadić and Krstić cases for their extensive historical interpretation of the causes of the conflict, adding that their "approach to historical interpretation forces a reconsideration of the long-standing view that the pursuit of justice and the writing of history are inherently irreconcilable".[70] However, as the ICTY itself elucidated in the Krstić case, in his final conclusion Wilson seems to leave the actual history writing to people outside the Tribunal who may use the ICTY records. The ICTY's judgments, Wilson writes, "could become an indispensable part of the process of writing a common, credible history of political violence in the 1990s."[71] Prosecutor Carla Del Ponte said, "Governments, NGOs and historians should use the millions of pages presented in court to recount history as it really happened."[72] Robert Donia (who appeared before the Tribunal as an expert witness several times) testified that the ICTY had "produced histories that are not only credible and readable, but indispensable to understand the origins and course of the 1990s conflicts in the former

---

68 United Nations International Criminal Tribunal for the former Yugoslavia (1997) Judgment IT-94-1-T, http://www.icty.org/case/tadic/4#tjug [accessed 22 June 2011] para.53; The Tribunal stressed that this exposé was exclusively based upon the evidence presented in court. Scharf concludes that the record of the Tadić trial "provides an authoritative and impartial account to which future historians may turn for truth, and future leaders for warning" (Scharf, *Balkan Justice*, 215).

69 United Nations International Criminal Tribunal for the former Yugoslavia (2001) Judgment IT-98-33-T, http://www.icty.org/x/cases/krstic/tjug/en/krs-tj010802e.pdf [accessed 22 June 2011] para. 2, 95.

70 R.A. Wilson, "Judging History: the historical record of the international criminal tribunal for the former Yugoslavia," *Human Rights Quarterly*, 27 (2005) 908-942, 922; see also Schiff, "Do Truth Commissions Promote Accountability or Impunity?".

71 . Wilson, "Judging History," 942.

72 United Nations International Criminal Tribunal for the former Yugoslavia (2007) *ICTY and the Legacy of the Past*, http://www.icty.org/sid/8829 [accessed 22 June 2011].

Yugoslavia," and that it provided "a detailed, thoroughly investigated and comprehensive account of what happened at critical times in the battle for Bosnia from 1992 to 1995."[73] Nevertheless, according to Donia, the judges' 'historical essentialism' took only those elements into account that they felt were essential to comprehend the atrocities, and that they heard about from witnesses in each case.

The Tribunal's time is in conflict with the time of history; the former emphasizes presence (justice here and now), the latter focuses on absence (justice in the past).[74] The law aspires to a degree of finality now and for the future. Therefore, a trial seeks closure through a full and final sentence. On the other hand, there "is no such expectation of relative fixity in the realm of historical understanding, or of the collective memory to which such understanding contributes."[75] Subsequent events, new interpretations, new sources—they will inevitably change the view, and reopen the case. The court's verdict is final, but its reading of the historical event is not. Court records have, therefore, not more value than other records.[76] Law's closure has to be rejected in favor of history's recurrence. History is never finished or final because with the passage of time historical interpretation undergoes change.[77] History is provisional and thereby allows a contrapuntal narrative doing justice to adversarial and contested stories.[78] Instead of asking for the truth or the history, one should show and teach that there are many truths and histories.

5. Memories

The psychologist Nico Frijda suggests that appropriating the past is an element in the construction of an individual's identity. It does so in a double way, by "shaping or affirming the identity of one's group, and by accepting or redefining membership within that group."[79] This argument is shared by James Booth who puts forward that gathering in the past, appropriating it, "gives us identity and a moral narrative of

73 R.J. Donia, "Encountering the Past: history at the Yugoslav war crimes tribunal," *Journal of the International Institute*, 11 (2004) 2-3, http://hdl.handle.net/2027/spo.4750978.0011.201 [accessed 22 June 2011].

74 B. Bevernage, "Time, Presence, and Historical Injustice," *History and Theory*, 47 (2008) 149-167. According to Booth, both the court and the historian depend on absence, on what is no longer present. However, justice, as Booth writes, seeks to act on the past by making it present: Booth, *Communities of Memory*, 113-115.

75 Osiel, *Mass Atrocity, Collective Memory, and the Law*, 217; see also Minow, *Between Vengeance and Forgiveness.*

76 Ketelaar, "Tacit Narratives: the meanings of archives."

77 Teitel, *Transitional Justice.*

78 C.S. Maier, "Doing History, Doing Justice: the narrative of the historian and of the truth commission," in *Truth v. Justice,* eds. R. Rotberg and D. Thompson (Princeton and Oxford: Princeton University Press: 2000) 261-278.

79 N.H. Frijda, "Commemorating," in *Collective Memory of Political Events: social psychological perspectives*, eds. J.W. Pennebaker, D. Paez and B. Rimé (Mahwah NJ, Lawrence Erlbaum: 1997) 103-127, 109.

pride, shame, and indebtedness, that ties us across time to our past and the burdens this past imposes simply by virtue of being ours."[80] The common, often mythical, past, sustained through time into the present, is what gives continuity, cohesion and coherence to a community.[81] Any community is therefore a community of memory, especially a community living after mass atrocities, where the past continues to torment because it is not past. They "are not living in a serial order of time, but in a simultaneous one, in which the past and present are a continuous, agglutinated mass of fantasies, distortions, myths and lies."[82] For victims and survivors of mass atrocities, the past stays on, as Frijda asserts, as "unfinished business": they and their families keep on searching for meaning to understand how the humiliations, the cruelties, the systematic destruction were ever possible.[83] They may label their search for meaning, searching for the truth or the history, but it is in fact no more and no less than a meaning-making process to confirm and reconfirm identity,[84] constructing and reconstructing their community's memories and narrative truths, engaging the community in rituals of commemoration. The ICTY cannot—or only minimally—live up to the expectations of a "secular ritual of commemoration."[85] Such a ritual with its beneficial effects on individuals and communities has to be set up elsewhere, with the help of people and institutions engaged in memory-practice.[86] Among these institutions are, of course, memorial museums, including sites, that are established in "the global rush to commemorate atrocities," as the title of Paul Williams's recent book on memorial museums includes. Williams acknowledges that we only have a fuzzy awareness whether and how "concrete spaces like memorials and museums are effective social spaces for aiding reconciliation."[87] But they provide space for rituals of commemoration, as for example the Srebrenica memorial and cemetery in Potočari (Bosnia), where annually on July 11 commemoration ceremonies are held.[88]

Archives could also become such spaces of memory-practice, where people can try to put their trauma in context by accessing the documents, not primarily seeking

80 Booth, "Communities of Memory," 254; Booth, *Communities of Memory.*

81 D. Morley and K. Robins, *Spaces of Identity: global media, electroniclandscapes, and cultural boundaries* (London and New York, Routledge: 1995); B. Stråth, ed., *Myth and Memory in the Construction of Community: historical patterns in Europe and beyond* (Bruxelles and New York, P.I.E.-Peter Lang: 2000).

82 Ignatieff, "Articles of Faith," 119.

83 Frijda, "Commemorating."

84 U. Fuhrer, *Cultivating Minds: identity as meaning making practice* (London: Routledge: 2004).

85 P. Akhavan, "Justice in The Hague, Peace in the Former Yugoslavia? a commentary on the United Nations war crimes tribunal," *Human Rights Quarterly*, 20 (1998) 737-816, 784: Here Akhavan writes about "the sacral aspect of remembrance" and the "public ritual of atonement."

86 Osiel, *Mass Atrocity, Collective Memory, and the Law.*

87 P. Williams, *Memorial Museums: the global rush to commemorate atrocities* (Oxford and New York, Berg: 2007) 170.

88 Ibid. 17-18.

the truth or searching the history, but transforming their experiences into meaning. Accessing the archives of the ICTY, and weaving them into private and public memories, may constitute a healing ritual. The archives become a space of shared custody and trust, where records are preserved through time—long enough perhaps to destroy the agony and heal the communities.[89]

6. A Living Archive

Even after completion of the primary mission of the ICTY the archive will continue to be a living archive, used by prosecutors and judges within and outside the former Yugoslavia, by defence counsel, and by other stakeholders. At the same time—and stretching far beyond the time the documents have to serve judicial purposes—the archive will be a living archive for the causes of truths, histories, and memories. The archive will be a living archive because it will continue to be challenged, contested, and expanded. I will deal with these issues successively.

According to one of the UN Human Rights Commission's principles, people are entitled to challenge the validity of the information in archives concerning them by exercising their right of reply.[90] The challenged document should include a cross-reference to the document challenging its validity and both must be made available together whenever the former is requested. A comparable right of correction, enshrined in the data protection legislation of all European Union states, should be given to people involved in trials before the ICTY, especially because in some cases discrepancies between the witness' evidence and the official record of it have been found.[91]

Any archive is a place of contestation (Harris, 2000,p. 80; Harris 2007). Like memorial museums, archives are spaces where battles about the politics of memory are fought. Like memory, an archive is not just an agency of storage, but a process, a mediated social and cultural practice.[92] A living archive allows for what Hayden White calls

> three different kinds of discourse about 'what happened' and 'what is to be done.' First, the disaster can be assimilated to communal memory by its mythification. Secondly, it can be assimilated to communal memory by the conventions of classification, cataloguing, and storage techniques of the rationalising sciences. And thirdly, the disaster can be

89 E. Ketelaar, "Archives as Spaces of Memory," *Journal of the Society of Archivists,* 29 (2008) 9-27.

90 E. Ketelaar, "Access: the democratic imperative," *Archives and Manuscripts,* 34 (2006a) 62-81.

91 Human Rights Watch. Justice at Risk: war crimes trials in Croatia, Bosnia and Herzegovina, and Serbia and Montenegro, 16, no. 7 (2004) http://www.unhcr.org/refworld/docid/42c3bcf70.html [accessed 22 June 2011].

92 E. Ketelaar, "Writing on Archiving Machines," in *Sign Here! handwriting in the age of new media,* eds. S. Neef, J. van Dijck and E. Ketelaar (Amsterdam: Amsterdam University Press: 2006) 183-195.

> assimilated to communal memory in such a way as to force a revision and delegitimation of traditionalised memory itself.[93]

Different as these kinds of discourse may be about what happened and what is to be done, they have to be related. Myth and rationality are not entirely independent of collective memory; they are mutually constitutive.[94] The third component—revision and 'delegitimation'—entails hospitality to contestation and renegotiation. As Michael Moss writes, the archive is

> a place of 'dreams' of re-enactment for both the user and the archivist (curator), who together always are engaged either passively or actively in the process of refiguration that is never ending.[95]

I believe that the archive is not merely (as White suggests) a rational storage technique but primarily a space to escape from a monolithic truth, history and memory, by allowing the questioning of myth and rationality—including the myth and rationality contained in the archive.

This is even more relevant in the former Yugoslavia, where the past is no common past. After the Second World War there was

> never a discourse on how a multiethnic society whose population consisted of extremely divergent individual and collective memories could manage this complex legacy sufficiently to come to terms with its complex past.[96]

And when the Yugoslav state disintegrated, the historical memory disintegrated too. The post-Yugoslav republics created "a new fragmented memory along not only ideological, but ethnic, borderlines."[97] Different ethnic groups each claim their own memory of suffering, to be framed in a space only trusted by and accessible to members of their own group. This "ethnization of memory"[98] may lead to "ghettoization

93 Hayden White adds: "Programmes for recovery from the disaster (or the reconstruction of the afflicted society) can thus be sublimated into public debates about the relative merits of different ways of construing the *causes* of the disaster." White, "Catastrophe, Communal Memory and Mythic Discourse," p. 55.

94 Olick, *The Politics of Regret.*

95 M. Moss, "Opening Pandora's Box: What is an Archive in the Digital Environment?", in *What are Archives? Cultural and Theoretical Perspectives: A Reader*, ed. L. Craven (Aldershot, Ashgate:2008) 71-87, 83.

96 W. Hoepken, "War, Memory, and Education in a Fragmented Society: the case of Yugoslavia," *East European Politics and Societies*, 13 (1999) 190-227, 204.

97 Ibid. 226.

98 D. Corkalo et al., "Neighbors Again? Intercommunity relations after ethnic cleansing," in *My Neighbor, My Enemy: justice and community in the aftermath of atrocity*, eds. E. Stover and H.M. Weinstein (Cambridge, Cambridge University Press: 2004) 143-161, 157.

of history."[99] The archives of the ICTY, however, cannot be split up according to the ethnic provenance of perpetrators, victims, and witnesses. It is a joint, albeit a contentious, heritage that should be accessible from any of the places in former Yugoslavia (and from anywhere in the world) where people live who want to use the archives. The contentiousness of the archive might even prove beneficial because it can show "how people can live with continuing disagreements about what exactly happened in the past and why, and still respect each other as fellow citizens."[100] Reconciliation, as Christodoulidis[101] argues, has to take risks, and one of them is that memories and identities are not arbitrated, that constituencies for communities are not fixed. I believe that the risk of contentiousness of the archives should be taken too.

The living archive should be expanded, in the first place by linking the content to the holdings of the broad range of governmental and nongovernmental agencies within and outside the former Yugoslavia who continue to collect material about the conflict.[102] Secondly, the archive should be expanded by gradually releasing the numerous classified documents, classified because of protection of witnesses, privacy, and state secrets. Most of the transcripts contain redacted passages, sometimes amounting to more than fifty percent, as in the case of Miletic et al, where 7.994 pages of the more than 16.000 pages of transcript contain redacted passages. And thirdly, by allowing people to enrich the ICTY record with their comments and stories. Witnesses, victims, as well as convicted and indicted people (and bystanders) should be allowed to tell their stories. Stories are not only vehicles for understanding, but they are also a means of remembrance.[103] Writing down and submitting their stories—co-creating and constituting the archive—allows people to articulate their own war histories and, in psychoanalytic terms, gives them an opportunity to express and thus begin to incorporate them into the present.[104] I propose permeating

99 Williams, *Memorial Museums*, 168.

100 A. Gutmann, and D. Thompson, "The Moral Foundations of Truth Commissions," in *Truth v. Justice*, eds. R. Rotberg and D. Thompson (Princeton and Oxford, Princeton University Press: 2000) 22-44, 35.

101 Christodoulidis, "Truth and Reconciliation as Risks."

102 D. Djordjevic, *Summary Report Regarding Local, Regional and International Documentation of War Crimes and Human Rights Violations in the former Yugoslavia* (New York, International Center for Transitional Justice: 2002) http://ictj.org/sites/default/files/ICTJ-FormerYugoslavia-Documentation-Violations-2002-English.pdf [accessed 22 June 2011].

103 B. Atwood and F. Magowan, eds., *Telling Stories: indigenous history and memory in Australia and New Zealand* (Sydney, Allen & Unwin: 2001).

104 C. Twomey, "'Impossible History:' trauma and testimony among Australian civilians interned by the Japanese in World War II," in *History on the Couch: essays in history and psychoanalysis*, eds. J. Damousi and R. Reynolds (Melbourne, Melbourne University Press: 2003) 155-165; D.B. Pillemer, "Can the Psychology of Memory Enrich Historical Analyses of Trauma?", *History and Memory*, 16 (2004) 140-155; N. Adler, et al., *Memories of Mass Repression: narrating life stories in the aftermath of atrocity* (New Brunswick N.J., Transaction Publishers: 2009).

the boundaries between what Hayden White calls the communal 'traditionalized memory' and the communal 'rationalized memory'; the first consisting of stories of the past, the second of "accounts of a community's past, contained in its archives and catalogued and processed in the form of written or visualized 'histories,' so that it can be 'accessed' on demand."[105]

Of course archival institutions, as the rationalized receivers of story, should, in Verne Harris's words,

> Be ever vigilant. Cherish what story gives us, but always probe its telling, explore other tellings and other stories. Know that as compelling as it might seem, as seamless and satisfying and healing, it remains story not truth. We should never allow story to be more than a platform to our own search for meaning.[106]

Archival institutions around the world are moving into new ways of capturing, storing, and using public and private documents, stories, images, and sound. Digital systems of distributed custody of the holdings of both public institutions and private individuals and communities are already in place. Web 2.0 applications stimulate social navigation, and uploading "evidence of me"[107] to an archival institution's server thus creats and maintains a living archive out of private and public documents.[108] The ICTY archive presents "an unprecedented challenge to use new technology and innovative finding aids to assure access and usability to future generations."[109]

7. Conclusion

The ICTY archives, as any other archives, allow for contestation. But paradoxically that quality may help members of a community not only to come to grips with their own past but also to acknowledge that the past they share with neighboring ethnic and political communities is not a monolithic truth, history, or memory, but allows—even requires—questioning and contestation. For this, the archive provides a space. As South African judge Albie Sachs stated, archivists are caring for archives "not as we used to think, to guard certainty: they are doing it to protect uncertainty

---

105 White, "Catastrophe, Communal Memory and Mythic Discourse," 53.

106 V. Harris, *Archives and Justice. A South African Perspective* (Chicago, Society of American Archivists: 2007) 415.

107 S. McKemmish, " 'Evidence of me' ", *Archives and Manuscripts*, 24 (1996) 28–45, at rcrg.dstc.edu.au/publications/recordscontinuum/smckp1.html.

108 E. Ketelaar, "Being Digital in People's Archives," *Archives and Manuscripts*, 31 (2003) 8-22; E. Ketelaar "Archives as Spaces of Memory", *Journal of the Society of Archivists*, 29 (2008) 9-27; M. Šajkaš, *Transitional Justice and the Role of the Media in the Balkans*, International Center for Transitional Justice (2007) http://ictj.org/sites/default/files/ICTJ-FormerYugoslavia-Media-Justice-2007-English_0.pdf [accessed 22 June 2011].

109 Donia, "The New Masters of Memory," 400; R.J. Donia, and E. Becirevic, *ICTY Archive Must Be Open To All* (2008) http://iwpr.net/report-news/icty-archive-must-be-open-all [accessed 26 June 2011].

because who knows how the future might use those documents."[110] Each community is a community of records, marking the limits to other groups and their members. The risk of 'ethnization' (or exclusiveness) of memories may be abated by giving each community in the former Yugoslavia not just a share in a joint heritage, but by making each community a co-custodian of the living ICTY archive, constantly challenged and challenging.

110 Sachs, "Archives, Truth, and Reconciliation," 14.

16. Truths, Memories and Historians in the Archives of the International Criminal Tribunal for the Former Yugoslavia

Robert Donia

Professor Ketelaar offers an admirable, visionary proposal to create a "living archive" of international tribunals—but achieving an open, accessible, and dynamic archive will not be easy. In this presentation I will identify some of the challenges that are likely to arise in transforming his vision into a reality.

The living archive he proposes will serve the needs of many different stakeholders in the work of the International Criminal Tribunal for the Former Yugoslavia (ICTY). Among those stakeholders, I would like to today focus on the community of public users: scholars, writers, human rights activists, and policymakers, who are constantly seeking to understand the nature, causes, and consequences of genocide and war crimes. My remarks will pertain mainly to the holdings of the Office of the Prosecutor (OTP). Those holdings include millions of documents and artifacts, which together constitute the world's largest collection of information about developments in the former Yugoslavia from its twilight period in late 1989 until 1999. The OTP gathered most of this material from various parties to the conflicts, frequently against their will. The collection includes millions of documents provided by various polities in the region, records of international organizations, documents seized by international peacekeeping forces, and many thousands of witness and victim statements.

The highly contentious public discussion of the archive's ultimate disposition has largely centered on where it will be located. But as Mayor of The Hague, Van Aartsen, noted earlier in this volume, the issue of access to the archive is ultimately more consequential and vexing than the question of its final physical resting place. Today I will argue that the mandate and operations of the ICTY during war crimes trials have been inherently inimical to a functioning, publicly-accessible archive. Unless its purposes are reoriented to those of an archive, the ICTY's policies, presently tailored to facilitate war crimes trials, could eventually lead to the archive's dismemberment or permanent inaccessibility.

I am at some risk of being misunderstood, so I want to emphasize in what follows that I am not criticizing any person or group of persons at the ICTY; I am solely characterizing the behavior of the institution as it has pursued its mandate to try those accused of war crimes in the territory of the former Yugoslavia. While the

H.G. van der Wilt, J. Vervliet et al., *(eds.)* The Genocide Convention: The Legacy of 60 Years.
 ISBN 978 9004 15328 8. pp. 223-228.

ICTY's primary mandate is incontrovertibly to prosecute war criminals, the institution was also tasked with contributing to peace and reconciliation in the region. Not unexpectedly, the ICTY has been consumed with fulfilling its primary purpose, and its other roles have been relatively neglected.

Judge Wolfgang Schomberg, in commencing the trial of Milomir Stakić on April 16, 2002 (the Stakić case), defined his hopes for the ICTY to reconcile old enemies, deter future war crimes, and reveal the truth:

> This Tribunal is not only a criminal court. . . . It is at the same time a peacekeeping mission. To quote from Security Council Resolution 827 of 1993, 'This Tribunal has to contribute to the restoration and maintenance of peace.' We have to do our very best to break the vicious and at the same time fatal cycle of vengeance, intolerance, and hate. We never should forget this additional mandate during trial ... To act in this spirit should encourage potential perpetrators in future to respect themselves, and the human rights of persons they regard as their enemies. . . . As human beings, we will never find the truth, but we have to try to come as close as possible to truth with the tools of a fair trial.[1]

These are ambitious and admirable goals, and the Tribunal cannot be held solely responsible for achieving them. As an institution, however, the ICTY has lost track of these goals in the single-minded pursuit of its primary objective—namely, trying the accused. Prosecutors and judges have vigorously pursued the truth by scouring the region for witnesses and acquiring a monumental collection of documents and records. One might note, for instance, the extraordinary efforts of a panel led by Judge Schomberg in calling additional witnesses in the Stakić case in an effort to determine if the accused was guilty of genocide. But this same resolve has led the institution to hoard and sequester documents that would enable outsiders, as well as trial participants, to "come as close as possible" to the truth. The ICTY tends to view its decisions (at the appeals stage) as irrevocable and incontrovertible. Many panels of judges jealously guard their exclusive role as "triers of fact" and seek to preclude further assessment and inquiry. Symptomatic of the Tribunal's syndrome of certitude, judges have assembled a list of "adjudicated facts," presumably uncontested by any party. Among these hundreds of "adjudicated facts" are at least a dozen that I would consider debatable, and one demonstrable falsehood, namely that Bosnia and Herzegovina declared independence in spring 1992. Most, but not all, source sequestration has been for legitimate and understandable reasons, and I am not proposing in this paper that the ICTY alter its basic policies during the trial and appeal phases of its life. But these policies must be radically altered if the ICTY is to be transformed from a court of justice into a living archive to serve a broad spectrum of stakeholders.

Behind the Tribunal's hoarding and sequestering policies lie the sovereign states upon which the Tribunal depends for its very existence. The Tribunal probably could not have begun its work without the cooperation of the government of Bosnia and

1 *Prosecutor v. Milomir Stakić*, ICTY (IT-97-24), April 16, 2002, 1589-91, http://www.icty.org/x/cases/stakic/trans/en/020416IT.htm, viewed December 1, 2008.

Herzegovina in identifying witnesses and turning over documents. But other states in the region have at one time or another contested the Tribunal's authority and defied its orders to turn over indictees and evidence; Serbia continues to do so—although its leaders' ambitions to join the European Union (EU) have made it much less acceptable for them to taunt the ICTY publicly, as did former governments of Serbia and Croatia.

Even the United Nations (UN) member states that helped create the Tribunal, by passing Security Council Resolution 827 in 1993, have at times declined to provide important information. Nor are consortia of those nations particularly inclined to transparency, as I learned in the late 1990s when I requested access to reports of observers of the European Community Monitoring Mission (ECMM), the famed "ice cream men" who arrived in Bosnia in the fall of 1991. I applied at the front gate of ECMM's Sarajevo compound and was immediately escorted into a room of document boxes, assigned a young officer who assisted me by retrieving documents, and given access to the files. I made a few notes, outlined a plan to accept their generous offer of copying documents, and returned the next day, only to be summoned to the commander's office. I could no longer examine the files, the commander politely told me; the names of ECMM monitors were sensitive and might put them at risk, so the documents would be closed for thirty years, at which point I was welcome to come back to examine them. I now regret not asking whether this was thirty years from then, or thirty years from the date the documents originated, as the latter period is more than half over. In any case, I was denied the benefit of these reports for my research on the background of the Sarajevo siege. I find this particularly ironic, since shortly thereafter I observed a former ECMM monitor testifying in open court at the Tribunal and submitting his own reports as evidence—as a witness for the defense. Evidently, the ECMM failed to tell its own monitors that their reports are to be treated as confidential.

The power of sovereign states to inhibit public disclosure of information is embedded in the Rules of Procedure and Evidence (RPE), which bestow on an "entity" providing evidence rights similar to those of a protected witness. Rule 70(b) states, inter alia:

> If the Prosecutor is in possession of information which has been provided to the Prosecutor on a confidential basis and which has been used solely for the purpose of generating new evidence, that initial information and its origin shall not be disclosed by the Prosecutor without the consent of the person or entity providing the initial information.[2]

The OTP's document collection—that is, the future Tribunal archive—is replete with Rule 70 documents, which are protected by virtue of their provider—usually a sovereign state or international organization such as the North Atlantic Treaty Organization (NATO), the United Nations High Commissioner for Refugees (UN-

---

2 ICTY, "Rules of Procedure and Evidence," IT/32/Rev38, June 13, 2006, http://www.icty.org/x/file/Legal%20Library/Rules_procedure_evidence/IT032_Rev41_en.pdf, viewed: December 2, 2008.

HCR), ECMM, the International Committee of the Red Cross (ICRC), or the European Commission/EU—rather than by virtue of their content or originator. Thus, even a newspaper clipping, if provided to the OTP by a Rule 70(b) source, could be considered protected.[3] Both the RPE and Tribunal practice raise the question of whether items under seal will remain under seal long after the Tribunal has passed from the scene, with no mechanism to unseal them.

The RPE give judges broad discretion to place evidence and testimony under seal. Rule 53 grants to a single judge or trial chamber the power, "in exceptional circumstances" and "in the interest of justice", to "order the non-disclosure to the public of any documents or information until further notice."[4] That provision in itself is problematic for transparency, but "until further notice" means that someone, presumably that same judge or trial chamber, must proactively remove the "under seal" status of a document or information, or it will remain inaccessible. Rule 54 bis provides that a state, if ordered by a judge or trial chamber to produce documents or information, may "raise an objection ... on the grounds that disclosure would prejudice its national security interests" and request "protective measures," including that a hearing on its request be held in camera with no transcript made. A state may also lead to the court "documents to be submitted in redacted form, accompanied by an affidavit signed by a senior State official explaining the reasons for the redaction."

The elevated status of sovereign states in this process was most recently and graphically demonstrated in the affair of the transcripts of the Supreme Defense Council (Vrhovni savjet odbrane), which the government of Serbia provided to the prosecution for use in the Milošević trial. The Tribunal made these documents available to the public, but only with substantial sections redacted at Serbia's insistence. The government of Serbia argued that the redacted segments were matters of its vital state interest, a reference to the then pending case of Bosnia and Herzegovina v. Serbia and Montenegro for genocide before the International Court of Justice (ICJ). This claim stretched the notion of national security interests beyond recognition; it was, in any case, a dubious claim given the amount of time that had passed since the war's end. Many critics have denounced the former Prosecutor, Carla Del Ponte, for acquiescing to Serb demands to keep portions of SDS (Demokratska Stranka Srbije, Serbian Democratic Party) minutes under seal, and additional public debate has centered on the refusal of the ICJ to subpoena the complete documents during the

3 The following text was prepared but not delivered at the conference:

> If I may again cite a personal experience, in one case before the ICTY I provided for the prosecution an assessment of an expert report prepared for the defense by a well-known participant in the events of the Bosnian war. For reasons unclear to me, the Trial Chamber placed that report under seal. Possibly because I had quoted brief excerpts from that report, my assessment was sealed as well. In other words, I was barred by the Chamber's decision from disseminating my own report. Happily, prosecutors in the case were kind enough to appeal to the Chamber to remove the provision of confidentiality, and the judges responded by making both reports public. But I am uncertain this would have been the case had prosecutors not been inclined to seek the order, or if the trial had ended and the Chamber for the case ceased to exist.

4 ICTY, RPE, Rules 53 and 54 *bis*.

case of Bosnia and Herzegovina v. Yugoslavia. I rather wish the debate had centered instead on the ICTY's proclivity for secrecy and non-transparency in its evidence disclosure procedures.

The public is presently kept from accessing the Tribunal's documentary resources by a rigorous regimen of control. The key principle, however, is that a representative of the public may have access to those documents once they are admitted into evidence, or marked for identification, in a trial. This is but a subset of all documentation in the possession of the OTP, and it is accessible by exhibit number of the case in question. Many trial chambers have routinely admitted into evidence entire documents in the interest of keeping evidence in context, but several have admitted individual sentences, paragraphs, and pages in the interest of limiting tangentially relevant material, leaving the bulk of a given document inaccessible to the public. When key items are admitted into evidence (or indictments handed down) journalists gather like hawks to sweep down and pick up copies (or, more recently, hover over computers like moths drawn to light), and immediately write a dispatch featuring whatever appears sensational—or not. From that moment forward, access becomes more difficult. A potential user must identify an exhibit within a case at the time that it is mentioned, and then request the document or exhibit from the registrar. I have personally found personnel in the Office of the Registrar to be consistently helpful in fulfilling my requests, but challenges remain for researchers to identify a particular exhibit when little or nothing of the content is known.[5] To my knowledge, the Office of the Registrar has not made available a list of exhibits admitted in the various cases, something which would be immensely helpful to a prospective researcher.

Further challenges arise from the several different record management systems adopted by the ICTY since its establishment in the 1990s. While each system has made these documents more accessible to authorized users, each has also added a layer of complexity. The primary system uses an eight-digit number-letter group—sometimes with a prefix or suffix of up to two letters—to identify each individual page in the vast archive. An almost impenetrable wall separates methods used internally for document management and those used for documents admitted into evidence. This is equivalent to managing a library with Library of Congress call numbers, but making its books available only to those who know their Dewey Decimal call numbers. I note that in recent proceedings the ICTY has begun to assign a number to each complete document prior to it being considered for admission, thus creating another layer of possible confusion for potential users. This practice is enshrined at the ICTY in "E-Court". I thought this stood for "Electronic Court," until I was subjected to it in testimony two weeks ago and concluded that it stands for "Eternal Court," as it is no more expeditious than submitting evidence engraved on stone tablets to the Court. This new set of numbers resembles organizing your books by height today and reorganizing them by thickness tomorrow. Happily, nearly all

5 Author's note, dated May 2009: "In April 2009, after this paper was delivered, the Registrar revamped the Tribunal's website and made a large number of documents accessible to the public, thereby rectifying some of the deficiencies noted above."

documents in the OTP's possession are now digitized, and most are searchable, but systems of internal usage will require adjustments to create a system suitable for the global community of users.

Some may find comfort in the standard UN practice of declassifying documents after thirty years. But that too is problematic, as a document's date of origin is almost always much earlier than its acquisition by the UN. The HDZ (Hrvatska Demokratska Zagednica, Croatian Democratic Party) was founded in Zagreb in February 1989, marking the beginning of the dense documentary record accumulated by the Tribunal; that event will be twenty years old in two months. To my knowledge, the ICTY has yet to encounter this issue, and it may be left for resolution once the document collection becomes a living archive. Meanwhile, document originators and providers, including sovereign states and individuals, may be expected to seek return of Rule 70(b) documents. Should their requests be granted, the archive of the ICTY will be a vestigial collection of judicial records without the evidentiary basis on which judgments and decisions were based.

The ICTY's current rules and practices lead me to suggest that a set of guidelines be established to assure that the archive is truly open, and that the "living archive" be subject to the decisions of an "ombudsperson" with the power to unseal and declassify documents in accordance with those guidelines.[6] Such a system is necessary because making documents available to the public will require a strong advocate to request and promote declassification from those originating or providing documents. The ombudsperson's function could be modeled on the US "Freedom of Information" procedures and similar legislation in many other countries. I further suggest that those archivists, historians, and jurists currently using the collections to support the trial process be utilized as consultants in the processes of shaping the future archive and overcoming the myriad of complex challenges to widespread access. With the benefits of a cadre of professional archivists, electronic search capabilities, digitization, and adequate financial resources, it will be possible to realize Professor Ketelaar's laudable vision of a living Tribunal archive.

6 In discussion, Professor Ketelaar noted that he has proposed a similar concept styled as a judicial official with the authority to perform the functions that I have described here.

Education

17. Sixty Years UN Genocide Convention – New Challenges for Genocide Education[1]

Martin Mennecke

1. Introduction

Reportedly, there were seven people at the funeral of Raphael Lemkin (1900-59), the father of the term 'genocide' and founder of the field of genocide studies. Lemkin's earlier attempts to publish a four-tome study of genocide were rejected because there would be no audience for a "book of this nature."[2] For many decades this kind of obscurity was representative of efforts to study genocide. While a few monographs were published in the first years following the drafting of the UN Convention on the Prevention and Punishment of Genocide in 1948, there was no sustained academic interest in what has been labelled the "crime of crimes."[3] At the political level, the Cold War buried all efforts to put life to the promise of 'never again;' the attempt to establish a permanent international criminal court stymied as did the work at the United Nations to codify an international penal code. Eventually, a small group of scholars began to study the Holocaust, leading to the formation of Holocaust studies. The first association of researchers that defined themselves as genocide scholars, continuing the work of Raphael Lemkin, was founded as late as 1994.

1 This essay is dedicated to the memory of the late Eric Markusen, a pioneer of genocide studies and education.

2 See Samantha Power, *'A Problem from Hell' – America and the Age of Genocide* (2002), 77f.

3 For examples of early works see Pieter N. Drost, *The Crime of State: Penal Protection for Fundamental Freedoms of Persons and Peoples* (vol. II, Genocide – United Nations Legislation on International Criminal Law, 1959); and Nehemiah Robinson, *The Genocide Convention – A Commentary* (1960). The term "crime of crimes" was used in one of the first judgements of the International Criminal Tribunal for Rwanda, *Prosecutor v. Kambanda*, 4 September 1998, para.16.

H.G. van der Wilt, J. Vervliet et al., *(eds.)* The Genocide Convention: The Legacy of 60 Years.
 ISBN 978 9004 15328 8. pp. 231-245.

Today, genocide studies have come of age.[4] There are countless conferences being held, two professional organizations,[5] several non-governmental organizations,[6] and a number of peer-reviewed journals[7] as well as research centers,[8] all focusing on the legacy of Lemkin's work. Genocide studies encompass inquiries into the role and motives of perpetrators, bystanders and rescuers, institutions and non-state actors, the fate of victims, as well as case-studies and comparative approaches. Meetings of genocide scholars bring together experts from a variety of disciplines, including history, law, political science, anthropology and psychology and many more.

In recent years, this growing interest in genocide studies has been paralleled by an increased demand for genocide education. This has in several countries led to the initiation of educational outreach programs which go beyond the scope of classic Holocaust education and specialise in devising teaching material and courses focused on genocide.[9] There is also a growing number of both undergraduate and graduate programs focusing on the study of genocide. Examples can be found in the graduate studies program at Clark University in the United States, the international Masters programs at Kingston University in London, United Kingdom, and Uppsala University, Sweden, and the newly established Masters in genocide studies at the

4 See on this development more generally Eric Markusen and Carol Rittner, "Beyond the Never Agains? Efforts to Confront Genocide," in *Beyond the 'Never Agains'*, ed. Eva Fried (2005), 152-159; and Scott Straus, "Second-Generation Comparative Research on Genocide," *World Politics*, vol. 59 (2007) 476-501.

5 The two scholarly organizations are the International Association of Genocide Scholars (http://www.genocidescholars.org) and the International Network of Genocide Scholars (http://www.inogs.com/).

6 See only the Committee on Conscience, a branch of the US Holocaust Memorial Museum (http://www.ushmm.org/genocide/); AEGIS Trust, a UK-based group (http://www.aegistrust.org) and Genocide Watch (http://www.genocidewatch.org/).

7 For example, Genocide Studies and Prevention (http://www.utpjournals.com/gsp/gsp.html); Zeitschrift für Genozidforschung (http://www.ruhr-uni-bochum.de/idg/unterseiten/zfg.html); and Revista de Estudios sobre Genocidio (http://www.untref.edu.ar/institutos/institutos_ceg_eng.htm).

8 In Europe, relevant research centres include the Dutch Centre for Holocaust and Genocide Studies (http://www.chgs.nl/) and the Norwegian Centre for Studies of Holocaust and Religious Minorities (http://www.hlsenteret.no/). In North America, mentioning could be made of the Montreal Institute for Genocide and Human Rights Studies in Canada (http://migs.concordia.ca/); the Strassler Family Center for Holocaust and Genocide Studies at Clark University (http://www.clarku.edu/departments/holocaust/); the Center for Holocaust and Genocide Studies at the University of Minnesota (http://www.chgs.umn.edu/); and the Center for the Study of Genocide, Conflict Resolution and Human Rights at the University of Rutgers (http://cghr.newark.rutgers.edu/) - the latter three all being situated in the United States.

9 There are several organizations promoting an inclusive form of genocide education. Suffice it to mention the innovative work done by the Swedish Living History Forum (http://www.levandehistoria.se/english), the Norwegian Holocaust Centre (http://www.folkemord.no/) and by the small section for Holocaust and Genocide Studies at the Danish Institute for International Studies (http://www.diis.dk/sw262.asp).

Centre for Conflict Management at the National University of Butare, Rwanda. Specific courses are also offered by the Holocaust Centre in Norway and the Centre for African Studies at Copenhagen in Denmark.[10]

Notwithstanding these significant developments, there are, of course, also areas which need further attention and improvement. The field of genocide education in particular has grown immensely over the past years without much specific research resulting or being sufficiently reflected in the literature. In fact, despite the aforementioned growth of genocide studies as a whole, there are only very few textbooks for courses in this area.[11] Even more striking is the dearth of literature on genocide education as such, addressing the challenges that arise from teaching on and after mass atrocities or from bringing survivors to the classroom.[12] Therefore in this essay we want to focus on the field of genocide education and raise some issues which ought to figure prominently on the agenda of educators working in this field.

2. Revisit the UN Genocide Convention

A classic feature of publications in the field of genocide studies and education is criticism of the UN Genocide Convention: it is considered toothless, held to entail a flawed, if not useless, definition, and it says, according to critics, too little on questions of prevention and intervention.[13] In this context it is interesting to note that the fight against genocide was initiated by a man who had turned to law to fight this "barbarity."[14] Contemporary genocide scholars simultaneously try to reject the law as insufficient and wrong, while placing themselves in the tradition of Raphael Lemkin.

Indeed, there are many critical things to be said about the UN Genocide Convention. Besides the well-known shortcomings such as the limited catalogue of groups

10 For further information consult the following websites: Clark University (http://www.clarku.edu/departments/holocaust/grad/grad_index.cfm); Kingston University (http://www.humanrightsandgenocidestudies.eu/); Uppsala University (http://www.valentin.uu.se/index_eng.htm); Butare University (http://www.nur.ac.rw/spip.php?article36); Centre for Studies of Holocaust and Religious Minorities in Norway (http://www.hlsenteret.no/Nyheter/7578) and Centre for African Studies, University of Copenhagen (http://www.teol.ku.dk/cas/summer_courses/).

11 The only textbook addressing both individual cases and general questions of genocide studies is Adam Jones, *Genocide – A Comprehensive Introduction*, 2nd edition (2010). A different approach, based on case-studies, is taken in Samuel Totten and William S. Parsons (eds.), *Century of Genocide*, 3rd edition (2009). For an innovative, interdisciplinary concept see Thomas Brudholm and Martin Mennecke (eds.), *Efter Folkedrab* ("The Aftermath of Genocide"), 2nd edition (2007).

12 The only monograph addressing relevant questions is Samuel Totten (ed.), *Teaching About Genocide* (2004).

13 Instead of many see the remarks by Holocaust scholar Yehuda Bauer, The November Pogrom, the Holocaust and Genocide, 10 November 2008, 7-9 (available at http://www.holocausttaskforce.org/speeches/details/2008-11-10-7/document.pdf).

14 See on this Power, *supra* note 2, 21ff.

protected against genocide, the lack of any provisions addressing the needs of victims and their concerns when seen from today's perspective is particularly startling. There are, however, good reasons for both genocide educators and scholars to revisit the Convention. Above all, Lemkin's treaty has finally been put to practice, making it relevant beyond academic discussions. And it turns out that it may be better than its reputation has suggested. Over the past decade, a number of international and national courts and organizations have given life to the Convention by issuing judgements as well as reports. This new and rich practice highlights that the Genocide Convention covers more aspects of genocide than just punishment of perpetrators after the fact, concerning also conspiracy and incitement.[15] This should prompt observers to revisit well-established truisms about the Genocide Convention. It is submitted that such reassessment will lead to the discovery of new and far-reaching perspectives, valuable to both genocide studies and genocide education.[16]

Let us start with the legal definition of genocide. Time and again it has been stated that the definition wrongfully omits political groups from the catalogue of groups protected under the Convention. Now this has not changed and probably never will. The legal definition has proven to be very resistant, going unchanged through the negotiations leading to the establishment of the two UN tribunals for respectively the Former Yugoslavia and Rwanda and the International Criminal Court. Only a tiny fraction of states expressed interest in amending and expanding the definition of genocide; the overwhelming majority wanted to retain it as it had been devised in 1948. Still, there are interesting developments vis-à-vis the question of protected groups to be discerned. In particular, the International Criminal Tribunal for Rwanda (hereinafter ICTR) has authored rich (if somewhat incoherent) case-law on this matter. The tribunal's judges were early on confronted with the question of how to classify the main victims of the mass killings—the Tutsi of Rwanda—as a separate, protected group, despite the fact that the Tutsi shared culture, religion and language with the Hutu of Rwanda, not to mention the frequency of intermarriage between the two groups. In the very first case to be decided by the ICTR, the judges truly struggled with what seemed to be a dilemma: if the Tutsi were not held as a separate group falling under the limited catalogue of the Genocide Convention, there could be no legal finding of genocide—and this seemed ludicrous in light of the massive crimes that had been committed throughout Rwanda. The judges found a way out of this conundrum by classifying the Tutsi as a "permanent and stable group" and deciding that it had been the will of the drafters of the Genocide Convention to include

15 See on the role of incitement in the Rwandan genocide the seminal judgement in the so-called "media case", *Prosecutor v. Nahimana et al.*, International Criminal Tribunal for Rwanda, Trial Chamber, Judgement, 3 December 2003.

16 A good example for how to use the Convention in the classroom can be found in Adam Strom (ed.), *Totally Unofficial: Raphael Lemkin and the Genocide Convention* (2007), produced by Facing History and available at http://www.facinghistory.org/sites/facinghistory.org/files/raphael_lemkin.pdf.

all such groups under the protection of the Convention.[17] This was certainly well-intended; the historical evidence supporting such finding, however, was ambivalent, at best, and the reasoning deeply flawed on a number of accounts.[18] Consequently, other judges of the Rwanda Tribunal distanced themselves from this approach and devised new interpretations of the protected-groups-element of the legal definition of genocide. Of specific interest in this context, one of the approaches put forward built on a view expressed early-on by two pioneers of genocide studies: Frank Chalk and Kurt Jonassohn had written in a seminal textbook on genocide back in 1990 that with regard to the definition "group and membership in it are defined by the perpetrator."[19] In one of the later judgements of the ICTR, the judges adopted this thinking and pronounced that a

> group may not have precisely defined boundaries and there may be occasions when it is difficult to give a definitive answer as to whether or not a victim was a member of a protected group. Moreover, the perpetrators of genocide may characterise the targeted group in ways that do not fully correspond to conceptions of the group shared generally, or by other segments of society. In such a case, the Chamber is of the opinion that, on the evidence, if a victim was perceived by a perpetrator as belonging to a protected group, the victim could be considered by the Chamber as a member of the protected group, for the purposes of genocide.[20]

This emphasis on the perpetrator's viewpoint opened up the protected-groups-element for new interpretations. Political groups are still omitted from the legal definition of genocide—and there is still little that can explain this omission, other than realpolitik. The existing catalogue of protected groups, however, is more flexible in its scope and reach than previously assumed. Therefore, it enables educators to explore new cases of genocidal violence in regard to the Genocide Convention, as well as to underscore the need for other social sciences in order to understand the process of victimisation.

The Rwanda tribunal authored another important finding concerning the legal definition of genocide. In the aforementioned first case against Jean-Paul Akayesu, the mayor of a small commune, the judges declared that

> the Chamber wishes to underscore the fact that in its opinion, [rape and sexual violence] constitute genocide in the same way as any other act as long as they were committed with the specific intent to destroy, in whole or in part, a particular group, targeted as such. Indeed, rape and sexual violence certainly constitute infliction of serious bodily and mental

17 *Prosecutor v. Akayesu*, International Criminal Tribunal for Rwanda, Trial Chamber, Judgement, 2 September 1998, para. 511.

18 For a comprehensive analysis of this question see Martin Mennecke, "At the Centre of the 'Crime of Crimes' – Who is Protected Against Genocide?", forthcoming.

19 Frank Chalk and Kurt Jonassohn, *The History and Sociology of Genocide* (1990) 23.

20 *Prosecutor v. Bagilishema*, International Criminal Tribunal for Rwanda, Trial Chamber, Judgement, 7 June 2001, para. 65.

harm on the victims and are even, according to the Chamber, one of the worst ways of inflicting harm on the victim as he or she suffers both bodily and mental harm.[21]

This was the first time that an international tribunal had singled out acts of sexual violence as genocidal. The recognition of the specific targeting of women and girls and the particular, destructive nature of the mass rapes carried out in Rwanda was widely hailed as historical. The most recent confirmation of this reading of the definition of genocide can be found in the case against the Sudanese president Al-Bashir before the International Criminal Court. Here the Prosecutor argued that with regard to the alleged genocide in Darfur rape "is used as a weapon, a silent weapon, to destroy the target groups."[22] These recent cases under the Genocide Convention illustrate well the role sexual violence can play during genocide and provide strong material, including witness testimonies, which can be used in genocide education.

Finally, another recurring litany about the Genocide Convention shall be addressed, i.e. the alleged failure of the Convention to realize the promise of 'never again.' All too often, genocide scholars have said the Convention seemed preoccupied with matters of punishment, neglecting that its second purpose was the prevention of genocide. Also in this regard, however, there are new developments of which note should be taken. On February 26, 2007, the International Court of Justice—the highest judicial organ of the United Nations which hears disputes between states and does not deal with the criminal responsibility of individuals—rendered a judgement in a case between Bosnia Herzegovina and Serbia. Bosnia had asked the Court to rule that Serbia had violated the UN Genocide Convention, and the judges did find that this was indeed the case. The Court specified that Serbia was not, in a legal sense, responsible for the genocidal massacre committed at Srebrenica in July 1995. Instead the Court ruled that Serbia had violated two legal duties enshrined under the Genocide Convention: first, the duty to punish genocidaires present on its territory; and secondly and independently, the duty to prevent genocide outside its own territory.[23]

This determination of a legal duty to prevent genocide, directly applicable to all 141 states that have ratified the Genocide Convention, came as a surprise. While

21 *Prosecutor v. Akayesu*, see *supra* note 17, para. 731 (footnotes omitted).

22 Situation in Darfur, Sudan, International Criminal Court, Public Summary of Prosecutor's Application under Article 58, 14 July 2008, para. 23. See also, ibid., paras. 24-8 (available at http://www.icc-cpi.int/iccdocs/doc/doc529671.pdf). The judges of the Pre-Trial Chamber of the ICC followed the Prosecutor's argumentation on this point. Cf. *Prosecutor v. Bashir*, Pre-Trial Chamber, Second Warrant against Omar Hassan Ahmad Al Bashir, 12 July 2010, page 6f.

23 *Bosnia and Herzegovina v. Serbia and Montenegro*, Case Concerning the Application of the Convention on the Prevention and Punishment of the Crime of Genocide, International Court of Justice, 26 February 2007 (hereinafter *Bosnia v. Serbia*, Judgement). The decision is available at http://www.icj-cij.org/docket/index.php?p1=3&k=8d&p3=4&case=91. Generally, on the duty to prevent genocide, see William Schabas, *Genocide in International Law*, 3rd edition (2009) 520ff.

the US government during the Rwandan genocide apparently had recognised such a duty, this was later dismissed by many observers as an overly legalistic reading of the UN Convention.[24] The International Court of Justice, conversely, saw this duty established under Article 1 of the Convention—pursuant to which the parties "undertake to prevent and punish" genocide—and spelt out some conditions to help measure whether states comply with their obligations. The Court held that states are expected "to employ all means reasonably available to them, so as to prevent genocide so far as possible." In fact, it is "irrelevant whether the State whose responsibility is in issue claims, or even proves, that even if it had employed all means reasonably at its disposal, they would not have sufficed to prevent the commission of genocide."[25] Accordingly, a state incurs legal responsibility for violating the Genocide Convention "if the State manifestly failed to take all measures to prevent genocide which were within its power, and which might have contributed to preventing the genocide."[26] The Court acknowledged that different states may have different capacities to prevent genocide from being committed: the scope of the duty therefore depends on factors such as geographic proximity and political influence.

This finding of the Court raises a number of questions to be addressed by genocide scholars and educators the like: did, for example, the United States meet the aforementioned requirements vis-à-vis the Darfur crisis? What about other member states to the UN Genocide Convention such as China, Russia and South Africa? Is there a particular responsibility resting with the permanent members of the UN Security Council both because of their special status and their factual influence on Sudan? The newly discovered legal duty to prevent is actionable before the International Court of Justice and strongly underscores the preventative capacity of the UN Genocide Convention.

3. Avoid Focusing on Genocide Alone

There is one crucial addendum to the plea for revisiting the UN Genocide Convention: educators should not stop there and limit their teachings to those cases 'officially recognised' as genocide. There is, admittedly, a certain temptation to fall for the rhetorical power of the 'g-word'—but there are at least two strong reasons for expanding the scope of what, here, is referred to as genocide education. First of all, the determination of whether a certain case meets the criteria of the UN Genocide Convention (or, for that matter, those of any other definition of genocide) is often difficult, to say the least. As the ongoing Darfur crisis has painfully illustrated there is

24 It may be recalled that the Clinton administration at the time avoided to call the crimes committed in Rwanda by their rightful name because there was a fear this "could commit the US [government] to actually do something." Cf. the Discussion Paper, Office of the Deputy Assistant Secretary of Defence for Middle East/Africa Region, Department of Defence, 1 May 1994. For an instructive analysis of the approach taken by the Clinton administration see Power, *supra* note 2, 329ff.

25 Bosnia v. Serbia, Judgement, *supra* note 23, para. 430.

26 Ibid.

the enduring danger of embarking onto a "definitional dance" where some quarters will claim that a given scenario is a clear-cut case of genocide and indeed disagreeing with this proposition is held to amount to outright genocide denial.[27] Other observers will reject the genocide label and instead speak of crimes against humanity and other massive human rights violations, perhaps, as in the case of Darfur, linked to a complex armed conflict. Many of the topics educators want to bring to the attention of their students under the heading of genocide education will be present in both scenarios: unimaginable atrocities; questions of why these crimes are committed and how ordinary people can participate in them, the politically motivated abuse of existing or alleged tensions between different groups of the populace; the international community intervening or ignoring a major humanitarian crisis, and so on.

A case in point is the protracted conflict in the Democratic Republic of Congo (abbreviated as the DRC).[28] In what has been dubbed Africa's first World War, more than five million people have perished since 1998, most of them due to malnutrition and diseases, but also many through killings and armed violence. Sexual violence against women and children has been a characteristic of the conflict, reaching at times staggering levels. In fact, a high-ranking UN official has called the sexual violence "the worst in the world."[29] Millions of people have become refugees, either internally displaced in the DRC or in neighboring countries. The conflict started at a time when the DRC was considered a failed state and was closely related to the genocide in Rwanda. It involves local massacres, child soldiers, different ethnic groups, neighboring countries, local militias and the currently largest UN peacekeeping force, MONUC. Yet, all that being said, the requirements of the legal definition of genocide have seemingly not been met.[30] Does that make the atrocities committed in the DRC less relevant to an educator than, for example, the protracted conflict in Bosnia where some 100,000 people died, about half of them believed to have been armed combatants? If the focus indeed was on genocide, genocide education should focus on the massacres at Srebrenica and not the Bosnia conflict as a whole, as both the International Criminal Tribunal for the Former Yugoslavia and the International Court of Justice only have held Srebrenica to constitute genocide.

A second strong reason to abort the traditional focus on recognised cases of genocidal violence is the overall goal of preventing genocide. Many educators will mention prevention as one of the main drivers behind their interest in teaching

---

27 Cf. Scott Straus, "Darfur and the Genocide Debate," *Foreign Affairs*, vol. 84 (2005) 132.

28 For a very brief overview of the DRC conflict see Jones, *supra* note 11, 368ff. The Bosnia conflict, conversely, takes up a whole chapter (ibid., 317-339).

29 John Holmes, UN Under Secretary General for Humanitarian Affairs, cited in Jeffrey Gettleman, "Rape Epidemic Raises Trauma of Congo War," *New York Times*, 7 October 2007, page A1.

30 This remains, however, somewhat controversial. See, for example, the UN Report of the Mapping Exercise documenting the most serious violations of human rights and international humanitarian law committed within the territory of the Democratic Republic of the Congo between March 1993 and June 2003, August 2010, pages 275ff., available at http://www.ohchr.org/en/Countries/AfricaRegion/Pages/RDCProjetMapping.aspx.

on genocide. It is believed that reaching a better understanding of these atrocious crimes will contribute to their prevention in the future.[31] Preventing genocide, however, does not depend on the determination of whether genocide is being committed. The opposite is the case. In order to prevent genocide, the international community needs to engage with a simmering crisis before it escalates into full scale genocide. The then Special Adviser to the UN Secretary General on the Prevention of Genocide, Juan Mendez, once remarked that "quite frankly many times the debate about whether something is genocide or not has substituted for the decision to act to prevent it, and that is a paralyzing, very sterile debate."[32]

This logic is also embodied in the aforementioned legal duty to prevent genocide. The International Court of Justice explained that it would be "absurd" in the context of prevention to wait till the crime of genocide has been committed and determined. Therefore, the Court held that "a State's obligation to prevent, and the corresponding duty to act, arise at the instant that the State learns of, or should normally have learned of, the existence of a serious risk that genocide will be committed."[33] The question is not whether a certain crisis constitutes genocide, but whether it could evolve into genocide. This move away from a sole focus on genocide is also expressed in the new, increasingly important concept of a responsibility to protect—often referred to as 'R2P.' According to R2P, state sovereignty entails the responsibility for governments to protect their people from genocide, war crimes, ethnic cleansing and crimes against humanity. Other states and the international community have a responsibility to support each individual government in this undertaking. If a state "manifestly" fails its responsibility, "the international community (…) [is] prepared to take collective action, in a timely and decisive manner, through the Security Council, in accordance with the [UN] Charter," to protect the affected people.[34] No immediate distinction is made between genocide and other international crimes.[35] A former senior adviser to the Clinton administration, David Scheffer, has developed the term 'atrocity crimes' to capture the essence of this approach to massive human

31 See, for example, the resolution by the UN General Assembly introducing a Holocaust memorial day at the United Nations, UN Doc. A/RES/60/7, 1 November 2005, para. 2.

32 Interview with Juan Mendez, Special Adviser to the UN Secretary General on Genocide Prevention, US Holocaust Memorial Museum, 16 February 2006 (available at http://www.ushmm.org/genocide/analysis/details.php?content=2006-02-16). See also the mandate of the UN Special Adviser on Genocide Prevention, which states that the Adviser will "not make a determination on whether genocide within the meaning of the Convention had occurred. The purpose of his activities, rather, would be practical and intended to enable the United Nations to act in a timely fashion" (UN Doc. S/2004/567, 13 July 2004, page 2).

33 Bosnia v. Serbia, Judgement, *supra* note 23, para. 431 (Emphasis added by the author).

34 Cf. World Summit Outcome Document, United Nations Document A/60/1, 24 October 2005, paras. 138-9.

35 The Security Council resolution justifying airstrikes by an international coalition against Libya in March 2011, for example, invoked the notion of "responsibility to protect", but did not refer to "genocide", but "crimes against humanity". Cf. UN SC Resolution 1973 (17 March 2011).

rights violations: in order to avoid lengthy, costly debates on the accurate label for a given crisis in which massive crimes are being committed, Scheffer submits to speak of atrocity crimes and to leave the final determination to subsequent judicial proceedings and analysis.[36] The inclusion of other instances of atrocity crimes would also allow the educator to ultimately distinguish between cases of genocide and case of other human rights violations—not to measure suffering, but to distinguish facts according to different definitions. This may be particularly helpful in scenarios where the history of a nation has seen several types of atrocity crimes. Rigorous, exclusive focus on genocide might mean to blank over an important, painful part of that nation's history—possibly at the cost of new tensions. A clear example for this scenario can be found in international attempts to force the Baltic nations such as Lithuania to face their role during the Holocaust. Not only were vast parts of the local Jewish population exterminated; in part this took place with significant help from local collaborators to Nazi Germany. If the focus of genocide education efforts is exclusively aimed at this part of a country's history—leaving aside the massive crimes committed by the Soviet occupiers and the suffering inflicted upon the locals—this would be incomplete and may prove counter-productive.

4. Make Genocide Studies and Genocide Education Truly Interdisciplinary

Virtually all genocide scholars and genocide educators are familiar with the pioneering work of Raphael Lemkin. Few may actually have read his 1944 work on Axis Rule in Occupied Europe, but it is commonly known that he derived the term 'genocide' from the Greek word 'geno' for 'race' or 'tribe' and the Latin word 'caedere' meaning 'to kill.' Much lower is the number of those who know that Lemkin not only was an international lawyer, but also an amateur historian, studying numerous historical cases of genocidal violence. Thus, Lemkin was himself an example for how genocide studies makes it necessary to look beyond one's own discipline in order to reach a holistic understanding. Now, it is often said—whether in introductions to relevant works or at genocide scholar conferences—that contemporary genocide studies is a "profoundly" interdisciplinary field.[37] It remains frequently unclear what exactly this attribute may embody, but the underlying assumption is certainly that this is positive. It is questionable, however, whether genocide studies or education can be held to be interdisciplinary. While the contributors to an edited volume on genocide or the speakers at an international meeting may stem from various academic disciplines, this can hardly per se be taken to attest for a truly interdisciplinary approach. Most often the different panels at such conferences will still separate historians from lawyers, as will the different sections of an edited volume. How much interdisciplinary work is there being carried out at the existing genocide centres? How many genocide scholars do engage with readings from outside their own discipline? Often the

36 See on this David Scheffer, "Genocide and Atrocity Crimes," *Genocide Studies and Prevention*, vol. 1 (2006) 229-50.

37 By way of example, Jones, *supra* note 11.

composition of the staff will already reflect a bias towards certain disciplines. Thus, the field is for the most part characterised by the simultaneous, but unconnected presence of several disciplines, reflecting at best a multidisciplinary approach.

The question to be asked, of course, is whether genocide studies and genocide education were to gain from a serious attempt to bring together different disciplines examining genocide and other massive human rights violations. And there are indeed numerous issues and limitations to confront: different methodologies, different theoretical frameworks, different terminologies, to mention just a few. Anybody who has spent considerable time working with colleagues from other areas will know the feeling of relief one senses when talking to colleagues from one's own field: there is no need to start out by explaining or justifying oneself; there is a lot of understanding.

Yet, having said that, there are a number of evident advantages to studying genocide across the traditional borders of existing academic disciplines. For example, with legal scholars, the past years of practice before the international criminal tribunals for the Former Yugoslavia and Rwanda have shown very clearly that lawyers need the input of anthropologists, historians and others to be able to understand the situation on the ground. There are certainly also expert witnesses in trials at the national level, but international trials have compounded this need. Taking into account the alleged, as well as the real, impact of international prosecutions, lawyers are hardly in a position to assess what a particular case or judgement may mean for the dynamics in a conflict-ridden society or for the history writing in that country.

Also other disciplines have much to gain from looking beyond the borders of their own framework. An obvious starting point could be the immense paper trail and record of testimonies, video and photographs created by the international criminal tribunals.[38] There is much to be read and analysed, way beyond the fractured stories judgements are capable of telling. This requires that historians and others develop a sound understanding of the judicial process and its limitations—otherwise there is plenty of room for misleading interpretations. Recently, such cross-cutting, thoughtful analyses have been presented both with regard to the Nuremberg trials and the effect of the international prosecutions in Rwanda.[39] An example for a mistaken reading of an international judgement can be found in the positive commentary one anthropologist appended to the earlier mentioned Akayesu judgement by the International Criminal Tribunal for Rwanda. The analysis concluded that "the chamber significantly expanded the kinds of populations that will be protected by the convention."[40] This understandably sounds tempting, but, as pointed out before,

38 Cf. for example the online archive created by the International Criminal Tribunal for the Former Yugoslavia at http://icr.icty.org/.

39 See, respectively, *Donald Bloxham, Genocide on Trial – War Crimes Trials and the Formation of Holocaust History and Memory* (2001); and Nigel Eltringham, *Accounting for Horror – Post-Genocide Debates in Rwanda* (2004).

40 Paul J. Magnarella, "Recent Developments in the International Law of Genocide," in *Annihilating Difference – The Anthropology of Genocide*, ed. Alexander Laban Hinton (2002) 318. See also Jones, *supra* note 11, 13 (asserting that the Akayesu interpretation

the judgement is widely considered among lawyers to be deeply flawed and was not adopted in subsequent judgements by the same tribunal. To make genocide studies interdisciplinary, therefore, is a difficult and challenging task.

The same applies to genocide education. To teach on genocide is by itself difficult and challenging. Thus any ambitions to go interdisciplinary will warrant careful preparation and well designed teaching material. Here lies an additional task for genocide scholars: while the number of monographs and journal articles dealing with genocide is burgeoning, there is need for further textbooks and material suitable for classroom use. This material should include works which embrace the interdisciplinary approach and provide for different angles and perspectives. A successful example for new ways to implement this philosophy can be found in Denmark. The small Holocaust and Genocide education unit at the Danish Institute for International Studies annually organises outreach events throughout the country for high school students to mark what in Denmark has been called "Auschwitz Day" —that is January 27, the day commemorating the liberation of the Nazi extermination camp. Every year, these events evolve around a new topic such as 'perpetrators,' 'causes of genocide' or 'the aftermath of genocide.' More than 2,000 students select two workshops to learn about the respective overall topic in regard to different instances of genocide. In some cases, the discussions will take place within one school subject—focusing, for example, on the historical analysis or ethical considerations—and in others, there will be an interdisciplinary approach. At the end of the day, all participants will have been exposed to different and yet interrelated perspectives to the study of genocide.[41]

5. Win New Audiences for Genocide Education

High school or university students are traditionally at the receiving end of genocide education. Virtually all of the aforementioned material and institutions fit into this category. The question is why genocide education remains by and large limited to these audiences? General Roméo Dallaire recalled that prior to taking up his job as commander of the UN peacekeeping mission to Rwanda he knew little about the country and little about genocide.[42] This turned out to be a serious problem during the mission, as Dallaire and other UN officials failed to realise that what they were witnessing was not simply the resumption of the armed conflict between Hutu regime and Tutsi rebels, but genocide. Shortcomings regarding training prior to their

"is likely to become the norm in future judgements"); and Bauer, *supra* note 13, 8 (stating that "[s]trictly speaking, the description of the Rwandan tragedy as a genocide could be challenged. But of course it was a genocide, so the thing that is wrong is the definition").

41 Most material on the Denmark's Auschwitz Day is only available in Danish. A brief English introduction can be found at http://www.diis.dk/sw13037.asp.

42 Cf. Roméo Dallaire, *Shake Hands with the Devil* (2003) 45-56.

deployment have also been reported from the Dutch peacekeeping unit that ended up unable to prevent the genocidal massacre at Srebrenica in Bosnia in July 1995.[43]

Despite of these experiences, the focus of Holocaust, as well as genocide, education lies clearly with students and their teachers. The Task Force for International Cooperation on Holocaust Education, Remembrance and Research, for example—an ever growing network of government officials and experts from currently twenty-eight nations—has an impressive record in supporting teacher courses and the design of teaching material.[44] Only recently, however, a pilot project by the Auschwitz Institute for Peace and Reconciliation was funded to educate a group of government officials on the contemporary significance of the Holocaust.[45] Similar efforts are undertaken by the Holocaust and the United Nations Outreach Programme established by the UN General Assembly. Since 2007, this small unit has together with relevant Holocaust institutions trained local staff from UN public information centres around the world.[46] Other institutions such as the US Holocaust Memorial Museum, the British Imperial War Museum and the German Haus der Wannseekonferenz run occasional programs for members of the armed forces. It is submitted, however, that these efforts do not suffice to address the current need. A recent study by the Stimson Institute in Washington D.C. has underscored that many Western nations lack both doctrine and training when it comes to preparing armed forces for missions where the protection of civilians against genocide and other atrocity crimes is at the heart of the mandate.[47] Thus, it is important for genocide scholars and educators to contribute to closing this gap.

6. Concluding Observations

There are more issues to be put on the future agenda of genocide education than the framework of this essays allows to discuss. What, for example, is the role of

43 See the report Srebrenica – A Safe Area, compiled by the Netherlands Institute for War Documentation (NIOD), 2002, available at http://srebrenica.brightside.nl/srebrenica/.

44 For more information on the work of the Task Force see the network's website http://www.holocausttaskforce.org/.

45 See the report on the Institute's activities at http://auschwitzinstitute.org/.

46 For information on the UN Holocaust Outreach Programme see the report of the UN Secretary General, United Nations Document A/63/316, 20 August 2008, and the website http://www.un.org/holocaustremembrance/.

47 Cf. Victoria K. Holt and Tobias C. Berkman, *The Impossible Mandate? Military Preparedness, the Responsibility to Protect and Modern Peace Operations* (2006) 101ff. See also the recent report by the Genocide Prevention Task Force convened by the US Holocaust Memorial Museum, the US Institute for Peace and the American Academy of Diplomacy which makes the same point (Preventing Genocide – A Blueprint for US Policymakers, 2008, 77, available at http://www.ushmm.org/genocide/taskforce/). An interesting project in this regard is the Mass Atrocity Response Operations Project initiated by the Carr Center for Human Rights Policy, Kennedy School of Government, Harvard University with support of the US Army Peacekeeping and Stability Operations Institute (see http://www.hks.harvard.edu/cchrp/maro/index.php).

activism and prevention in genocide education? This is already a difficult question to answer for genocide scholars. Can one study the horrors of the Holocaust or the Rwandan genocide without feeling the deep urge to contribute to the prevention of future atrocity crimes? Having reviewed the US response to genocide throughout the 20th century, Samantha Power remarked that "the most realistic hope for combating [genocide] lies in the rest of us creating short-term political costs for those who do nothing."[48] This has become the cause for more than a million students at US universities who have joined forces to be 'upstanders,' to speak out on the Darfur crisis. Has this activism helped - or been misleading? A good question for genocide educators outside the US is why this call for upstanders has seemingly gone unheeded elsewhere. Where was the European coalition to save Darfur? Who is the European counterpart to George Clooney and Mia Farrow, Hollywood actors who have become Darfur activists? While it is easy to belittle US student activists as naïve, it is striking that there has been only little public response to the Darfur crisis in Europe. Is there a role for genocide education in this?

Another important, under-researched issue is the influence of Holocaust education on genocide education, as well as the interplay between international and national efforts in this field. Some Holocaust scholars still consider the Nazi genocide of the European Jews "the most extreme genocide," "unprecedented" or the "paradigmatic case of genocide."[49] This understanding is promoted further by some of the leading educational actors in the field, including the aforementioned International Holocaust Task Force, the US Holocaust Memorial Museum and Yad Vashem in Israel. What are the effects of this for genocide education in countries that have their own history of genocide? There is little discussion of this, even though Holocaust education increasingly formulates international standards. The Organisation for Cooperation and Security in Europe (OSCE) has for example published guidelines highlighting good practice in the field of Holocaust commemoration, co-authored by Yad Vashem.[50] In Rwanda, the British Aegis Trust is deeply involved in the making of genocide memorials, significantly the central exhibition on the 1994 genocide in the capital Kigali. Aegis Trust has its origins in a UK Holocaust center and is still deeply involved in Holocaust education.[51] Another interesting example from Rwanda

48 Samantha Power, Raising the Costs of Genocide, Dissent, 1 April 2002, 13.

49 Cf. only Bauer, *supra* note 13. It shall be mentioned in this context that the universalist conception of the Genocide Convention—without any bias to any particular instance of genocide—is another strength of the treaty. An interesting introduction to the necessary and valuable practice of comparing genocides can be found in Alan S. Rosenbaum, ed., *Is the Holocaust Unique? Perspectives on Comparative Genocide*, 3rd edition (2009).

50 Yad Vashem and the Office for Democratic Institutions and Human Rights in the Organisation for Security and Cooperation in Europe, Preparing Holocaust Memorial Days – Suggestions for Educators, January 2006 (available at http://www.osce.org/documents/odihr/2006/01/17836_en.pdf). It should be stressed that the guidelines do refer to other victim groups of the Nazi regime as well as other cases of genocide (ibid., 8f.).

51 Cf. the information provided on the Aegis Trust website at http://www.aegistrust.org/index.php?option=content&task=view&id=35&Itemid=66.

is the cooperation between the Human Rights Center at the University of Berkeley and Rwandan partner institutions on how to teach history after the genocide.[52] As with all forms of international cooperation and assistance, questions of local ownership and space for different and differing narratives need to be addressed, deserving closer scrutiny in the future. There is a thin line between facilitating Vergangenheitsbewältigung and imposing foreign versions of 'truth.' At the same time, scholars as well as educators should highlight overly nationalistic or selective accounts and resist the convenience of forgetting uncomfortable truths or even outright denial.[53]

The practitioner might respond to all these suggestions that the reality in the classroom does not allow for pondering these fundamental questions. Above all, educators face a lack of time to address the Holocaust and other genocides beyond the superficial treatment, not to mention concerns about as interdisciplinary approaches and so on. Indeed, to teach on genocide is a difficult task for any educator. The topic is demanding both emotionally and intellectually. It is nonetheless hoped that more and more educators will respond to the growing interest in atrocity crimes and will take into account some of the issues discussed here.

52 On this project, titled "Education for Reconciliation: Creating a History Curriculum After Genocide," see http://hrc.berkeley.edu/rwanda.html.

53 See, for example, Susanne Buckley-Zistel, "Nation, Narration, Unification? The Politics of History Teaching After the Rwandan Genocide," *Journal of Genocide Research*, vol. 11, 2009, 31ff. Interesting research in this field is conducted by the Georg Eckert for International Textbook Research in Braunschweig, Germany (cf. http://www.gei.de).

18. Genocide and Education

Dirk Mulder

1. Why Did People Act as They Did?

Genocide and education, do these two go together? In other words, can pupils be educated about genocide? Although asking the question is valid, trying to find an answer is a waste of time. Why? Because teaching about genocide is a must!

If we as an international community have deemed it important to draft a Genocide Convention to try to prevent genocides, then education is a matter of course. The contemplation of people and the world, which is the basis of this Convention, is the same as the essence of education—history teaching. For, the most essential question one can ask about the past is: Why did people act as they did? And if this question to the past can be asked at all, it is certainly the case regarding genocide.

Thus, we can leave the why-question, and direct all attention to the question how and in which way this education could or should take form.

The starting point of my contribution is the presence of authentic places of persecution, especially those of the Holocaust. But in principle the educational story about other genocides is not a different one.

2. A Limit to Age?

Before going further into this matter, I wish to make a few observations on the public about whom we must speak. These comments relate to the ages of the public and the place of performing the educational activities.

Education is often defined as the activities developed and executed on behalf of the regular education, for children and adolescents of school-age. However, in my vision, education has to be put in a broader perspective; it should also be aimed at adults, individuals and also groups like military personnel, doctors, teachers or policemen. In other words, there is no upper limit to age as regards education.

However, and this is my second age-related point, one should place a question-mark regarding an under-age limit. I am of the opinion that we, as professionals in Holocaust and Genocide-education, lie down much too easy for an under-age limit. Simply the fact that this age can differ in several countries indicates that there is no

H.G. van der Wilt, J. Vervliet et al., *(eds.)* The Genocide Convention: The Legacy of 60 Years.
 ISBN 978 9004 15328 8. *pp. 247-251.*

consensus to be found. In some countries, an organized school-visit to a museum or memorial, related to the Holocaust, is not done under the age of fourteen years, whilst in the Netherlands in general an age-limit of ten years is observed. But even for me this age is not absolute.

In the Camp Westerbork[1] Memorial Centre, we have in recent years designed projects for children in the age-group between six and ten years. It has been proven that this is possible, only the level of treatment of the subject and the form in which this is done, is, of course, different from that for a twelve-year-old child.

3. Performing Places

The place where educational programs are performed, are often seen as taking place within the walls of a museum or a memorial or on the authentic place of persecution. I will address the first as a matter of course and the second as an exception.

My first point here is that it is far too often taken for granted that education has to take place in a museum building. Educators should wonder rather how the visit to the authentic place of persecution could be placed in the centre. And by this, I do not mean this should be in the usually form of a one hour or more tour, with only a transmission of facts and figures, or horrible stories.

Far too much meaning is given to this in all countries employing this much used method, while the value of a lasting transmission of information is very doubtful. I shall come back to the educational use of the authentic place later on.

A second remark in this respect is that education should not be restricted to the museum or memorial building and the present place of persecution itself. The education should be extramural and in a broader context. Educational Holocaust and Genocide programs, especially those designed for pupils, should also include components that can be performed in schools, to prepare for a visit to a memorial and/or an authentic place, to working up to a visit, and to serve as implementation for this visit. Thus, these programs follow the generally accepted teaching-principle: introduction – gist – working up.

Finally, museums and memorials also have the educational task to develop programs and projects that can be used in schools, without the pupils paying a visit to a place of persecution.

4. Educational Objectives

Now, I come to the educational objectives and didactic methods.

1 Camp Westerbork was a concentration camp in the Netherlands during World War II. The Nazi occupying forces deported 102,000 Jews via this transit camp. The camp was originally built in 1939 by the Dutch government as a Central Refugee Camp for Jews fleeing Germany. In 1942, it became a transit camp headed by the SS. From July of that year, the Dutch Jews, German refugees, 245 Sinti and Roma and dozens of resistance fighters were deported from this 'hell's gate' to death camps such as Auschwitz and Sobibor. Only 5,000 of those deported returned alive.

(1) By exemplifying the biography of one person, wartime history – in particular the persecution of the Jews – is paid attention to. The confrontation with one historic person can give the possibility of identification with the visitors' own experiences, and also can offer a vision for life.
For example, the history of Westerbork transit camp in the Netherlands. Its 102,000 deported and murdered Jews is a figure which has lost an individual dimension. To bring this figure back to human dimensions it has to become clear that it concerns 102,000 times a mother, a father, a grandmother, an uncle, a sister, a brother, a nephew, a friend, a neighbour and so on.
(2) The story of the persecution of the Jews has to be presented as the story of the murdered victims. Anne Frank has become a well-known symbol of those victims. This approach presents – pedagogically speaking – a dead-end road, destroying one's hope and perspective. On the other hand, the story of a survivor can give back hope and perspective.
(3) The story of the Holocaust does not only present as the story of the victims but also the role of other groups: the perpetrators and the bystanders. The genocide-triangle, formed by the victims, the perpetrators and the bystanders, is the framework for the genocide-education.

5. Didactic Methods

In the educational service, especially aimed at schoolchildren, these principles can be worked out regarding the following aspects.
(1) Starting point: the history of the visitor's hometown, especially of its Jewish community and the war-time period.
(2) The biography of an historic individual: in the case of school-pupils, specifically, a Jewish child from the visitor's hometown. Since it is about a period filled with extreme circumstances, personal stories are essential. Dramatic moments, real events, existential choices, but also accommodations obtain an actual and understandable substance.
A special project in Westerbork is 'A Name and A Face,' in which we want to tell the story of all the victims—102,000 people—on the internet. The research had to be done by schoolchildren as an educational learning.
(3) To centralize the authentic place of persecution, and not the museum or memorial:
a historic place, if it has been violated by a deep and human tragedy, has an expressiveness which can best be described as 'aura' or 'sense of place'. Almost nothing evokes more strongly the memory of the past than the locations where the past has happened. It is the authentic or historic dimension that gives the place this aura. The confrontation can produce 'a historic sensation,' according to the Dutch historian Johan Huizinga. It is this dimension that gives not only a guarantee for the past reality, but also an experience of the senses.
A renewing method in Westerbork is that of training the pupils as Junior-guides.

(4) Guest lectures of eye-witnesses: the real contact with the past comes through the living past. An ear- and eye-witness can sketch an image in an inimitable way of the historic and actual reality. In this person and in the meeting with young people a really felt bond between today and the past is created.
An ear- and eye-witness shows pupils and lets them experience that war and persecution are not equal to death, providing them with perspective and prospect.
There is a special project as part of the Westerbork museum: The National Institute for Guest Lectures of Eyewitnesses in Schools. The strength of this educational procedure lies in the cohesion between the story of the hometown of the visitor, a personal story (preferably live) and the connection of both with the authentic place. This integrated approach, through the connections that are being made, on an individual level and close to home, is in my view the obvious educational way.

6. 'Small' History

Let me go a little further in this matter of using biographies of individuals.

The didactic approach of personal stories prevents that history from becoming a series of notions, names and numbers. Human matters should not remain themes in books but subjects that can touch pupils. This can be reached by putting the individual person in the centre, by which identification becomes possible. Precisely if a time-period is marked by extreme circumstances, this approach is advisable. Dramatic moments, real events and existential or non-choices obtain an actual and understandable meaning. Only then, can there be talk of a learning effects on attitude: on the one hand, learning to recognize that daily forms of prejudices and 'light' discrimination can be the beginning of real catastrophes; on the other hand, learning that even in the most inhuman situations humanity can still exist.

These goals of learning cannot be reached by abstractions; they can be reached by events from the historic daily reality. With attention to the individual and the effect of world-shaking events by slow indoctrination or sneaking and continuing legislation with commands and prohibitions in his or her daily life, can be called the 'small' history.

The attention to the 'small' history, as it has occurred in the daily life of the individual, does not only relate to the 'lighter' forms of injustice and suppression, but especially elementary humanity. By this, we can prevent relatively too much attention to extreme cruelty from making a little cruelty seem less bad. Also, the speaking of human cruelty often activates new human cruelty; and, at any rate, it does not teach pupils to prevent this.

The "small" history also provides the possibility of a didactic translation to the pupils' own environment. Not only because it is part of the world of experience of the children, but also because it can be found near home and school. The meeting with several kinds of remaining historic substance in 'their own world' and on the very spot itself confronts the pupils very powerfully with the past. So try to translate the 'far' past to the pupils' own geographic world in which more traces of that past are to be seen and found than many people think.

7. It Can Happen Again

The goals of the educational service don't restrict themselves to only transmitting knowledge. Besides cognitive goals, affective goals had to be formulated as well. Holocaust- and Genocide-education must contribute to the awakening of consciousness and to the education of visitors by means of activities and projects. An important basis for that purpose is historic awareness, which is a necessary condition towards updating. Studying the past does not give a manual for solving present-day problems, but it does offer a possibility to place those problems in some kind of perspective.

Directors and educational services of museums and memorials should be conscious of the essence they wish to transmit to the visitor. It should be possible to express this essence in only one or two sentences. To me, it is the notion that the Holocaust has really taken place and that therefore genocides can happen again.

In general, I think we have in education concentrated ourselves on the groups and their relations in the Genocide-triangle. For most visitors and pupils, typically a non-specialized audience, the focus on the Genocide-triangle is complicated enough. Therefore, I think it's too complicated to connect Genocide-education with the problems of international law.

Let me end my contribution with the following words of Abel J. Herzberg, Dutch survivor of Westerbork and Bergen-Belsen: "If knowledge of an event added to an understanding of the things man is capable of and the things he can be driven to if he is not careful, then a lot would be gained."

Appendix

If the Whole Body Dies:

Raphael Lemkin and the Treaty Against Genocide

By

Robert Skloot

Raphael Lemkin (1900–1959)

Acknowledgments

I wish to thank the following people for their support and encouragement: John Wiley, Casey Nagy, Steven Jacobs, Steven Burch, Jim Fussell, Gary Sandefur, Norma Saldivar, David Stewart, Casey Martin, Lewis Leavitt, Evan Massou, the Evjue Foundation, and the University of Wisconsin–Madison Graduate School.

If the Whole Body Dies was given its first reading on December 15, 2005, at the University of Wisconsin–Madison with the following cast:

RAPHAEL LEMKIN	Donavon Armbruster
GIRL	Carrie Coon
MAN	Craig Jacobson
WOMAN	Susan Sweeney
MEN'S VOICES	Pete Bissen
WOMEN'S VOICES	Amy Sawyers

The reading was directed by Roseann Sheridan.

Introduction

Why this play? Why now?

If the Whole Body Dies was written with three objectives in mind. First, the play aims to give Raphael Lemkin his "due" by raising his extraordinary achievements to a higher level of recognition. The origin of the word genocide is not popular knowledge, just as few know that Lemkin was the author of the *U.N. Convention Against Genocide.*

Second, the play is my own attempt to add a small comment to the store of anti-genocide materials, a play that can stimulate discussion of the phenomenon that Lemkin worked most of his life to outlaw. If the scourge of genocide is to be diminished, the pressure to work toward that goal must involve all disciplines and professions, including artists whose public testimony is part of history's record against atrocity and killing. Euripides and Rabe, Verdi and Britten, Goya and Picasso, Maya Lin and Iri and Toshi Maruki have all contributed to our knowledge and feeling about the devastation of war and its tragic aftermath, and their work, in the aggregate, comprises a storehouse of compassion and horror, of anger and shame, of witness and memory we know is necessary to comprehending the world, past and future.

The (antiwar) work of artists, however, tends to be overlooked by many in politics and academe who carry a negative bias toward things freighted with idealism and emotion. The work is greeted as soft and starry-eyed, depressing and irrelevant, distractive and untrustworthy, and a host of other dismissive pejoratives. But artists know better, and so do the millions who over time have seen *Guernica*, heard the *Requiem* or stood in the confounding, deathly courtyard of the Berlin Jewish Museum. I hope that getting to know Lemkin and his work will show colleagues (especially in the social sciences) that knowledge can be obtained in ways grounded as much in feeling as fact, and that the power of theatrically communicated insights can assist in the work they do.

Third, plays do things to people. What the theatre can provide uniquely is a connection between human beings and among groups through the creation of empathy. It is a connection that, however brief, creates visible, remarkable humane possibilities that differ from the violent and terror-filled world too many know, even though many others are, with luck and resources, seemingly exempt from danger.

It's likely that the historical Lemkin of *If the Whole Body Dies* is a Lemkin who shares some of my own characteristics, which is why I was drawn to him: his Polish roots, his love of language (and puns), his passion for justice; we even share the same Hebrew name, though not the fate of family in

Hitler's Europe. (There are likely less positive characteristics too.) I think of a number of characters in Chekhov's plays whose disappointments with life provoke them to work harder for something tangible that will keep the world on the path to something better for the future, and I connect that to the way Lemkin lived and died with his one obsessional conviction: that in the law, universally endorsed, can be found the mechanism to prevent the wholesale slaughter of innocents. The problem, of course, is that people throughout history don't abide by that conviction, and behave in ways that recreate genocidal devastation with seemingly endless regularity.

As I have written elsewhere, the first problem of teaching about genocide is the challenge to maintain hope. Raphael Lemkin, ingesting heart medication in a cheap Manhattan walk-up, depressed that his adopted country refused to accept his plan to stop genocide, hounded by bill collectors and sustained by a few friends and not a little vanity, was battered by storms internal and outside himself. But in the darkness of another tempest, this time Shakespeare's, I hear, as he must have felt, Miranda's immediate, empathic connection watching the visitors' ship battered by the furious waves:

> "O, I have suffered with those I saw suffer....
> O, the cry did knock against my very heart!"

Robert Skloot
University of Wisconsin–
Madison

If the Whole Body Dies:[1]

Raphael Lemkin and the Treaty Against Genocide

> "The conscience of humanity is like that of a dying man. All his sins invade his mind in his last hour, when he is powerless to repair them."
>
> —Raphael Lemkin, from his unpublished autobiography

Cast
Raphael Lemkin
Girl
Man
Woman
Other occasional voices

Time
August 27, 1959, in and around the 1950s, and other times too.

The Setting
Lemkin's flat. A sparsely furnished studio apartment in upper Manhattan. Prominent features are a desk, telephone, and a back wall on which projections can be shown. Many books and papers, and boxes of "stuff" that can be consulted if necessary. Manual typewriter, fountain pen, and radio. On the desk is a pair of horn rimmed glasses, comb and small hand mirror, and a 1950s radio microphone with a table name sign identifying the speaker as "Dr. Lemkin." The room is neat despite the substantial clutter, though it might get messier as the play proceeds.

On the rear screen appears a picture of the Roman Coliseum as, before the play begins, we hear music from the "The Triumphal March" from the Miklos Rozsa soundtrack for the 1951 M-G-M movie *Quo Vadis* ©DRG Records #19060 (4 minutes). After the music concludes, the background image on the wall changes to a photo of an upper Manhattan apartment house of the time of the play. A man in his 50s with thinning hair is dozing in his desk chair in worn but neat clothes, including a white shirt, white pants, and white socks. His dark silk tie and white shoes are nearby.

(Music ends. Man startles awake. Rises slowly and with effort. Combs his hair. Puts on glasses. Sits. Begins to type.)

LEMKIN
(*With Yiddish/Polish accent throughout)*
In my early childhood I read *Quo Vadis* by Henryk Sienkiewicz dealing with the Romans' attempt to destroy the early Christians. It moved me greatly. I couldn't believe that people could be so cruel or understand why the murdered were so helpless. (*Stops typing*) The movie was highly praised for its pageantry but not very good otherwise. Ustinov was a travesty as Nero. There is in the nature of mankind something not to be trusted.

(*A young GIRL with dark hair about 13 or 14 appears in light that expands to include her. Image on wall changes to exterior shot of Prinsengracht 263, Amsterdam, from 1942.)*

GIRL
Bon jour, Professor Lemkin. Am I calling too early?

LEMKIN
Non, mademoiselle. I overslept. (*Thinks of the linguistic connection, as he will often*) Overslept. On top of the blankets. (*Smiles*) A little joke. It must be afternoon where you live. *Bon jour.*

GIRL
The world spins along and is everywhere at once. I'm not certain why I'm awake when you're asleep, but I am going to study more science to find out.

LEMKIN
Be patient. It will get clearer. Scientific laws are something you can't ever disregard… or shouldn't. If it were the same time everywhere, the world would run out of breakfasts.

GIRL
That's what I think too. (*Laughs*) But there are laws that aren't good. Bad laws made our lives miserable before we moved to where we are now. I would tell you where, but it's better if you don't know. Maybe if we only had a few good laws, we could obey them more easily.

LEMKIN
That's what I think too. (*Laughs*)

GIRL
Like not having to put up with people I'm fed up with, who always misinterpret my intentions.

LEMKIN
That's not exactly what I had in mind. (*Seriously*) Laws are serious. They are written to make it harder to do away with people you don't get along with.

GIRL
Cheer up, *monsieur*, we shall still have our jokes and tease each other, and our holidays to celebrate. It won't do us any good... to go on being gloomy. Chins up, stick it out, better times will come! Oh, we're going to have dinner now. I hope your breakfast is more ample and better tasting than mine was. We had *oeufs au chou*, but without the eggs. I call it a *sans omelette*.(*Laughs*) *Bon apetit*!

LEMKIN
Your French is getting very good, *tres bon*! *Auf wiedersehen, mein Mädchen.*

GIRL
Au revoir, Professor Lemkin. (*She leaves with her light.*)

(He tries to put on a shoe with great difficulty, gives up and instead puts on slippers. Puts on his tie. Combs hair. Glasses. Scenic image of U.N. building in New York. Gets document, reads.)

LEMKIN
"The Minister of Foreign Affairs of Syria, His Excellency Mr. Khalid El-Azem, has submitted 25 June 1955, in the office of the Secretary-General of the United Nations at the Veterans Building in San Francisco, the instrument of Accession of Syria to the Convention on the Prevention and Punishment of the Crime of Genocide. Genocide is defined as the deliberate destruction of national, religious, racial, or ethnic groups. This latest ratification is of special significance because it brings the number of ratifications of the Genocide Convention to fifty... (*He makes some corrections on the paper he is reading, indicates he is skipping through some text, and resumes.*)... The Genocide Convention came into force on January 12, 1951. Since then it became the best ratified convention among those adopted under the auspices of the U.N. It is hoped that more ratifications and more implementation through domestic legislation will come soon. The list of the 50... (*skips text*)...Roma-

nia, Saudi Arabia, Sweden, *(writes)* S-Y-R-I-A, Turkey, Ukraine, Uni... (*long pause*)...Vietnam..."
*(Stops. Squeezes his brow as if he had a bad headache, takes a pill with glass of water.*2 *Light expands as MAN walks into it.)*

MAN
Raphael Lemkin...?

LEMKIN
Yes, I'm Dr. Lemkin.

MAN
Hello. I'm William Proxmire... Bill... the new junior senator from Wisconsin.[3] The state shaped like your right hand. When you look at the palm. *(He shows that.)* I got your number from our U.N. people. They said you wanted to talk to me. Just what do you have in mind, Professor?

LEMKIN
First, congratulations on your victory.

MAN
Too bad you weren't there to run my campaign for governor. Or campaigns. There were a few of them. I admire the way you lined up all those countries for ratifying the convention. I very much admire the convention too. It's a brilliant and necessary piece of legislation. Congratulations to you.

LEMKIN
The work never ends, Senator. I look for assistance wherever I can. I'm going to count on you for the help I need to get the treaty through the Senate. As the law says in Latin, I do, *Facio [fa-ki-o]* that you might do, *ut facias [oot fa-kee-as].* Never mind. It's urgent that someone lead the way to convince your colleagues that it is the only hope for stopping the wholesale killing of innocent groups. President Truman sent it up years ago, but still no vote. It's a disgrace.

MAN
Once I move down to Washington, I'll do whatever I can. You know, I've got a sign on my kitchen wall with a Chinese proverb that kind of says it all: "The glory is not in never failing, but in rising every time you fall." I suppose you can say it in Chinese, Professor?

LEMKIN
No, Chinese isn't one of my languages.

MAN
It got me to Washington. The proverb, not the Chinese. It's not even the Chinese that concern me. I'll call you after I settle in and we can talk about all those innocent people who'll die without the ratification. You can count on me to help in any way I can.

LEMKIN
Thank you for calling, Senator... Senator, since you're here, maybe we could make the appointment now. (*He's looking for his appointment book.*) What about during the week of the fourteenth...

MAN
I hear it's real hot in New York. Keep up your spirits and strength. Eat lots of vegetables. And exercise. That's the real secret of keeping fit and on top of things.

LEMKIN
If that week won't work, what about...

MAN
(*Overlaps*) Broccoli. Try broccoli. I'll be in touch.

(*Light out*)

LEMKIN
(*Writes in his book*) William. Means "protector." Proxmire. "Close to a swamp." (*Laughs at his joke*)I read he's a Yale man. Well, I am too. We're together on the seal: Mr. Lux meet Mr. Veritas. (*Chuckle*) Likes Chinese proverbs, green vegetables, and exercise. (*He looks at his right hand.*) From Wisconsin.

(Massages his head. Drinks water. Takes off his tie. Puts on his glasses. Begins to type and then speak:)

"Estimado Presidente Rafael Trijillo Molina, No es porque tenemos el mismo nombre que escribo..."

No. It's got to be more formal. He's a general of the armies.

"Excelentísimo Señor Generalísimo Marcus Vinicius Molina,[4]

La trágica situacíon que ha vivido la humanidad, y que esta viviendo ahora..." (*Continues*)

I am writing to you, Mr. Axelrod, to acknowledge that the Foreign Economic Administration overpaid my salary in 1947, and to say I am anxious to liquidate this indebtedness before you refer it to the Department of Justice for collection. But I ask your patience because my work abroad has distracted me from this obligation that at the moment I am not able to pay. Before you begin a procedure we both want to avoid...

"de su Excelencia atentamente, Raphael Lemkin, fundador del movimiento mundial contra el genocidio." Basta!

(He turns on the radio. Quo Vadis *music. Scenic image of rural farm in Poland. A middle-aged WOMAN, dressed modestly, appears in light.)*

(*Quietly*)
Mama, why when the Roman emperor ordered the lions to kill the Christians did no one stop them? Why did they scream for blood and vengeance? Before Jesus was a Christian he was, and died, a Jew. To be slaughtered for what you believe, or believed, or just for being who you are, is to be victim of the worst evil man can commit. (*Radio off)*

WOMAN
(*Hebrew*)
"*Kum lech l'cha ayl eer ha-harega.*" Bialik.[5]

LEMKIN
"Come with me to the city of slaughter." Bialystock.[6] You and pappa died as Jews too. Not killed by lions, but by something even worse. Those were Christians ate your flesh. I want you to be proud of me, Mama. Like Kosciuszko, I came to America to fight tyranny and oppression. He was able to return to Poland. Here in America, I am condemned to loneliness. This is an essential condition of my life. I talk to the most important people in the world, and in their own language, but I'm still alone. I also talk to you, Mama, whom I miss so much.

WOMAN
(She hums a Yiddish lullaby.)
Ess mein Kind.[7] Pancakes and sour cream, Raphael!

LEMKIN
And your home-made jam!

(Scenic image of New York. He checks address book, old newspaper. At typewriter.)

Dear Mr. Ben Hecht, We have never met but I have not forgotten what I read about your pageant at Madison Square Garden, the one with Paul Muni and Edward Robinson. Szyk, Szyk who did your souvenir program drew the illustration for the review of my article entitled "Axis Rule in Occupied Europe" in the *New York Times*! Did you know that? I was only in this country three years then. In North Carolina.

WOMAN
If three people share a blanket, my son, make sure you're the one in the middle.

(She leaves. Light returns to usual.)

LEMKIN
The calling the roll of the famous Jews in history was your masterstroke, 119 names I read in the paper! And that is why genocide—do you know the word? I invented it the year after your pageant—must be stopped, because mass killing destroys the diverse, distinct cultures of groups and every one of these groups has its mission to fulfill and a contribution to make in terms of culture. Even Karl Marx, whom you left off the list, deserved mention. That would have made 120. *Me'a esrim.*[8] Your age in bibles. You called the show *We Will Never Die*, but six million is too many to lose… 49 of them were my family, Mr. Hecht. I am writing you to help me to stop genocide. Please write me at 504 W. 112th Street in New York. Perhaps we can meet? I'm sure you'll understand why my phone number isn't in the book…"

(Phone rings; LEMKIN answers.)

This is Dr. Lemkin.

VOICE
We're ready for the interview, Mr. Lemkin.

LEMKIN
Just a moment. (*He quickly puts on his tie.*) All right.

(Puts down phone; rear image of U.N. building.)

VOICE
We have before our microphone today Professor Raphael Lemkin who is known in the United Nations and the world over as the man who coined the word *genocide* and conceived the idea of the Genocide Convention….

LEMKIN
(*Ardently*)
Il pensiero legale italiano (*Woman's Voice translates*: "Italian legal thought"] mi ha interessato sempre ["has always interested me"], come il Diritto Romano su cui si basa… ["like the Roman Code on which it is based…"]); Nobody else has ever depicted human suffering and the abyss into which a human personality can be thrown better than Dante in *Pergatoria*…. But genocide is the greatest degradation to which humanity can be brought…

VOICE
(*Comic*)
Excuse me. Dr. Lemkin? This is John J. Carroll, the credit manager of the Henry Hudson Hotel. We wish to call attention to your account which amounts to $129.86 and is now past due. (*LEMKIN sags*) The management would appreciate you giving the payment of this account your immediate attention in bringing it up to date. (*He removes his tie*) It is… policy… that all accounts are paid when the bill is rendered.

(He hangs up phone. Image of apartment building. Drinks more water. Begins to type.)

Chapter three. In order to be successful with fellow men one must learn to be fully alone with an integration into the sublime world of feelings and faith. I learned to love the obstacles by making them a test of my moral strength. In this moral strength I believe fervently. It is stronger than temporal power. It is stronger than technology and government. It is life itself. Caleb was a hero in the Bible, but his name in Hebrew spells dog.

(*LEMKIN turns on radio. Some music from the* Quo Vadis *movie plus the piece of the soundtrack where we hear an English accent by a MAN's voice speaking the words of Nero [Ustinov]: "When I have finished with these Christians, Petronius, history may not know they ever existed."*)

LEMKIN

That is the issue, Petronius, the maniacs of history. How to stop them. I have an answer now. In law. The law can do what nothing else is capable of. The law is our best protector. And I have a wonderful friend in the Senate now. No, not the Roman one. Proxmire in Washington. He will help me get the ratification. "History may not know they ever existed." *[Radio off]* How will people know about the Jews if they are "finished off"? By what we leave to history that we created. Not our blood. Not our suffering. Our books. Our brains. Our dreams. *Hatikvah.*[9] Humanity is enlarged by the contributions of all. Killing one group diminishes all. That film was terrible and funny at the same time. No, not *Quo Vadis...* it got eight nominations! No, Hitler's film. Where Jews are "the plague that threatens the Aryan people.... a race of parasites" it said. Parasites. Parasites. Two footnotes. (*Laughs*) "Their homelessness is a matter of choice," it said. As if I chose to live like this and here, though I live here now, with less of a home than I deserve but more on $25.00 a week is not possible. *The Eternal Jew* was the film.[10] *Der Ewige Jude.* E-wig-e. E-wig-e. We are a head-covering people. (*Laughs*) We "assimilate and destroy from within... forever foreign bodies... regardless of appearance," it said. So I bought a white suit with white shoes and white socks all of which I wore with a dark silk tie in order to attend the dinners I was invited to.... In America, I saw that one first cut a piece of meat, then put the knife on the plate, shifted the fork to the other hand, and ate it. This did not fit well into my notions of American economy, and it slowed down the eating process considerably. (*Smiles*) We are like rats it said, no, we *are* rats, "that migrate everywhere,... cunning, cowardly, cruel." "What if my house be troubled with a rat...?" Einstein is "the relativity Jew," but I have no more relatives. "Jewish blood will never pollute the German nation," wasn't that what Nero said, Mama? So you were murdered. Is that why they hate us? Is that why they hate me? ". . . I can give no reason, nor will I not, more than a lodged hate and a certain loathing..."[11]

(Holds his head. His hands begin to shake. Image of Prinsengracht 263 on the back wall; light up on GIRL.)

GIRL
(*Cheery*)
Bon jour, Professor Lemkin. Are you well, today?

LEMKIN
My head aches a little. I take these pills. What do you want?

GIRL
Je voudrais de fromage et des saucisses.

LEMKIN
(*Laughs*)
Cheese and sausage? You are very silly, *ma cherie*.

GIRL
Oui. It is very silly to learn all the foods in the world when all we have are cabbages, potatoes, and beans. But one day I will go to the grandest restaurant and order everything on the menu… but only to test my vocabulary, you understand.

LEMKIN
The writer Victor Hugo said: As many languages you know, as many times you are a human being. (*Drinks some water*) Do you know about the brave Cyrano de Bergerac? He was a very proud Frenchman who once, rather than admitting he was too poor to buy anything to eat, only took a grape and a glass of water from a big banquet.

GIRL
Der Mann hat einen grossen Geist
Und ist so klein van Taten!

LEMKIN
The spirit of man is great,
How puny are his deeds.

(*Thinks*)
Wenig brauche, so ess, ich glaube, Nur Nip und kleine Traube.

GIRL
Little I need, I'll take a plate Have a sip plus one small grape.

(They laugh together.)

GIRL
I'll ask Daddy to ask Miep to bring the book so we can read it together. Now, excuse me, Professor. *Adieu.*

(Light out on GIRL*)*

LEMKIN
Do you know I worry about you? I have the way to save you all.... *(Pause)* Haiti. We don't have Haiti yet!

(*Writes*)"*Je formule cette requete au nom de l'humanite, Monsieur le President,* and please allow me to urge in the strongest possible terms that you use all the influence you have with your colleagues in Haiti.... (*Uses pen to sign.*) *Excellence, Professeur Raphael Lemkin, fondateur du mouvement mondial contre le genocide,* and five-time nominee, Nobel Peace Prize.

(Phone rings. Scenic image of New York apartment.)

VOICE
(*Comic*)
Dr. Lemkin, this is Francine Zeller. I represent Gates Ambulance and Oxygen Service, who has turned over to my office a claim against you for the sum of $18.00 for services rendered in moving you from 159 St. Paul Road, Hempstead to South Nassau Hospital. May I please have your remittance by return mail, and thank you. (*Click*)

LEMKIN
"So, when I win some triumph, by some chance,
Render no share to Caesar—in a word,
I am too proud to be a parasite,
And if my nature wants the germ that grows
Towering like the mountain pine,
Or like the oak, sheltering multitudes—
I stand, not high it may be—but alone!"
Ah, Cyrano...

(Drinks a glass of water)

Chapter seven. *(Types a bit, then*)

Through the open window an old oak tree, planted some 50 years ago in the Yale garden, looked quite indifferently at my disturbance. But the decision was made, not so much by me but by something inside me. Perhaps the destruction of the Moors... had influenced my decision to travel to Geneva. I had not been there since 1938.... In this city I buried the hopes for a better world in the sentimental and confusing days of the old League of Nations. There I had talked for days and nights to the paralyzed minds of men who were unable to stir themselves into action to save the peace of the world.

RECORDED VOICE
(We hear a tape recording from February 1949; as the Announcer starts, LEMKIN again puts on his tie and jacket, drinks, tries to quiet his shaking hands.)

And now we come to our third guest, who is a Professor of Law at Yale University and specializing in teaching matters about the United Nations. Dr. Lemkin is the man who created the word genocide and really he has fought this thing from long, long ago. Dr. Lemkin, can you give us a little background about how you came to be interested in this genocide fight, originally?

(He listens to his own voice on tape approvingly; combs hair.)

Gladly, Mr. Howe. It leads me very far back to my childhood. Everybody has sentimental memories from childhood. And everybody has a book they love the most. One of my inspirations in this field was by Sienkiewicz, *Quo Vadis*. It describes the terrible suffering of the early Christians...

(LEMKIN interjects over the tape.)
He won the Nobel Prize! "Later on I became interested in genocide because it happened so many times. It happened to the Armenians."

(The tape fades out.)

LEMKIN
I should win the prize too. Who will ratify me? I thought a crime should not be punished by the victims, but should be punished by a court, by international law. Saith the Jew: "For the intent and purpose of the law hath full relation to the penalty... By my soul I swear there is no power in the tongue of man to alter me."

(Light up on GIRL)

GIRL
Bon jour, Monsieur. Are you happy or sad today?

LEMKIN
"I'll not answer that... say it is my humor."

GIRL
I'd say you're in a very bad mood. The best remedy for those who are afraid, lonely, or unhappy, is to go outside, somewhere where they can be quite alone with the heavens, nature, and God. That's hard for me to do, but perhaps you can do that where you live. I want to tell you that lately I have developed a great love for family trees and genealogical tables. Did your family have any trees, Monsieur?
(*Laughs*)

LEMKIN
We had many on the farm. I loved the cherry trees most. And we had a white dog I called Riabczyk. He was shot by a passing rider.

GIRL
If you think of your fellow creatures, then you only want to cry, you could really cry the whole day long.

(He picks up a postcard. Light up on WOMAN.)

WOMAN
Dearest Raphael. We have been moved with the others of the town. Do not worry. The weather is hot. We are well and send our love, Mama.

(Light out)

LEMKIN
Postcards from the East.[12]

GIRL
The only thing to do is to pray that God will perform a miracle and save some of them. Now you've made me sad, Monsieur. *Adieu.*

(Light out)

LEMKIN
When Sienkiewicz accepted his prize in 1905 he said: "Nations are represented by their poets and their writers."... the Nobel Prize he said... "bears witness that that nation has a share in the universal achievement..." Pasternak, the coward, turned his prize back. (*He types*) Mr. Charles A. Hite, Storage Superintendent, Merchants Storage and Transfer Co., Washington 4, D.C. Dear Mr. Hite, The letter marked "LAST NOTICE" has reached me at my Yale Law School office. I am writing to request your forbearance, as my travel schedule and personal circumstances have prevented me from dealing with personal matters, no matter how urgent. Despite my neglect of payment of my account, I plan to have the bill paid forthwith, and I earnestly desire that you not sell my goods at your next sale as you indicate you plan to do. Thanking you in advance, I am sincerely yours, Professor Raphael Lemkin, Author of the Word Genocide and Founder of the World Movement Against Genocide.

(Image of Washington; light up on MAN)

MAN
Congratulations, Dr. Lemkin! I see you've got Ghana and Morocco to ratify.

LEMKIN
But the one I want most isn't there, Senator. The United States is missing. Why, Senator?

MAN
You must be nearing sixty ratifications now.

LEMKIN
No, Syria and Egypt have merged to become the United Arab Republic so we lost one by the count. America could make up for that loss.

MAN
I talked with the Bar Association folks.[13] They are leading the opposition and won't be moved. Reason is lost on them. They're worried that allowing foreign interventions into domestic matters would make us vulnerable here at home... some of my southern colleagues in the Senate even think we'll be invaded from four directions for our treatment of the Negroes, which I do admit is very bad. I don't think they're eating their vegetables.

(*Chuckle*)

LEMKIN
(*Angry*)
But genocide is an international issue. America must take the leadership in the world to prevent it.

MAN
And I'm determined that Wisconsin will take the lead for America.

LEMKIN
Wisconsin must become the shape of things to come. The strong right hand. With the palm facing you. Remember? (*They laugh.*) A friend once told me: "Chins up. Stick it out. Better times will come." Senator, do you know Ben Hecht, the writer? He's from Racine, in your Wisconsin.

MAN
I know the Hechts from Fond du Lac. Lyle and Rayleen. Their son is Ben. No, it's Bert. Or Buddy. You've done magnificent work and I hope you get the Nobel, Professor. Lots of people do. There's a sign on my Senate office wall that says: "It is not necessary to hope in order to undertake, or to succeed in order to persevere." Not as long as you get exercise, anyway. *Time* magazine called me "Quixote from Wisconsin." So, I won't give up if you don't.

LEMKIN
It's all I care about, Senator. In my line of work, I'm called a *nudnik*. That's a Yiddish word. For a pest. I could come down to Washington and see you this week. I have time on my calendar...

MAN
My secretary will call you next week, Professor. She's the one who deals with, uh, nude-niks... but only if they have their clothes on. (*Laughs)*

(Light out. Drinks. Takes pills. Finds old sandwich and eats it. Begins to type. Lights up on WOMAN; she sings the Yiddish song.)

LEMKIN
Was I not under a moral duty to repay my mother for having stimulated in me the interest in Genocide? Was it not the best form of gratitude to make a "Genocide Pact" as an epitaph on her grave and as a common recognition that she and many millions did not die in vain? Mama. You own what you name: genocide, geno... cide, to kill a people. You are what you are

named: Raphael, God has healed. You blot out the name of him who kills you: Amalek,[14] and remember instead… *Ama-lek, Ama-lek*: she loves milk.

(Smiles. Cries. He drinks. Light off on WOMAN. Types.)

Mr. Judah Shapiro, Conference on Jewish Material Claims Against Germany, 270 Madison Ave., New York, 16. Dear Mr. Shapiro, I was sorry to learn that the grant to me from the Conference cannot be made in a lump sum, but only in bimonthly payments through April. I shall try to carry on as best I can with the volume on the Genocide Pact. Though my situation is dire, your encouragement is received with gratitude. (*Pause*) Signed, Lemkin. (*Thinks*) No. Lambkin. God has healed his sacrifice.
(Smiles. He dials the phone.)

WOMAN'S VOICE
John Day Publishing.

LEMKIN
This is Dr. Lemkin. I want to speak with Richard Walsh. (*Pause*)

WOMAN'S VOICE
One moment please. (*Long pause*; *LEMKIN squirms.*) I'll put you through now.

MAN'S VOICE
Doctor Lemkin? Richard Walsh. I must apologize because we have taken so long about considering your material and ideas.

LEMKIN
They are good, not so?

MAN'S VOICE
This morning, my colleagues and I had a chance to discuss the sample chapters of your manuscript, which we found of great interest. Unfortunately, we had to come to the conclusion that it would not be possible for us to find a large enough audience of buyers for a book of this nature. It is a fascinating and important record, however, so we regret the commercial aspect prevents us from submitting a publishing offer.

LEMKIN
(This is a blow.)

Quo vadis, domine?

WOMAN'S VOICE
You have a call on line three, Mr. Walsh. It's Mrs. W.

MAN'S VOICE
I'm sorry, Professor.

(He hangs up.)

LEMKIN
You say that again and again, Petronius: "People will believe any lie if it is fantastic enough."

(LEMKIN hangs up. Light up on WOMAN.)

When I had the surgery, Mama, I knew that I would not die. I could not die for the simple reason that I was convinced that my work would have died without me. I did not have the good sense to prepare enough disciples to continue my work.

WOMAN
(Angry)
You did not have the good sense to find a wife, Raphael. We are not eternal, any of us. Jacob worked for fourteen years and got *two* wives. You've worked longer than that and don't have any.

(Light out; rear image: Prinsengracht 263, Amsterdam)

LEMKIN
I often felt deserted, but because I was on the go the whole day long, I didn't think about it and enjoyed myself as much as I could.

(Lights begin to come up on GIRL and she speaks softly these lines along with LEMKIN as his voice fades.)

Consciously or unconsciously, I tried to drive away the emptiness I felt with jokes and pranks. Now I think seriously about life and what I have to do. ... I can't just only enjoy myself as my serious side is always there. ... I couldn't understand it ... and the only way I could keep up some bearing was by being impertinent.

GIRL
I have done just like you. We won't win prizes for popularity. I'm working hard on my French and manage to add to my store five irregular verbs a day. Today's are: *ecrire, craindre, faillir, maudire* and *mourir.* There are so many of them, I don't think I can ever learn them all, Professor.

LEMKIN
To write, to fear, to fail, to curse, to die. You are a student a teacher would be delighted to have in class. What are you reading now, *ma cherie*?

GIRL
Lots and lots of history. Schiller's *Don Carlos.* But I'm going to read Shakespeare. He knows so much about people and places and evil and good and hate and love. Papa says the Germans love Shakespeare as much as they love Goethe. If I am to love anyone, above all I must have admiration for them, admiration and respect. Who do you love, Professor?

(Light up on WOMAN)

LEMKIN
I love justice. I love the law. *Sous les lois, nous devenons tous freres.* Perhaps I love it too much. Of course, I love Goethe and Shakespeare.

WOMAN
But are you sure that every book is more important than a friend, Raphael? More important than family?

LEMKIN
And I love language. I do have many books, it's true. I'm even writing one now, the story of my life.

GIRL
So am I. I say things in mine that I can't say to anyone else. I'm the best and sharpest critic of my own work. I know myself what is and what is not well written. (*She might go to him.*) *Courage, mon profeseur,* uphold your ideals, and I am sure you will be content... content in the end. If you love the law, and the laws are good, and the people who made them are good at heart, in spite of the suffering of millions, Finnin-II... I think it will all come right. *Au revoir.*

(Light out on GIRL and WOMAN. He drinks. His hands tremble.)

LEMKIN
(Whispers)
"I charge you by the law..." *bei dem Gesetz... (Louder) bei dem Gesetz!*

(Scenic image changes back to United Nations building. Puts on tie; hands shake.)

Mama, it was the most beautiful day of my life, January 12, 1951, the day when the Convention went into force. I told them, I told them: "The spiritual force of a humanitarian crusade is stronger than any obstacles so that individuals and governments must bow before this force.... I am sure that when the Genocide Convention will be fully understood in all its implications, nobody will oppose it. For example, in a certain country certain groups became cool to the Convention because they thought that the Convention deals with discrimination. ... The idea of discrimination is embodied not in the Genocide Convention but in the Declaration of Human Rights, and whoever confuses these two documents produced by the United Nations may do a great harm to both documents."
(
He collapses in chair.)

WOMAN
(Scenic image: Auschwitz. She might go to him and caress his brow.)
Of all of us you are the lonely and the loveless one, Raphael. Is a life of the law better than a life of the heart?

LEMKIN
I take my briefcases and confront them. In their halls, in their offices, in their languages. They look angry or exasperated or resigned when I approach. The *nudnik* cometh. But I would not let them escape. And I still don't. Yes, I fainted from hunger and ruined my health. At Yale, they complained I make too many phone calls, too many telegrams are sent. I have to pay bills for secretaries and office services. But that day, that day was a triumph for mankind, Mama, and more than that, it was an epitaph for your grave.

WOMAN
I have no grave, Raphael!

(He subsides. Rear image changes to Washington. Light on MAN.)

MAN
Hello Dr. Lemkin.

(WOMAN retreats and goes.)

It's Senator Quixote *(said "kay-hotie").*

(*Chuckle*)

LEMKIN
Not Quixote (*kay-hotie*), Senator, Que-sote (*kays-otie*)? (*Silence*) It was a little joke, Senator. *Queso* in Spanish means cheese. My research told me that cheese is very important in Wisconsin. So,...Quesote.

(Silence)

MAN
We don't speak much Spanish in Wisconsin, Professor. Sorry. How are you feeling these days? Those ratifications are still coming in. Great work. You must be very satisfied. People really talk about your persistence. The way you focus in on something and don't let up. Like a dog with a bone. That's one reason I'm keeping my optimism that the U.S.A. will sign the treaty too, though I admit it's harder work than I thought it was going to be. You know, we have a tuna treaty with Costa Rica, a halibut treaty with Canada, and a shrimp convention with Cuba. Maybe you need to name your treaty after a fish?

(Silence)

It was a little joke, Professor.

LEMKIN
The Human Rights people are saying now that their document is stronger than mine.[15]

MAN
Well, if it's Mrs. Roosevelt you're thinking of, I believe she'll come around. Eleanor is the most popular woman in America, and she sent me a check for $25 when I ran for governor. She's not what I worry about.

LEMKIN
Popularity means nothing. It distracts from what's important. What do you worry about, Senator?

MAN
And it's not the communists either, though that's all those McCarthy nutcases want to talk about. They've got cheese between their ears. Swiss, with lots of holes. I really worry about three things: mischief by big banks, government waste and... Professor... can you keep this confidential?... losing my hair.

(*They smile at each other.*)

LEMKIN
Then let's meet next week, Senator, and talk over our very mutual concerns. I've got my appointment calendar...

MAN
That's not the reason for the visit, Professor. I wanted to tell you about a movie I saw last night. Right up your New York alley.

LEMKIN
I don't have much time for movies, Senator. But I have plenty for appointments with treaty supporters...

MAN
Everybody's talking about it around the office.[16] It's about a girl being chased by the Nazis during the war. She hides in a secret annex with her family and boy friend and a cat. Only one of them made it through, Professor. Maybe you heard about the girl? She wrote a diary. She was Jewish like you, though the movie did-n't make a big deal out of that. And she was German, too! We have lots of Germans in Wisconsin. Milwaukee is full of them. I did my military service in Chicago, so I never got over to Europe. My secretary told me that Eleanor, the president's wife and my twenty-five dollar benefactor, wrote an introduction to the girl's book.

LEMKIN
Yes, I know the girl who you mean.

(LEMKIN and the GIRL look at each other.)

MAN
So, I decided I'm going to make a speech in the Senate sometime and I thought you'd like to get a chance to hear it first.

(LEMKIN combs hair)

It goes like this: "Mr. President"… that's the president of the Senate, not the President of the United States… "no treaty by this country could ever make up for the loss of Anne Frank and 6 million others who perished in the Holocaust. But we have an obligation to join with the other nations that have ratified the Genocide Treaty to make clear to them that we share their sorrow at the tragedy that claimed Anne Frank's life. We need to make clear, Mr. President, our intention to prevent such a tragedy from ever happening again. We need to make clear that we will bring those who would commit genocide to justice." What do you think, Professor?

LEMKIN
Very good, Senator, *muy bien*. Thank you for writing it. You are a very good man and a loyal ally.

MAN
This week a journalist called me "the number one jackass in the Senate." Now I like being number one, but he'll think differently when the treaty gets ratified. This is America. We're on the side of the good not the side of the barn. We'll win this one for that kid hiding from the Nazis.

(Pause)

My office will get back to you about setting a meeting, Professor. Maybe next week.

LEMKIN
Please don't go. Senator…

MAN
(Distracted)
Yes?

LEMKIN
(Pause)
Just one question more, Senator… Are potatoes counted as vegetables?

MAN
The ones grown in Wisconsin are. Don't forget to exercise, Professor. If you don't like broccoli, try spinach. Does wonders for Popeye.

(Pause. Light out. Scenic image: New York apartment house.)

LEMKIN
Popeye.

(Looks at his glasses)

Popeye... a.k.a. Kepler... Popeye Kepler... Father of spectacles.

(Smiles. Puts down glasses. He is exhausted. Radio on. The March from Quo Vadis *is heard. Slowly, he begins to type.)*

Mr. Guy W. Pearson, Collector of Taxes, Revenue Collection Enforcement Unit, District of Columbia. Dear Mr. Pearson, I am in receipt of Mr. Holler's letter referring to a delinquent and unpaid tax item identified as Personal Property Tax, Account No. 66909. I would like to arrange a meeting with you or Mr. Holler to identify the best method of satisfying the levy now totaling $20.16. I hope you will understand that my work forces me to spend long periods out of the country, and my attention to correspondence is not always timely. I will call you next week to schedule a visit. Thank you for your consideration. Raphael Lemkin, Inventor of the word Genocide, author of the *Convention Against Genocide*, five time nominee for the Nobel Peace Prize... and Good Friend of the Girl Hiding in the Secret Annex.

(Radio off. Dials phone.)

MAN'S VOICE
Charlie Pierce...

LEMKIN
This is Dr. Lemkin...

MAN'S VOICE
Oh, yes, the genocide book. The fact is that we have considered your materials very seriously... but our conclusions are... negative. That is, we don't feel that we could successfully sell a book about the history of genocide, whether condensed or at length. Furthermore, we now feel that in spite of our first impression, we could not sell successfully a biography of you.

(The next lines are overlapped and repeated to a crescendo.)

WOMAN'S VOICE
Your meeting will be starting in five minutes, Mr. Pierce...

MAN'S VOICE
If you pay the bill in full by the end of the month...

WOMAN
I have no grave, Raphael...

GIRL
Bad laws made our lives miserable, *Monsieur Professeur* ...

MAN
It was a little joke, Dr. You should try fish...

LEMKIN
(Pushes books off desk. Rises in fury.)

Jestem kontent![17]

(Pause. LEMKIN hangs up. Defeated.)

I am content.

(He drinks a glass of water. He is profoundly alone. Lights up on the WOMAN and the GIRL.)

I could not fail, because I spoke in the name and for the benefit of the innocent. This is the reason why heads of state, members of cabinets, senators, and other persons in power never refuse to talk to me, and they have always recognized me as a messenger of humanity.

(The two women embrace and exit. Light out. Pause. He begins to hum the Yiddish song.)

Mama, I promise I'll do better tomorrow. Oh, Mama...

(Lights fade. On the wall upstage appears the legend: "The Genocide Convention Implementation Act was adopted in the U.S. Senate in 1988 under the Reagan administration and called The Proxmire Act." Then, "Raphael Lemkin died on August 28, 1959. Seven people attended his funeral.")

END OF PLAY

Endotes

1 The play's title is taken from a passage in Primo Levi's *Survival in Auschwitz*: "... if you wound the body of a dying man, the wound will begin to heal, even if the whole body dies within a day." Some of the words spoken by the characters are taken from several documents and plays, the most important ones being Lemkin's unpublished autobiography and Anne Frank's *Diary of a Young Girl*. Lemkin's papers are housed at the American Jewish Archives, Cincinnati, Ohio; the Center for Jewish History, New York; and the New York Public Library.

2 Raphael Lemkin suffered from high blood pressure, which was treated in the 1950s with diuretics [Reserpine] to relieve the pressure of fluids and decrease the strain on his heart. The side effects of the medicine included: shaking, difficulty breathing, fatigue and even mental depression. Headaches were common. After some time, without successful treatment, heart attacks were possible. Lemkin's obituary in the *New York Times* reported that Lemkin died of a heart attack on August 28, 1959 in the office of a public relations consultant where he had gone to discuss the publication of his autobiography; others report that he died in his Manhattan apartment or in a New York hotel.

3 William Proxmire was the U.S. Senate's most ardent and persistent supporter of the Genocide Treaty. From 1967, eight years after Lemkin's death, until the Treaty was approved—though not implemented—nineteen years later, he delivered more than 3,200 speeches in favor of ratification.

4 Marcus Vicinius was the Roman general in *Quo Vadis*; here and later, Lemkin is "mixing things up."

5 Chaim Nachman Bialik (1873–1934). His poem *In the City of Slaughter* was written to commemorate the notorious and terrible Kishinev pogrom in 1903.

6 Lemkin's mind "hears" the city of Bialystock in eastern Poland whose Jewish population was destroyed in World War II.

7 "Eat, my child." (Yiddish)

8 One hundred twenty in Hebrew, the Biblical "long life."

9 Hebrew for "The Hope," the name of Israel's national anthem.

10 The most famous of the Nazis' antisemitic propaganda films, made in 1940.

11 Here, and elsewhere, Lemkin speaks Shylock's words from *The Merchant of Venice*.

12 The Nazis often ordered deported Jews, prior to their murder, to write postcards back to their families saying they were well.

13 Opposition to ratifying the Genocide Convention was led by the American Bar Association which felt the treaty would leave Americans vulnerable to arrest and penalty for their actions abroad and at home.
14 See *Exodus 17*: 8–16 and *Deuteronomy 25*: 17–19.
15 The Declaration of Human Rights, whose leading advocate was Eleanor Roosevelt, was advanced for ratification in the United Nations at the same time as Lemkin's Genocide Treaty. For political reasons, it came to be seen as a competing rather than a complementary document.
16 The Hollywood film based on Anne Frank's diary was released in 1959.
17 "I am content." (Polish) See *The Merchant of Venice*, IV, i.

Author's Note

The attention paid to Raphael Lemkin in recent years results directly from increased incidences of genocide in the world. Lemkin, of course, was the one who coined the word in 1944, and then who used it in the name of the *Convention for the Prevention and Punishment of the Crime of Genocide*, which he single-handedly shepherded through the United Nations in those early years of its existence. Today, nearly sixty years after its passage, historians are unanimous in their assessment of Lemkin's extraordinary achievement. The discussion continues, however, concerning the effectiveness of the Convention in the light of ongoing human savagery and mass murder everywhere in the world.

The play I have written approaches the subject of genocide from the perspective of the man, not the treaty. From the available evidence, Lemkin was obsessed with the creation and ratification of the *UN Genocide Convention* (as it is called) all of his professional life, from his early thinking in the 1930s at the League of Nations and continuing to his death on August 28, 1959. He had no time for personal entanglements and little time for his few friends, with whom he sought occasional respite from the intensity of his mission.

We know about Lemkin from those who knew and wrote about him, and from what he wrote about himself. Off and on throughout the 1950s, he put time into writing his autobiography, which he called *Totally Unofficial* after a phrase describing him in a *New York Times* editorial in 1957. It was a title full of truth and adversity (because he represented no government) and some irony (because it became a kind of badge of honor and a mark of his outsider status). The book was never finished and exists in several revisions, as if Lemkin couldn't stop himself from tinkering with a story that moved between remarkable personal experience and extended historical disquisition.

In truth, the many hundreds of pages are stylistically ordinary, a surprising result from an engaged man who was well educated, well read, and well spoken (in at least nine languages). Reading his autobiography gives the impression that he lived some of his life through literature. In addition, his correspondence (excerpts of which appear in this play) discloses several letters from publishers declining to consider his manuscript, surely one of a number of painful disappointments in a productive life both unofficial and, I believe, in an important way, unfulfilled.

Contemporary scholars of genocide and of Lemkin's part in getting the world to acknowledge it (Steven Schnur, Samantha Power, William Korey, Michael Ignatieff, Jim Fussell) focus on Lemkin's remarkable qualities: his perseverance, idealism, ethical imagination, linguistic brilliance, and his single-mindedness of purpose. They also refer to periods of ill health, loneliness, and professional frustration (most especially by the refusal of his adopted country to ratify the treaty), augmented by his precarious personal finances and, above all, by the murder of most of his family during the Holocaust. Power, who credits Lemkin's effectiveness, is perhaps harshest in her evaluation of Lemkin, but to her I owe the affirmation of a connection I had made, for different reasons, with a senator from Wisconsin. (See: *"A Problem From Hell,"* p. 79.)

If the Whole Body Dies tries to give a sense of who Lemkin was according to the experiences and various cultures that shaped and influenced him. If the play succeeds, I hope it will enlarge the "attention being paid" to him and to his incontrovertible achievements. (The phrase is famous from Miller's *Death of a Salesman*; Lemkin had seven people at his funeral, two more than Willy Loman did.) Lemkin was very human too, and wrote how the three things he hoped to avoid in life came "in implacable succession": wearing eyeglasses, becoming a refugee, and losing his hair.

Lemkin's thinking was determined by his status as an intellectual and an outsider. Perhaps the question I was most determined to answer was what might have made Lemkin laugh, or at least smile. Thus, in the play, he makes an identical connection to a person many Americans turned to in the 1950s as a way to feel better about themselves and the world. And his genius with languages helped too. In notes to the first part of another book Lemkin was writing, *Introduction to the Study of Genocide*, he lists a number of neologisms by writers from Cicero to others in the 20th century, and he is clearly well-aware of the inherent opportunities for pun-making in the word-coining work for which he will always be known.

"I always wanted to shorten the distance between the heart and the deed," wrote Lemkin in the unpublished autobiography, by which he meant "to live an idea" through action. That he did shorten the distance is beyond doubt, even though my interest is to know what lay under "the deeds" of this important, complicated, and (I hope) interesting figure at the very end of his difficult life.

Convention on the Prevention and Punishment of the Crime of Genocide

Adopted by Resolution 260 (III) A of the United Nations General Assembly on 9 December 1948.

Article 1
The Contracting Parties confirm that genocide, whether committed in time of peace or in time of war, is a crime under international law which they undertake to prevent and to punish.

Article 2
In the present Convention, genocide means any of the following acts committed with intent to destroy, in whole or in part, a national, ethnical, racial or religious group, as such:
(a) Killing members of the group;
(b) Causing serious bodily or mental harm to members of the group;
(c) Deliberately inflicting on the group conditions of life calculated to bring about its physical destruction in whole or in part;
(d) Imposing measures intended to prevent births within the group;
(e) Forcibly transferring children of the group to another group.

Article 3
The following acts shall be punishable:
(a) Genocide;
(b) Conspiracy to commit genocide;
(c) Direct and public incitement to commit genocide;
(d) Attempt to commit genocide;
(e) Complicity in genocide.

Article 4
Persons committing genocide or any of the other acts enumerated in Article 3 shall be punished, whether they are constitutionally responsible rulers, public officials or private individuals.

Article 5
The Contracting Parties undertake to enact, in accordance with their respective Constitutions, the necessary legislation to give effect to the provisions of the present Convention and, in particular, to provide effective

penalties for persons guilty of genocide or any of the other acts enumerated in Article 3.

Article 6
Persons charged with genocide or any of the other acts enumerated in Article 3 shall be tried by a competent tribunal of the State in the territory of which the act was committed, or by such international penal tribunal as may have jurisdiction with respect to those Contracting Parties which shall have accepted its jurisdiction.

Article 7
Genocide and the other acts enumerated in Article 3 shall not be considered as political crimes for the purpose of extradition.
The Contracting Parties pledge themselves in such cases to grant extradition in accordance with their laws and treaties in force.

Article 8
Any Contracting Party may call upon the competent organs of the United Nations to take such action under the Charter of the United Nations as they consider appropriate for the prevention and suppression of acts of genocide or any of the other acts enumerated in Article 3.

Article 9
Disputes between the Contracting Parties relating to the interpretation, application or fulfilment of the present Convention, including those relating to the responsibility of a State for genocide or any of the other acts enumerated in Article 3, shall be submitted to the International Court of Justice at the request of any of the parties to the dispute.

Article 10
The present Convention, of which the Chinese, English, French, Russian and Spanish texts are equally authentic, shall bear the date of 9 December 1948.

Article 11
The present Convention shall be open until 31 December 1949 for signature on behalf of any Member of the United Nations and of any non-member State to which an invitation to sign has been addressed by the General Assembly.
The present Convention shall be ratified, and the instruments of ratification shall be deposited with the Secretary-General of the United Nations.

After 1 January 1950, the present Convention may be acceded to on behalf of any Member of the United Nations and of any non-member State which has received an invitation as aforesaid.
Instruments of accession shall be deposited with the Secretary-General of the United Nations.

Article 12
Any Contracting Party may at any time, by notification addressed to the Secretary-General of the United Nations, extend the application of the present Convention to all or any of the territories for the conduct of whose foreign relations that Contracting Party is responsible.

Article 13
On the day when the first twenty instruments of ratification or accession have been deposited, the Secretary-General shall draw up a proces-verbal and transmit a copy of it to each Member of the United Nations and to each of the non-member States contemplated in Article 11.
The present Convention shall come into force on the ninetieth day following the date of deposit of the twentieth instrument of ratification or accession.
Any ratification or accession effected subsequent to the latter date shall become effective on the ninetieth day following the deposit of the instrument of ratification or accession.

Article 14
The present Convention shall remain in effect for a period of ten years as from the date of its coming into force.
It shall thereafter remain in force for successive periods of five years for such Contracting Parties as have not denounced it at least six months before the expiration of the current period.
Denunciation shall be effected by a written notification addressed to the Secretary-General of the United Nations.

Article 15
If, as a result of denunciations, the number of Parties to the present Convention should become less than sixteen, the Convention shall cease to be in force as from the date on which the last of these denunciations shall become effective.

Article 16

A request for the revision of the present Convention may be made at any time by any Contracting Party by means of a notification in writing addressed to the Secretary-General.

The General Assembly shall decide upon the steps, if any, to be taken in respect of such request.

Article 17

The Secretary-General of the United Nations shall notify all Members of the United Nations and the non-member States contemplated in Article 11 of the following:

(a) Signatures, ratifications and accessions received in accordance with Article 11;
(b) Notifications received in accordance with Article 12;
(c) The date upon which the present Convention comes into force in accordance with Article 13;
(d) Denunciations received in accordance with Article 14;
(e) The abrogation of the Convention in accordance with Article 15;
(f) Notifications received in accordance with Article 16.

Article 18

The original of the present Convention shall be deposited in the archives of the United Nations. A certified copy of the Convention shall be transmitted to all Members of the United Nations and to the non-member States contemplated in Article 11.

Article 19

The present Convention shall be registered by the Secretary-General of the United Nations on the date of its coming into force.

[The Convention was *entered into force* on January 12, 1951.]

Bibliography

Docker, John. "Raphael Lemkin's History of Genocide and Colonialism." A lecture to the U.S. Holocaust Memorial Museum, February 26, 2004.

Ignatieff, Michael. "The Legacy of Raphael Lemkin." A lecture to the U.S. Holocaust Memorial Museum, December 13, 2001.

Jacobs, Steven L., ed. *Raphael Lemkin's Thoughts on Nazi Genocide: Not Guilty?* Lewiston, NY: Edwin Mellen Press, 1992.

_______________, ed. "The Papers of Raphael Lemkin: A First Look." *Journal of Genocide Research* 1.1 (1999), 105–114.

Korey, William. *An Epitaph for Raphael Lemkin.* New York: Jacob Blaustein Institute for the Advancement of Human Rights/American Jewish Committee, 2001.

_____________, "Revisiting the U.N.'s Genocide Convention." *Forward,* August 10, 2001.

LeBlanc, Lawrence J. *The United States and the Genocide Convention.* Durham, NC: Duke University Press, 1991.

Power, Samantha. *"A Problem from Hell": America and the Age of Genocide.* New York: Basic Books, 2001.

Skloot, Robert. "*We Will Never Die*: The Success and Failure of a Holocaust Pageant," *Theatre Journal* (May 1985), 167–180.

www.preventgenocide.org website.

Biographical Note

Robert Skloot

Robert Skloot (rskloot@wisc.edu) has taught and directed plays at the University of Wisconsin–Madison since 1968 and served as an associate vice chancellor from 1996 to 2002. He is the author of *The Darkness We Carry: The Drama of the Holocaust* (1988) and the editor of the two-volume anthology, *The Theatre of the Holocaust* (1982, 1999). He served as a Fulbright Professor in Israel, Austria, Chile, and the Netherlands, and he holds a joint appointment in the UW–Madison's Mosse-Weinstein Center for Jewish Studies.

www.ingramcontent.com/pod-product-compliance
Lightning Source LLC
LaVergne TN
LVHW010631300926
849162LV00001B/126